HISTORIES

DUKE UNIVERSITY PRESS   DURHAM | LONDON 2005

OF THE FUTURE

EDITED BY Daniel Rosenberg and Susan Harding

© 2005 Duke University Press   All rights reserved
Printed in the United States of America on acid-free paper ∞
Designed by Mary Mendell
Typeset in Quadraat by Tseng Information Systems, Inc.
Copyright acknowledgments and Library of Congress
Cataloging-in-Publication Data appear on the last
printed pages of this book.

FOR BEA, ED, AND MARCO—
our futures past and present

CONTENTS

ACKNOWLEDGMENTS

Many people contributed much to the design and content of this book over the course of several years. The *Histories of the Future* project was conceived and organized by Susan Harding as a research workshop at the University of California Humanities Research Institute in Irvine in 1997. Over the course of the next several years, the workshop grew and changed as we were joined by new participants and generated new areas of research. In 1998 we held a follow-up conference at the University of California, Santa Cruz, with the support of UCHRI and the Center for Cultural Studies at UCSC. We also received generous support from the Oregon Humanities Center to prepare the manuscript. Finally, we are grateful to UCHRI, the Institute for Humanities Research, the Social Sciences Division, and the Department of Anthropology at UCSC, and the Robert D. Clark Honors College at the University of Oregon, for granting subventions to make this book possible.

In addition to all the authors in the volume, we would also like to acknowledge and thank Mai-Lin Cheng, Valerie Hartouni, Stephen Best, Liisa Malkki, Hayden White, Michael Taussig, Karen Ho, Paulla Ebron, Emily Martin, Patricia O'Brien, James Clifford, Donna Haraway, Ken Wissoker, Mary Murrell, Richard Randolph, Sina Najafi, Brian Conley, David Serlin, Jeffrey Kastner, Frances Richard, and two anonymous reviewers for Duke University Press. We received wonderful technical support from Debra Massey, Deanna Nunez, Chris Aschan, Katy Eliot, Theresa Champ, and Jon Kersey. Special thanks to Jeremy Campbell for the index, and to Brian McMullen and Tal Schori of *Cabinet* magazine for the graphic design for the original Timeline of Timelines. All original art for "Global Futures: The Game" is by Elizabeth Pollman. All uncredited images are by Daniel Rosenberg.

HISTORIES OF THE FUTURE

CHAPTER

Introduction: Histories of the Future

Daniel Rosenberg and Susan Harding

We have been living through boom times for the future. Even before the escalating storms of 2001 and the conflicts that followed, our cultures and industries collaborated in a remarkable proliferation of words and images about the future. And none of this has shown any sign of slowing down. Whether in modes of progress or apocalypse, the media flow over with anticipations of things to come, with utopias, dystopias, stories of time travel and artificial intelligence, with accounts of acceleration and progress, of doom and imminent destruction, with scenarios, predictions, prophecies, and manifestoes. In this swirl of uncertainty, even the benighted "science" of futurology has come back into style.[1]

In the first years of the twenty-first century, representations of the future have cycled wildly through a historical repertoire from the ray-gun gothic of the 1930s to the noir and the endism of the 1940s and 1950s to the plastic op-art modularity of the 1960s and back again. As if following a kind of Moore's Law scaling principle, futures today seem to be reproducing themselves faster and more cheaply than ever. At the same time, their shelf lives appear to be getting shorter. Any child can historicize them for you, can tell you in a minute which future is up to date and which is already over, which doesn't run fast enough on the current microprocessor and which doesn't run at all.

More and more, our sense of the future is conditioned by a knowledge of, and even a nostalgia for, futures that we have already lost. Indeed, nostalgia for the future has become so pervasive today that it has even developed a distinctive set of commercial uses. As Arjun Appadurai suggests, contemporary mass consumption "is not simply based on the functioning of simulacra *in* time, but also on the force of the simulacra *of* time."[2] If, as E. P. Thompson argues, different modes of production imply different

Future junk mail.

forms and experiences of temporality, our current mode of consumption appears to imply a nostalgia for productivity in general and for all the different experiences of temporality that it might be able to produce.[3] Today our futures feel increasingly citational—each is haunted by the "semiotic ghosts" of futures past.[4]

Whether ultimately this phenomenon will turn out to be an expression of the logical limits of the progressive chronotype (what, after all, comes after progress?) or simply another version of the Baudrillardian hyperreal (simulacra in yet another realm), the rise of future-nostalgia has already brought to light phenomena of formal and historical importance.[5] From a formal point of view, future-nostalgia reminds us that the future is not, and has never been, an empty category. Even as we accept a skeptical critique of prophecy, we must acknowledge that for us the future is not so much underdetermined as overdetermined. Our lives are constructed around knowledges of the future that are as full (and flawed) as our knowledges of the past. Often these future knowledges are profoundly freighted, since they involve anticipatory hopes and fears. As one commentator recently put it, our futures are junkyards of memories we have not yet had.[6] They are not merely geometrical extensions of time. They haunt our presents, obeying architectural laws that look more like Gaudí than Euclid. They arise in the most diverse and peculiar ways.

In historical terms, the development of future-nostalgia also points to a kind of crisis in modern futurity. From the beginning, the modern was constituted through a rejection of prophecy. The philosophy of the Enlightenment required that time would be open to human achievement and that events could gain meaning from their interrelation, rather than from their relationship to absolute, biblical beginnings and ends. As Fredric Jameson has argued, by bracketing eschatological questions, the Enlightenment effectively "sealed off" the future from prophetic knowledge.[7] But this development had paradoxical consequences. In no way did it amount to a going out of business for futurological workshops. The Enlightenment proscription against traditional prophetic practices turned out to produce new and intensified imaginative demands on the future and new techniques of narration and prognosis.[8] The very possibility of an open-ended time elicited an outpouring of grand narratives from Condorcet and Kant to Hegel and Comte. This effect was by no means limited to high philosophy. In the arena of fiction, for example, the late eighteenth century saw an efflorescence of future fantasies. And for the first time in literary history, these futures took place not in some vague hereafter but in a chronological expanse freed from the finitude of sacred history, in the profane historical future, in the years 2440, 1850, 1900, and 7308.[9]

Of course, these future narratives were also morality tales for the present, but in them the present is materialized through striking new kinds of proleptic imagining.[10] The new futurisms of the eighteenth and nineteenth centuries allowed—and even required—the thinking of alternative timelines: in them, the present was not just the past of the future but the "the past of future, contingent presents."[11] It is difficult to overestimate the implications of this new possibility. But it is equally crucial to note that its victory was only ever partial. Even in the twentieth and twenty-first centuries, the contingent futures that emerged during the Enlightenment never fully displaced the necessary futures of prophecy. In some instances, such as the case of Auguste Comte (and, arguably, much of American pub-

Early-twentieth-century futures. Chromolithography. Villemard Publishers, 1910. Courtesy of the Bibliothèque Nationale de France.

lic culture), modern visions of progress themselves took on a providential character.[12] In others, such as the nineteenth-century *Uchronie* of Charles Renouvier, contingencies piled on contingencies seemingly without end.[13] Moreover, the religious prophets did not oblige anyone by going away. As it turns out, what most characterizes the modern problem of the future is not its historical distance from the mode of prophecy but rather its hybrid and contradictory relationship to it.

The modern period saw a proliferation of techniques for imagining, predicting, and narrating futures — many in an importantly ambiguous terrain "between science and fiction" — and a developing cultural consciousness of the instability of this new temporal landscape.[14] By the end of the nineteenth century, according to contemporary observers, time itself appeared to be accelerating, and futures — big and small alike — seemed to be coming and going with breathtaking speed.[15] In the memorable words of Henry Adams, thinking historically in 1900 evoked the feeling of having one's neck broken.[16] And this sense of acceleration did not go away. Instead it became something like second nature, so that by the late twentieth century, the problem was no longer how to account for historical acceleration, but how to account for the acceleration of acceleration itself.

In recent years, futurological upheavals have continued to take place with much ado, as in our recent and paradigmatic turn of the millennium. Although the coming of the new millennium did not occasion the level of crazy cult activity or terrorism anticipated by many observers and political leaders, it did provoke a remarkable outpouring of speculation. Prophets, prognosticators, predictors, fortunetellers, astrologers, millennialists, apocalyptics, visionaries, seers, and their journalistic and academic fellow travelers clogged the airwaves, magazines, newspapers, bookstores, and pews with their wares. As we approached 2000, the clock of discourse ticked louder and louder. The future itself seemed to shrink to fit the narrowing frame of time left until the calendar turned over. As one observer put it, "When I was a child, people used to talk about what would happen by the year 2000. Now, thirty years later, they still talk about what will happen by the year 2000. The future has been shrinking by one year per year for my entire life."[17] When all was said and done, though, 2000 could not have been anything but an anticlimax to the countless stories in which it played an anticipatory role. There was something vampiric about it: a thousand flashbulbs popped, but nothing showed up in the picture. Still, it was everywhere. There was no escaping it. It haunted us.

In the months leading up to the turn of the millennium, anticipations of the year 2000 transformed into anticipations of the "Year 2000 Problem," or the "Y2K bug," or simply "Y2K," and for a while the future was now.

Peering Into the Abyss of the Future

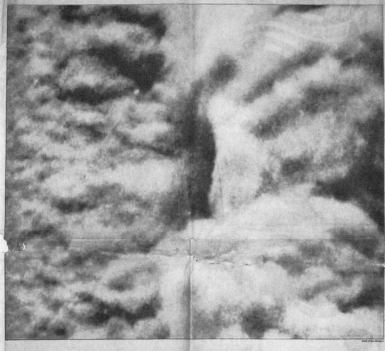

By JOHN ROCKWELL

> Like the rest of us, artists, so sensitive to our dilemmas and dreams, have lost their bearings.

Continued on Page 4

As Y2K, it had a technical and a rational and, especially, an economic content. Its importance was to be measured in the amount of money that was spent on preventing it, or cleaning up the mess that it created. It gave us something to believe in and to anticipate when we were barred from hoping for something mysterious. It also had the effect of spectacularizing a new world order, as, according to the experts, only the hypertechnologized and the primitive would be spared.

As some skeptics had predicted, at Y2K, the big story turned out to be the nonstory. Early on there were reports of problems here and there released from the bunker-style headquarters of our own federal "Y2K Preparedness Center," but none of these turned out to be serious. Yet the failure of the Y2K apocalypse to materialize did not lessen its historical importance. Like the nuclear tests of the 1950s, Y2K, in all its dimensions—cultural, commercial, and political, as well as technological—energized an entire economy of anticipation and produced a powerful expressive performance of a still-unstable global culture business vying for metanarrative control over the future.[18] Not surprisingly, this moment also saw a prose explosion: ten years after the declared "end of history," we were still "zeroing in on the millennium" and having "conversations about the end of time."[19]

Shortly after the turn of the millennium, the same dynamic was repeated with greater and graver intensity in the wake of the terrorist attacks on the World Trade Center and the Pentagon. The attacks utterly suspended our futures, big and small, public and private, local and global. For Americans on 9/11, it was as if time had stopped, or at least stood terribly still. The sensation was strikingly evoked by a graphic artist's drawing for the *New York Times*. Shortly after the attacks a full-page image of the the terrible smoke cloud rising from the burning World Trade Center declared us "Peering into the Abyss of the Future." Two years later a calendar image still finds us stuck on 9/11. An event as big as 9/11, calling on such resources of collective imagination, virtually commands us to consider "The Future" as a singular story and as a singular presence in national and international life. But at the same time, it reminds us how decisively our imagination of futures can change in response to changing times. And it leads us to ask what sorts of cultural work are necessary to make new futures cohere. The problem of futures after 9/11 is not just the problem of deciphering big narratives; it is also the problem of mapping networks of small stories and practices changing with place and time.

In the end, the events of Y2K and 9/11 lavishly demonstrate that the future in the modern West is not the empty category that it is supposed to be— that the conflict of futures present and past is as central an element of modern temporality as was the adaptation and confirmation of futures before

New York Times Book Review, April 20, 2003.

the eighteenth century—that our uncertainties are at every moment themselves positive cultural expressions. This is the paradox of modern futurity: while we are taught to believe in the emptiness of the future, we live in a world saturated by future-consciousness as rich and as full as our consciousness of the past. There is abundance everywhere, in big narratives and in small acts, and in every place where hopes and doubts are mobilized, in everything that we know and are not supposed to know. "The future" is a placeholder, a placebo, a no-place, but it is also a commonplace that we need to investigate in all its cultural and historical density.

This is what *Histories of the Future* sets out to do. Through a selection of essays and artifacts, the book maps sites where big futures—metanarratives that foresee, predict, imagine, divine, prognosticate, promise, and reveal the future—make contact with everyday lives. It traces a variety of small futures, some pervasive and some fugitive, all haunting their presents. It examines the densities and overdetermination of our futurizing imaginations. It tries to understand what "the future" is by looking at what "the future" does when it is called upon in practical situations in art and politics and in everyday life. The essays that make up this volume are themselves densely interlinked, and the volume is intended to operate as a hypertext, opening up analytic paths among disparate temporal experiences of modernity, links between technology and messianism, life and half-life, panic and nostalgia, waiting and utopia, conspiracy and linearity, prophecy and trauma.

Each of the essays presented here was written in relation to the others and grew out of a series of seminars, conferences, and collaborative research experiences. The authors first convened during a six-month residency at the Humanities Research Institute at the University of California, Irvine, in 1997. This turned out to be consequential in itself. From our arrival, Irvine appeared to us a remarkable example of American corporate futurism in all its complexity and self-contradiction, and our collective experience of the place served as a jumping-off point for many of our reflections.

At the time of our arrival, Irvine was still the largest entirely planned community ever built in the United States. Like many planned communities, it depended from the start on its own industry, in this case, an especially clean industry, well suited to the developing information and service economies of the late twentieth century. Before the chartering of the city, the land on which it would be built was held by a private corporation that had obtained ownership of much of the large rancho that had formerly extended through Orange County and beyond. In the 1960s, as farming in the area declined, the Irvine Corporation donated a substantial property to the University of California system to establish a new university which would become the "economic engine" at the heart of this clean city. The local signage pays homage to the division of industry and residence and to the protection of local residents from the possible harms of both industrial and urban life. The seal of the City of Irvine, visible from the roads that lead in and out, does not proclaim a future in so many words, but the future is called up in other ways, through the figures of a child on the left and a cultivated tree on the right.[20] In its shield, Irvine defines itself as a project of control, protection, and culture that is echoed in the layout of every subdivision and the architecture of the campus. In Irvine, geographic, economic, and social futures were mapped in every possible detail. But, as Anna Tsing argues in her essay here, grand futurizing schemes "never fully colonize the territories on which they are imposed."[21] Even in Irvine, where wealth has grown unabated since the earliest days, futures have not been fully controlled. There are little signs of this everywhere, found inside closets and tucked under tables. As you drive south from Irvine toward San Diego, the child of the future changes shape. No longer firmly protected by a paternal corporate arm, this immigrant child figured on a Caution sign on the highway is clinging for dear life to the hand of her mother and father who are sprinting across the freeway, hoping not to get hit as they race into an uncertain and perilous future. Even in its earliest days in the 1960s and 1970s, the fantasy landscape of Irvine was colored by a lingering dystopian haze. It is strange to look back on the production

Seal of the City of Irvine. Photograph © Daniel Rosenberg.

stills from the *Planet of the Apes* film shot on the campus of UCI. Actors in sci-fi ape costumes are off to lunch with humans of the everyday variety. And nothing really looks so wrong with this scene.

As we read the futures unfolded and still unfolding in Irvine and its environs, our group developed a tool kit for thinking about the future. We paid attention to plans, predictions, and narratives about the future, but also to the everyday purposes and situations in which they were conjured. We came to see futures all around, not only in explicit forms of futurism but in the manners of talking, doing, and imagining that get us through from day to day. Futures in this sense lie not only in a segregated, marked domain (characterized by practices such as forecasting, planning, and speculation) but in the domain of social practice generally. The particular environment of Irvine attuned us to the pervasiveness and diversity of these future-making practices. In places designed to express corporate uniformity—behind the berms and hedgerows, around traffic islands and sculpture gardens, in commercial plazas and recreation areas—we saw signs of practices that complicated and resisted the single vector of Irvine's master plan. There are postcards to the future carved into the smooth surfaces of this futuristic city and counterterritorializations mapped in skateboard wax on every concrete plaza and stair.[22]

During the course of our work in Irvine, we became interested in the proliferation of these sorts of contrasts and conflicts and the problem of

Planet of the Apes movie set, Irvine, California. Courtesy of Special Collections, University of California, Irvine.

Migrant Futures. Photograph © Daniel Rosenberg.

explaining them. How to account for the sort of corporate and political futurism that built the city without obscuring the complex trajectories that grew out of it, drawing on it and challenging it all at once? How to describe and analyze the acts of small resistance and interpretation all around us without losing sight of the imaginary, structural, and bureaucratic power of the place? How, in general, to think *grands récits* with local acts? How to think strategy with tactics? Narrative with practice? These questions led us to read and to study Irvine, but they led us many other places, too.

Our conception of futures developed further when we traveled as a group across Southern California to several sites in and around Las Vegas. We visited the casinos, the Hoover Dam, the Liberace Museum, the Nevada Nuclear Waste Site, the Nevada Nuclear Test Site, and the desert town of Rachel, Nevada, at the edge of the storied secret government installation at Area 51. We sought to explore the American West as a spatial metonym for the post-Enlightenment future—a region at once empty, being emptied out, already filled up, and always filling up with unfolding futures and futures past. For our group, this region became a laboratory, an imaginary, in which we explored the cultural and sentimental microdynamics of future making.

This research collaboration is represented directly in this volume. Several of the essays draw their topical material from our excursions in the American West, and the exploratory work that we did there influences every

Near Rachel, Nevada. Photograph © Daniel Rosenberg.

essay. This takes many forms and focuses—from the play of memory, re-pression, and return, to the uncanny, messianic expectation, unintended excess, and the operation of myriad desires and fantasies—for justice, di-rect communication, getting outside or inside, or elsewhere, for the other, another life, wealth, democracy, power, or revisable pasts and a universe of total information. In a Western terrain that makes claims of narrative priority and independence, we found a dense network of futurisms from the past and from elsewhere, a network that demanded an approach that was at once global and local. In this way, our initial work on the American frontier opened doors to other frontiers—to Indonesia, the Philippines, and Japan; to France, Spain, and Italy—on the other sides of the oceans that are supposed to separate and punctuate the course of history.

In the essays assembled here, the prognosticators, speculators, utopi-ans, prophets, imagineers, and all the other architects and visionaries of big futures have their say. But our accent here is decidedly on the side of the small. In contrast to the many books that have focused on the big story of the future, *Histories of the Future* foregrounds everyday attitudes, images, stories, performances, debris, movement, lifestyles, and work. The grands récits and their characteristic mechanisms (prophecy, prediction, etc.) ap-pear in this book, but always and only in relation to the places, practices, and objects through which they take shape.[23] The aim of *Histories of the*

Future is to explore the relationship between expectation and experience on the level of everyday life.

While the essays and interludes that follow defy simple summary and classification, they abound in conceptual linkages, shared themes, and common sites. We have ordered them in a way that highlights certain connections, but they may easily be read in another order. The volume as a whole represents all the intensities of an ongoing conversation that may be joined and rejoined at various points.

Histories of the Future begins with the question of frontiers. Joseph Masco's essay on the nuclear frontier in the American West may be read as a companion piece to Anna Tsing's essay on the resource frontier in Borneo. Masco focuses on popular and military cultures in and around Las Vegas from the 1950s onward, providing a postnuclear revision of Turner's "frontier thesis" as he explores the play of amnesia, conspiracy theory, and spectacle that constitute the "desert modern." Tsing, too, provides a retake on the frontier thesis, arguing that on the Indonesian "resource frontier," a local discourse of wildness functions in concert with powerful and decentered logics of capital, creating rifts in the big narratives of "the future of the environment." Both essays examine the material and cultural waste that frontier futurizing practices leave in their wake.

The following two essays by Vicente Rafael and Daniel Rosenberg explore the relationship between technology and modern or postmodern futurisms. Rafael, in his study of protest and revolution in the Philippines, examines a new site of messianic expectation and action—a "fantasy of direct communication" and collective justice—created through practices of electronic communication, particularly the use of cell phones and instant messaging. In his analysis of the work of the information theorist Theodor Holm Nelson, Rosenberg demonstrates the simultaneous intensification and disavowal of problems of memory and nostalgia in information culture. Each of these essays brings into focus and troubles the prevailing eschatology of information technology.

The next three essays revolve around imaginations of the future in literary and artistic movements. Jamer Hunt's essay focuses on futurist and surrealist happenings in Europe in the early decades of the twentieth century, especially on the futurist banquets. He argues that these events provide a crucial counterpoint to the technophilic rhetoric of the movement and that the aesthetic of the banquet arose from its premonitions of degeneration and rot as much as from those of speed and strength. Pamela Jackson leads us through the baroque temporal landscape of the recession-era Southern California of Philip K. Dick. Jackson shows how Dick cobbled together a new kind of prophetic language out of the discarded materials of a commercial culture. Miryam Sas, too, focuses on space and place in her account of the futurist art movement in Japan. She shows how the Japanese futurists grappled with the problem of cultural translation and with the difficult manipulations involved in mapping new ideas onto bodies and landscapes with palpably distinct histories.

The final four essays in the volume deal with risk, paranoia, and fatalism as practices of everyday life. Christopher Newfield examines the culture of investment in the bubble economy of the 1990s, arguing that what looked from the outside like a new kind of orientation toward the future was more a translation of long-standing hopes and fears into a new situation and language. Susan Lepselter takes up another such translation in her study of the stories and rumors circulating through Rachel, Nevada, a small, economically depressed town on the edge of a high-tech military base, Area 51. She shows how everyday stories of losses, wounds, and broken dreams resurfaced, coalesced, and became more *real* than ever in the form of an elaborate and marketable conspiracy between alien invaders and the federal government. Susan Harding examines still another folk technology of time in her essay on the end-of-the-millennium wanderings of the Heaven's Gate group. In the group's writings, recordings, media artifacts, and suicidal performances, Christian and UFO or alien visions mingled to produce an expectation of impending apocalypse. It is a quintessentially premodern time scene, a classic if thoroughly heterodox episode of socially enacted prophecy, and at the same time an exemplary moment in the crisis of modern futurity. For Kathleen Stewart, all these sites and problems represent versions of fallout from the modern trauma of attempting to live in linear time. This temporal friction creates moments of crisis, or "trauma time," when past meets future and time stands still. Stewart renders and evokes such moments in a series of "still lifes" portraying practices, objects, encounters, actions, stories in which past- and future-making technologies converge on and constitute a scene, a pause, a moment of aperture in the modern order of things.

Four interludes break up and reconfigure the relations among the essays. The first interlude, "Global Futures," is a boardless board game designed by Anna Tsing and Elizabeth Pollman. They, like Newfield, evoke problems of choice and risk in the construction of futures. Like Rosenberg, they thematize the multiplicity of possible narrative trajectories toward the future. Like Lepselter and Stewart, they emphasize the social and political power of storytelling. The second interlude is an experiment in genre fiction by award-winning novelist Jonathan Lethem. Lethem's story "Access Fantasy" at once evokes and comments on the dystopian visions of

Philip K. Dick conjured by Jackson. It also resonates with Harding's implicit tale of the self-novelization of a contemporary religious group and with Rafael's preoccupation with the place of communications technology in the utopian and dystopian landscape. The third interlude is Miryam Sas's translation of Hirato Renkichi's Japanese Futurist Manifesto. This translation, the first ever in English, flows directly from Sas's essay on Japanese futurism but may also be read in relation to the Global Futures game and essays by Rafael, Masco, Tsing, and Harding, each of which raises the problem of mobilization in a different way. The final interlude, Daniel Rosenberg's collection of timelines, graphically displays the ongoing and laborious cultural work necessary to maintain our visions of linear time. This is the central theme of Stewart's essay, but it pervades all the pieces gathered in *Histories of the Future*. We find it in the confrontation of big and small narratives in Masco's and Tsing's essays; in the problem of hypertext linkages that Rosenberg and Harding pose; in the practices of repetition, haunting, and degeneration that Sas and Lepselter examine; and in the dynamics of risk and fatalism explored by Newfield, Jackson, and Stewart.

With this foretaste of things to come, we invite you to pursue your own tracks through our volume, exploring its futures at once open-ended and overdetermined.

Notes

1   For a recent overview of secondary literature on millennial and apocalyptic movements, see Harding and Stewart, "Bad Endings." On the return of futurology, see, for example, the reissue of the 1967 study edited by Daniel Bell, *Toward the Year 2000*.

2   Appadurai, *Modernity at Large*. Fredric Jameson makes a related argument in "Nostalgia for the Present," 253–73.

3   E. P. Thompson, "Time, Work-Discipline, and Industrial Capitalism."

4   William Gibson, "The Gernsback Effect." See also McCaffrey, *Storming the Reality Studio*.

5   Bender and Wellbery, *Chronotypes*; Baudrillard, *America*; Kathleen Stewart, "Nostalgia—a Polemic."

6   James Gleick, *Faster*.

7   Jameson, *A Singular Modernity*, 27.

8   Koselleck, *Futures Past*. See also Daniel Rosenberg, "An Eighteenth-Century Time Machine" and "Condillac's Exemplary Student."

9   Clarke, *The Pattern of Expectation, 1644–2001*; Aldiss, *Billion Year Spree*; Bronislaw Baczko, *Utopian Lights*.

10   Jameson, *Singular Modernity*, 27.

11   Luhmann, *The Differentiation of Society*, 321–22.

12 Blumenberg, *The Legitimacy of the Modern Age*; Tuveson, *Redeemer Nation*; Fitz-
    gerald, "The American Millennium"; Harding and Stewart, "Bad Endings."

13 Renouvier, *Uchronie (l'Utopie dans l'histoire)*. The same impulse animates contem-
    porary discussions of counterfactual history which are central to the popular
    imagination of historical studies. See Niall Ferguson, *Virtual History*.

14 Certeau, "History," 199–221.

15 Kern, *The Culture of Time and Space*.

16 Henry Adams, "The Dynamo and the Virgin" and "Acceleration of History,"
    in *The Education of Henry Adams*, 379–90, 489–98.

17 Brand, *The Clock of the Long Now*, 2–3. This tone is characteristic of many of
    the popular works published at the time. Stephen Jay Gould's *Questioning the
    Millennium*, for example, begins with a reminiscence of the idea of the millen-
    nium being "burned into my cortex" as an eight-year-old child (39–40). For
    related psychoanalytic readings of apocalyptic prophecy and science fiction,
    see especially Martin Jay, "The Apocalyptic Imagination and the Inability to
    Mourn," 84–98; and Constance Penley, "Time Travel, Primal Scene, and the
    Critical Dystopia."

18 Joseph Masco, in this volume.

19 To name only a few of the key texts in the millennium debates: Carrière et al.,
    Conversations about the End of Time; Marcus, *Zeroing In on the Year 2000*; Strozier
    and Flynn, *The Year 2000*. On the problem of "posthistory," see especially Perry
    Anderson, "The Ends of History."

20 Liisa Malkki, "Children, Futures, and the Domestication of Hope," unpub-
    lished essay.

21 Anna Tsing, in this volume.

22 On postcards to the future, see Vicente Rafael, "The Undead: Notes on Pho-
    tography in the Philippines, 1898–1920s," in his *White Love and Other Events in
    Filipino History*. For a useful comparison to the problem of inhabiting Irvine,
    see Holston, *The Modernist City*.

23 Lyotard, *The Postmodern Condition*.

CHAPTER

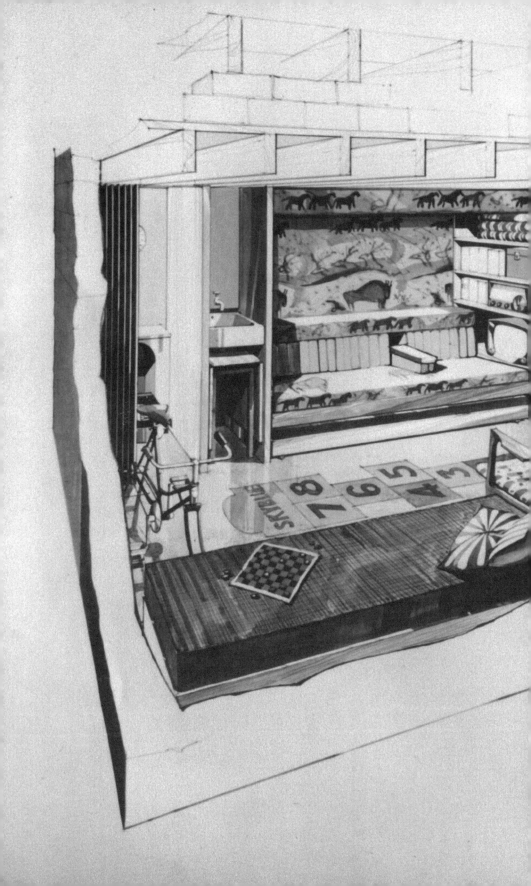

FAMILY ROOM OF TOMORROW
FALL-OUT SHELTER

designed by
MARC T. NIELSEN.   F. A. I. D.
CHICAGO, ILLINOIS

A Notebook on Desert Modernism:
From the Nevada Test Site to Liberace's
Two-Hundred-Pound Suit

Joseph Masco

Too much of a good thing is wonderful. —Liberace

The modern American desert is a place where curious things seem possible. It exists as (post)modernist frontier and as sacrifice zone, simultaneously a fantasy playground where individuals move to reinvent themselves on their own terms and a technoscientific wasteland where many of the most dangerous projects of an industrial, militarized society are located. In the twentieth century, the desert Southwest became a space of modernist excitement, where the challenge of an expansive wildness was met by monumental efforts to dislocate its indigenous inhabitants, to redirect its rivers, to populate its interior with cities and roads, and to fill its airspace with jet and missile contrails. Part neon oasis, the modern desert now dazzles with a phantasmagoria of electric lights, presenting monuments of distraction that offer up the wonder of the built for intimate comparison with that of the natural.

At century's end, Las Vegas is the fastest-growing city in the United States, consuming water as if it were surrounded by ocean. It is also a desert island within a military-industrial crypto-state, a place where secret military machines are designed, where atomic bombs are detonated, and where chemical weapons and nuclear waste are stored; it is a home, in other words, to all the "national security" technoscience supporting a superpowered military state. Nevertheless, for those caught in the spell of American desert modernism, the desert can still take on the appearance of a pristine possibility, an existential blank page awaiting a script to provide it with an essential meaning. This ability to reinscribe the desert West requires constant imaginative work, as the pursuit of utopian potential relies on a continual emptying out of the dystopian projects of the nuclear security state. It is this capacity to invest in monumental projects through practices of cognitive erasure that I call "desert modernism," a conceptual enterprise that perennially reinvents the desert as dream space for a spectacular idea of progress.

The desert has always captured American imaginations by offering citizens the hope of leaving behind the past in favor of an endlessly renewable frontier, forever open to new possibilities. But this migration away from self and nation is now doubly fraught as refugees to the interior run headlong into an equally imaginative military-industrial economy that constructs the desert as a hyperregulated national sacrifice zone, a "proving ground" for the supersecret, the deadly, and the toxic. A national-cultural excess is evident in the shared nature of this desert modernism, visible not only in the official images of nuclear nationalism but also in the afterimages of American Cold War culture. In the slippages between the form and content of American desert modernism, we can see how a careful crafting of appearances has been mobilized to endow everyday life with an epic quality. In the desert West, both citizens and officials have come to rely on tactical amnesias and temporal sutures to enable a precarious—if addictive—cosmology of progress, one fueled by high-octane combinations of risk, secrecy, utopian expectation, and paranoid anxiety in everyday life.

During the Cold War, desert modernism took on a decidedly masculine form, combining military science with corporate capitalism in a highly gendered national performance. What follows is a reflection on this particular blending of utopian desire and toxic practice in American culture, a narrative experiment provoked by a post–Cold War research tour of Nevada in the spring of 1997. Presented in the form of an ethnographic notebook, the following four biographical sketches offer a dialectical image, a composite portrait of the masculinist afterimages of Cold War culture. What is at stake in these distinct articulations of male mastery (each linked through practices of mirror imaging or inversion in an overarching attempt to define and control the future) is the nature of modernity itself as a knowable enterprise. For we can see in the American desert today a national-cultural arena in which the high modernism of the Cold War—sustained by a powerful belief in an unlimited possibility for self-reinvention and an unending technological progress—circles back to confront itself in the everyday lives of nuclear weapon designers, tunnel engineers, conspiracy theorists, and sequined entertainers. As survivors of that expressive national performance known as the Cold War, which offered the delirious rush of participating in a universe-making or universe-breaking cosmology, desert dwellers are left now to negotiate the accumulating residues of desert modernism in the here and now, even as they mobilize to reinvent the future. Indeed, we can see in the following fragmentary moments how the contradictions of a disabled master narrative of progress have come to saturate everyday life with unruly new forms of imaginative agency, simultaneously exhilarating, excessive, apocalyptic—American.

Day One. On Mythic Masculinity:
The Nevada Test Site

Our guide is utterly charming.[1] A thirty-five-year career at the Nevada Test Site (NTS) building detonating mechanisms for nuclear weapons has obviously been good to him. He carries himself today with the cool assurance of someone who has performed well at the center of an important national project, a cold warrior in the truest sense of the term. Even after the demise of the Soviet Union and while in retirement, he upholds the mission of the test site, educating the public about "what really went on," articulating the continued need for weapons of mass destruction, and reiterating the critical role the NTS plays in managing a global order of proliferating danger and constant threat. Physically strong, crystal clear in thought, and with a great sense of cowboy humor, our guide's manner is, in and of itself, a political counter to many of the popular images of weapons scientists, the NTS, and the nuclear security state. This is no Dr. Strangelove but more a favorite story-telling relative.

Driving us through the NTS, he relates stories of Cold War excitement, pointing out project details: "That's Sedan Crater (second biggest crater in the U.S.—part of the nonmilitary use of nuclear explosives program—astronauts trained there before going to the moon); that's the Chemical Spill Test Facility (the only place in the country where you can create a major toxic accident to study how to clean it up); that's the new Device Assembly Facility (it's got miles of underground tunnels—*we* can't go there)." He presents a seamless history of work at the test site, mediated by an understated, if undeniable, patriotism. I ask him when, in his experience, was the best moment to be working on nuclear weapons at the test site. "From 1962 to 1988," he replies without hesitation. This is roughly the period from the implementation of the above-ground nuclear test ban to the near collapse of the nuclear narrative in 1988, when revelations about the scope of environmental damage at places like Hanford, Washington, Rocky Flats, Colorado, and Fernald, Ohio, brought heightened public suspicion and new regulatory restraints on work at the test site. During this twenty-six-year period, the only pause he mentions in a narrative of pure techno-national progress was for President John F. Kennedy. "He was as-

Railroad bridge section, Nevada Test Site. U.S. Department of Energy photograph.

sassinated on a test day," our guide tells us. "We postponed the 'shot' for twenty-four hours in his memory, but then got back to work."

For our guide, working at the test site provided access to the very best minds in the world, the weapons scientists at the national laboratories (Los Alamos, Livermore, and Sandia), but it also demanded a constant negotiation of the military mind-set. He confides that he had to put an army colonel or two in his place who didn't understand the technoscientific logistics of the test site. During one such confrontation, he simply pulled the detonating mechanism out of the nuclear device, placed it in the trunk of his car, and drove away—putting the whole multi-million-dollar test on hold until he felt confident of its success. In the realm of Cold War masculinity, the buck stops here. But it was also obviously so much fun. Our guide populates his stories with tales of adventure, of midnight helicopter rides across the desert test site, hints at secrets he's not allowed to share, and reiterates the pleasures of commanding earthshaking technoscience. "I could wreck twenty thousand marriages," he proclaims, the isolation and excitement of nuclear science at the NTS creating a culture of hard work, drink, and (intermarital) play. His commentary constantly registers the pleasure of the Cold War, the satisfaction of having a significant job, all the resources the nation-state could muster to support it, and a race with a real enemy to give military science meaning in everyday life.

Much of our tour focuses on remnants of the "weapons effects tests" from the 1950s, consisting of tanks, bridges, and buildings that were placed near a nuclear blast to see what would happen to them. The torn wreckage that remains documents a particular moment in the Cold War, when in order to understand how to fight a nuclear war with the Soviets, U.S. military officials actually waged one at the NTS. We look at twisted steel girders, whose original shape has been lost to the bomb and the shifting sands of the desert, and learn about kilotonnage and blast effects. But our guide continually emphasizes moments of survival over all. Ignoring that which was vaporized by the nuclear blast, he shows us a safe, which was filled with money and used in a 1957 nuclear effects test called Priscilla. The building was completely destroyed by the thirty-seven-kiloton explosion, but the safe and the money inside it, he notes with clear satisfaction, came through just fine. (This was an important discovery in the early days of the Cold War: the monetary system might just survive a nuclear exchange after all.)

Next we visit the nuclear waste storage site at the NTS, which consists of an enormous trench filled with neatly stacked wooden boxes and metal drums filled with radioactive refuse. In the accompanying office building, we immediately encounter a poster board presentation detailing how site workers mobilized to relocate a family of foxes that were living inside the

Priscilla Shot, June 25, 1957. U.S. Department of Energy photograph.

Nevada Test Site Radioactive Waste Disposal Facility.
U.S. Department of Energy photograph.

nuclear waste dump. Thus, while asking questions about radioactive waste and pondering the 100,000-year threat posed by some nuclear materials at the NTS, we are presented with images of baby foxes and overtly documented signs of worker environmentalism. When we ask about radiation contamination, our guide steps in to say that he has walked "every inch of this site" and suffered "no ill effects." Here his own vitality is used as political commentary: thirty-five years at the test site without a cancer. Yes, there is some contamination at the test site, he acknowledges, but it is readily contained by the desert and poses no risk to the public. He soon counters the reference to radioactive contamination with a story about a rattlesnake that attacked him one day while he was wandering the test site. It bit into his cowboy boot and wouldn't let go. He fought back and then had the boots—snake included—bronzed. In his presentation, dangers at the test site are natural or international, but not radioactive or technoscientific—*that's* well under control.

Our final stop on the tour is the Apple II site, where the U.S. military built a "typical" American suburb in 1955 for the sole purpose of detonating a nuclear bomb on it. A fire station, a school, a radio station, a library, as well as a dozen homes were built and furnished with everyday items (televisions, refrigerators, furniture, carpets, and linens). They were then stocked with food, populated with white-skinned mannequins, and neatly incinerated. Today two remnants of the test remain: a brick ruin and what looks like an abandoned wooden house. Our guide describes the latter as "a real fixer-upper" but soon suggests that it wouldn't take much work to bring the house back to life after all. This is a curious place; the only real sign that something dramatic happened here is that the brick chimney is significantly cracked and wildly off center, suggesting a powerful blast but only hinting at the force of the twenty-nine-kiloton bomb that was detonated one mile away; it vaporized the rest of "survival town." After the explosion, scientists held a feast in which they ate the food that survived the test, again, as our guide informs us, "suffering no ill effects." The food had been flown into the NTS by special military charter from Chicago and had been neatly laid out on kitchen tables before the test. In the serious play of the test site, this was a kind of reverse last supper, where any signs of life after the nuclear explosion were celebrated as an absolute victory.

I ask our guide if the United States could survive a nuclear war. "Oh, yes, I believe we could," he replies confidently, but at another moment he seems unsure, stating that a nuclear war would be, of course, an "act of insanity—the end of everything." This is the only ambiguity in a nearly perfect performance, a slight slippage about what the end would look like. The seamlessness of his narrative, in fact, is a register of his Cold War discipline: he neither confirms nor denies anything that makes work at the NTS suspect. To that end, he focuses on certain historical events in our tour while scrupulously avoiding others. His history of the test site, for example, is largely restricted to the era of above-ground nuclear testing (1951–1962), after which testing—and most of the *visual* consequences of nuclear explosions—went underground. This was, however, also the era of the most extreme environmental damage, when studies of nuclear blast effects included experiments not only on banks, tanks, houses, and airplanes but also on soldiers (ordered to march into fallout clouds) and civilians (hit by the fallout from this era of nuclear testing). We know now that most of the continental United States was covered with radioactive fallout from above-ground testing at the NTS, contributing significantly to national thyroid cancer rates. But when I ask about fallout, he simply states, "That was before my time," and moves on in his narrative.

But isn't this simply desert modernism in its purest form, a profound belief in the possibility of an unending and conceptually clean progress, but one made possible only by tactical amnesias and sublimated technophilia? The Cold War nuclear complex required a constant surveillance and regulating of discourse to retain its narrative purity. For just as the desert

Nevada Test Site, nuclear blast effects. U.S. Department of Energy photograph.

Survival Town house today. U.S. Department of Energy photograph.

constantly threatens to overrun the activities of the test site, introducing weeds and blowing sand where shiny metal should be, so the cosmology of the cold warrior required a constant self-monitoring, a patrolling of the cognitive field, to prevent multiplicity or ambiguity from taking root. As we leave the NTS, I ask our guide about the future of nuclear weapons after the Cold War. He states unequivocally that the United States will need to return to nuclear testing, that a world without an active NTS producing new and improved nuclear weapons is a more dangerous and uncertain world. "The Soviets" he states, then corrects himself with a private half smile that we hadn't seen previously, "I mean Russians" are still unpredictable and dangerous.

Our guide reiterates that developing nuclear weapons is a means of protecting the "free world," a means of producing stability and security in everyday life. However, his narrative does not acknowledge the local consequences of nuclear testing or assess the legacy of nuclear waste produced by that mission—in a perceived fight to the death, one doesn't have time to think about such things. Historical displacement and tactical erasure have enabled a strategic renarration of America's nuclear-powered national security in his presentation. Thus the signs of nuclear nationalism revealed to us in our tour are not drawn from the current nuclear complex, which is busily reinventing itself and prospering in a post–Cold War world, but are instead a displaced and carefully edited reiteration of 1950s nuclear culture. By the end of our visit to the NTS, it's difficult not to conclude that nuclear weapons, despite our guide's proclamations about the future, are now located in the past, part of an abandoned project likely to be completely reclaimed by the desert sands. We've seen no real evidence that nuclear weapons remain the foundation of U.S. national security or a multi-billion-dollar-per-year operation in the United States, with budgets in 1997 exceeding the height of Cold War levels. The vast desert landscape of the test site, the aged quality of the buildings we visit, and the lack of any substantive sign of ongoing nuclear science reduce the scale of the nuclear project at the NTS and, seemingly, its claim on the future.

In the end, this may be a public relations tactic (a strategy to reduce public concern about activities at the test site during a time of institutional change), but it might also be one structural effect of desert modernism. It might well be that those inhabiting the center of this kind of techno-national project cannot assess their own history, or terms for being, or recognize their own historical excess. For that, we might have to look more closely at the borders, look to neighboring communities that live with the effects of nuclear nationalism but are excluded from the internal logics of the national security state. In other words, we might have to turn to those who reflect back the mission of the NTS but do so from radically different perspectives, revealing nuclear weapons science at the NTS to be productive of far more than a particular form of international relations.

Day Two. On the Poetics of Rock Bolts:
The Yucca Mountain Project

On the western periphery of the Nevada Test Site, overlooking the desert proving grounds where nuclear devices were detonated throughout the

Cold War, is Yucca Mountain, which is currently in preparation to become the principal nuclear waste storage site in the United States.[2] If the narrative of weapons scientists at the NTS presents desert modernism in its positive form (that is, still invested in a conceptually pure narrative of progress), then the Yucca Mountain Project represents its flip side, an arena where the dream space of absolute technical mastery and control of nature slips out of joint, revealing other processes also to be at work. In this mountain, a spiritual center for the displaced indigenous cultures of the desert Southwest, the industrial waste of a nuclear-powered state proves to be uncontainable, exceeding the power of the nation-state that produced it to predict its future effects. From a distant coast, the Department of Energy has ruled that any permanent nuclear waste depository in the United States must have an operative plan that would make it safe for ten thousand years. Such a plan is unprecedented in human history, though still accounting for only a fraction of the life span of the most dangerous nuclear materials, which will remain radioactive for hundreds of thousands of years. Nevertheless—a *ten-thousand-year* safety plan—consider the astonishing confidence this regulation reveals, as well as the certainty it registers about the future and the eternal reliability of the nation-state.

We arrive at Yucca Mountain from Las Vegas at midmorning, just in time for a safety lecture before plunging into the thirty-foot-diameter cave that U-turns in a great arch through the center of the mountain. We don red hard hats, put on huge fluorescent orange earplugs, fit ourselves with eye protection, and strap an emergency-breathing filter around our waists. We have been told to wear long-sleeved shirts and good shoes and are now briefed on emergency procedures. We are told that in case of a fire, we should use our breathing filters, even though they might scorch our lungs. Weighted down with our awkward new gear, we move slowly past the work trucks and walk single file along the railway tracks into the darkness of the tunnel. Deafening machine noise mixed with the long shadows produced by artificial light and the smell of stale earth greet us. We walk about seventy-five yards into the mountain and move into a large chamber off the main tunnel.

Here we meet the tunnel engineer, a middle-aged man who wears his protective gear with practiced ease, and learn about the technical aspects of the Yucca Mountain Project. He explains to us how the waste is to be shipped to the site in barrels, where and how it will be stacked within the mountain, as well as contingencies for retrieving specific barrels once stored. Our tunnel engineer is nervous talking with us, the intense politics around the Yucca Mountain Project having undoubtedly brought many confrontations to his workplace. He immediately has my sympathy, for he is

Yucca Mountain Project, southern entrance. U.S. Department of Energy photograph.

not a public relations expert or a nuclear policy maker; he builds things—tunnels, to be precise. Shouting over the machine noise echoing through the mile-long project, he seems to be most comfortable providing technical information about the tunnel itself, and he does so in great detail. Eventually our attention moves to the chamber walls and ceiling, which are covered with countless metal spikes, secured by netting. It looks as though project engineers feared that the entire surface of the cave might crumble and sought to shore it up with hundreds of metal spikes each set about a foot apart. A strange place for a public conversation about nuclear safety, the overwrought performance of the cave begs immediate questions about the nature of its technology as well as its long-term stability.

The engineer, who has seemed tentative up to this point in our conversation, lights up with a newfound enthusiasm to our questions. "Well you see, there are two kinds of rock: good rock and bad rock. This is bad rock." We learn that "bad" rock crumbles and needs mechanical reinforcement, while "good" rock is internally stable and reliable from an engineering point of view. Yucca Mountain, he tells us, has both good and bad rock, and the tunnel has been engineered, through the use of rock bolts, to compensate for both. "There are three different kinds of rock bolts," the tunnel engineer offers, and then, in a moment of technoscientific reverie, proceeds to introduce us to the engineering cosmology of the rock bolt. In the next few minutes, we learn that rock bolts differ by length, thickness, head type, and means of insertion. Some can be removed, some can't. Some are stronger than others and are used on certain kinds of rock, but not on others. We learn that rock bolts are a very important technology and that this tunnel is largely dependent on them. With alarming ease, in fact, all the debates about the scientific viability of Yucca Mountain as a nuclear waste site, the twenty-plus years of acrimonious technical and political debate, the hundreds of thousands of pages of technical reports that argue with specificity the potential risks and advantages of the site, the entire ten-thousand-year modernist plan for ensuring safety at the site, are reduced to the (conceptual and engineering) power of the rock bolt. Rock bolts, a brilliantly simple technology, present desert modernism in its primordial form, for they seem to offer the possibility of holding Yucca Mountain together, of disciplining the earth itself through the millennia.

I ask the tunnel engineer if the ten-thousand-year safety plan required by federal law for the Yucca Mountain Project has affected his engineering in any way, if it has made this tunnel different or more difficult than other tunnels he has built. "No, it hasn't," he replies testily. Startled by his answer, I ask, "Do you ever feel like you are building something for the ages here, like the pyramids in Egypt, because it will last for thousands of years?" "I

Yucca Mountain Project, interior. U.S. Department of Energy photograph.

don't like to think about those kinds of things," he replies. Then, looking me directly in the eyes, he says, "I'll guarantee this tunnel for one hundred years. After that I hope they'll have someplace else to put this stuff." *After that I hope they'll have someplace else to put this stuff.* It soon becomes clear that the tunnel engineers do not believe the ten-thousand-year plan is attainable. In fact, they readily dismiss the ten-thousand-year program as a product of a political, not a technoscientific, process. We also learn from our guide that Yucca Mountain lies on top of several major fault lines and that the underground water supply for much of the Southwest runs underneath the project. Neither our guide nor our tunnel engineer will say that Yucca Mountain is a good place to permanently store nuclear waste; they just say it will happen and that much of the reason for it is politics: there is simply nowhere else to put the nation's radioactive garbage. As the zeros drop off the ten-thousand-year master plan, the Yucca Mountain Project assumes for many of us the appearance of a national hoax, and its desert modernism, once seemingly perfected, fractures unredeemably.

We leave Yucca Mountain knowing that the ten-thousand-year safety plan maintains a very public secret. The narrative of absolute technical mastery and control of nature, propagated by work on nuclear weapons at the NTS and now necessary to legitimate the power of the state to deal with its nuclear waste, is revealed at Yucca Mountain to be a political tactic, not a technoscientific reality. The excesses of nuclear nationalism, the tons of nuclear waste located all around the country, thus remain unpredictable despite the rhetorical effort by the state to contain them within a ten-thousand-year institutional plan. What will happen a thousand years from now at Yucca Mountain, and who will be around to watch over the radioactive waste of the twentieth century? Can we imagine a nation-state that lasts one thousand years, let alone ten thousand?

Leaving the Iron Age technology of the rock bolt to grapple with the unpredictable products of the nuclear age, the future is being reinvented at Yucca Mountain. The nuclear apocalypticism of the Cold War, the fear of a sudden fiery end that propelled nuclear weapons science and the creation of deterrence theory, assumed that the nation was going to end abruptly with a nuclear flash, requiring radical action in the here and now. The Yucca Mountain Project, however, now assumes an eternal nation-state, one that will diligently uphold twentieth-century laws and watch over twentieth-century nuclear waste across the millennia. Thus the nuclear waste storage project at Yucca Mountain is where the desert modernism of the NTS formally confronts its own apocalyptic excess and, in an effort to control that excess, is expanded—exponentially—to the point of self-contradiction and failure. The same modernist logic that made the nuclear complex blind to its own waste in the first place, to nuclear contamination in all its forms, continues to inform the Yucca Mountain Project, which is now attempting a massive compensation for the unprecedented physical effects of the Cold War nuclear complex by maintaining the fiction of a ten-thousand-year operative plan.

But in the American desert, reality is mandated not only by modernist planning and official discourse but also by wild processes. Over the millennia, Yucca Mountain is an object in motion, a living being, subject to tectonic shifts, erosion, and unseen planetary forces. In the Yucca Mountain Project, we see desert modernism transformed into a new kind of mystic vision, an arena in which human control is assumed to be eternal, even as our tunnel engineer articulates the tenuous power of the rock bolt, as emblem, exemplar, and limit of modernity. The poetic call of the rock bolt may be the conceptual limit of Yucca Mountain, but the logic that supports it—the search for a master narrative that denies the uncontainability of the future—proliferates in modern American life and, like the unpredictable course of nuclear materials, radiates, catching individuals outside the center in its mutating glow.

Day Three. Paranoid Surveillance: Rachel

If nuclearism at the Nevada Test Site represents the center of a certain kind of modernist planning, of big science protected and enabled by government secrecy, what is it like to live on the outside, to be surrounded by nuclear nationalism but to be denied access to its internal logics or lines of power?[3] One need drive only ninety minutes north of Las Vegas to find just such an outpost on the frontier of desert modernism. In the little town of Rachel, which consists of a dozen or so mobile homes parked on the side of a two-lane desert highway, one encounters an important cultural side effect of Cold War military technoscience. Apparently surrounded by wilderness, the desert calm of Rachel—population one hundred—is broken primarily by the military aircraft that fly overhead from Nellis Air Force Base, the Nevada Test Site, and the mysterious Area 51, also known as Dreamland, where stealth fighter technology was covertly invented, some locals say, by a process of reverse-engineering crashed UFOs. On the outer periphery of military-industrial airspace, Rachel is a center for conspiracy theorists and UFO believers, a point of pilgrimage for those caught up in another aspect of American desert modernism. In Rachel an important cultural legacy of the Cold War intermingling of secrecy, security, and science at the NTS becomes visible. Indeed, we can see in Rachel how a century of revolutionary technological progress has combined with a half century of intense

Rachel, Nevada. Photograph © Joseph Masco.

government secrecy to permeate everyday life, encouraging those on the periphery to assume the existence of a secret master narrative that controls everything, one that is busy regulating and reinventing the terms of existence from a hidden center of power.

We go into the Little Ale'Le'Inn cafe, where you can buy conspiracy theory and a hamburger. The walls are covered with hundreds of photographs of fuzzy, disc-shaped things that might be spaceships, and talk here frequently turns to tracking the signs of coverup, of misinformation, of why "they" are here and "what's going on." Here you can discuss government black budgets, and black helicopters: are they disguised UFOs or part of a covert military project? You can explore the latest theories on cattle mutilations in the desert West or on human abductions, covert genetic experimentation, and the coming New World Order. Who is secretly behind the United Nations, the International Monetary Fund, and the Trilateral Commission, and when will they reveal their true purpose? Was the Cold War really a battle with the Soviets, or merely a way for both countries to secretly arm themselves against an invading extraterrestrial source? Is the current fascination with UFOs a giant misinformation campaign to hide *The Truth*, or is the government slowly preparing us for the news that *They* have been here for a long, long time? Whose soldiers are training under the cover of the desert night and using that vast underground network of tunnels connecting U.S. military sites in order to stay hidden during the daytime? Why did JFK need to be silenced, and which government entity invented AIDS? And above all—what's coming next?

While we eat lunch in the cafe and discuss the strange desert context of life in Rachel (a curious mix of pure Americana and paranoid utopia), a conspiracy theorist takes center stage, literally. He begins singing country and western songs over a microphone while playing an electric organ. One

Photographs on the wall of the Little Ale'Le'Inn cafe. Photograph © Joseph Masco.

of the two waitresses joins him for a song. They are having a good time, and the public space has been made intimate by their performance. Between tunes, he introduces himself and spins a conspiracy.

I recognize him, having seen one of his self-financed videos on UFOs. On tape he argues that all UFO sightings are masterminded by an "international cabal" of men who are planning to take over the world. UFOs, he believes, are human made, a ruse to distract people from the real conspiracy, from the men who are positioning themselves to take control of everyday life and implement a "new world order." He warns that sometime in the late 1990s, a "major UFO incident" will be staged at Area 51, a carefully planned media distraction to enable the global takeover. Today he has some new information he wants to share, identifying perhaps the first salvo in this upcoming campaign of public misdirection and conspiracy. He holds up an 11-by-14-inch color photograph, an aerial image of a parking lot, which is surrounded by trees and populated with several olive green U.S. army vehicles and one discordant bright yellow Ryder moving van. "This photograph was taken in April of 1995 at a military base near Oklahoma City a few days before the Oklahoma City bombing." Then he holds up another photograph of the same parking lot, same visual perspective, same olive green army jeeps, but no Ryder moving van. "This photograph was taken a few days after the Oklahoma City bombing. Now, I think this is very interesting. Now what is a Ryder moving van doing in a military parking lot? I'm not saying the government was directly involved in the bombing of the Oklahoma federal building, but I think this is very interesting. Before the bombing of the Murrah Federal Building there is a Ryder van on the military base, and after, it is gone. I think this is very significant." Having set the conspiratorial narrative in motion, he returns to his music, leaving his audience to contemplate what it would mean to their everyday lives if a secret organization with access to U.S. Army facilities had bombed a U.S. federal building and implicated a white-supremacist group for the crime as part of a calculated plan to take over the world.

Conspiracy theorists are one of the unexpected side effects of the desert modernism pursued at the NTS and Area 51. Excluded from the internal logics of state power, but well aware of the effects of these military sites—nuclear fallout, a militarized space, lights in the night sky—conspiracy theorists mobilize to fill in the gaps in their knowledge. The conspiracy theorist patrols everyday life for the signs of a hidden master narrative, a master narrative that he endlessly constructs out of the strange details of modern life, attempting to make visible that which is hidden, making rational the national cultural excesses within desert modernism. The very lack of proof becomes evidence of conspiracy as the personal observations of a

Area 51. Satellite image © 2001Terraserver.com and Spin-2.

vast cross section of America sees that which the government denies. The people of Rachel, for example, live only a few miles from Area 51, a military base that everyone knows about. Some residents have even worked at the base and trace their current health problems to toxic exposures on the job. For years, one of the best, and most readily available, photographs of Area 51 was made by a Cold War–era Soviet surveillance satellite. Yet despite the worker histories and the toxic lawsuits, the Soviet photographs and a significant presence in American popular culture (as, for example, in the film *Independence Day*), the U.S. Air Force will acknowledge only an "operational presence" in the Groom Lake area.[4] Officially, Area 51 does not exist.

For citizens in Rachel, the engine of modernity has become a giant conspiracy, requiring those who want to "live free" in the desert West to track the signs of military-industrial life that impinge on everyday life, and search for the truth behind the coverup and misinformation. It should not be surprising that places like Rachel exist. A half century of government policy to "neither confirm nor deny" questions about nuclear nationalism has forced the question of "security" to remain open and unanswered. An ironic effect of the effort to control technical information about military science in a world of competing nation-states has been to produce a prolif-erating discursive field where citizens who confront the effects of nuclear nationalism are left to rely on their own imagination for information. The reality of black budgets and apocalyptic technologies, the possibilities of a ten-thousand-year safety plan and its obvious propaganda, the history of nuclear fallout and covert human plutonium experiments on U.S. citizens, and always the wild new technologies that arrive unannounced (especially during wartime)—all of these realities have demonstrated that government planning can indeed take the shape of conspiracy. The problem in Rachel is how to negotiate that knowledge, how to resolve the effects on everyday life of living side by side with covert and dangerous government projects, how to make sense of it all with only the peripheral effects and those strange lights in the sky as one's muse. In this way, the citizens of Rachel present merely the displaced mirror image of nuclear nationalism, for the logics informing work at the NTS, Yucca Mountain, Area 51, and life in Rachel all assume that the world is ultimately knowable, that there are no coinci-dences in modernity, and that careful observation of the details of everyday life can reveal the hidden master narrative of existence. This fixation on the scripting of appearances in the desert West, however, now exceeds the logics of the national security state, evolving into a resilient new kind of American expressive culture—apocalyptic, narcissistic, sensational.

Day Four. Delirious Excess: Las Vegas

One of the most remarkable attributes of the Nevada Test Site is its loca-tion. Founded on the need for concealment (of military technoscience and environmental ruin), it is nonetheless bordered by the one city in the world most famous for its embrace of extravagant public display. Contrary to the NTS, where every act is supposedly regulated by a national security state, and where the foremost experience of place involves fences, gates, and guards, Las Vegas is known as the town where quite literally "anything goes" (gambling, prostitution, the Mafia), a place where there are few bar-riers to the imagination, and the nation-state is somehow conceptually

Courtesy of the Liberace Museum.

absent. If there is a seam in the structure of desert modernity that links the introverted world of the NTS and the extroverted world of Las Vegas, it should be visible in any number of sites, but perhaps most powerfully in the cultural exemplars of Las Vegas itself. We enter just such a site on day four of our tour through the afterimages of American Cold War culture, the Liberace Museum, which is located in a shopping complex just off Tropicana Avenue. Inside this museum/shrine, one can move through room after room filled with the material traces of a Cold War life uniquely devoted to visual excess. Near the end of our visit, our senses increasingly dulled and bored with ostentatious display, we are nevertheless stopped dead in our tracks, caught in the shimmering reflection of a room filled with an entirely new form of desert modernism. Dazzled by the sheer visual power of tens of millions of glittering sequins, we stare at Liberace's fantastic suits and are forced to contemplate how Liberace, and the broader Las Vegas culture of excess he embodies, participates in the desert modernism of the Cold War.[5]

As one of the most popular attractions in Las Vegas, the Liberace Museum, which houses the entertainer's famous costumes, his jewel-encrusted pianos and candelabra, his custom-built cars, and other mementos from a career that resides within the temporal limits of the Cold War, provides a unique window into American Cold War culture. Indeed, Liberace, Las Vegas, and the Nevada Test Site were structurally linked right from the beginning. The NTS opened in 1951, about the time Liberace first played Las Vegas, and by the mid-1950s the two biggest shows in Nevada were the nuclear explosions at the test site and Liberace, who by then was making $50,000 a week at the brand-new Riviera casino performing in a black tuxedo jacket studded with 1,328,000 shimmering sequins. We can begin to see here how the serious politics of concealment at the NTS and the seemingly frivolous politics of display in Las Vegas are mutually reinforcing, sharing in a common modernity. Indeed, a favorite pastime of that era was to take a cocktail to the top of a Las Vegas casino in the early morning hours, and from that vantage point search the northern horizon for a flash of light or the shape of a mushroom cloud emanating from the test site, and thereby offer a toast to America's ascendancy to superpower status. Could it possibly be that Liberace, whose career is both a Cold War and a Las Vegas artifact, never partook in that premier spectacle of the nuclear age?

Whereas the public/secret world of the desert nuclear complex, as we have seen, denies its own excess, the public/private world Liberace created so successfully for himself delights in presenting a delirious excess. Linked with that other icon of Cold War masculinity, JFK, Liberace's fame was, in part, drawn not only from a public fascination with his sexuality but also from the explicit constructedness of his public persona, which constantly offered audiences the chance to participate in the act of its construction. Living at a moment when to be gay was to occupy the structural position of the communist in the United States (and therefore to be subject to all the assaults of the McCarthy era), Liberace successfully sued newspapers that questioned his heterosexuality in print, even as he lived with male partners. (And we might note here that it was not until 1993 that U.S. security clearance guidelines for those working within the nuclear complex were revised to take homosexuality off the list of things that make a potential employee, by definition, a national security risk.) Liberace's over-the-top stage performances and fantastic costumes, however, constantly registered his acute awareness of the normalizing structures in Cold War life, and his charm lay, in part, in how explicit his scripting of appearance was, enabling audience after audience to enjoy his overt class transgressions and mimetic gender play without feeling in any way challenged by them.

In the realm of Cold War masculinity, Liberace's life reveals something important, both inverting an imagined white, heterosexual norm, and through expressive cultural performance becoming a site of release, where the excesses of Cold War identity politics were put onstage and manipulated for pleasure. As an intensely private person who paradoxically made a living displaying himself as spectacle, Liberace rejected the Cold War logics of white, middle-class masculinity that emphasized self-sacrifice and capitalist production above all. This is evident both in his stage persona and in the nature of his musical performance. Liberace commingled musical genres, high classical and contemporary popular music, in his stage show, cutting and pasting musical types as a gag. Mixing works by Liszt, Chopin, and Debussy with the "Beer Barrel Polka" and "Cement Mixer (Put-Ti Put-Ti)," Liberace played with the division between classical and popular music and showed a keen attention to the power of transgressing and marking the artificiality of such boundaries. In his early performances, one of Liberace's famous acts was to play duets with recordings of famous classical pianists onstage. His perfect bodily synchronization with the virtuoso recordings of Vladimir Horowitz, Arthur Rubinstein, and other classical artists demonstrated for all his musical technique, but also his ability to mimic official culture, thus drawing attention to the constructed discourse of high classical art. His fantastic financial success, and his unrelenting public display of wealth, cut against serious logics of Cold War consumption and suggested that money could be fun. Not tied to "serious" art production, mocking notions of class standing, rejecting the need to produce a traditional "nuclear" family (the most prominent woman in his life remained his mother, who was ritually evoked in every performance), and ridiculing Cold War notions of utilitarian consumption through his baroque lifestyle, Liberace offered relief from the seriousness of the Cold War nuclear standoff while nonetheless sharing in its (desert) modernity.

So one need not be a conspiracy theorist to wonder today at the vast global intrigue that must have been in place to bring down two exemplars of Cold War masculinity on the same November night in 1963. As news of John F. Kennedy's assassination swept the country, Liberace promised to put special energy into that evening's performance to console his audience.

Courtesy of the Liberace Museum.

However, his own life was soon put into jeopardy by his fabulous wardrobe—which, quite simply, tried to kill him. In the midst of that evening's memorial performance and while the nation mourned, Liberace collapsed, having been poisoned by the chemicals used to dry-clean his costumes. The toxic shock brought on by the chemicals took Liberace into complete kidney failure. Unconscious, and on life support, he was eventually given last rites, and thought lost.

In its pure form, I've suggested, desert modernism is necessarily blind to its own excess. And just as the toxins produced by the nuclear complex are somehow conceptually absent from the narrative of our nuclear weapons scientist at the NTS, so too was Liberace's brush with a toxic death taken by him not as an invitation for critique, requiring at least a moment of reflection, but instead as a new authorization of his act. Liberace claimed afterward that in a vision, a white-robed nun had not only healed him but actually blessed his love of opulent display. After this near-death experience, his outfits only got more lavish, and he embraced his love of visual excess with no restraint. Indeed, Liberace sought to reinvent himself with each new costume and was soon fighting a cold war of his own with entertainers like Elvis Presley and other Las Vegas superpowers for command of the most over-the-top performance. Liberace's love of sequins continued to escalate, and by the 1970s, his sequined outfits had attained truly epic proportions—often weighing over two hundred pounds.

Sequins serve no purpose other than to be pretty. But consider their power when sewn together in the hundreds of thousands; they shimmer brilliantly, becoming luminous. To achieve this visual effect, Liberace performed nightly in sequined suits that could, like his poisonous outfits, certainly kill him. The nature of this public display, its perilous tightrope act, was always a metacommentary on Liberace himself, who was always on the verge of crashing, of turning into a spectacular ruin. In this light, his Las Vegas career provides an index of American Cold War culture, in which the hyperproduction of nuclear weapons (70,000 in all, enough to destroy every city on the planet dozens of times over) also registered a national fascination with excess and display and involved a precarious dance with death. The shared nature of this desert modernism allowed Liberace's stage performances in Las Vegas and the serious work at the NTS to mirror-image each other, as both provided distractions from the desert landscape (and from each other) through specific forms of technosocial power. It is important to remember that (after Hiroshima and Nagasaki) the U.S. nuclear arsenal was officially designed never to be used; it was intended

Frenchman's Flat test craters, Nevada Test Site. U.S. Department of Energy photograph.

merely to display American might to the Soviets and thereby to be a tool in foreign relations. Thus the Cold War nuclear explosions at the NTS were not merely tests; *they were the entire performance*, communicating to the world the U.S. possession of, and commitment to, weapons of mass destruction. From this perspective, the Cold War logics of "containment" that energized the U.S. nuclear economy also produced a powerful scripting of appearance that can today be read as a kind of expressive national cultural performance. To suggest that Liberace shared in the logic of this Cold War display, inverting and revealing its excess, making playful that which was so deadly serious (particularly in the 1950s when he began), and reinventing Las Vegas in the process, is only to wonder at the danger and discipline required to perform in a life-threatening mass of sequins.

Notes

My thanks to Susan Harding for organizing and directing the *Histories of the Future* project, and to the University of California's Humanities Research Institute for enabling our discussion. This essay is part of a collective research project; thus many conversations and shared experiences inform these pages. I want to thank all the participants in the *Histories of the Future* seminar—as well as the terrific staff at HRI—for a great experience in Irvine. I'm indebted to the public relations staff at the DOE-Nevada and the Yucca Mountain Project for facilitating our research on those sites. Thanks also to anonymous reviewers for helpful comments, and to fellow traveler Dan Rosenberg for his intellectual engagement and editorial care with this essay. Finally, I'm grateful to Shawn Smith, who has been a generous reader and critic of this work.

1   For a remarkable introduction to the Nevada Test Site as an environmental site, see Center for Land Use Interpretation, *The Nevada Test Site*; as well as Kathleen Stewart, "Bitter Faiths." For a historical analysis of the era of aboveground nuclear testing at the test site, see Richard L. Miller, *Under the Cloud*; Fradkin, *Fallout*; and Hacker, *Elements of Controversy*. For studies of communities suffering the most severe health effects from work at the Nevada Test Site, see Gallager, *American Ground Zero*; and Kuletz, *The Tainted Desert*. For an assessment of Cold War human radiation experiments in the United States, see Advisory Committee on Human Radiation Experiments, *The Human Radiation Experiments*. For a 10,000-page, county-by-county dose reconstruction of radioactive fallout from nuclear testing, and its impact on national thyroid cancer rates, see National Cancer Institute, "Estimated Exposures and Thyroid Doses Received by the American People from Iodine-131 in Fallout following Nevada Atmospheric Nuclear Bomb Tests," Cancer.gov, 1997, http://i131.nci.nih.gov/ (accessed April 9, 2003). For a global assessment of the environmental impact of military nuclear technology, see International Physicians for the Prevention of Nuclear War and the Institute for Energy and Environmental Research,

Radioactive Heaven and Earth; and see Schwartz, *Atomic Audit*, for a detailed accounting of the nearly $6 trillion spent on U.S. nuclear weapons in the twentieth century.

2   On July 23, 2002, President George W. Bush approved Yucca Mountain as the nation's primary commercial nuclear waste repository. Barring the numerous lawsuits that still have to work their way through the courts, Yucca Mountain will open in 2010. See Kuletz, *The Tainted Desert*, for a complex reading of the cross-cultural politics of the Yucca Mountain Project; and Michael Taussig, who in *Defacement* defines a public secret as "that which is generally known but cannot be spoken." For a trenchant analysis of desert monumentalism, see Rosenberg, "No One Is Buried in Hoover Dam."

3   See Susan Lepselter's sublime essay on Rachel in this volume, as well as Darlington, *Area 51*, on Area 51 beliefs. See Stewart and Harding, "Bad Endings," on American apocalypticism; and Fenster, *Conspiracy Theory*, on conspiracy theory in the United States. See Welsome, *The Plutonium Files*, for a discussion of covert human experimentation during the Cold War; Weart, *Nuclear Fear*, for a cultural history of nuclear anxiety in the United States, and Moynihan, *Secrecy*, for an analysis of U.S. secrecy since World War II. See Masco, "Lie Detectors," for a discussion of post–Cold War secrecy and security concerns within the U.S. nuclear complex.

4   See the Federation of American Scientists study of satellite imagery of Area 51, "Area 51—Groom Lake, NV," Federation of American Scientists Web site, April 17, 2000, http://www.fas.org/irp/overhead/ikonos_040400_overview_02-f.htm (accessed April 9, 2003). In September 2001, President George W. Bush renewed a Clinton administration executive order exempting an "unnamed" Groom Lake Air Force facility from environmental laws. This rule has been justified under national security protocols as a way to keep state secrets, but it also has the effect of suppressing the lawsuits filed by former Area 51 workers over toxic exposures. In other words, the state can now argue that since the base does not formally exist, how could anybody have worked there, let alone been poisoned on the job?

5   Biographical information on Liberace in this section is based on the presentation at the Liberace Museum (Las Vegas), as well as *Liberace: An Autobiography*; and Thomas, *Liberace: The True Story*. For an analysis of gender roles during the height of the Cold War, see Nadel, *Containment Culture*. For a policy assessment of U.S. security clearances and sexual orientation, see U.S. General Accounting Office, *Security Clearances*. For more on Las Vegas and the culture of aboveground nuclear testing at the NTS, see Titus, *Bombs in the Backyard*.

CHAPTER

How to Make Resources in Order to Destroy Them (and Then Save Them?) on the Salvage Frontier

Anna Tsing

A frontier is an edge of space and time. A frontier is a zone of unmapping: even in its planning, it is imagined as unplanned. Frontiers are not just discovered at the edge; they are projects in making geographic and temporal experience.

The late twentieth century saw the creation of new "resource frontiers" in every corner of the world. Made possible by Cold War militarization of the Third World and the growing power of corporate transnationalism, resource frontiers grew up where entrepreneurs and armies were able to disengage nature from its previous ecologies, making the natural resources that bureaucrats and generals could offer as corporate raw materials. From a distance, these new resource frontiers appeared as the "discovery" of global supplies in forests, tundras, coastal seas, or mountain fastnesses. Up close, they replaced existing systems of human access and livelihood and ecological dynamics of replenishment with the cultural apparatus of capitalist expansion. This essay explores the making of a resource frontier in the eastern part of South Kalimantan, Indonesia, in the 1990s.

Most descriptions of resource frontiers take the existence of resources for granted. Most descriptions label and count the resources and tell us who owns what. The landscape itself appears inert: ready to be dismembered and packaged for export. In contrast, the challenge I have set myself is to make the landscape a lively actor. Landscapes are simultaneously natural and social, and they actively shift and turn in the interplay of human and nonhuman practices. Frontier landscapes are particularly active: hills are flooding away, streams are stuck in mud, vines swarm over fresh stumps, ants and humans are on the move. On the frontier, nature goes wild.

The place I describe is a mountainous, forested strip of southeastern Kalimantan. My companions in traveling and learning this landscape are

Meratus Dayaks, old inhabitants of the area, whose livelihood has been based on shifting cultivation and forest foraging.[1] For Meratus, the frontier has come as a shock and a disruption; it is with their help that I experience the trauma of transformation. There are other perspectives: for some, such as migrants and miners, the frontier is an opening full of promise. They come in expectation of resources, and so they can ignore how these resources are traumatically produced. I leave their stories for other chronicles, of which there are many.

In the mid-1990s, the political regime in Indonesia was called the New Order. The New Order was a centralized and repressive political machine that depended heavily on the power of its military, particularly to control the countryside. In the 1970s and 1980s, the regime flourished through a rhetoric of state-led development. In the 1990s, however, privatization became a regime watchword; in practice, the new policies further concentrated economic power in the hands of the president's family and close cronies. In Kalimantan, state policy privileged corporate control of natural resources; huge tracts were assigned to logging companies, mining companies, and pulp and paper as well as oil palm plantation companies. The military played an important role in transferring these tracts from previous residents to their corporate owners; military men also took their own interest in resources. It seems fair to say that the military had a central role in creating the "wildness" of the frontier. This seminal period, which has gone on to shape the wildness of the early twenty-first century, is the moment I describe.

In the Violent Clarity of the Abandoned Logging Road

An abandoned logging road has to be one of the most desolate places on earth. By definition, it doesn't go anywhere. If you are walking there, it is either because you are lost or because you are trespassing, or both. The wet clay builds clods on your boots, if you have any, sapping your strength, and if you don't have any boots, the sun and the hot mud are merciless. Whole hillsides shift beside you, sliding into the stagnant pools where mosquitoes breed. Abandoned roads soon lose their shape, forcing you in and out of eroded canyons and over muddy trickles where bridges once stood but now choked by loose soil, vines crawling on disinterred roots, and trunks sliding askew. Yet, ironically, the forest as a site of truth and beauty seems clearer from the logging road than anywhere else, since it is the road that slices open the neat cross section in which underbrush, canopy, and high emergent trees are so carefully structured.

In 1994 I walked on many abandoned logging roads in the eastern sector of South Kalimantan, Indonesia, between the Meratus Mountains and the coastal plains now covered with transmigration villages—Block A, Block B, Block C—and giant, miles-square plantations of oil palm, rubber, and acacia for the pulp and paper trade. The region was transformed from when I had last seen it in the 1980s. Then, despite the logging, I had thought the forest might survive; local villagers were asserting customary resource rights, and transmigration here was just a gleam in one engineer's eye— and he wasn't in charge. Now, even beyond the newly planted industrial tree plantations lay miles of scrub and vines. These were landslides of slippery red and yellow clay, with silted-up excuses for water. The logging roads had eroded into tracks for motorcycles, water buffalo, and the still-streaming mass of immigrant and local blood and sweat that the government calls "wild": wild loggers, wild miners, and bands of roving entrepreneurs and thieves. I had seen resource booms before: when the prices for rattan shot up in the 1980s, for example, people went crazy cutting rattan until all the rattan had been cut to the ground. But this was something different. Something easy to call degradation was riding through the land. It was the kind of scene that informs so many powerful theories of resource management: the human presence was leaving the landscape all but bare. This, they say, is ordinary behavior on the resource frontier, where everything is plentiful and wild. It's human nature, they say, and the nature of resources.

In the violent clarity of the abandoned logging road, questions come to mind that might seem simple or even idiotic elsewhere. How does nature at the frontier become a set of resources? How are landscapes made empty and wild so that anyone can come to use and claim them? How do ordinary people get involved in destroying their environments, even their own home places?

This is business that gets inside our daily habits and our dreams. Two complementary nightmares come into being; the frontier emerges in the intertwined attraction and disgust of their engagement. I considered this question first while writing with the "Histories of the Future" seminar that germinated this volume in Southern California. Orange County is full of planned communities, industrial tree plantations of neatly spaced condominiums, row on row on row, which give way only to identical roads and shopping malls. There is truly no there there, no directions, no place marks, only faceless serenity, time on hold. Like game in a tree plantation, I felt caught out in the open there, an easy target. Orange County is one kind of nightmare. Its flip side is South Central Los Angeles, the mere thought of which drives masses of whites and Asian Americans behind the Orange Curtain. Time is not on hold in that bastion of short lives. Yet these two

Orange County, California. Photograph © Daniel Rosenberg.

nightmares play with each other: just as the fear of hell drives the marketing schemes of paradise, so too does the desire of paradise fuel the schemes of hell. Both rise and fall on the spectacular performances of savvy entrepreneurs.

The same is true in Kalimantan. The giant monocrop plantations are the flip side of the wild resource frontier: on one side, endless rows of silent symmetry and order, biopower applied to trees; on the other side, wild loggers, miners, and villagers in the raucous, sped-up time of looting. Each calls the other into existence. Each solves the problems put in motion by the other. Each requires the same entrepreneurial spirit. In that spirit, gold nuggets, swifts' nests, incense woods, ironwood posts, great logs destined to be plywood, and whole plantations of future pulp are conjured. Here I find the first answer to my impertinent questions. Resources are made by "resourcefulness" in both plantation and wild frontier. The activity of the frontier is to make human subjects as well as natural objects.

The frontier, indeed, had come to Kalimantan. It had not always been there. Dutch plantation schemes mainly bypassed Kalimantan in the colonial period, allowing colonial authorities to treat their natives as subjects of kingdoms and cultures. Kalimantan's Dayaks, to them patently uncivilized, were still seen as having law and territorial boundaries, not a wilderness that needed to be filled up. In its first years, the postcolonial nation maintained Kalimantan's villages, fields, and forests. Commercial logging only got under way in the 1970s. Administrative expansion and resettlement followed, with the goal of homogenizing the nation. In the 1980s, conflicts broke out between village people and commercial loggers. Massive fires and waves of immigration disrupted emergent localisms. Through the 1980s, however, it was possible to see rural Kalimantan as a landscape of villages, small cultivations, and traditional agro-forestry, with discrete patches of estate agriculture and large-scale logging and mining here and there.

The late 1980s and the 1990s witnessed a national wave of entrepreneurship. Spurred on by economic "liberalization," with its international sponsors, and a consolidating regional capitalism, entrepreneurs shot up at every level, from conglomerates to peasant tour guides. In this great surge of resourcefulness, Kalimantan became a frontier.

The frontier, then, is not a natural or indigenous category. It is a traveling theory, a blatantly foreign form requiring translation. It arrived with many layers of previous associations. "Indonesian Miners Revive Gold Rush Spirit of 49ers," proclaimed a headline in the *Los Angeles Times*.[2] Indonesian frontiers were shaped to the model of other wild times and places. Nor was 1849 California the only moment of frontier making available to be reworked and revived. There is the dark Latin American frontier: a place of violence, conflicting cultures, and an unforgiving nature driving once-civilized men to barbarism, as Domingo Sarmiento, soon to be president of Argentina, argued in 1845.[3] This savage vision of the frontier has continued

Neatly planted tree stock, row on row on row. South Kalimantan, Indonesia, 1997. Photograph © Anna Tsing.

to percolate through later frontier optimism. There is the nation-making frontier, as famously articulated by Frederick Jackson Turner in his 1893 address "The Significance of the Frontier in American History."[4] Wild, empty spaces are said to have inspired white men to national democracy and freedom in the United States. Amazing for its erasures, the power of this formulation is suggested by the fact that U.S. historians remained in its thrall for nearly a hundred years. Finally, in the 1960s, frontier chroniclers dared to mention that there were Native Americans, Asians, Hispanics, and women in these empty spaces, and they may not have benefited from that nation-making freedom quite as much as Anglo-American men. Finally, in the 1980s, environmental historians dared mention that someone had despoiled the land, forests, and rivers.[5] But the proud frontier story of the making of "America" will probably be around a long time, particularly because it was remade in an internationally colonizing form after World War II in the concept of the technofrontier, the endless frontier made possible by industrial technology. The closing of national borders, dense settlement, and resource scarcity need no longer lead to frontier nostalgia; the technofrontier is always open and expanding. In the guise of development, the dream of the technofrontier hit Indonesian centers hard in the late 1960s. By the 1990s, it had dragged its older frontier cousins, those entangled stories of the wild, to the rural peripheries.

Frontiers are notoriously unstable, and it is fitting that Kalimantan landscapes should have a role in forging new frontier conceptions. The frontier arrived in Kalimantan *after* environmentalism had already become established not just among activists but also among government bureaucrats and corporate public relations agents. No one could be surprised this time to find that frontier making is destructive of forests and indigenous cultures. Susanna Hecht and Alexander Cockburn write that in the Amazon, heroic development plans unexpectedly turned to smoke, mud, and violence: "The generals had unleashed forces beyond their control, and now the Amazon faced its apocalypse."[6] But in New Order Kalimantan, the Amazon apocalypse was already known. Plans were set in motion to save the environment in the process of destroying it. Tree plantations were introduced to restore deforested and degraded land. Only then was the landscape deforested and degraded to make way for the restorative tree plantations. Giant mining conglomerates were licensed to save the land from the pollutions and depredations of wild miners, yet legal and illegal prospectors were inseparable. "They go where we go," a Canadian engineer explained, "and sometimes we follow them."[7] The national timber king, also czar of plywood and crown prince of mines, hosted the ten-kilometer "Run for the Rainforest" and produced a glossy coffee-table book of disappearing species. This is the salvage frontier, where making, saving, and destroying resources are utterly mixed up, where zones of conservation, production, and resource sacrifice overlap almost fully, and canonical time frames of nature's study, use, and preservation are reversed, conflated, and confused.

By this point it should be clear that by "frontier" I do not mean a place or even a process but an imaginative project capable of molding both places and processes. Turner describes the frontier as "the meeting point between savagery and civilization."[8] It is a site of transformations; "the wilderness masters the colonist. . . . Little by little he masters the wilderness."[9] It is a space of desire: it calls; it appears to create its own demands; once it is glimpsed, one cannot but explore and exploit it. Frontiers have their own technologies of space and time: their emptiness is expansive, spreading across the land; they draw the quick, erratic temporality of rumor, speculation, and cycles of boom and bust, encouraging ever-intensifying forms of resourcefulness. On the Kalimantan salvage frontier, frontier intensification and proliferation lurch forward in a hall of mirrors, becoming showy parodies of themselves. Time moves so quickly that results precede their causes, and the devastation expected behind the line of frontier expansion suddenly appears, as it seems, ahead of its advance.

The Kalimantan frontier is not the enactment of a principle of commodification or conquest. The commodification of forest products is centuries old in this area, and while the new frontier draws on the earlier trade, it is not a logical intensification of this earlier trade. The frontier is not a philosophy but rather a series of historically nonlinear leaps and skirmishes that pile together to create their own intensification and proliferation. The most helpful scholarship, then, is to be found not in abstract treatises but in historical descriptions and ethnographies. Thus accounts of the U.S. West tell us how the rush to grab one landscape element can jump off into another, as when gold prospectors made property claims on stream water. Legal precedents unexpectedly link one region to another. Aesthetic models are carried to new homes, as colonial conservation inspired the national parks movement.[10]

As these kinds of moves are repeated, they gain a cultural productiveness even in their quirky unpredictability. Thus Marianne Schmink and Charles Wood describe frontiers in Amazonia as a series of ironic twists. Planned communities lead to unplanned settlement; resource nationalization leads to private control; land titling leads to forgery; military protection leads to generalized violence.[11] Such twists are more than irony: they predict and perform their own reversals, forming productive confusions and becoming models for other frontiers. In Kalimantan, related paradoxes produce frontier degradation and salvage. The frontier is made in the shifting terrain between legality and illegality, public and private ownership, brutal rape and passionate charisma, ethnic collaboration and hostility, violence and law, restoration and extermination.

Legal, Illegal

Shifting cultivation is illegal in Indonesia, despite the fact that it is the major subsistence technology for many rural people in Kalimantan, including Meratus Dayaks. Perhaps that is why, as I hiked down the Meratus Mountains into the eastern coastal plains with Meratus friends, the lines of legality were not clear to me, and I was hardly aware that the immigrant loggers I passed were out of bounds, wild men. As soon as we hit the old logging roads, we found them, singly or in groups of three or four, each with a small chain saw or a water buffalo to haul out the logs. Their living places were bed-sized bamboo platforms along the road with only a sheet of plastic hung over to keep out the rain; they seemed to have no possessions but a coffeepot and a can of mackerel, the poor man's sardines. We stopped to drink sticky, thick coffee, loaded with sugar, and to talk of the pleasures and dangers of the forest world they knew. They chanted the prices of wood, the names of logs. They spooked themselves, and us, with tales of stolen chain saws and armed men on the roads. They were always planning to leave in a few days, when the earnings looked good, and before fiercer men arrived. Even as quick-moving transients, they gave us a human face for the frontier.

My friends thought the men worked for Inhutani, a government forest company, and while this turned out to be technically wrong, they were right that the lines between public, private, and criminal enterprise were unclear. These loggers have both legitimacy and access. They sell their logs to the properly concessioned logging companies or to small construction firms. Where environmental regulations keep the companies off mountain slopes, or where village claims push them back, that's where the wild loggers go. They fill out logging economies of scale, and their earnings are the only prosperity that logging is likely to bring to the province. Their chain saws come to them through networks of renting and profit sharing that cross local, ethnic, and religious lines. They form the slender end of channels of capital reaching from rich Chinese entrepreneurs, conglomerates, and — at that time — the family of the president, flowing in ever-narrowing channels out into the forest. Usually, the police and the army do not bother them, although the police and the army can be unpredictable. Many loggers pay fees to official Meratus village heads to give them permission to cut in village forests, and while villagers complain that village heads keep it all for themselves, this privatization is common, even proper, for government village subsidies.

And yet, both despite and because of all this respectability, these lonely loggers carried and spread the wildness of the frontier. Even in sitting with them, chatting with them, we partook of that wildness. They encouraged our fears of armed men; Oh, no one will attack you, they joked, because they will assume you are carrying a lot of guns. And who can tell the difference between a logger and an armed thief? Each time we came upon another man, another logger or thief, we stopped, hoping to domesticate him with our chatter. Perhaps he wouldn't attack us; perhaps he would alert us to the presence of other loggers or thieves. Soon our nerves were jangling from all those cups of coffee, and by then we had formed a silent pack, each huddling in his or her own unspoken fear.

They modeled frontier behavior for us, teaching us the value of wood until my Meratus companions began looking at familiar forest trees with eyes like cash registers. Oh, that one could bring me a million rupiah, Ma Salam sighed, interrupting our conversation about environmentalism. In writing their names or initials on the logs they cut, the wild loggers had introduced the new practice in this area of writing one's name on trees—to claim the tree to hold it or sell it to a logger with a chain saw before someone else did. The proliferation of naming brought new identities for trees and men, wrapping both in fearless assertion and violence, for, people said, armed men came by and cut the name off the tree, or cut the tree above the mark, and wrote their own names on the logs. If you confront them with five men, my friends said, they will come at you with ten or twenty. Sell quickly and move on to write your name again.

Who were these men, so human and yet so transiently identified? They came from everywhere and spoke the common language of trade and calculation based on the hope of a quick windfall. They were called penyingso, "chain saw men," or pembaluk, "square log men," after the shape of their logs. No one knew them as wild, but they were men without ordinary culture. Appendages to their equipment and their products, they had names, but no houses, families, meals, work schedule, or ordinary time. And in this stripped-down human form, they communicated across cultures, arranging ethnic collaborations. They offered a hot human connection to still the chills of fear. This thrilling connection was an anesthetic, blocking out the damaged world in which they operated—a world already left behind by bigger frontier makers, the soil sloughing off the hills, trees falling, waters muddied. Looking in and through that damaged world, can't you see the resources waiting to be claimed?

It is difficult to find the words to discuss this kind of transethnic, trans-local collaboration and the regional resource dynamics it sets in motion. Resource economists and bureaucrats recognize no localisms; to them, the world is a frontier. There is no point in asking how frontiers come to be; they are nature itself. To counter that perspective, anthropologists, rural sociologists, and geographers have drawn attention to non-frontier-like (or even anti-frontier) environmental social forms, such as common property, community management, and indigenous knowledge. They have returned attention to the cultural specificity of capitalism and state bu-reaucracy.[12] This important and quite wonderful work has come to domi-nate local and regional analyses of environment and society in Kalimantan; scholars point to the long-term social making of the rain forest, to a com-munity "ethic of access" that sustains forest commodities, and to the bizarre stereotypes of government planners.[13] My own work has developed within this dialogue.

Yet in contrasting community conventions with state and corporate schemes, there is little room for discussing the call of the wild, with its regionwide collaborations for aggressive resource grabbing and the seem-ingly unstoppable spread of the frontier. One might call this "the tragedy of the tragedy of the commons," that is, the tragic result of state and cor-porate policies that assume and enforce open-access conventions as the flip side and precondition of private property.[14] By refusing to recognize alternative forms of access, these policies will alternatives to disappear-ance. But this is a tragedy that cannot be well described with the vocabu-lary of management, property, and access rules. From the perspective of the abandoned logging roads, the divide between community and state-corporate standards feels nostalgic: too little, too late. The logging road and its illegal-legal loggers from everywhere call me toward more danger-ous country.

One look back: Grand schemes never fully colonize the territories on which they are imposed. If the frontier is an environmental project, not a place, it can never fill the landscape. Away from the logging road, there are trees, fields, and villages, and not everyone is so caught up in frontier schemes. The frontier could move on, and something else could happen in its place. The forest might regenerate. Although . . . those industrial tree plantations are truly huge, and through them the frontier claims powerful national and international players.

The Public Private

Riding from the provincial capital up the east coast and in toward the mountains in an airless, overcrowded van with the music so loud it closes down my senses, there is more than enough anesthetic; yet the difference between legal resource concessions and the wild is perfectly visible here. The road runs for miles through land without underbrush or animal life but only neatly planted tree stock, row on row on row. The transmigration villages recently placed here to provide the labor force for these future trees are similarly orderly, blank, and anonymous; in striking contrast to everywhere else I have been in Indonesia, the passengers get on and off at these nameless stops without looking at us or speaking. Sometimes we stop in noisy frontier towns, full of gold merchants, truckers, and hungry, aggressive men. But soon enough we are back among the silent army of young trees. This is the kind of discipline that boosted Indonesia—for a while— among the so-called Asian dragons. Under the name of political stability, discipline made economic indicators soar.[15]

Appearances are important here. No weeds, no trash timber. Indeed, it is unclear to what extent appearances were not the New Order economy's most important product. Oil palm, the darling of the export-crop set, was sponsored by foreign and domestic plantation subsidies;[16] perhaps the companies will have moved on before the oil is pressed. The pulp plantations were financed by the national reforestation program, the answer to environmentalists' concern for the rain forest. New international agreements offered plantation timber as the solution to rain forest destruction; timber companies put in plantations, sponsored by the government, to earn the right to cut down more forest, useful for future plantations. Meanwhile the young trees await future pulp factories. And as they wait, what will befall them? Many of the acacias are cloned from the same parent stock, making them highly vulnerable to disease.[17] They are also affected by a rot that causes hollow boles, an apt image for an economy of appearances.

There were government corporations here, and there were private ones, but most fell awkwardly across this distinction. In 1994 the oil palms were said to belong to the wife of then-president Suharto, Mrs. Tien Suharto, who died in 1996 but before her death was widely parodied as Mrs. Tien (Ten) Percent, after her voracious interest in the economy. The loggers told villagers who complained about the invasion of village forests to "go ask Mrs. Tien." The president's family served both a material and a mythical role in the plantation economy. The capital they controlled was both public and private. And it was the confusion of these categories that allowed frontier investment to flourish. For whom were these resources discovered and developed: the national interest, the army, the president, the foreign corporations, or, perhaps, all of them?

Even the staunchest of neoclassical economists admit that it was difficult to distinguish among domestic, foreign, and government ownership in New Order Indonesia, given the mix of investors, the central importance of patronage, and the slippage back and forth between military and private enterprise. The confusion proliferated at every level. Foreign was domestic: foreign aid formed a major portion of domestic revenue, and foreign firms worked through domestic partners. Public was private: the explicit goal of the government was to sponsor entrepreneurship at every level. Even peasant subsidies in the 1990s were individual entrepreneurship loans. Licenses and concessions were both public and private. Civil servants were paid a low base salary and expected to gain the rest of their living from perks and benefits of their discretionary authority.

You could call this corruption, or you could call it, as one North American corporate executive, gracefully submitting to government demands for a share of his company's enterprise, dubbed it, "Indonesia's political, economic, and social environment."[18] One must also consider these public-private arrangements in relation to the worldwide post–Cold War infatuation with the market. Soon after the collapse of the Soviet Union in 1989, nearly every nation-state redoubled its endorsement of the market, or at least the appearance of the market, and New Order Indonesia was exemplary. The bureaucracy was the market; its goal was to promote entrepreneurship. The military was the market; generals and common soldiers, at different levels, had the muscle to make the best deals. Environmental management was the market, offering another chance to claim resources and improve free trade. In this context, the fluidity between public and private was a fertile space for the capital, the deals, the plans, and the appearance of the economy itself. The president's family and friends were exemplars of what every citizen was supposed to be doing; and their capital flowed out through transregional networks in small deals that complemented the large ones. Furthermore, this was a dynamic that supposedly sped up modernization and development, the stated goal of the state. Secrets, passed through personalistic ties, encouraged speculation in which investments preceded contracts; for those tracking money and resources, an impatient anticipation emerged, speeding up the experience of time. A boom-time excitement was stimulated by the fluidity of deals, trickling down and then streaming between official coffers, foreign firms, and those-in-the-know. Rumors spread the excitement, and the wild men flocked to the frontier, following or anticipating news of gold strikes and quick timber harvests, before the plantations rolled in. In this productive space, quick, erratic, anticipatory frontier time intensifies and spreads, ricocheting back and forth between centers and peripheries, and getting ahead of itself in death-defying leaps. Here alternative appearance-based scams—disciplined or wild—are born, and the only promise that must surely be kept is of fabulous, unearned wealth.

Between the tree plantations and the mountains are networks of more- and less-maintained logging roads, with their heavy cargoes of legal logs by day and illegal logs by night. For bosses and managers, the roads shrink and simplify the territory, making it quicker to get from here to there. For most everyone else, the logging roads expand landscape emptiness, separating off- and on-road sites and creating obstacles between once-connected forest places even as they speed the trip to town. The roads are also conduits for migrants, fugitives, and thieves, who expand both danger and wildness for everyone who lives or visits there.

Natural treasures themselves become fugitive in this landscape of movement and flight, just as once, people said, a man stumbled over a nugget of gold as big as a rice mortar and marked the place oh so carefully to come back later with help—but when he did, nothing was there. Masculine magic and charisma are required, for even safe in one's possession, treasures disappear. Thus every man on the road with a splinter of gaharu incense wood or a palmful of immature swifts' nests unwraps it from its plastic bag, shows it like a secret talisman, wraps it, stows it carefully in his pocket, chants the price, pulls it out again to rewrap it, trying thereby to stabilize its presence on his person. And how much more flighty are the incense trees and swifts themselves.

Take the swifts, for example. The saliva nests they build in limestone caves are the key ingredient of Chinese bird's nest soup and fetch startling prices even locally: Rp 1.5 million for a kilo of the white clean ones, and Rp 800,000 for the debris-filled black.[19] In this area, they have long been associated with fugitive luck and danger. In the 1980s people told me that the only way to find birds' nests was to bring a freshly sacrificed human head to the spirits who could reveal them. Now, with armed men on the roads, the birds' erratic flight has intensified beyond the reach of headhunters, as have attempts to hold them in place. Where military men have found productive caves, they have posted guards and signs: This is the property of the army. And so Meratus who consider themselves rightful traditional owners hurry to guard remaining caves, building their homes and clearing swiddens in the dark glens directly in front of the caves, never leaving them. Still, they are outmaneuvered by the men on the roads, who come around with guns and flashlights and demand entry, peeling off the birds' nests long before they are fully built and indeed ensuring that the birds will not return. Quick harvesting leads to quicker harvesting, and nests the size of nail clippings are removed, depriving the birds of any place to raise their young. In this fugitive landscape, armed men are the best part of the law, and parodies of property appear. One Meratus man who built his house in front of a cave to guard it showed me the letter written by the most recent gang to have come by to rob the cave, which warned off future gangs on the principle of this group's precedence. My host got nothing, as did the swifts, who could only fly to other fugitive locations.

Men arm themselves with old war stories, and invulnerability magic from the 1958 rebellion has been revived, with its metaphors of penises as weapons and semen as spent bullets. As much as I tried to steer around the concerns of a simple ecofeminism, it was difficult not to conclude that an emergent masculinity fueled this regionally spreading dynamic, with its ability to unite men across lines of local culture and religion in a competitively intensive virility. Men arouse each other on the roads with stories of women who will do anything (And then, he said, she tore off her bra). They work themselves and each other into a constant state of masculine anxiety, forever talking about deals and opportunities and prices in the sped-up time of the chase. They forget day cycles, life cycles, seasons. They call to and challenge each other to greater efforts.

Hiking the logging roads in the hot sun, I find it difficult to refuse a ride from the men in the truck. But crammed into the cab with the crew behind a windshield covered with stickers of busty naked ladies and my male Meratus friends stuck in the back with the water buffalo, fear hits me like an avalanche. Within thirty seconds, they are feeling my arms and legs and breasts, and I must concentrate on how to get them to let me off at the next crossroads, where I heave a sigh of relief that I made it out, again, this time. Yes, says a wizened Meratus friend, they grab your breasts even if you are a wrinkled old woman, they must have no eyes, and every woman longs and must learn to jump out of the truck. But a younger friend responds to my stories with bravado: Why didn't you do it? Weren't they handsome enough? I had heard similar bravado from young men when a peer was cowed by soldiers: If they had come at me, I would have shown them something! And indeed, one's only choices are to hide or to play. Women can be resourceful too, and prostitution brings new resources to the frontier. But this is a world made by an intensive, peculiar, exaggerated masculinity.

This is a masculinity that spreads and saturates itself with images and metaphors, amulets, stickers of naked women, stories based on the confusion between rape and wild sex. Its moving force is perhaps best seen in the imagistic effects of the "water machine," the high-pressure hydraulic pump, small enough for one man to carry and connect to any local stream, but whose power in the spray emerging from the taut blue plastic piping can gouge a hole four feet deep into the land and thus expose the gravel underneath the clay, gravel in which, perchance, small flakes or nuggets

The plastic piping can gouge a hole four feet deep. South Kalimantan, Indonesia, 1994. Photograph © Anna Tsing.

of gold can be found. What charismatic force! And what possibilities it unveils.

The water machine, introduced in this area around 1990, is the key technology of small-scale or "wild" gold mining. It's much too expensive for an ordinary Meratus man, but networks of renting and share splitting, with borrowed funds and imagined profits split among more and more, make it possible for many ambitious men to join a mining group, or more aggressively yet, to bring the machine and a team upstream toward home. Nor are Meratus the only players. The miners, like the loggers, come from everywhere, building makeshift settlements along the logging roads with names like "Kilometer 105 and a half." At their excavations, they erect camps of bamboo platforms hung with plastic sheets; they have coffeepots, sugar, mackerel cans. But I know some of these people; they are Meratus farmer-foragers. I know they are perfectly capable of stopping anywhere in the forest and, in half an hour, building a cozy, rain-tight shelter of bamboo, palm leaves, or bark. I know, in other circumstances, they would carry rice; they would hunt and fish and gather wild fruits and vegetables and make a tasty meal. But here, surrounded by familiar forest, they observe the proprieties of rain-soaked plastic sheets and a nutrition of coffee and rancid fish. It feels like nothing so much as "culture" in its most coercive, simplistic form: a way of life that draws us in, ready or not, sensible or not.

Among the huddled mining shelters, men and women disagree. Women join the profit-sharing groups, panning the gravel with men until their own jealous menfolk arrive, sending them back to the village. The men attack the land with new vigor, sharing the washing with other women, and women sneak back to join the gold parties of strangers.

But what is the result of all this passion? Despite obsessive attention to secrets and signs, much of the gravel exposed yields no metal at all; and when it does, the gold flakes are quickly spent on the exorbitant prices of coffee, sugar, and cigarettes. No one I heard of had made much money; meanwhile, water machines broke, and huge debts were accrued. Most strikingly, the land lay pockmarked and deeply eroded beyond recovery. Those trees that remained clung tottering by the tips of their roots, their bases exposed. Broken streams formed muddy pools; even grass was banished. "They have ruined the land for many generations," said the old people. But perhaps it doesn't matter if the industrial tree plantations and their transmigrant labor force are coming anyway. Their mission is to make and restore degraded lands; why not get started?

Frontier Citizenship

Frontier men and resources, I have argued, are made in dynamics of intensification and proliferation. Confusions between legal and illegal, public and private, disciplined and wild, are productive in sponsoring the emergence of men driven to profit, that is, entrepreneurs, as well as the natural objects conjured in their resourceful drives. These men and objects are contagious, recharging the landscape with wildness and virility. The frontier then appears to roll with its own momentum.

The frontier is a globally traveling project, but it requires localization to come to life. I have tangled with this restless localization by moving back and forth between the intense physicality of the frontier landscape, its guiding models, and its unplanned insights. Let me resite it one more time in the hesitant emergence of frontier politics.

The frontier has been associated with distinctive political models of citizenship and culture. Most famously, frontier conditions are said to have made a freewheeling white male democracy in the New World. There is ongoing populist appeal here, not just in nostalgia for the U.S. West, but more recently in respect for the independent miners of Brazil, who found their representatives and fought for their rights. Frontier fears of apocalypse have also stimulated models of protection: extractive reserves, indigenous reserves, nature reserves; each, at its best, produces an alliance among small collectors, native peoples, and forest advocates. Neither of these models made an easy entry into the cultural politics of Indonesia's

New Order. In New Order models for the countryside, ethnic groups gained respect for cultural difference only with political submission: custom to keep farmers in their place. Yet frontier dynamics can unseat the obedience of custom to create a wider, wilder citizenship. Drawing men from everywhere, frontier culture can mobilize them both for and against each other.

A rhetoric of democracy is possible in official acts of protection of frontier culture, as when a governor of South Kalimantan once defended illegal logging as the livelihood of the people. Of course, this is a particular kind of democracy, in which women and indigenous residents — and, more firmly still, nature — are excluded. Then there is the question of race and ethnic violence, even genocide. This is the way frontier democracy has been made from below, at least historically. Thus far I have stressed transethnic collaboration, but this history alerts me to the lines and limits it also creates. Indeed, ethnic violence has come to fill out the Kalimantan frontier. In the mid-1990s, Dayaks mobilized in violent clashes with Madurese migrants in West Kalimantan. The year 2001 brought an eerily self-conscious echo in even more dramatic violence in Central Kalimantan; for a few days, Dayak-Madurese clashes dominated international news. In the distorted lens of international journalism, one might imagine the scene as the return of the U.S. Wild West — in its Hollywood version — with Dayaks as bloodthirsty savages scalping encroaching but civilized settlers. This is ridiculous parody; the clashes have their own political and cultural histories.[20] Yet the emerging frontier is a place for the historical repetition of reimagined savagery. Sometimes the army stages it; sometimes young men find themselves in its wild tropes. One's only choices are to hide or to play.

The reserve model has also attracted global attention. It arises in places where environmentalists are panicked by the possibility of total destruction; it argues that *something* must be saved. The most promising feature of this model is the mobilization it has inspired, which brings the possibility of citizenship claims to those who never had them before: small collectors, tribes, trees. In Brazil, a moment of alliance between rubber tappers and Indians offered conservationists a strategy to save the forests. Yet in Indonesia, the alliance between frontiersmen and indigenous residents has only recruited the latter to the frontier. This has not been an alliance that saves forests.

Conservationists, in turn, have taken their pleas to corporations and the state, and these, indeed, have found some use for reserves. Resource companies support nature reserves because they cordon off a small area in exchange for permission to destroy the remaining countryside. Given the collusion between legal and illegal, disciplined and wild, and the new frontiersmen who come to complement development, corporate giants can rest assured they will get those reserves back, once appropriately degraded from below. Then too, in an age of natural simulation, it is never quite clear what is being preserved, what is degraded, and what is restored. The zones overlap and tease each other, and Indonesia now has national parks zoned as logging concessions. It is hard to know what one is seeing. Environmental activists say that tree nurseries of hard-to-grow indigenous species are really cut-back natural forest, with young trees disguised as nursery seedlings. This, after all, is the salvage frontier. Meanwhile, maps contradict each other: A nature reserve sketched on one map is a production forest on another map, and a village territory on a third. A community forest designation is assigned to a treeless plain on which only dry stumps left by loggers recall living trees. The worst social coercions of conservation politics have been avoided in the areas I know best by not conserving anything at all.

In the late 1990s, the frontier began to spin out of control even from the perspective of capitalist investors and migrant entrepreneurs. In 1997 great fires broke out across Kalimantan, many of them set by the plantation companies who hoped to use this cheap method to clear their land. Since drought had been predicted due to the El Niño southern oscillation, the Ministry of Forests had warned the companies not to burn. But why consider regulation or prudence on the frontier? The fires spread beyond all expectation, destroying settlements and forests and forming a dangerous haze across Southeast Asia. Then the financial crisis that had begun in Thailand spread to Indonesia and wiped out the promises of the New Order economic boom. Kalimantan villagers were most hurt by the crisis in the "wildest" frontier areas, where subsistence agro-forestry had already been threatened or ruined by corporate and immigrant expropriations as well as destruction of the forest landscape. Meanwhile in West Kalimantan, ethnic violence between indigenous Dayaks and immigrant Madurese flamed into a war. In 1998 demonstrations in Jakarta, together with international pressure, toppled the government. In the ensuing moment of political freedom, community groups, entrepreneurs, and gangsters seized corporate resource sites. Mines were occupied. Logging camps were destroyed. The wildness sponsored by the New Order had veered out of control.

With the passing of the New Order, great possibilities opened up. Finally there was hope for an Indonesian democracy. Students and activists in Jakarta were jubilant. In Kalimantan, nongovernmental organizations and activist alliances took a newly assertive role in advocating for the rights of rural communities. Yet the frontier sponsored by the New Order only proliferated, taking off in new leaps and bounds. The resources were surely there; who could ignore them? Decentralization of resource rights, begun

Neatly planted trees, John Wayne Airport, Orange County, California.
Photograph © Daniel Rosenberg.

in 2000, pitted government officials at different levels against each other, such that the provincial governor and the regency assembly might fight continually over what forms of resource exploitation should be allowed— and who would get the proceeds. Meanwhile, regional groups within the military—no longer the tool of the central government—provoked ethnic violence and disorder. In 2001, Dayaks and Madurese became bloodily embroiled in Central Kalimantan. Still, hope rested on the possibility of new kinds of politics—as long as international powers allowed it. The U.S. government's decision in 2002 to rearm the Indonesian military for domestic surveillance in the "war against terrorism" was a painful reminder of the international sponsorship of frontier violence. The frontier is no neighborhood storm. It gathers force from afar, entangling multiple local-to-global scales.

Back in California, I remember the frontier hero John Wayne—a man who wasn't even a Wild West cowboy but instead an actor who made his living *pretending* to be a Wild West cowboy. He never served in the military, but a congressional medal honored him as the embodiment of American military heroism.[21] Orange County has dedicated its airport to him, attracting visitors to the frontier—where adventure still leads to wealth, and a man with guns can stand tall. The frontier, like a film, can be played and replayed. That's resourcefulness on the salvage frontier.

Notes

This chapter was conceived at the 1997 "Histories of the Future" seminar at the Institute for Humanities Research, University of California, Irvine. The influence of the other members of the seminar, and of our common readings and discussions, is reflected everywhere throughout the essay. I am most grateful for the opportunity the seminar offered to write using playful and experimental styles and to address our individual research projects from new directions. My thanks to Susan Harding and Daniel Rosenberg, who have taken this project forward, as well as to Stephen Best, Liisa Malkki, Joseph Masco, Vicente Rafael, and Kathleen Stewart. I gave a version of this chapter for the Boas-Benedict annual symposium plenary address at Columbia University in April 1997, and I thank my sponsors there for a most stimulating conversation. Kathryn Chetkovich, Paulla Ebron, and Lisa Rofel have been particularly helpful in the rewriting process.

1   See Tsing, *In the Realm of the Diamond Queen.*

2   Nick Williams, "Indonesian Miners Revive Gold Rush Spirit of 49ers," *Los Angeles Times,* December 12, 1988, sec. 1, p. 1.

3   Sarmiento, *Civilization and Barbarism.*

4   Turner, "The Significance of the Frontier in American History."

5   For an introduction to these literatures, see Limerick, *The Legacy of Conquest*; and Worster, *Under Western Skies*.

6   Hecht and Cockburn, *The Fate of the Forest*, 141.

7   Williams, "Indonesian Miners," 1.

8   Turner, "The Significance of the Frontier in American History," 32.

9   Ibid., 33.

10 Worster, *Rivers of Empire*.

11 Schmink and Wood, *Contested Frontiers in Amazonia*.

12 For an introduction to this literature, see Bryant and Bailey, *Third World Political Ecology*; and Peet and Watts, *Liberation Ecologies*.

13 See, for example, Li, "Marginality, Power and Production"; Peluso, "Fruit Trees and Family Trees in an Anthropogenic Rainforest"; and Dove, "Representations of the 'Other.'" In the last few years, Kalimantan scholars have turned much more intensively to problems of ethnic violence and resource conflict. See, for example, Peluso and Harwell, "Territory, Custom, and the Cultural Politics of Ethnic War in West Kalimantan, Indonesia."

14 I am referring to the much-discussed thesis called "the tragedy of the commons" (see Hardin, "The Tragedy of the Commons"), which argued that common property—in contrast to private property—is invariably degraded by its users. Many commentators have shown that this thesis is wrong, despite the fact that it has considerable authority among policymakers. (See, for example, McKay and Acheson, *The Question of the Commons*.) Indeed, as I suggest here, the thesis itself as applied in policy can be destructive to the environment.

15 Consider the relationship between mass murder and "banking output" suggested by figure 9.1 in Hill, *The Indonesian Economy since 1966*, 180, which shows the soaring line of growth exactly on the years of the army-sponsored massacre of 1968–1969.

16 Hill, *The Indonesian Economy since 1966*, 124.

17 Brookfield, Potter, and Byron, *In Place of the Forest*, 105.

18 The quotation is from David Walsh, the president of the ill-fated gold-mining company Bre-X, as reported in Richard Borsuk, "Bre-X Minerals Defends Pact with Indonesia," *Wall Street Journal*, February 2, 1997, B3A. For more on this company and its arrangements with the Indonesian government as well as its actions on the Kalimantan frontier, see Tsing, "Inside the Economy of Appearances."

19 These are prices from the mid-1990s, before the currency devaluation of 1997. At the time, one U.S. dollar was worth a little over Rp 2,000.

20 See Peluso and Harwell, "Territory, Custom, and the Cultural Politics."

21 Slotkin, *Gunfighter Nation*, 243.

CHAPTER

SH B'GOSH

WHAT THE FUTURE WEARS

The Cell Phone and the Crowd:
Messianic Politics in the
Contemporary Philippines

Vicente L. Rafael

This essay explores a set of telecommunicative fantasies among the middle classes in the contemporary Philippines within the context of a recent historical occurrence: the civilian-backed coup that overthrew president Joseph Estrada in January 2001. It does so with reference to two distinct media, the cell phone and the crowd. Various accounts of what has come to be known as "People Power II" (as distinguished from the populist coup that unseated Ferdinand and Imelda Marcos in 1986) reveal certain pervasive beliefs on the part of the middle classes. They believed, for example, in the power of communications technologies to transmit messages at a distance and in their ability to possess that power. In the same vein, they had faith in their ability to master their relationship to the "masses" of people with whom they regularly shared Manila's crowded streets, using the power of crowds to speak to the state. They thus conceived of themselves as capable of communicating beyond the crowd, but also with it, transcending its sheer physical density by technological means while at the same time ordering its movements and using its energy to transmit middle-class demands. At its most utopian, the fetish of communication suggested the possibility of dissolving, however provisionally, existing class divisions. Communication from this perspective held for the middle class —which has since the anticolonial revolution of 1896 long conceived of itself as the vanguard of nationalism and progress—the messianic promise of refashioning the heterogeneous crowd into a people addressing and addressed by the promise of justice. But as we shall see, such telecommunicative notions were predicated on the putative "voicelessness" of the masses, for once heard, the masses called attention to the fragility of bourgeois claims to shape the sending and reception of messages about the proper practice of politics in the nation-state. Media politics (understood in both senses of that phrase as the politics of media systems, but also politics as the inescapable event of mediation) in this context reveal the unstable workings of Filipino middle-class sentiments. Unsettled in their relationship to social hierarchy, such sentiments at times redrew class divisions, at other moments anticipated their abolition, and at still others called for their reinstatement and consolidation.[1]

Calling

Telephones were introduced in the Philippines as early as 1885, during the last decade and a half of Spanish colonial rule.[2] Like telegraphy before it, telephony provoked fantasies of direct communication among the colonial bourgeoisie. They imagined that these new technologies would afford them access to those on top, enabling them to hear and be heard directly by the colonial state. We can see this telecommunicative notion, for example, in a satirical piece written by the Filipino national hero Jose Rizal in 1889. Entitled "Por Telefono," it situates the narrator as an eavesdropper. He listens intently to the sounds and voices that travel between the Spanish friars in Manila—regarded as the real power in the colony—and their superiors in Madrid.[3] The nationalist writer wiretaps his way, as it were, into the walls of the clerical residences, exposing their hypocrisy and excesses. In this sense, the telephone shares in the capacity of that other telecommunicative technology, print, to reveal what was once hidden, to repeat what was meant to be secret, and to pass on messages that were not meant for those outside a particular circle.[4]

It is this history of tapping into and forwarding messages, often in the form of ironic commentaries, jokes, and rumors, that figured in the civilian-led coup in the Philippines known as "People Power II." From the evening of January 16 to January 20, 2001, over a million people massed at one of Metro Manila's major highways, Epifanio de los Santos Avenue, commonly called Edsa, site of the first People Power revolt in 1986, which overthrew the Marcos regime. A large cross section of Philippine society gathered to demand the resignation of president Joseph "Erap" Estrada after his impeachment trial was suddenly aborted by the eleven senators widely believed to be under his influence. These senators had refused to include key evidence that would have shown the wealth Estrada had amassed from illegal numbers games while in office. The impeachment proceedings had been watched avidly on national TV and listened to on radio. Most viewers and listeners were keenly aware of the evidence of theft and corruption on the part of Estrada and his family.[5] Once the pro-Estrada senators put an abrupt end to the hearing, however, hundreds of thousands of viewers and listeners were moved to protest in the streets. Television and radio had fixed them in their homes and offices attending to the court proceedings. But at a critical moment, these media also drew them away from their seats. Giving up their position as spectators, they now became part of a crowd that had formed around a common wish: the resignation of the president.

Aside from TV and radio, another medium of communication was given credit for spurring the coup: the cell phone. Nearly all accounts of People Power II available to us come from middle-class writers or by way of middle-class-controlled media with strong nationalist sentiments. And nearly all point to the crucial importance of the cell phone in the rapid mobilization of people. "The phone is our weapon now," says one unemployed construction worker, quoted in a newspaper article. "The power of our cell phones and computers were among the things that lit the fuse which set off the second uprising, or People Power Revolution II" (*Ang lakas ng aming mga celfon at computer ay isa sa mga nagsilbing mitsa upang pumutok ang ikalawang pag-aalsa o people power revolution II*), according to a college student in Manila. And a newspaper columnist relayed this advice to "would-be foot-soldiers in any future revolution: As long as [your cell phone] is not low on battery, you are in the groove, in a fighting *mood*."[6] A technological thing was thus idealized as an agent of change, invested with the power to bring forth new forms of sociality.

Introduced in the latter half of the 1990s, cell phones in the Philippines had become remarkably popular by around 1999.[7] There are a number of reasons for their ubiquity. To begin with, there is the perennial difficulty and expense of acquiring land line phones in the Philippines, along with the erratic service provided by the Philippine Long Distance Company (PLDT) and the more recent, smaller Bayan Tel. Cell phones seemed to promise to fill this pent-up need for connectivity. Additionally, cell phones cost far less than personal computers, which less than 1 percent of the population own, though a larger proportion have access through Internet cafes. By contrast, as of 2001, there were over 8 million cell phone users in a population of about 77 million, a number that has not ceased growing to this day. The great majority of them buy prepaid phone cards, which, combined with the relatively low cost of the phone (as low as $50 in the open market and half this amount in secondary markets), make this form of wireless communication more accessible and affordable than regular telephones or computers.

Even more significant, cell phones allow users to reach beyond traffic-clogged streets and serve as a quicker alternative to slow, unreliable, and expensive postal services. Like many Third World countries recently opened to more liberal trade policies, the Philippines shares in the paradox of being awash in the latest technologies of communication such as the cell phone while mired in deteriorating infrastructures such as roads, postal services, railroads, power generators, and land lines. With the cell phone, one seems able to pass beyond these obstacles. And inasmuch as such infrastructures are state run, so that their breakdowns and inefficiencies are a direct function of governmental ineptitude, passing beyond them also feels like overcoming the state, which to begin with has long been overcome by corruption.[8] It is small wonder, then, that cell phones could prove literally handy in spreading rumors, jokes, and information that steadily eroded whatever legitimacy President Estrada still had amid his impeachment hearings, along with those of his congressional supporters. Bypassing the complex of broadcasting media, cell phone users themselves became broadcasters, receiving and transmitting both news and gossip and often confounding the two. Indeed, one could imagine each user becoming a broadcasting station unto him- or herself, a node in a wider network of communication that the state could not possibly even begin to monitor, much less control.[9] Hence, once the call was made for people to mass at Edsa, cell phone users readily forwarded messages they received even as they followed what was asked of them.

Cell phones thus were not only invested with the power to surpass crowded conditions and congested surroundings brought about by the state's inability to order everyday life. They were also seen to bring a new kind of crowd about, one that was thoroughly conscious of itself as a movement headed toward a common goal. While telecommunication allows one to escape the crowd, it also opens up the possibility of finding oneself moving in concert with it, filled with its desire and consumed by its energy. In the first case, cell phone users define themselves against a mass of anonymous others. In the second, they become those others, assuming anonymity as a condition of possibility for sociality. To understand how the first is transformed into the second, it helps to note the specific form in which the vast majority of cell phone messages are transmitted in the Philippines: as text messages.

Texting

Text messages are e-mails sent over mobile phones and transferable to the Internet. Recently, the term "texting" has emerged to designate the act of sending such messages, indicating its popularity in places such as England, Japan, and Finland (where Nokia first began offering it, and where it is referred to as SMS, or Simple Message Service). In the Philippines, texting became the preferred mode of cell phone use once the two major networks, Globe and Smart, introduced free, and then later low-cost, text messaging as part of their regular service in 1999. Unlike voice messages, text messages take up less bandwidth and require far less time to convert into digitized packets available for transmission. It thus makes economic sense for service providers to encourage the use of text messaging in order to reserve greater bandwidth space for the more expensive—and profitable—voice messages. From an economic standpoint, then, texting offers one of those rare points of convergence between the interests of users and providers.[10] But obviously cost is not the only thing that makes text messaging popular among Filipino users. In an essay sent over the Internet signed "An Anonymous Filipino," the use of cell phones in Manila is described as a form of "mania." Using Taglish, the urban lingua franca that combines Tagalog, English, and Spanish, this writer, a Filipino *balikbayan* (that is, one who resides or works elsewhere and periodically returns to visit the motherland), remarks:

> HI! WNA B MY TXT PAL? They're everywhere! In the malls, the office, school, the MRT [Manila Railroad Transit], what-have-you, the cellphone mania's on the loose! Why, even Manang Fishball [i.e., Mrs. Fishball, a reference to older working-class women vendors who sell fishballs, a popular roadside snack] is texting! I even asked my sisters how important they think they are that they should have cells? Even my nephew in high school has a cell phone. My mom in fact told me that even in his sleep, my brother's got his cell, and even when they have a PLDT [i.e., land line] phone in the house, they still use the cell phone.[11]

"Mania," according to the *Oxford English Dictionary*, is a kind of madness characterized "by great excitement, extravagant delusions and hallucinations and its acute stage, great violence." The insistence of having cell phones nearby, the fact that they always seem to be on hand, indicates an attachment to them that surpasses the rational and the utilitarian, as the foregoing remarks indicate. The cell phone lends to its holder a sense of being someone, even if he or she is only a street vendor or a high school student. Someone, in this case, who can reach and be reached and is thus always in touch. The "manic" relationship to cell phones is thus this ready willingness to identify with it, or more precisely with what the machine is thought capable of doing. One not only has access to it; by virtue of its omnipresence and proximity, one becomes like it. That is to say, one becomes an apparatus for sending and receiving messages at all times of the day and night. An American journalist writing in the *New York Times* observes as much in an article on Manila society:

"Texting?" Yes, texting—as in exchanging short typed messages over a cell phone. All over the Philippines, a verb has been born, and Filipinos use it whether they are speaking English or Tagalog. . . . The difference [between sending e-mail by computers and texting] is that while chat-room denizens sit in contemplative isolation, glued to computer screens, in the Philippines, 'texters' are right out in the throng. Malls are infested with shoppers who appear to be navigating by cellular compass. Groups of diners sit ignoring one another, staring down at their phones as if fumbling with rosaries. Commuters, jaywalkers, even mourners—everyone in the Philippines seems to be texting over the phone. . . . Faye Siytangco, a 23-year-old airline sales representative, was not surprised when at the wake for a friend's father she saw people bowing their heads and gazing toward folded hands. But when their hands started beeping and their thumbs began to move, she realized to her astonishment that they were not in fact praying. "People were actually sitting there and texting," Siytangco said. "Filipinos don't see it as rude anymore." [12]

Unlike users of computers, cell phone users are mobile, immersed in the crowd, yet communicating beyond it. Texting provides them a way out of the very surroundings they find themselves in. Thanks to the cell phone, they need not be present to others around them. Even when they are part of a socially defined group—say, commuters or mourners—they are always someone and somewhere else, receiving and transmitting messages from beyond their physical location. It is in this sense that they become other than their socially delineated identity: not only cell phone users but cell phone "maniacs." Because the phone rarely leaves them, it becomes part of the hand, the keys an extension of their fingers. In certain cases, the hand takes the place of the mouth, the fingers that of the tongue. Writing about his Filipino relative, one Filipino American contributor to Plaridel, an online discussion group dealing with Philippine politics, referred to the former's cell phone as "almost a new limb." [13] It is not surprising, then, that the consciousness of users assumes the mobility and alertness of their gadgets. We can see how this process of taking on the qualities of the cell phone comes across in the practice of sending and receiving messages:

The craze for sending text message by phone started [in 1999] when Globe introduced prepaid cards that enabled students, soldiers [and others] too poor for a long-term subscription to start using cellular phones. . . . People quickly figured out how to express themselves on the phone's alphanumeric keypad. . . . "Generation Txt," as the media dubbed it, was born. Sending text messages does not require making a call. People merely type in a message and the recipient's phone number, hit the phone's send key and off it goes to the operator's message center, which forwards it to the recipient. Because messages are exchanged over the frequency the network uses to identify phones rather than the frequencies their owners talk on, messages can be sent and received the instant a phone is turned on—and can even be received when a phone call is in progress.

Sending text messages by phone is an irritating skill to master, largely because 26 letters plus punctuation have to be created with only 10 buttons. Typing the letter C, for example, requires pressing the No. 2 button three times; an E is the No. 3 button pressed twice; and so on. After the message is composed it can be sent immediately to the phone number of the recipient, who can respond immediately by the same process. People using phones for text messages have developed a shorthand. "Where are you?" becomes "WRU." And "See you tonight" becomes "CU 2NYT." People have different styles of keying in their messages. Some use their index fingers, some one thumb, others both. . . . [Others] tap away with one hand without even looking at [their] phone.[14]

As is frequently the case with e-mail, conventions of grammar, spelling, and punctuation are evaded and rearticulated with texting. The constraints of an alphanumeric keypad mean that one goes through numbers to get to letters. As a result, counting and writing become closely associated. Digital communication requires the use of digits, both one's own and those of the machine, as one taps away. But it is a tapping that is done not to the rhythm of one's speech and in tempo with one's thoughts but in coordination with the numbers through which one reaches a letter: three taps on 2 to get C, for example, or two taps on 3 to get to E. It is almost as if texting reduces all speech to writing, and all writing to a kind of mechanical percussiveness, a drumming that responds to an external constraint rather than one that emerges from and expresses an internal source. In addition, as it were, there are no prescribed styles for texting: one or two fingers will do, or one can use a thumb and look at the screen, while those adept enough can text while looking elsewhere, as in the case of skilled typists. Neither are standardized body postures required with texting: one can sit or walk or drive while sending messages. Where handwriting in the conventional sense requires learning proper penmanship and body postures under the supervision of teachers within the confines of desk and classroom, texting frees the body, or so it seems, from these old constraints.

Mimicking the mobility of their phones, texters move about, not moored to anything except the technological forms and limits of the medium. The messages they receive and send are condensed versions of whatever language—English or Tagalog, and more frequently Taglish—they are using and so belong to neither. The hybrid form of this language comes from the demands of the medium itself rather than reflecting the idiosyncrasies of its users. The introduction of a limit on the number of free text messages one can send and the assessment of a fee per character of text has meant the further shortening of words and messages. Instant messaging, along with the mechanical storage and recall of prior messages, requires only the most drastically abbreviated narrative constructions with little semantic deferral or delay. Using the cell phone, one begins to incorporate its logic and technics to the extent of becoming identified with what appears to be a novel social category: "Generation Txt."

An obvious pun on Generation X, "Generation Txt" began as an advertising gimmick among cell phone providers to attract young users to their products. Defined by their attachment to, and skill with, the cell phone, Generation Txt also troubled the older generation uneasy about the rise of texting. An anthropologist from the University of the Philippines, for example, writes about the dangers of texting in terms that have appeared in other countries where the practice has become popular, especially among youth: its propensity to stifle literacy by "[wreaking] havoc" on spelling and grammar, and "working in tandem with mindless computer games and Internet chat rooms . . . eroding young people's ability to communicate in the real world in real time." [15] Rather than promoting communication, texting in this view actually obstructs it, cultivating instead a kind of stupidity. Such can be seen in young people's gullibility and willingness to surrender to the marketing ploys of cell phone providers, so that they end up spending more, not less, in sending messages of little or no consequence. Furthermore, cell phones actually lead to "anti-social" behavior, as users "retreat to their own cocoons," while parents who give their children cell phones in effect avoid the responsibility of "interacting" with them in any meaningful way.[16] Other writers report the occasional use of texting by students to cheat on exams, or the use of cell phones to spread rumors and gossip that may ruin someone's reputation.[17] As one Filipino online writer put it, cell phones are like "loaded weapons," and their avid use needs to be tempered with some caution. Another writes that "if the text [I received] felt like a rumor masquerading as news, I didn't forward it." An office worker from Manila writes, "Sometimes whenever you receive serious msgs, sometimes you have to think twice if it is true or if perhaps someone is fooling you since there is so much joking [that goes on] in txt." [18]

Part of the anxiety surrounding texting arises from its perceived tendency to disrupt protocols of recognition and accountability. Parents are disconnected from their children, and children are able to defy parental authority. Cheating is symptomatic of the inability of teachers to monitor the communication of students via cell phone. And the spread of rumors and gossip, along with irreverent jokes, means that the senders of messages readily give in to the compulsion to forward messages without, as the writers previously quoted advise, weighing their consequences or veracity. Indeed, it is the capacity to forward messages almost instantaneously that proves to be the most dangerous feature of this "weapon." The urge to forward messages one receives seems difficult to resist. And under certain conditions, this urge becomes irrepressible, as the events leading to People Power II proved. We can see this happening, for example, in a posting by Bart Guingona, a theater actor and writer, to the Plaridel Listserv. As part of a group that planned to stage demonstrations at Edsa on January 18, he initially expressed doubts about the effectiveness of texting for popular mobilization. "I was certain it would not be taken seriously unless it was backed up by some kind of authority figure to give it some sort of legitimacy. A priest who was with us suggested that [the church-owned broadcasting station] Radio Veritas should get involved in disseminating the particulars. . . . We [then] formulated a test message . . . and sent it out that night and I turned off my phone. . . . By the time I turned it on in the morning, the message had come back to me three times . . . I am now a firm believer in the power of the text!" [19]

The writer is initially hesitant to resort to texting, thinking that messages sent in this way would be no different from rumors. They would lack authority by themselves. Anonymously passed on from phone to phone, texts seemed unanchored to any particular author who could be held accountable for their contents. Only when the church-owned radio station offered to disseminate the same information did he agree to send a text. Waking up the next day, he sees the effect of this transmission. Not only does his message reach others at a distance; it returns to him threefold. From a doubter, he is converted into a "believer" in the "power of the text." Such a power has to do with the capacity to elicit numerous replies.

There are two things worth noting, however, in this notion of the power of texting: first, that it requires, at least in the eyes of this writer and those to whom he sends messages, another power to legitimate the text's meaning; and second, that such a power is felt precisely in the multiple transmissions of the same text. The power of texting here has less to do with the capacity to open interpretation and stir public debate as it does with compelling others to keep the message in circulation. Receiving a message, one responds by repeating it. One forwards it to others who, it is expected, will do the same. Repeatedly forwarding messages, one gets back one's exact message, mechanically augmented but semantically unaltered. They crowd one's phone mailbox just as those who read and believe in the truth of the call they've received end up crowding the streets of Metro Manila. In this view, the formation of crowds is a direct response to the repeated call of texts now deemed to have legitimacy by virtue of being grounded in an authority outside the text messages themselves: the electronic voice of the Catholic Church. Such a voice in effect domesticates the dangers associated with texting. Users can then forward texts and feel themselves similarly forwarded by the expectations they give rise to. Finding themselves called by the message and its constant repetition, they become "believers," part of Generation Txt.

Generation Txt thus does not so much name a new social identity as it designates a desire for seeing in messages a meaning guaranteed by an unimpeachable source residing outside the text. Most of the people who gathered at Edsa and marched toward Mendiola, the road leading to the Presidential Palace, were united in their anger at the corrupt regime of President Estrada and their wish to replace him with a more honest leader. Doing so, however, did not mean changing the nature of the state or doing away with class divisions. Indeed, everything I have read about these events is at pains to stress the legality and constitutionality of these transitions, looking toward the Supreme Court and the Catholic Church (rather than either the army or left-wing groups) for institutional legitimacy. In the end, Estrada was replaced not by a new leader but by one who was part of the same old leadership: his vice president, and daughter of a former Philippine president, Gloria Macapagal-Arroyo. It would appear, then, that Generation Txt comes out of what its "believers" claim to be a "technological revolution" that sets the question of social revolution aside.

Texting is thus "revolutionary" in a reformist sense. If it can be said to have a politics, it includes seeking the cleanup and consolidation of authority, both that of the state and the source of messages. We can see an instructive instance of this politics in a manifesto that appeared in what was until recently one of Manila's more widely read tabloids, *Pinoy Times*. "Voice of Generation Txt" (*Tinig ng Generation Txt*), by Ederic Penaflor Eder, a twenty-something University of the Philippines graduate, credits the "power" (*lakas*) of "our cellphones and computers" with contributing to the "explosion" of People Power II. Texting became the medium with which "we" responded quickly to the "betrayal" (*kataksilan*) of the pro-Estrada senators who had sought to block the impeachment hearings. Elaborating on the "we" that is Generation Txt, Eder writes in Taglish:

We are Generation Txt. Free, fun-loving, restless, insistent, hard-working, strong and patriotic.

We warmly receive and embrace with enthusiasm the revolution in new technology. Isn't it said that the Philippines rules Cyberspace and that the Philippines is the text messaging capital of the world? Our response was rapid to the betrayal of the eleven running dogs [tuta] of Jose Velarde [aka Joseph Estrada]. The information and calls that reached us by way of text and e-mail was what brought together the organized as well as unorganized protests. From our homes, schools, dormitories, factories, churches, we poured into the streets there to continue the trial—the impeachment trial that had lost its meaning.

. . . Our wish is for an honest government, and a step towards this is the resignation of Estrada. We are patriotic and strong and with principles, since our coming together is not merely because we want to hang out with our friends, but rather to attain a truly free and clean society brought by our love for the Philippine nation. . . .

There were those from our generation that have long since before the second uprising chosen to struggle and fight in the hills and take up arms, trekking on the harsh road towards real change. Most of us, before and after the second uprising, can be found in schools, offices, or factories, going about our everyday lives. Dreaming, working hard for a future. Texting, internetting, entertaining ourselves in the present.

But when the times call, we are ready to respond. Again and again, we will use our youth and our gadgets [gadyet] to insure the freedom of our Motherland. . . . After the second uprising, we promise to militantly watch over the administration of Gloria Macapagal Arroyo while we happily push Asiong Salonga [aka Joseph Estrada] into the doors of prison.

We are Generation Txt.[20]

This statement of identity, curiously enough, does not identify this "we" except as those who "warmly accept and embrace" the "revolution" in new technology. The "we" that is invoked here comes about through its identification with technology and its purported newness that situates the country globally as the "text messaging" capital of the world. It is perhaps for this reason that the message reads as if it was meant to be received then forwarded: it begins and ends with exactly the same lines: "*Kami ang Generation Txt*" (We are Generation Txt).

Rather than develop ideas or put forth an analysis of social relations, Generation Txt has attitudes and affects: *malaya* (free), *masayahin* (fun-loving), *malikot* (restless), *makulit* (insistent), *masipag* (hardworking), and so forth. They pride themselves in having principles and courage, and unlike the rudderless and Westernized Generation X, they have direction. They stand for "transparent" government and a "free" and "clean" society. In this sense, they are really not that different from their elders, for they are patriots (*makabayan*) dedicated to using their "gadgets" for the sake of the motherland (*Inang Bayan*). Such commitment comes in the form of a "militant" readiness to watch over the workings of the new government in order to ensure "justice" (*katarungan*). Unlike those who have chosen to take up arms and go to the mountains, Generation Txt can be found in schools, offices, and factories, ready to respond to the call of the times. They watch, they wait, and they are always ready to receive and forward messages.

The interest of Generation Txt lies not in challenging the structures of authority but in making sure they function to serve the country's needs. This reformist impetus is spelled out in terms of their demand for accountability and their intention of holding leaders under scrutiny. Through their gadgets, they hold on to this holding, keeping watch over leaders rather than taking their place or putting forth other notions of leadership. Thus does Generation Txt conceptualize its historical agency: as speedy (*mabilis*) transmitters of calls (*panawagan*) that come from elsewhere and have the effect of calling out those in their "homes, schools, dormitories, factories, churches" to flood the streets in protest. Rather than originate such calls, they are able to trace them to their destination, which, in this case, is the nation of middle-class citizens as it seeks to renovate and keep watch over the state. Like the first generation of bourgeois nationalists in the nineteenth century I cited earlier, Generation Txt discovers yet again the fetish of technology as that which endows one with the capacity to seek access to, and recognition from, authority.[21]

Crowding

From the perspective of Generation Txt, a certain kind of crowd comes about in response to texting. It is one that bears, in both senses of that word, the hegemony of middle-class intentions. Texting, in its apolitical mode, sought to evade the crowd. But in its reformist mode, it is credited with converting the crowd into the concerted movement of an aggrieved people. In the latter case, the middle class invests the crowd with a power analogous to that of their cell phones: the power to transmit their wish for a·moral community, whereby the act of transmission itself amounts to the realization of such a community. Such a notion assumes the possibility of endowing the crowd with an identity continuous with that of middle-class texters. However, this assumption had another aspect. Not only did it lead to the fantasy of ordering the masses under bourgeois direction, middle-class interest in ordering the crowd also tended to give way to a different development. At certain moments, we also see the materialization of another kind of desire, this time for the dissolution of class hierarchy altogether. How so?

To understand the contradictory nature of middle-class ideas about crowds, it helps to look at the streets of Manila at the beginning of the twenty-first century. The city has a population of over 10 million, a large number of whom are rural migrants in search of jobs, education, and other opportunities unavailable in the provinces. Congested conditions — packed commuter trains, traffic-clogged roads, crowded sidewalks, teeming shopping malls — characterize everyday life in the city, making travel from one place to another slow and tedious throughout the day and late into the night. Such conditions affect all social classes. And because there is no way of definitively escaping them, they constitute the most common and widely shared experience of city life.

Just as the roads are clogged with vehicles, so the sidewalks seem unable to contain the unending tide of pedestrians who spill out onto the highways, weaving in and out of vehicular traffic. Indeed, among the most anomalous sights on Manila sidewalks are signs for wheelchair access. Given the uneven surfaces and packed conditions of sidewalks, such signs can only be the traces of a possibility that has never been realized, a future overlooked and forgotten. It is as if at one point, someone had the thought of organizing urban space along the lines of a liberal notion of accommodation. Instead, that thought itself quickly gave way to what everywhere seems like the inexorable surrender of space to people who use it and use it up.

Urban space in Manila thus seems haphazardly planned. It is as if no central design had been put in place and no rationalizing authority at work to organize and coordinate the movement of people and things.[22] Instead, such movement occurs seemingly of its own accord. Pedestrians habitually jaywalk and jump over street barriers. Cars and busses belch smoke, crisscrossing dividing medians, if these exist at all, inching their way to their destinations. Drivers and passengers find it difficult to see a few feet beyond their vehicles. The windshields and windows of jeepneys, tricycles, and cabs are usually filled with decals, curtains, detachable sun shades, and other ornaments that make it difficult to get a view of the road, in effect obstructing one's vision and further heightening the sensation of congestion. Indeed, given Manila's topographical flatness, it is impossible to get a panoramic view of the city except on the commuter trains and atop tall buildings. In the West, the "view" is understood as the site for evacuating a sense of internal unease and a resource for relieving oneself of pressure, both social and psychic. Such a notion of a view is not possible in Manila's streets. Caught in traffic, one looks out to see the view of more stalled traffic, so that the inside and the outside of vehicles seem to mirror each other.

Adding to the sense of congestion is the presence of garbage. The disposal of garbage has long been a problem in Manila owing to, among other reasons, the difficulty in finding adequate landfills. As a result, trash seems to be everywhere, as if it were dumped indiscriminately on street corners or around telephone poles, some of which have signs that explicitly ask people not to urinate or dump garbage there. What appears are thus scenes of near ruin and rubble. While certainly not exclusive to Manila, such scenes bespeak a city giving in to the pressures of a swelling population. Rather than regulate contact and channel the efficient movement of people and things, the city's design, such as it is, seems to be under constant construction from the ground up and from many different directions. No singular and overarching authority seems to be in charge. To walk or ride around in Manila is to be impressed by the power of crowds. Their hold on urban space appears to elude any attempt at centralizing control. It is perhaps for this reason that the largest private spaces open to the public in Manila, shopping malls, play what to an outsider might seem to be extremely loud background music. A shopping mall manager once told me that turning the volume up was a way of reminding the crowd in malls that unlike in the streets, someone was in charge and therefore watching their actions.[23]

The anonymity characteristic of crowds makes it difficult, if not impossible, to differentiate individuals into precise social categories. Clothes are at times clues to the social origins of people, but with the exception of beggars, it is difficult to tell on the basis of looks alone. The sense that one gets from moving in and through crowds is of a relentless and indeterminable mixing of social groups. This pervasive sense of social mixing contrasts sharply with the class and linguistic hierarchies that govern political structures and social relations in middle-class homes, schools, churches, and other urban spaces.[24] One becomes part of the crowd by becoming other than one's social self. Estranged, one becomes like everyone else. Social hierarchy certainly does not disappear on the streets. But like the police who are barely visible, appearing mostly to collect payoffs (tong or lagay) from jeepney drivers and sidewalk vendors, hierarchy feels more arbitrary, its hold loosened by the anonymous sway of the crowd.

The power of the crowd thus comes across in its capacity to overwhelm the physical constraints of urban planning and to blur social distinctions by provoking a sense of estrangement. Its authority rests on its ability to promote restlessness and movement, thereby undermining the pressure from state technocrats, church authorities, and corporate interests to regulate and contain such movements. In this sense, the crowd is a sort of medium, if by that word one means the means for gathering and transforming elements, objects, people, and things. As a medium, the crowd is also the site for the generation of expectations and the circulation of messages. It is in this sense that we might also think of the crowd not merely as an effect of technological devices but as a kind of technology itself. It calls incessantly, and we find ourselves compelled to respond to it. The crowd as a kind of technology refers then not merely to its potential as an instrument of production or as an exploitable surplus for the formation of social order. It also constitutes the context of, and the content for, a technic of engaging the world. The insistent and recurring proximity of anonymous others creates a current of expectation, of something that might arrive, of events that might happen. As a site of potential happenings, it is a kind of place for the generation of the unknown and the unexpected. Centralized urban planning and technologies of policing seek to routinize the sense of contingency generated in crowding. But at moments and in areas where such planning chronically fails, routine can at times give way to the epochal. At such moments, the crowd takes on a kind of telecommunicative power, serving up channels for sending messages at a distance while bringing distances up close. Enmeshed in a crowd, one feels the potential for reaching out across social space and temporal divides.[25]

As we have seen, middle-class discourses on the cell phone tend to set texting in opposition to the crowd precisely as that which overcomes the latter during normal times. But in more politically charged moments such as People Power II, cell phones were credited along with radio, TV, and the Internet for calling forth the crowd and organizing the flow of its desire, turning it into a resource for the reformation of social order. Other accounts, however, indicate the crowd's potential for bringing about something else, transmitting messages that at times converged with, but at other times submerged, those emanating from cell phones. For at times, the crowd made possible a different kind of experience for the middle class, one that had to do less with representing the masses than with becoming one with them. In so doing, the crowd becomes a media for the recurrence of another fantasy that emanates from the utopian side of bourgeois nationalist wishfulness: the abolition of social hierarchy.[26]

We can see the recurrence of this fantasy and the desire to do away with hierarchy in one of the more lucid accounts of the crowd's power from a posting by "Flor C." on the Internet discussion group Plaridel.[27] The text, originally in Taglish, is worth following at some length.

"I just want to share my own way of rallying at the Edsa Shrine" (*Gusto ko lang ibahagi ang sarili kong siste sa pagrali sa Edsa Shrine*), Flor C. begins. She invites others to do the same, adding, "I am also eager to see the personal stories of the 'veterans' of Mendiola" (*Sabik din akong makita ang mga personal na kuwento ng mga beteranong Mendiola*). Here the urge to relate her experiences at the protests comes with the desire to hear others tell their own stories. What she transmits is a text specific to her life, not one that comes from somewhere else and merely passes through her. Yet by signing herself "Flor C.," she makes it difficult to tell who this story pertains to outside that signature. Neither is it possible to tell who authorizes its telling. In this way, she remains anonymous to her readers, the vast majority of whom similarly remain unknown to her.[28] What is the relationship between anonymity and the eagerness to tell and hear about experiences, one's own as well as those of others?

Flor C. recalls the practice of protest marchers from the 1970s and 1980s of having what is called a "buddy system" for guarding against infiltration from fifth columnists and harassment by the military and police. But because "my feet were too itchy so that I could not stay in the place that we agreed to meet" (*masyadong makati ang talampakan ko imbes na tumigil sa puwesto namin*), she ends up without a "buddy" at Edsa. Instead she finds herself swimming in the "undulating river, without letup from Edsa and Ortigas Avenue, that formed the sea at the Shrine" (*ilog na dumadaloy, walang patid, mula sa Edsa sa Ortigas Avenue at bumubuo ng dagat sa Shrine*). She can't keep still. She feels compelled to keep moving, allowing herself to be carried away from those who recognize her. At Edsa, she knows no one, and no one knows her. Yet the absence of recognition is cause for neither dismay nor longing for some sort of identity. Instead she relishes the loss of place brought about by her absorption into the movement of the crowd. She finds herself in a community outside any community. It fills her with excitement (*sabik*). But rather than reach for a cell phone, she does something else: she takes out her camera.

> And so I was eager to witness [*kaya nga sabik akong masaksihan*] everything that was happening and took photographs. Walking, aiming the camera here and there, inserted into the thick waves of people who also kept moving and changing places, walked all day until midnight the interiors of the Galleria [shopping mall], around the stage and the whole length of the Edsa-Ortigas flyover. Sometimes stopping to listen for a while to the program onstage, shouting "Erap resign!" and taking close-ups of the angry, cussing placards, T-shirts, and posters and other scenes; "Good Samaritans" giving away mineral water and

candy bars, a poor family where the mother and child were lying on a mat while the father watched over, a group of rich folks on their Harley Davidsons, Honda 500s, and Sym scooters that sparkled. . . . And many other different scenes that were vibrant in their similarities but also in their differences.

Immersed in the crowd, Flor C. begins to take photographs. The camera replaces the cell phone as the medium for registering experience. In the passage just quoted, she initially refers to herself as *ako*, or "I," the first-person singular pronoun in Tagalog. But once she starts to take photographs, the "I" disappears. The sentences that follow do not contain any pronouns at all. It is as if there is no person performing the acts of walking, moving, listening, and looking. While we can certainly read these sentences to imply a person carrying out these activities, we could just as easily infer the agency of some other thing at work: an "it" rather than an "I." That "it," of course, is the camera that Flor C. takes out and begins to aim (*tinutok*). Led by her desire to be among the crowd, she begins to act and see like her camera. She stops to listen, then moves on, taking close-ups of "scenes" (*eksenas*) made up of the juxtaposition of various social classes. She is thus drawn to the appearance of sharp "contrasts" (*pagkaiba*) that are thrown together, existing side by side without one seeming to dominate the other. The juxtaposition of contrasts, the proximity of social distances, the desire to come up close to all manner of expressions and signs, to bring these within a common visual field, but one whose boundaries and focus keep shifting—these become the vocation of Flor C.'s camera. They are also the very features associated with the crowd. The crowd drives Flor C. to take out her camera; and the camera, in registering the mixing of differences, reiterates the workings of the crowd. Becoming the camera that brings distances up close and holds differences in sharp juxtaposition, Flor C. begins to take on the telecommunicative power of the crowd. Yet unlike the cell phone, whose political usefulness requires the legitimation of messages by an outside authority, the crowd in Flor C.'s account seems to draw its power from itself. It does not look outside itself, at least in this instance, precisely insofar as the crowd tends to erode the border between inside and outside. We can further see this blurring of boundaries in Flor C.'s account of entering the Galleria shopping mall next to the center stage of the Edsa protest:

During one of my trips there, I was shocked and thrilled [*kinilabutan ako*] when I heard "Erap resign!" resonating from the food center, cresting upwards the escalator, aisles and stores. The mall became black from the "advance" of middle-class rallyists wearing the uniform symbolic of the death of justice. But the whole place was happy [*masaya*]. Even the security guards at the entrance simply smiled, since they could not individually inspect the bags that came before them.

She is thrilled and shocked (*kinilabutan ako*) by a sonic wave making its way up from the bottom of the shopping mall. Middle-class "rallyists" dressed in black surged through the aisles, protesting rather than shopping. Like all modern retail spaces, the shopping mall is designed to manufacture novelty and surprise only to contain them within the limits of surveillance and commodity consumption. But during these days, the mall is converted into a site for the wholly unexpected and unforeseen. Ordinarily, the mall is meant to keep the streets at bay. Now it suddenly merges with them, creating a kind of uncanny enjoyment that even the security guards cannot resist. Formerly anonymous shoppers, middle-class protesters now come across en masse. As shoppers, they had consumed the products of others' labor. But as demonstrators, they now shed what made them distinct. They set aside their identity as consumers. They are instead consumed and transformed by the crowd. While still recognizably middle class, they nonetheless appear otherwise, advancing in their black shirts and chanting their slogans. To Flor C., their unfamiliar familiarity produces powerful effects. In the mall, Flor C. finds herself to be somewhere else. And as with the scenes in the streets, the intensification of this sense of displacement becomes the basis for the sensation of a fleeting and pleasurable connection with the crowd.

It is worth noting, however, that displacement as the source of pleasure can also, at certain moments, become the occasion for anxiety and fear. What is remarkable about Flor C.'s narrative is the way in which she takes on, rather than evades, this fear. The result, as we will see in the concluding section of her story, is neither the mastery nor the overcoming of the crowd's disorienting pull. Rather, it is the realization of what she conceives to be the saving power of the crowd. Back on the streets, she wanders onto a flyover, or an on-ramp at the Edsa highway.

When I first went to the flyover, I was caught in the thick waves of people far from the center of the rally. I could barely breathe from the weight of the bodies pressing on my back and sides. I started to regret going to this place that was [so packed] that not even a needle could have gone through the spaces between the bodies. After what seemed like an eternity of extremely small movements, slowly, slowly, there appeared a clearing before me [*lumuwag bigla sa harap ko*]. I was grateful not because I survived but because I experienced the discipline and respect of one for the other of the people—there was no pushing, no insulting, everyone even helped each other, and a collective patience and giving way ruled [kolektibong pasensiya at pagbibigayan ang umiral].

The night deepened. Hungry again. Legs and feet hurting. I bought squid balls and sat on the edge of the sidewalk. . . . While resting on the sidewalk, I felt such immense pleasure, safe from danger, free, happy in the middle of thousands and thousands of anonymous buddies.

Finding herself in the midst of a particularly dense gathering of bodies, Flor C. momentarily fears for her life. She can barely breathe, overwhelmed by the weight of bodies pressed up against her. Rather than a medium for movement, the crowd in this instance becomes a kind of trap, fixing her in place. But ever so slowly, the crowd moves as if of its own accord. No one says anything, no directives are issued, no leader appears to reposition bodies. Instead a kind of "collective patience and giving way ruled" (kolekti-bong pasyensya at pagbibgayan ang umiral). The crowd gives and takes, taking while giving, giving while taking, and so suffers the presence of all those who make it up. For this reason, the crowd is "patient," which is to say, forbearing and forgiving while forgetting the identities of those it holds and who hold on to it. Forbearance, forgiveness, and forgetting are always slow, so slow in coming. They thus share in, if not constitute, the rhythm of the work of mourning, which in turn always entails the sharing of work.

After what seems like an eternity of waiting and very little moving, Flor C. suddenly arrives at a clearing. "Lumuwag bigla sa harap ko" (It suddenly cleared in front of me), she says, which can also be glossed as "the clearing came before me." Who or what came before whom or what remains tantalizingly uncertain. Earlier, she had started to regret being trapped in the crowd. But thrown into a sudden clearing by a force that came from within that which was radically outside her, yet of which she had become an ineluctable part, Flor C. is grateful. She survives, but that is not the most important thing for her. Rather, what matters is that she was given the chance to experience the "discipline and respect" of the crowd where no one was pushed or pushing, no one was insulted or insulting, and everyone seemed to help one another, a condition that in Tagalog is referred to as damayan (cooperation), the same word used to connote the work of mourning.[29] Flor C.'s account also brings to mind the experience of crowding in certain religious gatherings, notably the all-male procession of the image of Black Nazarene that marks the high point of the fiesta of Quiapo, a district of Manila, on January 9.[30]

It is a strange sort of discipline that she undergoes. It is one that does not form subjects through systematic subjugation en route to establishing hierarchies of recognition. Instead it is a kind of discipline born of mutual restraint and deference, which, inasmuch as it does not consolidate identity, sets aside social distinctions.

Crowding gives rise to an experience of forbearance and a general economy of deference. At the same time, it does not result in the conservation of social identity. Rather, it gives way to a kind of saving that Flor C. refers to as the experience of "freedom" (*kalayaan*). Far from being a mob, the crowd here is a principle of freedom and incalculable pleasure. It is where a different sense of collectivity resides, one that does away momentarily with hierarchy and the need for recognition. Constraint gives way to an unexpected clearing, to a giving way that opens the way for the other to be free, the other that now includes the self caught in the crowd. And because it is unexpected, this freeing cannot last, just as it cannot be the last experience of freedom. Emancipation, however brief—and perhaps because it is felt to be so—depends here not on submission to a higher authority that guarantees the veracity of messages. Rather, it relies on the dense gathering of bodies held in patient anticipation of a clearing and release.

Accounts of People Power II indicate that over 1 million people gathered in the course of four days at Edsa. These included not only the middle classes. As Flor C.'s earlier remarks show, many from the ranks of the working classes as well as the urban and rural poor who opposed Estrada were also there. A heterogeneous crowd formed not simply in response to texting, for obviously not everyone had cell phones. It emerged primarily, we might imagine, in response to a call for, and the call of, justice. Put another way, the crowd at Edsa was held together by the promise of justice's arrival. Here justice is understood not simply in terms of a redistributive force acting to avenge past wrongs, one that in its use of violence is productive of more injustice. The nonviolent nature of People Power II suggests instead that the crowd formed not to exact revenge but to await justice. To do so is to dwell in a promise that, qua promise, is always yet to be realized. Like freedom and no doubt inseparable from it, justice is thus always poised to arrive from the future. And it is the unceasing uncertainty of its arrival that constitutes the present waiting of the crowd. The crowd in this case is a gathering that greets that whose arrival is never fully completed, forbearing this coming that is always deferred. Yet it is precisely because justice comes by not fully coming, and coming in ways unexpected, that it comes across as that which is free from any particular sociotechnical determination. It is this promise of justice that is conveyed by Flor C.'s experience of the crowd. The promissory nature of justice means that it is an event whose eventfulness occurs in advance of, and beyond any, given political and social order. Evading reification and exceeding institutional consolidation, such an event entails a telecommunication of sorts. It is what Jacques Derrida might call the messianic without a messiah. It would be "the opening up to the future or to the coming of the other as the advent of justice. . . . It follows no determinable revelation. . . . This messianicity stripped of everything, this faith without dogma." [31] In the midst of messianic transmissions, Flor C., along with others around her, imagines the dissolution of class differences and feels, at least momentarily, as if it were possible to overcome social inequities. She sees in crowding, therefore, a power that levels the power of the social as such. Past midnight, Flor C. finds herself no longer simply herself. Her body hurting, bearing the traces of the crowd's saving power, she sits on the sidewalk, eating squid balls, happy and safe, free in the midst of countless and anonymous "buddies."

Postscript

Utopias, of course, do not last, even if their occasional and unexpected happenings are never the last. Some three months after People Power II, the recently installed government of president Gloria Macapagal-Arroyo made good on its promise to arrest former president Estrada on charges of graft and corruption. On April 25, 2001, he was taken from his residence, fingerprinted, and photographed, his mug shot displayed for all to see in the media. The sight of Estrada treated as a common criminal infuriated his numerous supporters, many of whom came from the ranks of the urban poor and had given him the largest majority in any presidential election in the country. Spurred by the middle-class leaders of Estrada's party, Puwersa ng Masa (Force of the Masses), and swelled by the ranks of the pro-Estrada Protestant sect Iglesia ni Cristo and the populist Catholic group El Shaddai, a crowd of up to 100,000 formed at Edsa, raucously demanding Estrada's release and reinstatement. Unlike those who had gathered there during People Power II, the demonstrators in what came to be billed as the "Poor People Power" were brought in by the truckload by Estrada's political operatives from the slums and nearby provinces, provided with money, food, and, on certain occasions, alcohol. Rather than cell phones, many were reportedly armed with slingshots, homemade guns, knives, and steel pipes. English-language news reports described this crowd as unruly and uncivilized and castigated them for strewing garbage on the Edsa shrine, cursing at reporters, and urinating on the walls by the giant statue of the Virgin Mary of Edsa.[32]

Other accounts qualified these depictions by pointing out that many of those in the crowd were not merely hired thugs or demented loyalists but poor people who had legitimate complaints. They had been largely ignored by the elite politicians, the Catholic Church hierarchy, the middle-class-dominated left-wing groups, and the NGOs. They saw in Estrada a kind of patron who had given them hope by way of occasional handouts and who spoke to them in their vernacular even as he manipulated them. And unenlightened as they presently were, they deserved "compassion" from "us," the nationalist middle class, whose duty it was to uplift them to a higher level of political and moral consciousness. The great majority of middle-class opinion thus shared the view that the pro-Estrada crowd was profoundly different from the one that had gathered in January during People Power II. Where the latter was technologically savvy and politically sophisticated, the pro-Estrada crowd was retrograde and reactionary. In the earlier case, Generation Txt spoke of democratization, accountability, and civil society; in the other, the "*tsinelas* crowd," so called because of the cheap rubber slippers many of them wore, were fixated on their "idol." In their mystified state, they seemed to the middle class barely articulate, incapable of formulating their sentiments except in terms of seeking vengeance on those they deemed responsible for victimizing their leader. If those in People Power II responded to the circulation of messages sanctioned by a higher authority, as well as to the prospect of justice as the promise of freedom, the *masa* in People Power III were merely playing out its tragically mistaken identification with Estrada. They sought, or so it was assumed, a kind of crude payback characteristic of the plots of many of the movies in which the former president had acted.[33]

Middle-class accounts of this other crowd regularly made mention of the "voicelessness" of the urban poor. At the same time, such accounts showed a relative lack of interest in actually hearing, much less recording, any distinctive voices. By remarking on the masses' lack of voice, the middle class in effect redoubled the former's seeming inarticulateness. It is almost as if the masses, without anything intelligible to say, could only say the same thing. "Voiceless," the masses could only riot in the streets. Indeed, in the early morning of May 1, they marched from the Edsa shrine to the Presidential Palace, destroying millions of pesos of property, resulting in several deaths and scores of wounded, until they were dispersed by the police and palace guards. It is important to note, though, that while marching to the palace, the masses chanted slogans. Newspaper reports quote these slogans and in so doing give us a rare chance to actually hear the crowd. On the move, the crowd addresses us with statements such as "*Nandito na kami, malapit na ang tagumpay*" (We're here, our victory is close at hand!) and "*Patalsikin si Gloria! Ibalik si Erap! Nandyan na kami! Maghanda na kayo!*" (Get rid of Gloria! Return Erap! We are coming! Get ready!).[34]

Here the crowd is fueled by the desire to give back to Gloria what they think she has given to them. In exchange for unseating Estrada, they want to unseat her. She took his place, and now they want him to take hers. Through these slogans, the crowd expresses this giving back of a prior taking away. It says: "We are here, our victory is close at hand"; "We are coming, you better be ready!" The crowd thereby takes for itself an apocalyptic power. "We" here has already arrived even as it continues to come. Certain of its arrival, it asks those who hear to be ready. Having arrived, they will settle their debts, collect what is owed to them, and thereby put an end to their—the crowd's and the listeners'—waiting. Where the crowd in People Power II clung to the sense of the messianic without a messiah, this other crowd comes as a messianic specter delivered by resentments whose satisfaction could no longer be deferred. It is perhaps for this reason that middle-class observers repeatedly referred to it in English as a "mob," a "rabble" made up of "hordes." These words imply not only "savagery" and disordered appearance and speech. As the word "horde" indicates, the masses were also seen to be irreducibly alien: foreign invaders stealing up on a place they had no place in.[35]

Eschewing a stance of forbearance, this crowd demanded recognition without delay. "Here we are," it shouted. "Be prepared." For many among the middle class, to hear this crowd was to realize that they were not quite ready to hear them, and that they will always have been unprepared to do so. The masses became suddenly visible in a country where the poor are often seen by the middle class to be unsightly, spoken about and down to because they are deemed incapable of speaking up for themselves. They are thus acknowledged in order to be dismissed. Marching to the palace, however, and chanting their slogans, they assumed an apocalyptic agency. They threatened to bring about a day of reckoning that was simultaneously desired and dreaded by those who saw them. In their uncanny visibility, the masses did not so much gain a "voice" that corresponded to a new social identity. Instead they communicated an excess of communication that could neither be summed up nor fully accounted for by those who heard them. Unprepared to hear the crowd's demand that they be prepared, the middle class could only regard it as monstrous. Hence the bourgeois calls for the conversion of the masses and their containment by means of "pity," "compassion," and some combination of social programs and educational reform. But such calls also demanded that those who made up this crowd, one that was now totally other, be put back in their place, removed like garbage from the Edsa shrine and from the periphery of the Presidential Palace.[36] By the late morning of Labor Day, the military, spooked by the specter of "poor people power," had dispersed the marchers. Their violent outbursts, like their abandoned rubber slippers, were relegated to the memory of injustices left unanswered, fueling the promise of revenge and feeding the anticipation of more uprisings in the future.

Notes

My thanks to Pete Lacaba and the contributors to Plaridel, and to RayVi Sunico, Tina Cuyugan, Lita Puyat, Karina Bolasco, Jose and David Rafael, Carol Dahl, Chandra Mukerji, Matt Ratto, Paula Chakrabarty, Teresa Caldeira, James Holston, Jean-Paul Dumont, Adi Hastings, and Michael Silverstein for providing me with a variety of sources and insights that proved invaluable for this essay. I am especially grateful to Rosalind Morris and Michael Meeker for offering thoughtful comments on earlier drafts.

All translations are mine unless otherwise noted. Also, all newspaper citations without page numbers are drawn from plaridel_papers@yahoogroups .com.

1   The link between telecommunications technologies and the politics of belief that I pursue here is indebted partly to the work of Jacques Derrida, especially in writings such as "Faith and Knowledge," "Signature Event Context," and *The Politics of Friendship.*

2   See the bundle entitled *Telefonos, 1885–1891* at the Philippine National Archives, Manila, for sketches of a plan to install a telephone system in the city as early as November 1885. By December 1885, an Office of Telephone Communication (Communicacion Telefonica) had been established, and the first telephone station was set up on the same date at Santa Lucia, Manila.

3   Jose Rizal, *Por Telefono,* and various other anthologies of Rizal's writings. For an extended discussion of telegraphy and the formation of a wish for a lingua franca among the first generation of nationalists, see Rafael, "Translation and Revenge."

4   For an elaboration of other modalities of these telecommunicative fantasies and their role in shaping nationalist consciousness, see Rafael, *White Love and Other Events in Philippines History,* especially chapters 4 and 8 on rumor and gossip as populist modes of communication in Philippine history.

5   For a useful collection of documents and newspaper articles relating to the corruption case against Estrada, see Coronel, *Investigating Estrada.*

6   These quotations come respectively from Uli Schmetzer, "Cell Phones Spurred Filipinos' Coup," *Chicago Tribune,* January 24, 2001; Ederic Penaflor Eder, "Tinig Ng Genertion Txt," *Pinoy Times,* February 8, 2001; Malou Mangahas, "Text Messaging Comes of Age in the Philippines," *Reuters Technology News,* January 28, 2001.

7   See Celdran, "Text Revolution." See also Wayne Arnold, "Manila's Talk of the Town Is Text Messaging," *New York Times,* July 5, 2000, C1.

8   For a succinct historical analysis of the Philippine state, see Benedict Anderson, "Cacique Democracy in the Philippines." See also Sidel, *Capital, Coercion, and Crime;* and Hutchcroft, *Booty Capitalism.*

9   The technologies for monitoring cell phone use do exist, and there is some indication that the Philippine government is beginning to acquire them. It is doubtful, however, that such technology had been available under Estrada. It is also not clear whether the current regime of Gloria Macapagal-Arroyo has begun monitoring or intends to monitor cell phone transmissions.

10 See Arnold, "Manila's Talk," C1; Mangahas, "Text Messaging"; and Schmetzer, "Cell Phones." See also Leah Salterio, "Text Power in Edsa 2001," *Philippine Daily Inquirer* (hereafter cited as *PDI*), January 22, 2001, 1; Conrad de Quiros, "Undiscovered Country," *PDI*, February 6, 2001, 6; Michael L. Lim, "Taming the Cell Phone," *PDI*, February 6, 2001, 8.

11 This article was being circulated around the Listservs of various NGOs in the Philippines and bore the title "Pinoy Lifestyle." I have no knowledge about the original source of this piece, and so it exists in some ways like a forwarded text message. Thanks to Tina Cuyugan (tinacuyugan@mindanao.org) for forwarding this essay to me.

12 Arnold, "Manila's Talk," C1.

13 rnrsarreal@aol.com, online posting, January 25, 2001, on Plaridel Philippine political discussion group, plaridel_papers@egroups.com.

14 Arnold, "Manila's Talk," C1; See also Richard Lloyd Parr's untitled article on People Power II and cell phone use in the *Independent* (London), January 23, 2001.

15 Michael Tan, "Taming the Cell Phone," *PDI*, February 6, 2001, 8.

16 Ibid.; de Quiros, "Undiscovered Country," 6.

17 Arnold, "Manila's Talk," C1.

18 These messages were forwarded by rnrsarreal@aol.com, online posting, January 25, 2001, Plaridel discussion group, plaridel_papers@yahoogroups.com.

19 Bart Guingona, online posting, January 26, 2001, Plaridel discussion group, plaridel_papers@yahoogroups.com. Texting is widely credited with bringing about the rapid convergence of crowds at the Edsa shrine within approximately seventy-five minutes of the abrupt halt of the Estrada impeachment trial on the evening of January 16. Even before Cardinal Sin's and former president Corazon Aquino's appeal for people to converge at this hallowed site, it has been estimated that over twenty thousand people had already arrived there, perhaps lured by text messages they received. As Danny A. Gozo, an employee at Ayala Corporation, points out in his posting on Plaridel (January 23, 2001, plaridel_papers@yahoogroups.com), Globe Telecom reported an average of 42 million outgoing messages and around an equal number of incoming ones as well, while Smart Telecom reported over 70 million outgoing and incoming messages texted through their system *per day* during the days of People Power II. Gozo observes enthusiastically that "the interconnectedness of people, both within the country and outside, is a phenomenon unheard of before. It is changing the way that we live!"

20 Eder, "Tinig Ng."

21 I owe this term to James T. Siegel in his *Fetish Recognition Revolution*, perhaps

one of the most important and incisive works on the relationship between nationalism and technology.

22 My remarks on Manila's streets were gleaned from the notes and observations I made in the 1990s. On Manila's urban forms, see the excellent essay by Neferti X. Tadiar, "Manila's New Metropolitan Forms." For a lucid portrait of Manila's fantastic street life, see the novel by James Hamilton-Paterson, *The Ghosts of Manila*. Contemporary Philippine films, which often traverse the divide between rich and poor and acutely explore the spaces of their habitation, are excellent primary source materials for the study of Manila's urban forms. For a recent collection of essays on Philippine cinema, see Tolentino, *Geopolitics of the Visible*.

23 I owe this information to Mr. David Rafael, former manager of the Glorietta shopping mall in the Ayala Center in Makati.

24 For a discussion of the historical link between linguistic and social hierarchies, see Rafael, "Taglish, or the Phantom Power of the Lingua Franca."

25 Here I draw from Heidegger, "The Question concerning Technology." See also the illuminating commentary in Samuel Weber, "Upsetting the Setup." My remarks on the crowd are indebted to Walter Benjamin, *Charles Baudelaire*.

26 For a discussion of the history of this nationalist fantasy, see the introduction to Rafael, *White Love and Other Events*, 1–18. For a comparative approach to the radical potential of nationalist ideas, see Benedict Anderson, *Imagined Communities*.

27 Flor C., online posting, January 24, 2001, Plaridel discussion group, plaridel_papers@yahoogroups.com.

28 "Flor C.," I have subsequently learned, is Flor Caagusan. She was formerly editor of the editorial page of the *Manila Times* and at one point served as the managing editor of *Diliman Review*. I owe this information to the journalist Pete Lacaba. While she would be known to a small group of journalists who are part of the Plaridel discussion group, she would presumably be unknown to the majority of participants in this group. The matter of her anonymity thus remains crucial.

29 For an elaboration of the notion of *damayan*, see Ileto, *Pasyon and Revolution*. See also the important work of Fenella Cannell on Bikol province, south of Manila, *Power and Intimacy in the Christian Philippines*.

30 For a description of the 1995 procession that conveys some sense of the dangers and pleasures experienced by both onlookers and practitioners alike in the experience of crowding, see Laya, "The Black Nazarene of Quiapo."

31 Derrida, "Faith and Knowledge," 56–57. The relationship among politics, promise, and technology as intimated by Derrida is the key preoccupation of this essay. Promises arguably lie at the basis of the political and the social. The possibility of making and breaking pledges, of bearing or renouncing obligations, of exchanging vows and taking oaths, forges a sense of futurity and chance, allowing for an opening to otherness. It is this possibility of promising that engenders the sense of something to come, of events yet to arrive. With-

out promises, neither covenants nor consensus nor conflicts could arise, and neither would the sense of contingency these invariably foster. But promises can only be made and broken if they can be witnessed and sanctioned, confirmed and reaffirmed. They must, in other words, be repeatable and citable, capable of being performed again and again. Repetition underlies the making of promises, and thereby the practices of politics. We can gloss this iterative necessity as the workings of the technical and the mechanical that inheres in every act of promising. Technology as the elaboration of the technical, including the technics of speech and writing, is then not merely an instrument for engaging in politics. It is that without which the political and the futures it claims to bring forth would simply never emerge along with the very notion of emergence itself.

32 See, for example, the news reports and opinion columns of the *Philippine Daily Inquirer* from April 26 to May 5, 2001, for coverage of the "Poor People Power," or as others have referred to it, "People Power III." In particular, see the following: Alcuin Papa, Dave Veridiano, and Michael Lim Ubac, "Estrada Loyalists Overwhelm Cops on Way to Malacanang," May 2, 2001, 1; Amando Doronilla, "The State Defends Itself," May 2, 2001, 9; Doronilla, "Now the Fight over Semantics," May 4, 2001, 9; "Exchanges on Edsa 3," May 3, 2001; Blanche S. Rivera and Christian Esguerra, "Edsa Reclaimed by Edsa II Forces," May 2, 2001, 1; Blanche Gallardo, "Tears of Joy for Tears of Sadness," May 6, 2001. See also Jarius Bondoc, "Gotcha," *Philippine Star*, May 5, 2001; Howie G. Severino, "The Hand That Rocks the Masa," *Filipinas Magazine*, June 2001, 70–72; and Pete Lacaba, "Edsa Puwersa," *Pinoy Times*, April 29, 2001.

33 See, for example, Conrado de Quiros, "Lessons," *Philippine Daily Inquirer*, May 4, 2001, 6; Walden Bello, "The May 1st Riot: Birth of Peronism RP Style?" *Philippine Daily Inquirer*, May 7, 2001; La Liga Policy Institute, "Poor People Power: Preludes and Prospects," online posting, May 6, 2001, Quezon City, La Liga Policy Institute, as it appears in filipino-studies@yahoogroups.com; Ferdinand Llanes, "Edsa at Mendiola ng Masa," online posting, May 3, 2001, filipino-studies@yahoogroups.com.

34 Papa, Veridiano, and Ubac, "Estrada Loyalists Overwhelm Cops," 1.

35 "Horde" comes from the Turkish *ordi, ordu* (camp), and referred to "troops of Tartar or other nomads dwelling in tents or wagons and moving from place to place for pasturage or for war and plunder," according to the *Oxford English Dictionary*.

36 See Rivera, "Edsa Reclaimed by Edsa II Forces," 1, which reports, among other things, how people involved in People Power II "brought their own towels, sponge and scrubs" to clean the garbage that had been left behind by the pro-Estrada crowd, hosing "the filth from the ground" and "disinfecting" the shrine with chlorine. "They heaped mounds of garbage, sang and danced lustfully over the Edsa shrine marker, rammed a truck into the landscape and directed huge loudspeakers to the shrine door," fulminated Monsignor Soc Villegas, the shrine rector. See Pete Lacaba, "Edsa Puwersa."

INTERLUDE

Global Futures: The Game

Anna Tsing and Elizabeth Pollman

Why is Thai food so spicy? (The Portuguese brought chili peppers to Southeast Asia from Brazil.)

How did inexperienced British planters start a booming rice economy on the Carolina coast without the help of Asian farmers? (They enslaved West African rice farmers, who remade the landscape for rice production.)[1]

How did Arab and Chinese tools help sixteenth-century Europeans aim their guns? (The concept of triangulation was introduced by combining European versions of the Arab astrolabe and the Chinese compass into a surveying plane table with which target distances could be measured.)[2]

Unexpected connections can make new things come into being. New technologies, new economies, new identities and political visions: futures of all sorts are forged in the contingencies of strange connections. At a time when our future seems foreclosed in the narrow channels of corporate expansion, on the one hand, and clashing state and popular terrorisms, on the other, we might look for our best hopes (as well as our inchoate terrors) in the possibilities of something different. There are futures about which we have never even dreamed. "Global Futures" is a game that develops our ideas of the productivity—for better or worse—of contingency. It's also a chance to tell a good story and amuse your friends. You are free to make the world a better place, hatch a nefarious scheme, or narrate a true story. Your imagination opens up the possibilities of contingent connections.

Contingency surrounds us, but we ignore its power to shape the future. For more than a millennium, Europeans have tended to imagine the future as the fulfillment of prophecy. Since the Enlightenment, the most powerful future-making stories have told of the fulfillment of principles of progress and rationality. The driving force of technology will transform society. The ideal of democracy will be progressively encoded in law. Education will enlighten the next generation. In dialogue with such storytelling, anti-progress prophecy has developed equally formulaic tropes for encapsulating time. The national genius of a chosen people will blossom. Human nature will reestablish historic gender roles and racial hierarchies. The essence of ancient civilizations will rise again to vie and clash. There is no room for contingent connections in any of these predictions.

As the second millennium drew to a close, secular prophecy reached a fever pitch in the story of globalization. According to that story, the world is entering a global era without political or economic rifts. Nation-states and cultures are increasingly irrelevant. A global menu of consumer desires and entrepreneurial standards frames identity and sets individual and collective goals. Like most charismatic storytelling, there is something that touches us here. Much has been happening since the end of the Cold War. We are witness to the global expansion of a few giant corporations, the great flows of people from one continent to another, the forging of transnational standards for economics and politics, and the development of widely spread audiences for once parochial forms of popular culture. Yet the twenty-first century so far has shown that globalization cannot be regarded as a foregone conclusion. Global capitalism is not as seamless and successful as its promoters made it sound. The leapfrogging financial crises of the turn of the century have not disappeared. "Antiglobalization" politics have sprung up, deflating policymakers' hopes for a smooth transition to corporate empire. New wars and skirmishes make tall tales of an era without politics less believable. Nor do these disruptions of the dream appear to be part of a more complex evolutionary plan. But what about contingency and interconnection? Speculation on the Thai bhatt ricocheted to crash not just the Thai economy but then Indonesia, Korea, Japan. The unlikely alliance of "turtles and teamsters," the environmental activists and labor unions who shut down World Trade Organization negotiations in Seattle in 1999, made it impossible for global economic planners to imagine serene and celebrated public meetings. And since September 11, 2001, airplanes are no longer just transportation vehicles but also potential missiles. Before each of these events, their combination of elements would have seemed unpromising as historical agents. Now they are making the future. Are you tired of stale and dangerous predictions? It's time to appreciate contingent connections.

In this game, you imagine a global future that might develop from the possibilities of what we call a "coalescence"—the historical force that arises from a transformative coming together of disparate groups, institutions, or things. You tell the story of this coalescence, and if your fellow players accept the story, it makes history: it becomes a part of the world of the game. Your goal is to develop a set of coalescences that fulfills a preassigned mission—and changes the world. Whoever tells the best story while completing the mission wins. The game shows off a way of thinking, but it's also meant to be playable and fun.

What do we mean by coalescence? A coalescence is a historical force that derives from an unexpected connection.[3] The connection transforms the parties involved—thus creating the new historical force. The parties might be groups, institutions, ideas, identities, things, or beings. Chili peppers and Thai cuisine; African rice producers and the Carolina coast; astrolabes, compasses, and plane tables: each of these was transformed in the process of connection. Each "coalescence" made new futures possible.

In the game, you tell the story of an imagined coalescence. This coalescence must involve a coming together of two or more elements that transform each other. To say that a cat and a goldfinch are both animals is not to posit a coalescence; nor is it a coalescence to imagine a pet store that sells both. But if you posit a cat-feeding fad that requires that cats eat nothing but goldfinches to give the cats a sleeker coat, while goldfinches become seriously endangered because of the program, this is a coalescence. Both cats and goldfinches are changed in the encounter. As the example suggests, coalescences in this sense do not require intentional cooperation between the parties. They do not need to promote each party's interests. They can seriously damage collaborators—and the world. Nonhumans as well as humans participate. Your job as a player is to imagine how such an encounter might change the world. (That's what we mean by "historical force": something that might change the world.)

How to Play

At the start of the game, each player receives a *mission card* that defines his or her objective for forming a global future. For example, you might be asked to "create a revolution," "corrupt a nation's government," "use a natural resource to create havoc," or "revitalize an ancient philosophy." Players then take turns using *future-making cards* (as spelled out hereafter, these are icons of historical agency) to develop their missions. During his or her turn, a player describes a coalescence. In each subsequent round, the player's coalescence must grow and change with the addition of new future-making cards. After players have earned the required number of future-making cards, each player has a chance to tell his or her final narrative. Players evaluate each other's narratives by assigning points on a 1 to 5

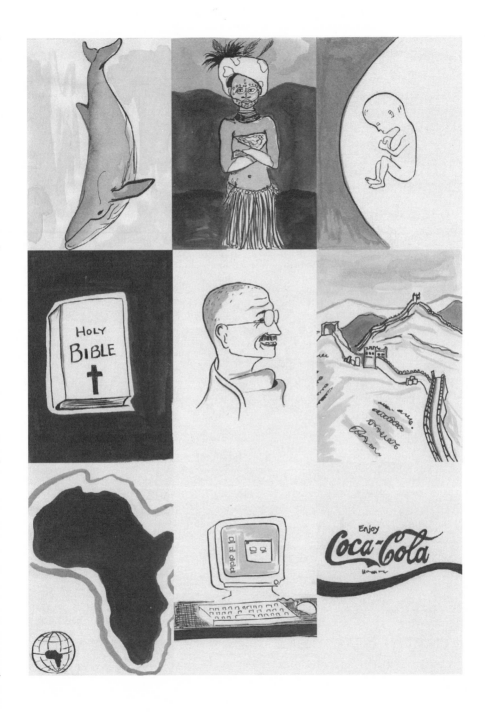

MISSION

Enable a marginalized group to gain power in a particular geographical location (not necessarily its own) in the midst of international conflict.

MISSION

Create a revolution with a coalition of at least two unlikely allies.

MISSION

Corrupt a nation's government. Tie into your narrative a threat to national security, an incidence of insider trading, and presidential impropriety.

MISSION

Create an entrepreneurial scheme in which one object is used in at least four different applications on at least three continents.

MISSION

Invent a plausible new technology that transforms the relationship between two species, improving the well-being of each.

MISSION

Force the scattering of a group (human or otherwise) that currently has health and autonomy in its own territory.

MISSION

Foster a democratic experiment in a traditionally undemocratic nation-state or social sector.

MISSION

Use a natural resource to create havoc among international agencies or corporations because of its association with the well-being of a disempowered social group.

MISSION

Save an endangered animal that is threatened by local inhabitants, and revitalize the local economy. Create a new system for sustaining the animal and the local economy.

MISSION

Launch an exploration venture that succeeds in becoming an allegory for a utopian future.

MISSION

Bring down a large international corporation or institution as a consequence of its expropriation of a natural resource previously used in a different way by local residents.

MISSION

Expose and neutralize a set of evildoings covered up by a rhetoric of goodness.

MISSION

Create a world economy based on an underappreciated natural resource and illegitimate trading.

MISSION

Forge a trade agreement between minor nations or their subgroups that shifts religious practices in powerful nations or global cities.

MISSION

Revitalize an ancient philosophy that changes stock markets, scholarly research, and official histories of science.

MISSION

Return a treasure to an original owner or nation through a chain of events that involves transnational negotiations and public scandal.

MISSION

Foment a conflict over health care that cripples the efficacy of state power.

MISSION

Bring together urban and rural schemes to save (or destroy) civilization as we know it.

scale based on the quality of coalescences imagined and articulated, the degree to which the narrative accomplishes its mission, and the cohesiveness and connectedness of the narrative in the collectively imagined world. The player with the most points wins.

The forty-nine future-making cards provided with this game are icons. They represent the world through stereotypes and symbols. They do not represent the complexity of historical agency and consciousness. Play with them as icons. Use them as an ideology about X (rain forests, biotechnology, France, pacifism, patriotism) rather than as the real thing. Some cards can be interpreted to refer to a historical legacy: cards with religious icons, cards picturing historical figures, cards with heavy symbolic loads. (A card with Einstein's picture might be interpreted as the scientific tradition; a card with Mickey Mouse might be interpreted as U.S. popular culture.) Most of the cards are ambiguous. It is up to you to interpret them and use them in a creative way. Feel free to use them literally or to stretch and refigure them—and to add them together in eccentric ways.

Once a coalescence is suggested and accepted, every player's narrative must accept it as a part of the game. This means that subsequent scenarios must be plausible in relation to these past narratives, or else the new story must change past parameters. Each player's narrative does not have to address or include other players' narratives. However, narratives that include other players' coalescences can add to the fun of the players sharing in a global future.

Round 1

Distribute one of the eighteen mission cards to each player. Players should not show their mission cards to other players. One player takes the role of dealer and shuffles the future-making cards. The player to the left of the dealer takes the first turn, which starts by the dealer giving the player three future-making cards, laid face up on the table. The player chooses two cards for his or her coalescence. The player then gives a short explanation of what the cards represent in his or her narrative. The story should articulate a connection that changes each of the elements to produce a new historical force. Is the story an acceptable coalescence? The other players may offer ideas for improvement before they decide whether or not to accept this coalescence. If accepted, the coalescence becomes part of the collectively imagined world of the game. It is now the next player's turn. The unused future-making card (from the original three dealt) is passed to this next player; the dealer adds two more, for a total of three. This next player chooses two from these three cards and repeats the process of telling the story of coalescence, hearing the evaluation of the other players, and passing one unused card to the next player.

After each player has had one turn, move on to the next round.

Rounds 2 and 3

In rounds 2 and 3, players continue taking turns narrating coalescences. However, instead of being offered three cards and choosing two, each player is offered two cards and chooses one. (The first player uses the last unused card from round 1, plus one dealt from the pack; unused cards from each turn are passed to subsequent players.) In round 2, each player gains a third future-making card, which must be incorporated into his or her narrative, forming a coalescence with the two cards earned in the first round. In round 3, each player gains a fourth future-making card; it must be worked into the story with the other three cards already earned. In each case, the new card must change the future-making prospects of the whole combination. Don't just add an element; rework the significance of the package. Players again judge the acceptability of each coalescence according to whether all the elements are transformed in forming a new historical force.

Round 4

This is the final round. To add a challenge, each player is dealt one more future-making card. There is no choice of cards in this round. (The last unused card from round 3 is returned to the bottom of the dealer's deck.) Each player must include this fifth future-making card into his or her final narrative and reveal his or her mission card. After the first person takes a turn in this round, the other players rate this player's narrative on a scale of 1 to 5 (the highest rating). Players should base the scores on the quality of coalescences narrated, the degree to which this narrative accomplishes its mission, and the cohesiveness and connectedness of the narrative in the collectively imagined world. Players write down the name of the player and the score on a piece of paper and fold the paper like a secret ballot to be counted after all players have taken their final turns and are evaluated. Players do not rate their own narratives. When the round is over, unfold the papers and total each player's points. The player with the most points wins.

If playing with five or more players, skip round 3 and move directly to round 4. Each player will have a total of four instead of five future-making cards.

The following suggestions are meant to help you understand what we have in mind as a coalescence:

- A card showing Hollywood's letters (interpreted as the U.S. film industry) and a card showing the Taj Mahal (interpreted as India) could be articulated together in the Bollywood film industry.
- A card showing a teapot and a card showing the tropical rain forest might be articulated in the story of a conservation project involving the development of a rain forest herbal tea.
- A card showing a Yanamami boy could be articulated to the rain forest herbal tea combination to tell a story of an indigenous marketing initiative to sell herbal teas. You could articulate the whole thing with Bollywood to create a song-and-dance musical about the importance of indigenous knowledge in forging twenty-first-century businesses.

In coming up with stories that connect cards, players should balance creativity and real knowledge of the world. Use the cards to expand what politics and culture might mean. You might solve real problems (peace in the Middle East, police brutality in Los Angeles) or make up new conundrums for the world. Meanwhile the game asks you to think beyond what you hear as news. What new historical forces might come into being? What else might develop for life on earth—or beyond? However, the game is less fun if the stories disintegrate into wild fantasies where everything is possible. Your stories should be plausible, although not necessarily real.

Players must satisfy each other in telling the stories that establish a connection between cards. In judging the worth of another's story, each player should ask him- or herself: "Does the story make a connection that transforms both parties?" "Does this transformation create a new kind of historical force?" It is not enough to establish that the agent represented on one card has met the agent on the other card. If you have a card with the Eiffel Tower and another with the Great Wall of China, it is not enough to imagine a travel agency that brings people to both places. Instead think of some way that each transfigures the other. French Maoism? A joint commission on historical preservation? An illegal arms sales scandal?

As you play, you'll see the need for new future-making cards. Making new cards adds variety to the game and widens the spectrum of play for the entire group. Sources for new cards could include pictures from newspapers and magazines or drawings made by the players. Players could also simply write down a few words representing their card idea on an equal-size piece of paper. New mission cards can also expand the game or make it more relevant for a particular audience or direction of play.

Beyond the Pleasures of Winning

The game is intended to amuse and stimulate a variety of audiences — but of course in different ways. The graduate students we've played with use it to debate theories of culture and globalization, as well as to invent sinister plots to destroy civilization. Our biochemist friends experimented with eerily plausible, as well as hysterically funny, biotechnologies. One twelve-year-old used the game as a vehicle for outrageous stories. Sober faculty colleagues imagined how it might be useful in classes, workshops, or teach-ins. One could use the game to open discussions of world history, or social movements, or globalization, as well as antiglobalization. Furthermore, there is no reason to limit the game to these issues. To customize the game, one merely adds new mission and future-making cards with appropriate topics. Coalescence forges the force of all kinds of future making, in the realms of theory, technology, society, and more.

"Global Futures" is less particularly addressed to the rhetoric of the future and more to the process of making actual, alternative futures. The game requires us to think about our conceptualization of time and change. At its most obvious, the game shows what is wrong with theories that require that things don't change — for example, because they have eternal essences as natural objects or cultural codes. It also argues against theories of change that bind time as the rungs of an evolutionary ladder. This includes theories that left-leaning intellectuals are proud to call progressive (supportive trellises of flowering liberalism; critical charts of intensifying capitalism), as well as those that have been exposed as repressive (coercive international development; civilizational paternalism; free-market bullying). These frameworks all require us to accept that we will enter the future in lock-step progress; our only alternative is to be "left behind." They tell us that we already know what historical forces will propel us toward our common fate. These historical forces are, of course, the ones we recognize in the present: the forms of human and nonhuman possibility imagined within current discussions of politics and culture.

Everything interesting about future making has been omitted from these theories of progress. Moreover, these omissions are biased by the geopolitical structure of our theories of time. Current imperial arrangements are reproduced in these theories of the future: Today's world centers continue to lead the globe into the future; today's "backward" margins continue to trail after. It is "common sense" to imagine the future by looking over the shoulders of cosmopolitan elites in New York and Los Angeles; the view from rural villages in Africa or Asia is, of course, behind. Why do we continue to confuse world power and world time? There is something wrong with this commonsense idea of time and change, which forecloses the future and the past—and closes our imaginations. Political cultures depend on directing and disciplining our sense of time and change. As long as we imagine the future along the set trajectories of today's categories, we will find ourselves treading in the ruts they have set out for us.

Instead, the game looks for the alternative trajectories that *might* spring up. We turn to contingent connections to disengage our stories of the future from current geopolitics and knowledge hierarchies. We would like people in the world to have other ways to imagine the future as well as the past. The game offers some tools for reimagining the forces of change.

Are the rules of the game themselves a theory of future making? Only in the sense that we have responded to the contingent encounters of each time we played the game. Everyone has a different idea of how the game should be played. We have shifted the rules of play at least a little after every encounter, and we hope you will too. This places the game somewhere between a "finite" game and an "infinite" game. In a finite game, the pleasure is to do one's best to win the particular round; in an infinite game, such as art or scholarship, the pleasures involve pushing forward the state of play indefinitely into the future.[4] If scholarship has a role in our global future, it must revitalize the ways it can be fun in both senses.

Notes

Many friends have helped us develop this game. Susan Harding and the "Histories of the Future" seminar inspired the game, and we owe the participants in that seminar for their generosity and good humor in playing and discussing it. Daniel Rosenberg offered many suggestions. Many graduate students in the departments of anthropology at the University of California, Santa Cruz, and at Harvard University gave the game their attention and sense of play. The students of the 2001 "Graduate Core Course" (UCSC) and 2002 "Reading Theory through Ethnography" (Harvard) thoughtfully played and commented. We owe long historic debts to Joanie McCollom and Tim Choy. Friends, family, and colleagues also helped out. Thanks to Jean-Paul Labrosse for his ideas about future-making cards. Thanks too to Ky Lowenhaupt, Daniel Sullivan, and Jesse Sullivan for an especially helpful round of play. We are also grateful for the ideas that inform the three questions that begin the game instructions. For the first we owe Michael Herzfeld; for the second Paulla Ebron; the third we owe to Daniel Sullivan.

1   Carney, *Black Rice.*

2   Burke, *Connections*, 27, 122, 259–60.

3   Tim Choy suggested the term "coalescence" to describe the global-local process of forming new historical agents. Our conceptualization of coalescence is informed by Laclau and Moffe, *Hegemony and Socialist Strategy*, and Grossberg and Hall, "On Postmodernism and Articulation." Each of these scholars theorizes the "articulations" that give rise to social movements. Judith Butler's *The Psychic Life of Power* and Bruno Latour's *Aramis, or the Love of Technology* variously show us how "translation" and contingency form identities and objects, respectively. These scholars, and others, have turned attention to the continual making of new social forces.

4   Susan Harding and Daniel Rosenberg suggested this point to us.

CHAPTER

Electronic Memory

Daniel Rosenberg

The Future is not what it used to be. —Theodor Holm Nelson

Welcome to the Xanadu™ Millennium

"We stand at the brink of a new age, a new time," says one of the voices of the information millennium. Soon the written word will change, "and civilization will change accordingly." A universal hypertext network will make "stored text and graphics, called on demand from anywhere, an elemental commodity." In only decades, "there will be hundreds of thousands of file servers—machines storing and dishing out materials. And there will be hundreds of millions of simultaneous users, able to read from billions of stored documents, with trillions of links among them." Within a few decades, a network of this sort may even bring "a new Golden Age to the human mind." [1]

The voice belongs to Theodor Holm Nelson, inventor of the terms "hypertext" and "hypermedia," apostle of the home computer, Web visionary, self-appointed "officer of the future," seer of so much that we now take for granted in our experience of the electronic universe. If the tenor of this statement from the 1980s is somewhat stronger than usual, the discourse is nonetheless one that we readily recognize. Indeed, by now, the rhetoric of information explosion must strike us as less strange than the forecast: decades, didn't that seem an awfully long time to wait?

Since the 1960s, Ted Nelson's prescience has been his trademark. Before the first home computers, he called for a home computer revolution. He dreamed of a word processor before the first was designed. Already in the sixties, he argued that the information future would materialize in the form of an Internet. And most famously, he dreamed that the computer might

"Computer Lib." © Theodor Holm Nelson. Courtesy of Theodor Holm Nelson.

free writing from the strictures of linearity, that electronic text would take the form of an open and multidimensional linking structure, of what in 1965 he named "hypertext."

Nelson has never been known principally as a technical innovator. He has mostly been thought of as a seer. His most famous work of writing, a cut-and-paste hypertext manifesto called *Computer Lib/Dream Machines*, which he self-published in 1974, has remained for a quarter century one of the underground classics of hackerdom.[2] His more recent work, and especially his 1980 *Literary Machines*, has revolved around his still-in-progress initiative to design a universal transclusive hypertext network called Xanadu. To many, this dream seemed chimerical before the rise of the Internet and then the graphical and textual interfaces of the World Wide Web. Since then, perceptions of the information universe have changed, and perceptions of Nelson have changed with them. Indeed, to some, it appears that Nelson's vision of a universal hypertext network has already been achieved in the form of the World Wide Web. For reasons that I will explain, Nelson himself disagrees with that idea. But one way or the other, the Web made it clear that the electric word was going to change many of our tacit assumptions about the ways in which textuality and information work. All of this gave Nelson's work a new currency. With the rise of the Web, Nelson was cited more and more in academic and popular journals. He was invited to address major conferences. His older work was reissued in new editions. As Nelson himself put it, with the explosion of the Web, he was "abruptly promoted from Lunatic to Visionary."[3]

But for all its resonance, the label "visionary" has never quite fit. In the first place, Nelson's vision of the future was always paradoxical. Like many of his contemporaries, in the 1960s and 1970s, Nelson regarded the future with both fear and hope. He envisioned the future as a coming social and ecological disaster that only the swiftest and most general change of direction might avert. But it is precisely the tyranny of this prediction against which Nelson has always seen himself struggling. As he suggested in discussions of ecological and demographic trends of the day, predictions of the future based on rational calculation pointed toward disastrous futures for the planet. Thus, as he put it, "It is . . . up to us to make . . . predictions come out wrong."[4] Or quoting another computer theorist, "the best way to predict the future is to invent it."[5] Whatever hope we have, Nelson argued, lies in a (computer-aided) multiplication of intellectual paths and possibilities, in the system of "envisioning complex alternatives" that he named "hypertext."[6]

What Is Hypertext?

The term "hypertext" conjures something futuristic and technological, four dimensions perhaps like a hypercube, or space-time distortion as in hyperspace. Hypertext is in fact an ordinary and recognizable kind of writing. The term refers simply to text that is interconnected in nonlinear ways. You use hypertext, for example, every time you click on a link in a Web browser and travel to a different text or to a different place in the text that you are reading. But it is not necessary to use a computer to read or to write a hypertext. A printed book presenting two versions of a text side by side (as in a critical literary edition, for example) is a kind of hypertext insofar as the texts are intercompared.[7] The same might be said of footnotes or of marginalia, of nested commentaries such as those of the Talmud or of medieval manuscripts, or of "choose your own adventure" books that allow the reader to pursue one or another trajectory through a numbered series of narrative episodes. All these texts are designed to allow readers to travel by leaps, shifts, and returns that confound the notion of textual linearity.

Pierre Bayle's *Dictionnaire historique et critique* (1697) might be thought of as an exemplary print-era hypertext. Bayle was an innovator of the footnote.[8] In fact, as Diderot and d'Alembert, editors of the great eighteenth-century *Encyclopédie* (1751–1766) noted, Bayle was so interested in his footnotes that he multiplied them to the point of nearly excluding his primary text altogether.[9] His "historical" dictionary treats linear time as only one possible indexing system among others. The *Encyclopédie* too is a kind of hypertext, and as I have argued elsewhere, a very thoroughly theorized one at that.[10] The encyclopedists were electrified by the critical work of Bayle and his contemporaries. But they reacted against the difficulty and the formal constraints of these texts. In their own work, they sought to smooth the space of representation, to present knowledge in such a way as to make it available to as many readers as possible and according to any imaginable set of intellectual concerns. To do this, they designed their encyclopedia to look like a conventional dictionary. Though this had been done before, most notably by the Englishman Ephraim Chambers, for Diderot and d'Alembert, it had an epistemological as well as a practical importance.[11] Their "encyclopedic dictionary" aimed to express and to activate the infinitely dense network that links together all possible knowledge. By presenting their encyclopedia in the highly accessible format of the alphabetic dictionary, they hoped to encourage readers to jump from entry to entry and idea to idea, wherever their interest and concerns might take them. To this end, the encyclopedists also employed a variety of other techniques for text linking, including hierarchical charts, embedded cross-references, and graphic explanatory schemes. The result of these various mechanisms was to upset the apparent linearity of textual structures and to emphasize the role of the reader in constructing the effective text. Mark Olsen and Gilles Blanchard's map of the referential densities in the *Encyclopédie* captures this complexity.[12]

But as Ted Nelson argues, at a deep level, there is nothing new in Bayle or Diderot (or on the Web, for that matter). Rather, these writers highlight and activate elements constitutive of all texts, what Nelson refers to as their

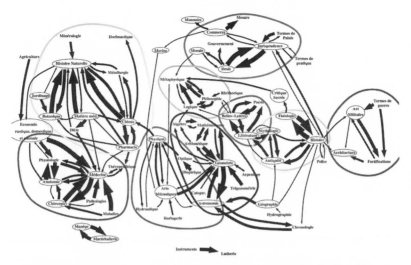

Linking structures in the *Encyclopédie* of Diderot and d'Alembert. The density of the cross-references is indicated by the thickness of the connecting arrows. © Mark Olsen and Gilles Blanchard. Courtesy of Mark Olsen and Gilles Blanchard.

hypertextuality. According to Nelson, with the exception of the simplest and most rudimentary examples, all text is run through and through with pointers to other texts and textual places that stand outside the supposed linear sequence and encourage the reader to make explicit or implicit comparisons, mental leaps, and intellectual choices.[13] As he explains in *Literary Machines*, "Many people consider [hypertext] to be new and drastic and threatening. However, I would like to take the position that hypertext is fundamentally traditional and in the mainstream of literature. Customary writing chooses one expository sequence from among the possible myriad; hypertext allows many, all available to the reader. In fact, however, we constantly depart from sequence, citing things ahead and behind in the text. Phrases like 'as we have already said' and 'as we will see' are really implicit pointers to contents elsewhere in the sequence."[14] This broad conception of hypertext allows us to see the ways in which electronic writing can be understood as sharing the basic characteristics of other forms of writing while accenting aspects that are often less visible in those forms. Nelson writes: "Hypertext can include sequential text, and is thus the most general form of writing. (In one direction of generalization, it is also the most general form of language.)"[15]

For Nelson, no text or utterance travels in a straight line, and none stands alone. The general and theoretical usage of the term "hypertext" (as opposed to the more specific usage that refers only to electronic text linking of the sort that occurs on the Web) foregrounds these characteristics. The concept "hypertext" points us toward the interconnective tissue of *lexias* that make up a given textual unit such as a "book," and at the same time, toward the complex web of external references out of which every text must draw its filaments. From this perspective, literature appears not as a collection of independent works but as "an ongoing system of interconnecting documents." [16] As Nelson explains, "Within bodies of writing, everywhere, there are linkages we tend not to see. The individual document, at hand, is what we deal with; we do not see the total linked collection of them all at once. But they are there, the documents not present as well as those that are, and the grand cat's-cradle among them all." [17] From Nelson's point of view, the computer and the Internet heighten the visibility of these structures and facilitate their use. But as Hillis Miller, George Landow, and others have noted, literature is full of fine and well-recognized examples of textual multiplicities, discontinuities, and links, whether implemented in the form of textual devices such as those I have mentioned or through the operation of prose itself, as, for example, in the writing of Proust, Joyce, or Borges. [18] Along these lines, one might also think of Roland Barthes's injunction to readerly erring in his *Pleasure of the Text*. [19]

For Nelson, we read and write in a world bigger than books, a world he refers to as the "docuverse," the theoretical realm in which all textual interreference takes place. While the concept of the docuverse comes from thinking about the implications of an electronic network of texts, it applies to all texts, electronic, printed, and written. For Nelson, hypertextuality works fluidly through dimensions often considered distinct, inside and outside a given text. Indeed, from a technical point of view, in the docuverse there is quite literally no *hors-texte*. The reference, the parallel text, and the entire paratextual apparatus all inhabit the same space on equal terms. Though still somewhat counterintuitive when it was first proposed (in the days of the ARPANET), the concept of a docuverse has become almost second nature today. Indeed, it forms a crucial part of our common cultural imagination of the Internet. Signs of this can be found just about everywhere in the hyperbolic rhetorics of information revolution. And it is exactly these rhetorics and this imaginary that Nelson helps us decode.

Back to the Future

As we see in the quotation that opens this essay, Ted Nelson has never avoided the futuristic rhetorics of information revolution. At the same time, his own notion of what computers may enable looks as much backward as it does forward. In the first place, Nelson makes it clear that he respects and cherishes what works in traditional textualities. Indeed, viewed the right way, Nelson argues, traditional literature may offer a more sophisticated picture of hypertextuality than do electronic writing and networking as we currently know them.[20] And for this reason, in his later work, Nelson reverts consistently to what he calls "the literary paradigm."

> Our design [for a new hypertext system] is suggested by the one working precedent that we know of: literature. A piece of writing—say, a sheet of typed paper on the table—looks alone and independent. This is quite misleading. Solitary it may be, but it may be also part of a literature. . . . A literature is a system of interconnected writings. We do not offer this as our definition, but as a discovered fact. And almost all writing is part of some literature. These interconnections do not exist on paper except in rudimentary form, and we have tended not to be aware of them. We see individual documents but not the literature. . . . The way people read and write is based in large part on these interconnections. . . . Writings in principle remain continuously available—both as recently quoted, and in their original inviolable incarnations—in a great procession. . . . We cannot know how things will be seen in the future. We must assume there will never be a final and definitive view of anything. And yet this system functions. LITERATURE IS DEBUGGED.[21]

This formulation captures a great deal of what makes Nelson different from so many of his technologically oriented peers in information theory. Nelson's account of information is formulated as much for books as for computers. And while an electronic enthusiast, he has always insisted that the study of hypertext begin from the study of literature. Technology, he argues, allows us to see dimensions of literature that remained obscure in the print era. At the same time, literature and scholarship traditionally construed offer a model of an intellectual and cultural system that, while far from perfect, has nonetheless proved capable of expressing complexity, ambiguity, and responsibility.

Nelson's "systems humanism" is echoed in the work of a number of contemporary critics who have taken a middle road in what is often a depressingly binary debate on the value of electronic writing. As I have noted, Hillis Miller appreciates the Proustian possibilities inherent in hypertextual erring and the hypertextual qualities of Proust's own meditations. At the same time, he warns against a naive implementation of hypertext literature and especially against naive readings in it. For example, in his review of Brown Intermedia's hypertexted Tennyson, Miller writes that the very structure of the system (its paths and links) implies that "a Victorian work . . . is to

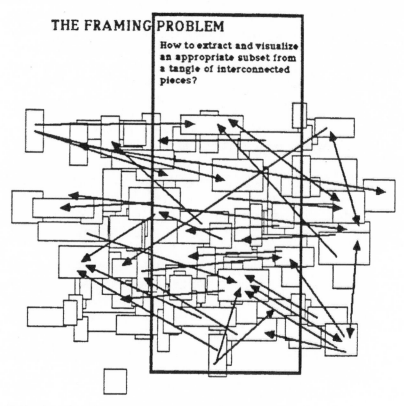

THE FRAMING PROBLEM

How to extract and visualize an appropriate subset from a tangle of interconnected pieces?

© Theodor Holm Nelson. Courtesy of Theodor Holm Nelson.

be understood by more or less traditional placement of the poem in . . . its socio-economic and biographical context, by reference, for example, to the building of canals in England at the time. The apparent freedom for the student to 'browse' among various hypertext 'links' may hide the imposition of predetermined connections. These may reinforce powerful ideological assumptions about the causal force of historical context on literary works. . . . Hypertext can be a powerful way to deploy what Kenneth Burke called 'perspective by incongruity,' but it can also be conservative in its implications."[22] Terrence Harpold's concern with modeling our reading on the technologized version of linking is more purely deconstructive. To treat "the link as purely a directional or associative structure is . . . to miss—to disavow—the divisions between the threads in a hypertext. 'Missing' the divisions is how the intentionality of hypertext navigation is realized: the directedness of the movement across the link constitutes a kind of defense against the spiraling turn that the link obscures. What you see is the link as link, but what you miss is the link as gap."[23] Both Miller's and Harpold's concerns raise questions that we will want to hold on to as we continue to read Nelson. And Harpold's questions in particular may trouble some of the more utopian moments in Nelson's work. At the same time, both point to advantages in the structure of Nelson's vision of Xanadu as opposed to electronic hypertext and the Internet as they are currently constituted. As we will see, the point of Xanadu is in a way to make intertextual messiness maximally functional, and in that way to encourage its proliferation and elaboration. Moreover, for both Miller and Harpold, the key to reading and writing hypertext well is to emphasize the ways in which the text is constructed, what is included and excluded, what sorts of choices and structures determine possible routes through it, and to teach a kind of critical reading and writing that keeps these problems first and foremost.[24] All these suggestions reinforce Nelson's argument for thinking simultaneously in two directions, from literature and scholarship (with their conventions of citation, critique, and so forth) toward electronic writing, and from electronic writing (with its attention to the literal mechanisms of textual construction) toward traditional textual fields.

Transclusion

While the general concepts of hypertext and docuverse apply equally to all textual mechanisms, it is still the case that not all textual mechanisms function in the same way. Diderot's alphabetical *Encyclopédie* employs a mechanism that is different from that of the subject-oriented Renaissance encyclopedias that he criticized, and the full-text searchable electronic *Encyclopédie* mounted on the Web by the ARTFL project operates with a different mechanism than does Diderot's print version.[25] In both cases, the latter example attempts to facilitate modes of textual reorganization that would be cumbersome if not impossible otherwise. Similarly, Nelson's proposal for a universal hypertext network functions differently from the World Wide Web. The key feature that distinguishes Xanadu from the Web is the principle that Nelson calls "transclusion."[26] Traditional print texts work by a principle of "inclusion." In a typical printed text, external references are included in the form of quotations. In this way, they become an integral part of the referring text itself. While quotation is employed on the Web, a different technical principle is also at work. When you use a typical Web link, you move from one place to another or from one electronic document to another, changing context and engaging with a new text in the way that you might if you went to the library to follow a citation from one print text to another. As an alternative to both of these possibilities, Nelson proposes a different system combining aspects of inclusion and linking that he calls "transclusion." A transclusive network implements links in such a way as to combine documents dynamically, allowing them to be read together while remaining integrally distinct. "When you cite something," Nelson writes, "you ordinarily insert a copy of the quoted material from the original, or quoted, document into the new, or quoting, document. In the Xanadu model we use transclusion instead: now you have a hidden pointer in the data structure of the second document, which points to the original and tells the computer based reading machine where to get it. So the material is not copied from the original; it remains in the documentary space of the original and is brought anew from the original to each reader."[27] Such a structure has a variety of advantages. For example, Nelson conceives of this system as a guarantee of intellectual property: "This system allows all the appropriate desiderata of copyright to be achieved: one, payment for the originator; two, credit for the originator; three, nothing is misquoted; four, nothing is out of context."[28] The goal of Xanadu, on the one hand, is total and instantaneous information access; on the other hand, it is the continuous revelation of the specific interconnectedness of all text.

For Nelson, the problem with conventional forms of writing is that they tend to limit and to discourage our options in thinking. Electronic hypertext is a promising medium for nonlinear thinking. Or as Nelson puts it (fishing Vonnegut-like for a name that might capture the mirth and complexity of the hypertextual possibility), "*grandesigning*, piece-whole *diddle-work*, grand fuddling, *metamogrification*, and for that most exalted possibility, *tagnebulopsis* (the visualization of structure in the clouds)."[29] At one pole of Nelson's world is the dream of the grand hypertext, the universal archive, and the historical tree. At the other pole is the fragmented and nomadic appropriation of knowledges of all sorts, hypertext as a system for the production and management of "loose ends."[30]

The question of loose ends has always been of crucial importance to Nelson. A meticulous taker and retaker of notes, his original inspiration for Xanadu came when as a sociology student at Harvard in the early sixties, he first encountered computers. In this age before word processing, it was evident to Nelson not only that computers could be used as glorified typewriters but that they could function as spontaneous archiving, database, and communication systems. And Nelson is often credited with theoretical innovations in this area.[31] From the beginning, Nelson set out to formulate a way of writing that would operate on an associative rather than a linear principle, that would in that way mirror and supplement the lightness of thinking opposed by linear writing and condemned by "regularity chauvinists." Like many of us, Nelson himself has difficulties remembering. He carries notecards and tape recorders with him wherever he goes and lectures from a portable archive carried in a binder. His life is an archive of fragments. In an interview, a reporter once asked Nelson whether his Xanadu design might not be connected to a kind of generalized attention deficit disorder. Nelson responded, "We need a more positive term for that. *Hummingbird mind*, I should think."[32] And it may be that hummingbird mind has finally found its technology.[33] The striking success of hypertext and hypermedia systems in all sorts of applications, from reference works and technical manuals to works of literature, art, and games, attests to the generality of Nelson's vision. But Nelson, vivid and sensitive writer that he is, also captures something like the unconscious of these practices.[34]

Magic Place of Literary Memory

In one respect, for Nelson the problem of hypertext is profoundly historical. It is the history of his life. He writes in *Literary Machines*, "This is a Caper story—a beckoning dream at the far edge of possibility that has been too good to let go of, and just too far away to reach, for half my life."[35] There is an important relation between biography and history in all of Nelson's works, and it is from this relation that hypertext draws much of its force and necessity. Biography for Nelson is a way of arguing against Historical (with a capital H) time. Perhaps this should remind us that the "caper" story (the adventure story or the detective story, in somewhat different ways) is something of a hypertext itself and that its resolution requires an imposition of narrative authority held in suspense. The effectiveness of narrative in these genres, no less than in the science fiction story (which thematizes the problem in metahistorical terms), relies on a constructed tension between the openness of the possible and the expectation of narrative closure.[36]

The story of Nelson's life, by his own account, is the story of the Xanadu project, his attempt to design a universal transclusive hypertext network. For Nelson, Xanadu, the promise of creative openness, exists as an imaginary structuring end to both an autobiographical and a technical story. It is the grail of his life's work. The very name Xanadu expresses the problem of narrative as Nelson sees it.

> Xanadu™
> One of the great unfinished dreams of the computer field . . . : Literary System, Storage Engine, Hypertext and Hypermedia Server, Virtual Document Coordinator, Write-Once Network Storage Manager, Electronic Publishing Method, Open Hypermedium, Non-Hierarchical Filing System, Linked All-Media Repository Archive, Paperless Pub-

lishing Medium, and Readdressing Software. The Magic Place of Literary Memory™.

Xanadu, friend, is *my dream*.

The name comes from the poem; Coleridge's little story of the artistic trance (and the Person from Porlock) makes it an appropriate name for the pleasure dome of the creative writer. The Citizen Kane connotations, and any other connotations you may find in the poem, are side benefits.

I have been working on Xanadu, under this and other names, for fourteen years now.

Make that twenty-seven years.[37]

According to Nelson, the name Xanadu refers to Coleridge's vision of a magic place accessible only by memories, a vision that Coleridge had in a poem that he always insisted had been interrupted irretrievably and would forever remain unfinished. "I have been working on Xanadu, for fourteen years now," Nelson writes in the 1974 edition of *Dream Machines*. In the 1987 edition, he adds, "Make that twenty-seven years." And these days, we could add more years to that. Despite notable funding setbacks, intercontinental displacements, movements in and out of private industry and academia, Nelson is still at it. A number of years ago, a writer for *Wired* magazine angered Nelson tremendously when he referred to Xanadu as the "greatest vaporware project in the history of computing."[38] Nelson took offense, pointing out that the project had produced notable results already. Still, vision after vision and revision after revision, the project continues.

For Nelson, the story of Xanadu goes back to youth, a youth that he hypereventually relives through his experience with a New Jersey elementary and junior high school computer group called the RESISTORS, recounted in his early book *Computer Lib* (1974). Nelson's accounts of the RESISTORS are hypermediated versions of the childhood he did not himself have. He contrasts his own experience in school with the free play of ideas that he observes among his junior friends. In Nelson's memory, school was the first place where the disaster of linear temporality was imposed on him. This is what he calls "the school problem." "The very system of curriculum, where the world's subjects are hacked to fit a schedule of time-slots, at once transforms the world of ideas into a schedule ('Curriculum' means 'little racetrack' in Latin). A curriculum promotes a false simplification of any subject, cutting the subject's many interconnections and leaving a skeleton of sequence which is only a caricature of its richness and intrinsic value."[39] It is in school that Nelson discovers the tragedy of history.[40] In the face of time, reason is always too late. Nelson sharply

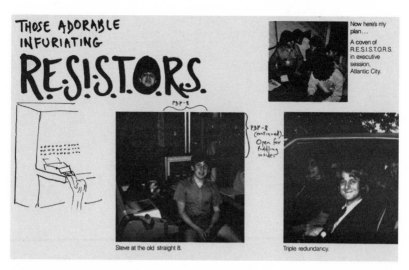

© Theodor Holm Nelson. Courtesy of Theodor Holm Nelson.

criticizes the restraints that institutions place on the imaginations of the young. "We are all born geniuses," writes Nelson, quoting Buckminster Fuller.[41] And rewriting Rousseau, "The human mind is born free, yet everywhere it is in chains." The goal of Xanadu, he says, is to make the world "safe for smart children." He might just as well have said, "smart children of all ages," for among smart children, he clearly includes himself.[42]

For Nelson, writing or reading is always restoring something lost. If, in the more mundane sense, every act of composition is an act of creation, in the terms of the docuverse, every act of creation is, in effect, a mapping of forgotten hypertextual space. At a deeper psychic level, every linguistic act is an act of contact with a lost body, contact through a "magic place of literary memory." Info-discourse provides us with an accidental metaphor, and maybe a useful one: memory. Of course, what Nelson is thinking of when he talks about memory is system storage. But it is also the problem of consciousness slipping from our grasp.

This is the essence of the question of "versioning." Xanadu operates as prosthetic memory. It stores everything in alternative versions, and nothing need be lost. A mistaken path can always be retraced, a lost reference recovered, a silenced voice revived. Nelson even compares the process of versioning to time travel in science fiction in which "the past can be changed."[43] In the world of ideas, texts, and images, versioning is effectively an antidote to linear time. And the design of Xanadu refers to it as such. Users of the prototype Xanadu system notice that the cursor on the computer screen takes the shape of an hourglass "with a softly fall-

☒ ANADU

© 1974 T. NELSON

FAIL-SAFE AND HISTORICAL FEATURES.

In systems for naive users, it is essential to safeguard the user from his own mistakes. Thus in text systems, commands given in error must be reversible. (For instance, Carmody's system (see P. DM¹/₇) requires confirmation of deletions.)

Another highly desirable feature would allow the user to view previous versions, to see the current versions, and even go back to the way particular things were and resume work from the previous version.

In the Parallel Textface this is all comprised in the same extremely simple facility. (Extremely simple from the user's point of view, that is. Inside it is, of course, hairy.)

In an egregious touch of narcissistic humor, we use the very trademark on the screen as a control device (expanded from the "X" shown in the first panel),

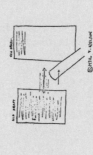

© 1974 T. NELSON

Actually the X in "Xanadu™," as it appears on the screen, is an hourglass, with a softly falling trickle of animated dots in the lower half, and Sands of Time seen as heaps above and below. These have a control, as well as a representative, function.

TO UNDO SOMETHING, YOU MERELY STEP "BACKWARD IN TIME" by dragging the upper part of the hourglass with the lightpen. One poke, one editing operation undone. Two pokes, two operations.

... and see them displayed collaterally; and revise them further.

© 1974 T. NELSON

Materials may be copied between versions. (Note that in the copying operation of the Parallel Textface, you actually see the moved text moved bodily as a block.

© 1974 T. NELSON

GETTING AROUND

The user may have a number of standby layouts,

Separate portions of the Edit Rose invoke various edit operations. (You must also point with the lightpen to the necessary points in the text: once for Insert, twice for Delete, three or four times for Rearrange, three times for Copy.)

GENERALITY.

The system may be used for comments on things,

© 1974 T. NELSON

for organizing by multiple outlines or tables of contents;

> Insert
✗ Delete
∿ Rearrange
⌐ Copy

Operation applies to Link

Operation applies to file (old version of file operation)

☐

© 1974 T. NELSON

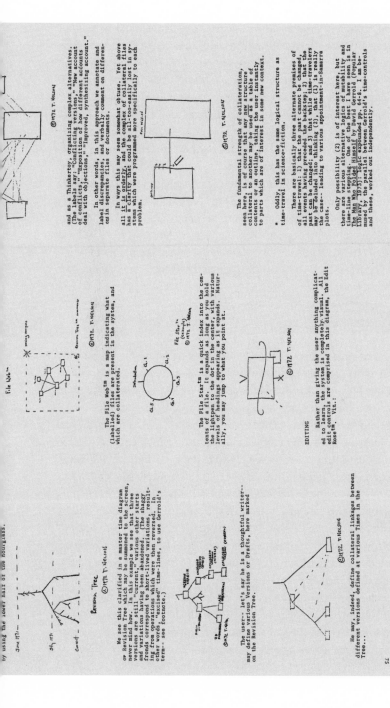

by using the lower half of the hourglass.

We see this clarified in a master time diagram or Revision Tree which may be summoned to the screen, never mind how. In this example we see that three versions are still "current," various other starts and variations having been abandoned. (The shaggy fronds correspond to short-lived variations, resulting from operations which were then reversed, in other words, "excised" time-lines, to use Gerrold's term-- see footnote.)

The user-- let's say he is a thoughtful writer-- may define various Versions or Drafts, here marked on the Revision Tree.

He may, indeed, define collateral linkages between different versions defined at various times in the Tree...

The File Web™ is a map indicating what files are present in the system, and which are collaterated.

(labelled files are present in the system, and which are collaterated.)

The File Star™ is a quick index into the contents of a file. It expands as long as you hold the lightpen to the dot in the center, with various levels of headings appearing as it expands. Naturally, you may jump to what you point at.

EDITING

Rather than giving the user anything complicated to learn, the system's various individual edit-controls are comprised in this diagram, the Edit Rose™. Viz.:

and as a Thinkertoy, organizing complex alternatives. (The labels say: "Conflicting versions," "New account of conflicts," "Exposition of how different accounts deal with objections," "Improved, synthesizing account."

In other words, in this approach we annotate and label discrepancies, and verbally comment on differences in separate files or documents.

In ways this may seem somewhat obtuse. Yet above all it is orderly, and the complex of collateral files has a clarify that could be all-too-easily lost in systems which were programmed more specifically to each problem.

The fundamental strength of collateration, seen here and elsewhere, is that any new structure, collateral to another may be used as a table of contents or an outline, taking the user instantly to parts which are of interest in some new context.

* Oddly, this has the same logical structure as time-travel in science-fiction.

There are basically three alternate premises of time-travel: 1) that the past cannot be changed, all events having preceded the backstep; 2) that the past can be changed; and 3) that while time-travelers may be deluded into thinking (2), that (1) is really the case-- leading to various appointment-in-Samarra plots.

Only possibility (2) is of interest here, but there are various alternatives in the logic of mutability, and time-line stepping. One of the best I have seen is in The Man Who Folded Himself by David Gerrold (Popular Library, 1973); logic expounded pp. 64-8. I am bemused by the parallel between Gerrold's time-controls and these, worked out independently.

75

Hypertext as time travel. © Theodor Holm Nelson. Courtesy of Theodor Holm Nelson.

ing trickle of animated dots in the lower half, and Sands of Time seen as heaps above and below." In the Xanadu system, this image of an hourglass has "a control, as well as a representative function." As Nelson explains, in Xanadu, "TO UNDO SOMETHING, YOU MERELY STEP 'BACKWARD IN TIME' by dagging the upper part of the hourglass with the lightpen. . . . You may then continue to view and make changes as if the last . . . operations had never taken place. This effectively creates an alternative timeline."[44] The temporal rhetoric here is extremely dense. Historically, writing has often figured as a transit across time. As Friedrich Kittler puts it, "every book is a book of the dead."[45] In this respect, electronic writing is no different from other forms of writing. But at the same time, electronic writing, as figured by Nelson, energizes a fantasy that death might not be so permanent. Through the chiasmic X of Xanadu, the sands of time pass back and forth: "TO UNDO SOMETHING, YOU MERELY STEP 'BACKWARD IN TIME.' " The X of Xanadu has a "control, as well as a representative function."

Screen Memory

What is the relationship between the compulsive return to the problem of memory and to the prophecy of the future? Italo Calvino poses the problem in *Invisible Cities*: in the following dialogue between Marco Polo and Kublai Khan, Polo describes cities that he has visited to Kublai Khan, who imagines seeing them or conquering them. " 'Journeys to relive your past?' was the Khan's question [to Marco Polo] . . . , a question which could also have been formulated: 'Journeys to recover your future?' . . . And Marco's answer was: 'Elsewhere is a negative mirror. The traveler recognizes the little that is his, discovering the much he has not had and will never have.' "[46] Nelson's Xanadu caper acts as a negative mirror of the narrative of his own life, or rather, forms a chiasmus (a giant X) pivoting around an act of reading-writing. Nelson figures this as literally as possible: the book(s) *Computer Lib* and *Dream Machines* are distinct texts bound back to back and upside down, so that when you reach the end of either text, you arrive at a page called "pivot," which instructs you to turn the book over and to start again. The text at the pivot reads: "The first edition was dedicated to my grandfather. This second edition is dedicated to my son. With my apology that these toys were not ready when he was a boy."[47] The pivot condenses the problem of linearity. In fact, in Nelson's imagination, there are two worlds, refracted and reversed through the chiasmatic prism of the computer screen. "Mine is a parallel universe," he writes. "I share the physical universe with other people, but it seems I see it very differently."[48] In linear time, the future is

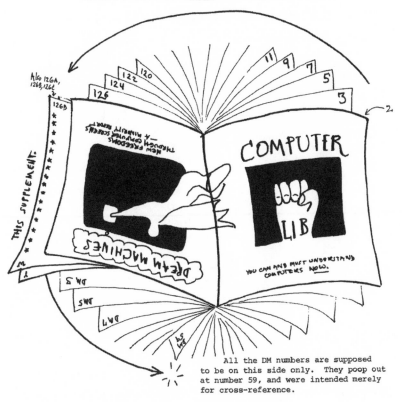

anywhere amongst these <u>plain</u> numbers, you got a lemon.

All the DM numbers are supposed
to be on this side only. They poop out
at number 59, and were intended merely
for cross-reference.

Pivot. © Theodor Holm Nelson. Courtesy of Theodor Holm Nelson.

an "endgame."[49] But in hypertextual time, the future is an endlessly revisable archive.

In another way, hypertext embodies the fantasy that the screen might open. In this respect, there is a literal dimension to the subtitle of *Computer Lib*, "New Freedoms through Computer Screens."[50] In Nelson and others, the metaphor that so often serves to replace linear time as an organizing principle is the human body. To date, perhaps the most interesting meditation on this linkage is Shelley Jackson's pioneering "hypertext novel" *Patchwork Girl*, which self-consciously weaves together elements of Mary Shelley, L. Frank Baum, and varieties of poststructuralist criticism. Jackson explicitly energizes the body metaphor by leading the reader through phrenological maps and anatomical graveyards, inciting the reader to construct for herself or himself (through itineraries of reading) a "patchwork girl" of her or his own creation.[51] Jackson's novel simultaneously employs and undermines intuitive unities of the body.

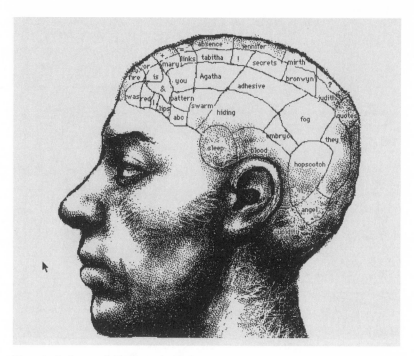

Phrenological menu. © Shelley Jackson. Courtesy of Eastgate Systems.

In *Dream Machines*, Nelson calls hypertext "a new home for the mind." [52] He figures the light pen (which he uses rather than a mouse) as a scalpel, to cut across the body of the screen, to open it. [53] "The notion of sequential presentation is deep in our thinking. The TV show, the movie, even the fireside tale, are sequential. . . . Yet there are many reasons for wanting to create non-sequential explorable media. TO REPRESENT THE TRUE STRUCTURE OF THINGS. Your body is not sequentially interconnected, but neither is everything connected to everything else. There are many specific places and forms and aspects of interconnection, each of which needs to be understood." [54] Of course, the body metaphor is in no special way the province of hypertextual representation. From the cabalistic mapping of scripture onto the human body to metaphors like the ship of state, the body provides a natively comprehensible metaphor for functional interconnection and hierarchy. But as Anne Balsamo and others have pointed out, the human body plays a stressed role in fantasies of cyberspace because these fantasies so often rely on the assumption of a simultaneous negation or evacuation of the body. [55] This is no different for Nelson. "New freedoms through computer screens" literally means through computer screens, on the other side.

Consider, for example, "fantics," Nelson's term for the study of "presentation to mind," a science including the theoretical structure of virtualities of all sorts, but also the old terrain of psychology, physiology, and epistemology, everything that concerns the possible address of our perception. It is "the art and science of getting ideas across, both emotionally and cognitively."[56]

Should I have called it TEACHOTRONICS? SHOWMANSHIPNO-GOGY? INTELLECTRONICS? . . . THOUGHTOMATION? MEDIA-TRONICS? . . . Okay, so I wanted a term that would connote, in the most general sense, the showmanship of ideas and feelings—whether

"Dream Machines." © Theodor Holm Nelson. Courtesy of Theodor Holm Nelson.

or not handled by machine. I derive 'fantics' from Greek words 'phani-nein' (show) and its derivative 'phantastein' (present to the eye or mind). You will of course recognize its cousins fantastic, fantasy, phantom. ('Phantom' means what is shown; in medical illustration it refers to an opaque object drawn as transparent; a 'phantom limb' is an amputee's temporary feeling that the severed limb has been restored.) And a fantast is a dreamer. The word 'fantics' would thus include the showing of anything.[57]

Nelson's argument for the reality of "fantic space" should not come as much of a surprise to us, steeped as we are in current promotions of "virtual reality."[58] What is interesting about Nelson's presentation is, first of all, that he attempts to dispense with any hard and fast distinction between the presentation of "reality" and the presentation of "virtuality." There is no theoretical distinction between the two in fantic terms. What is interesting in his metaphorical construction of fantics is, if you will, the ghost of the physical body. It is there in the term itself, like a phantom limb, viscerally present despite it all. As much as the fantasy of the computer screen is supposed to be an addition to consciousness, a new domain of freedom for consciousness, there seems always also to be an echo of amputation or atrophy. In the Xanadu universe, the electronic Rapture is principally supposed to take place in word and image: "We are approaching the screen apocalypse. The author's basic view is that RESPONSIVE COMPUTER DISPLAY SYSTEMS CAN, SHOULD AND WILL RESTRUCTURE AND LIGHT UP THE MENTAL LIFE OF MANKIND."[59] But our bodies as well as our minds link up with these machines. As Nelson explains, "Everything has a reality and a virtuality. Good examples are buildings, equipment, cars. . . . The extreme cases are the movie, which is all virtuality, and the fishhook, which has no virtuality—no conceptual structure or feel to the victim—until too late."[60] Nelson is aware of the problem of the human body on this side of the screen. In his early work, he treats it with studied reverence, too. One of the interesting things about the revision of *Dream Machines* is that in 1974 Nelson argues that technology should stop at the limits of the human body. Our communing with the computer should be through the eyes and ears (and at the limit the skin).[61] But by the 1987 edition of the work, the proliferation of body-machine interfaces makes such a position look obsolete. And Nelson rejects it.

The computer is supposed to help us in this world, but it is hard not to notice the fantastic or fantic reconstitution of bodies on the other side of the screen, as well. The computer, Nelson admits, is not itself a dimension of our sensory apparatus. The computer is a kind of prosthetic. But, Nelson asks, in a sense, what isn't? Everything that we sense and know, we get through a complex psychic mediation. We already experience more rudimentary technologies this way. Indeed, our experience of our own bodies is no different. "The fingernail is an excrescence with no nerves in it; yet somehow you can feel things with your fingernails—tying together disparate sensations into a unified sense of something in the world (say, a coin you're trying to pick up). In the same way, an experienced driver feels the road; in a very real sense, the car's wheels and suspension become his own sensory extensions." [62] It seems to me that there are at least two important observations to make about this move in Nelson's thought. From a critical point of view, Nelson probably has something right. And without question, discourses on virtual reality take Nelson's perspective for granted. As George Landow and others have pointed out, one of the virtues of our developing discourses on technology is that increasingly we are able to understand the mediated and technological aspects of activities such as speech and handwriting, which in other contexts have remained relatively naturalized. [63] At the same time, however, here and elsewhere Nelson's vision of the fantic body tends to reify a distinction between intentionality and embodiment that feeds a fantasy of electronic transcendence.

In Nelson's world, the body out there is under threat: the coming "golden age" of the mind should not be mistaken for a golden age in all dimensions of environmental and social existence. To the contrary, according to Nelson, "It is a safe prediction that the horrors of the future will be unprecedented, and will make the horrors of the twentieth century look modest." [64] It is precisely the tyranny of this prediction against which Nelson sees himself struggling. "The Future is not what it used to be," writes Nelson. [65] And "whatever chance remains for the survival of anything good may be in the preservation and availability of information, the only commodity that will be cheaper and more convenient." [66] Tragically, for Nelson, at the same time that a kind of "hyperreality" becomes possible, it also becomes necessary. There is an ominous part of this history of the future: what happens off-screen, in the unilluminated extratextual world of "the *favelas* of Brazil, the barrios of Mexico, the South Bronx of New York." [67]

Although the language is apocalyptic and futurological, the passage through the computer is not so much a passage into the future. Nelson's linear futures threaten horrors. The passage through the screen into a hypermediated future is, rather, a passage into a certain kind of past, a passage into the childbody of the mind. What we see in the image of the child glued to the computer screen (an image repeated throughout Nelson's works) is a primal experience of communion, body and mind reunited.

Almost everyone seems to agree that Mankind (who?) is on the brink of a revolution in the way information is handled, and that this revolu-

Kids glued to the screen. © Theodor Holm Nelson. Courtesy of Theodor Holm Nelson.

tion is to come from some sort of merging of electronic screen presentation and audio-visual technology with branching, interactive computer systems. . . . Professional people seem to think this merging will be an intricate mingling of technical specialties. . . . I think this is a delusion and a con-game. I think that when the real media of the future arrive, the smallest child will know it right away (and perhaps first). . . . When you can't tear a teeny kid away from the computer screen, we'll have gotten there.[68]

This is the present experience toward which all of Nelson's work aims. Hypertext is a name for the physical pleasure of thought, for a kind of representation that reinforces and operationalizes hummingbird mind.

The "school problem" is another name for the problem of growing up. A friend of Nelson's named Mark Miller, referred to with admiration in *Computer Lib*, proposed to Nelson that his goal in computer programming was to make himself immortal, to pass entirely into the machine. Miller, Nelson writes, was the first reader "to take any interest in the Historical Tree section" of *Dream Machines*, that is, Nelson's discussion of the relationship between hypertext and time travel. The most unusual thing about Mark Miller, Nelson continues, "is his personal plan for immortality. He genuinely expects to live forever. It is Rev. Miller's belief that he will be converted to, and reborn as a computer program, to live and to prosper, in superior, immortal and generalized form. . . . If his brain has to be minced up in the conversion to software, so be it. He says, 'That's just an I/O [input/output] problem.' "[69] Nelson speaks of his friend's proposal with some amusement and some seriousness. The fantasy is one we all recognize. It is also one that, Susan Harding argues, was very dramatically enacted in the Heaven's Gate ritual suicide/ascension into the Web firmament.[70] It is, of course, a principal fantasy attached to writing itself. (In France, for example, to become a member of the Académie française is to become "one of the immortals.") Nelson's construction of the relationship between computer and body is different. His work revolves around the fantasy not of the dissolution of the body into data but rather of the reaccess of the lost childbody through the medium of fantic space.[71]

This is the special sense of Xanadu as a "magic place" of memory. Xanadu names a memory of an unchained childishness that is always hypereventually there. Xanadu expresses Nelson's imagination of the information future as a chiasmatic return through the mirror (looking glass) of the computer screen into the before-school world. Hypereventuality is time travel in the very specific sense of a return to childhood (to a time before choices and the impossibility of choices take hold on us). The future for Nelson is a hyperexperience of childhood, of the act rather than the story of prediction. For Nelson, hypertext revives a way of inhabiting ourselves which is nonlinear, which precedes any "curriculum." Through a kind of time travel, it gives body (back) to acts of imagination. As it turns out, the model for this kind of hypereventuality is less Borges's "The Garden of Forking Paths" than it is Shelley Jackson's operationalized L. Frank Baum: encyclopedic dream as electronic storybook. In one respect, this kind of observation might be made of much of the hypertext writing and theory that has appeared in the last thirty years. In this domain there has been

The computer manual as electronic storybook. Courtesy of Theodor Holm Nelson.

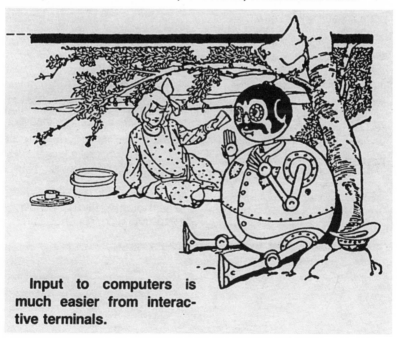

Input to computers is much easier from interactive terminals.

a general movement to highlight the intellectual and imaginative potential of nonlinear form. Literary utopia has given way to heterotopia or hypertopia. But what is most interesting about Nelson is not his role in propelling this movement (a role that should not be underestimated) but the kinds of problematization present in Nelson's work, which are often absent from the work of more recent writers. Even as Nelson's work unveils and releases the multidimensionality of seemingly traditional and linear texts, it insists on the material claims of the universe of so-called traditional writing on everything that might seek to supplant it. In this respect, Nelson's work may also be valuable in understanding and mapping the terrain of everything that claims to be new by virtue of its nonlinearity.

There are other ways, too, in which the Baum analogy suits Nelson. It seems to me that reading Nelson's work may help us desubtlize the rhetorics and practices of our information futures. In reading Nelson, we get a clear picture of how these networks are stitched together out of traditional fabrics of future and past: fabrics of progress, revolution, and millennium; of nostalgia, memory, and return. In this respect, what is important about Nelson's work is not the practice of nonlinearity per se but the insistence that our futures were never all that linear to begin with. In Nelson's writing, the seams of the formal patchwork are still showing. And not accidentally. Whatever else it is, Xanadu is a system for marking intellectual paths. Unlike so many theorists of our information future, Nelson's primary concern has never been speed, access, or totality per se. What distinguishes Nelson's vision is an attention to the link itself. This is at the heart of his concept of transclusion and the rationale behind his quixotic rejection of the Web and other current hypertext systems. The "school problem" is not just the problem of the inexorability of time but also the problem of the illusion of seamless and spontaneous intellectual, literary, and historical emergence. Xanadu is distinctive (and so far unmanageable) principally because it insists that all the seams be left showing, because it presents itself as patchwork.

Of course there are aspects of Xanadu that are utopian and nostalgic. And we can recognize these things for what they are. But if Xanadu is something of a phantasm, and if time will never really turn backward because we touch a floating hourglass with a magical cursor, it may equally be true that our futures make no sense unless we reckon with our regular suspension of disbelief on these counts, suspension that may have drifted into denial in more recent articulations of info-discourse. Reading Ted Nelson may give us a way of reframing this discourse, of demonstrating its historical embeddedness, of tracing and foregrounding its links.

Notes

1   Nelson, *Literary Machines*, 0.11–0.12.

2   Nelson, *Dream Machines* (self-published, 1974), *Computer Lib* (self-published, 1974), *Dream Machines* (Microsoft, 1987), and *Computer Lib* (Microsoft, 1987). Unless otherwise noted, citations are from the 1987 editions.

3   Nelson, *Computer Lib*, 16. On hypertext, see Landow, *Hyper/Text/Theory*, *Hypertext 2.0*, and "Twenty Minutes into the Future."

4   Nelson, *Computer Lib*, 175–76.

5   Nelson, *Dream Machines*, 151.

6   Ibid., 50.

7   Ibid.

8   On notation and indexing, see Grafton, *The Footnote*; and Blair, "Annotating and Indexing Natural Philosophy," 69–89.

9   See d'Alembert, "Dictionnaire," 967.

10 Rosenberg, "An Eighteenth-Century Time Machine," 45–66, and "We Have Never Been Interdisciplinary."

11 On Chambers, see especially Yeo, *Encyclopaedic Visions*. On the early modern question more generally, see Rosenberg, "Early Modern Information Overload." See also the articles in the January 2003 issue of *Journal of the History of Ideas* by Richard Yeo, Ann Blair, Brian Ogilvie, and Jonathan Sheehan.

12 Olsen and Blanchard, "Le système de renvois dans l'Encyclopédie."

13 See also Barthes, "The Discourse of History," 127–39.

14 Nelson, *Literary Machines*, 1.17.

15 Ibid., 0.3. This statement is among Nelson's most provocative, and it is one that suggests certain sympathies with a poststructuralist position. Nelson's use of the conventions of electronic language to highlight general but suppressed conditions of language in general extends also to include a great number of linguistic, rhetorical, compositional, and presentational questions. See also Nelson, *Dream Machines*, 37, and *Literary Machines*, 4.51–4.55.

16 Nelson, *Literary Machines*, 2.2. On this question from the point of view of the history of networks, see Mattelart, *The Invention of Communication*; and Headrick, *When Information Came of Age*. From the point of view of the history of documentation, see Day, *The Modern Invention of Information*.

17 Nelson, *Literary Machines*, 2.11.

18 See, for example, J. Hillis Miller, "The Ethics of Hypertext"; and Landow, *Hypertext 2.0*.

19 Barthes, *The Pleasure of the Text*.

20 The Internet is not the docuverse. Nelson's term "docuverse" refers only to a theoretical ideal. The Internet exists in a docuverse that is not limited to what is online. Moreover, for all its protean characteristics, the Internet is a network of particular computers. "Docuverse" refers to all the information potentially conveyed over such a network. In a docuverse, there is no redundancy, as every document exists only once and only at one theoretical loca-

tion. In principle, any bit of text that recurs in one document and another is a quotation and therefore does not assimilate completely into the new text. From a theoretical point of view, this is the case regardless of whether it happens this way in practice. On the distinction between Xanadu and the Web, especially as regards transclusion and transcopyright, see "What Is Xanadu," Xanadu Australia home page, April 4, 1998, www.xanadu.com.au (accessed December 17, 2002).

21 Nelson, *Literary Machines*, 2.9–2.11.

22 J. H. Miller, "The Ethics of Hypertext," 27–28.

23 From Harpold, "The Contingencies of the Hypertext Link," 134.

24 Miller is interested here in what is referred to as a "closed hypertext," whereas Xanadu is meant to be the paradigm case of "open hypertext." But the very distinction begs the application of Miller's question. What is "open" anyway? How do we evaluate the relative openness of a given hypertext configuration? What sorts of tools should we employ to understand the various factors that condition their arrangement? In a conventional closed hypertext such as a CD-ROM or a given Web site, these questions are relatively easy to answer (if not always posed). On the Web, or in the application of a search engine, the problem becomes much more elusive. Users of these resources are most often unaware of sorting protocols that generate their results. In Google, to take just one important example, the engine privileges search results that have been popular in the past. This feature of the search engine may be useful for answering some sorts of questions (where do I buy my airline ticket?) and problematic in others (what are the Illuminati?).

25 Andreev, Iverson, and Olsen, "Re-engineering a War Machine"; Iverson, Morrissey, and Olsen, "L'Encyclopédie de Diderot sur Internet"; Morrissey and Roger, *L'Encyclopédie, du réseau au livre et du livre au réseau*.

26 See also Nelson, "Opening Hypertext: A Memoir."

27 Ibid., 55.

28 Ibid., 55–56.

29 Nelson, *Dream Machines*, 37.

30 Ibid., 33–34.

31 Although credit for the word processor itself is frequently given to Douglas Engelbart, Nelson is frequently mentioned in the same breath. See, for example, Joyce, *Of Two Minds*; or Rheingold, *Tools for Thought*.

32 Gary Wolf, "The Curse of Xanadu," *Wired* 3.06 (June 1995), http://www.wired.com/wired/archive/3.06/xanadu.html (accessed December 17, 2002).

33 Ibid. Nelson's original response to Wolf was published at www.hotwired.com but was later removed for legal reasons. See also "Nelson Response to *Wired* Libel," *Xanadu News and Announcement Mailing List*, May 25, 1995, http://xanadu.com.au/mail/xanews/msg00003.html (accessed December 17, 2002); and Theodor Nelson, "Errors in 'The Curse of Xanadu' by Gary Wolf," *Ted Nelson: Ararat*, April 4, 1998, http://www.xanadu.com.au/ararat (accessed December 17, 2002).

34 See Moulthrop, "Polymers, Paranoia, and the Rhetoric of Hypertext," 156–57; Harpold, "Conclusions," 209–10; and Hunt, "Paranoid, Critical, Methodical."

35 Nelson, *Literary Machines*, 6.6.

36 See McConnell, "You Bet Your Life," esp. 227; and Jameson, "Progress versus Utopia," 240–41.

37 Nelson, *Dream Machines*, 141.

38 Wolf, "The Curse of Xanadu," 4.

39 Nelson, *Literary Machines*, 1.20.

40 "I have been talking revolution all these years—not political revolution, but intellectual and social revolution—fixing education, enticing all children to be smart (and making the world safe for smart children), and giving us all access to the panoply of thought and knowledge. The human race has to get very smart very fast." A telling anecdote: "Not all kids who play with computers are quite as law abiding as the RESISTORS. And the temptations are very strong. One such youngster went on a high school field trip to a suburban Philadelphia police station, and saw a demonstration of the police remote information system. The police who were demonstrating it, not being computer freaks, didn't realize how simple it was to observe the dial-in numbers, passwords and protocol. When this lad got home, he merrily went to his computer terminal in the basement and *proceeded to enter into Philadelphia's list of most-wanted criminals the names of all his teachers.* A few days later a man came to his house from the FBI. He was evidently not a regular operative but a technical type. He asked very nicely if the boy had a terminal. Then the FBI man asked very nicely if he had put in these names. The boy admitted, grinning, that he had. (Everyone in the school knew it had to be he.) The FBI man asked him, very, very nicely not to do it again. 'Of course it didn't do any harm,' says the culprit. 'I had them down for crimes like 'intellectual murder' ' " (Nelson, *Computer Lib*, 112).

41 Nelson, *Dream Machines*, 130.

42 See also Theodor Holm Nelson, "Barnumtronics," *Swarthmore College Alumni Bulletin*, December 1970, 13–15 (cited in Nelson, *Dream Machines*, 5).

43 Nelson, *Dream Machines*, 43.

44 Ibid., 49.

45 Kittler, "Gramophone, Film, Typewriter," 107.

46 Calvino, *Invisible Cities*, 29.

47 Nelson, *Dream Machines*, 153; Nelson, *Computer Lib*, 178.

48 Theodor Nelson, "My Parallel Universe," *Parallel Universe*, November 29, 1998, http://ted.hyperland.com/myU/ (accessed December 17, 2002).

49 Nelson, *Computer Lib*, 175.

50 Many writers have pointed out that the argument for "abandoning" linear time rarely means abandoning linearity altogether. They argue that some rudimentary linearity at least is necessary to all language. (Conversely, as Nelson shows, there is hypertexting in all language and writing, even so-called linear language and writing.) The psychologists and the social scientists echo the

hesitations of literary theorists in this domain. See, for example, Rouet et al., *Hypertext and Cognition*. The cognitive argument for nonlinear writing basically develops Vannevar Bush's argument about association in his classic article "As We May Think."

51 Jackson, *Patchwork Girl*. Also see Landow, "Twenty Minutes into the Future," 230–31.

52 Nelson, *Dream Machines*, 33, 150.

53 Ibid., 135.

54 Ibid., 30.

55 Balsamo, *Technologies of the Gendered Body*. For a pre-electronic version of this problem, see the discussion of dollhouses in Susan Stewart, *On Longing*. In the realm of fiction, compare James Tiptree (Alice Sheldon), "The Girl Who Was Plugged In."

56 Nelson, *Dream Machines*, 75.

57 Ibid.

58 Ibid., 78. It is interesting to note that the term "alternate world syndrome" has already been coined to refer to the loss of perceptual stability (like a vertigo) that sometimes accompanies exiting a virtual environment. See Heim, "The Design of Virtual Reality," 67–68. See also Lévy, *Becoming Virtual*; and Hayles, *How We Became Posthuman*.

59 Nelson, *Dream Machines*, 74.

60 Ibid., 68.

61 See sections on technodildonics and pornography, e.g., Nelson, *Dream Machines*, 139.

62 Nelson, *Dream Machines*, 77.

63 Mark Dery develops this question in a very interesting way in his analysis of a performance by the artist Stelarc, who uses a prosthetic arm wired to his nervous system to write by "hand" (Dery, *Escape Velocity*, 160–68). See also the discussion of "handwriting" fonts on computers in Bukatman, "Gibson's Typewriter"; and the more general meditation on the future of the body in Hockenberry, "The New Brainiacs."

64 Nelson, *Computer Lib*, 176.

65 Nelson, *Literary Machines*, 0.11.

66 Nelson, *Computer Lib*, 176.

67 Nelson, *Literary Machines*, 0.11.

68 Nelson, *Dream Machines*, 74.

69 Nelson, *Computer Lib*, 108.

70 Susan Harding, "Living Prophecy at Heaven's Gate" (in this volume).

71 This is why Nelson calls himself a "systems humanist." The physical body is still there, hence his disdain for Norbert Wiener, the founder of cybernetic theory, who reputedly was unable to recognize his own children (Nelson, *Dream Machines*, 126). On Wiener, see Tomas, "Feedback and Cybernetics."

CHAPTER

All That Is Solid Melts into Sauce:
Futurists, Surrealists, and Molded Food

Jamer Hunt

We affirm this truth: that we think, dream and act according to what we eat and drink. — Filippo Tommaso Marinetti, *The Futurist Cookbook*

Beauty shall be edible or nothing. — Salvador Dali, *Dali on Modern Art*

Food rots. It becomes waste matter. Its shelf life is momentary, even though its presence is universal. Its ubiquity across time, place, and culture notwithstanding, food has rarely functioned as an instrument for radical social change.[1] In the history of the avant-garde movements of the twentieth century, however, food does make a surprising appearance. In *The Futurist Cookbook* and in a few early writings by the surrealist Salvador Dali, food, or more precisely the consumption of food, takes on a critical role that belies its usual modesty. That is, eating emerges as an ordinary practice ripe with the potential for altering our perceptions of everyday life and politics. It offers a recipe for subversive action.

The quotidian qualities of food made it an apt vehicle for the futurists and the surrealists because each imagined movements that would spark revolutions in everyday life, not just salon culture, and each envisioned themselves laying waste to hidebound cultural values. Associations enveloping food occupy a wiggly place somewhere between the traditional and the lasting, on the one hand, and the fleeting and the ephemeral, on the other. This uneasy dialectic—quivering between the enduring and the evanescent—is, as Henri Lefebvre would later point out, the mark of the everyday. That is, it illustrates two competing temporal vectors: on the one hand, the cyclical, which ties us back to more traditional repetitions (birth and death, seasons, day and night); on the other hand, the modern, which is linear, productive, and transformative (business, fashion, news). The everyday, according to Lefebvre, came into existence as a concept only with the advent of the modern. As he writes, "Modernity and everydayness constitute a deep structure that a critical analysis can work to uncover." [2] This means that we will continually struggle to comprehend the role of the everyday in social change, but that we must pay particular attention to it, since it balances so precariously between the conservative and the radical.

What is especially striking, though, is that both the futurists and Dali couple their meditations on cuisine with connections to architecture and the built environment. Buildings are typically made to last. They can transform a landscape for years, decades, and even centuries and outlast generations. For this reason the practice of architecture inspires visions of immortality and transcendence. It freezes time, congealing the present into (semi-) permanent physical form. Consuming food is not so grandiose. It is a common ritual practice—ordinary, domestic, sensual, and repetitive. It engages taste and waste, the senses and the body, but also the digestive system, elimination, and then, ultimately, even more food. It is a corporeal act mostly, a cerebral one occasionally. A subject's relation to the object of desire is less mediated, or abstracted. We take food in, consume it, and it becomes us. Then we repeat. Each meal is an act of production and consumption, creation and destruction. It is a practice that is both cyclical and linear—repetitive and corrosive.

What unites the futurists and Dali—in addition to an appetite for fascism—and places them into a minor modernist lineage (along with Georges Bataille and, later, Fluxus) is their fixation on the ordinary forces of consumption and decay at the expense of the "timeless" object of design. In this way they both gnaw away at the atemporal conceits of the reigning architectural orthodoxies of the early twentieth century: the classical tradition, which traced a nearly unimpeachable formalist vocabulary back to antiquity; and the modern international style, which grew out of the presumption of a universalist geometry and mathematical purism. Both movements inclined toward architectural monumentalism, grounding themselves in transcendental values. The Futurist Cookbook and Dali's writing, on the other hand, juxtapose to this a common and ephemeral act—eating—and in the process throw into high relief the former's puffed-up attempts to trump time.

Futurism

The Futurist Cookbook is uproarious. Composed in 1932 primarily by F. T. Marinetti, the "field general" of the futurists, this multiform text occasions the unleashing of his powers of poetic invention and political dissension on the unsuspecting, humble cookbook form. It incorporates genres ranging from pamphlets and recipes to jeremiads, short stories, and poems by Marinetti and his sympathizers. Perhaps struggling with the relevance of the futurist movement twenty-three years after its inception, Marinetti assaults that most elemental of Italian concerns—pasta—in order to shock, yet again, the Italian masses. His agenda, however, is hardly trivial. What better way to profoundly change the direction of a nation than by revolutionizing its most common practices? And if so, why not food? Not content to let futurism devolve into an aesthetic movement alone, Marinetti weaves the futurist project into the fabric of Italy's daily life.

Marinetti vents his unique outrage at pasta in its many forms. What could possibly be the harm of pasta? Speed, light, color, motion: these are the qualities of a new futurist Italy, and pasta—flabby, starchy pasta—deadens that revolutionary spirit. It is a vestige of an old-fashioned, nineteenth-century style of life for which Marinetti has only bitter contempt:

> Pastaciutta, 40% less nutritious than meat, fish or pulses, ties today's Italians with its tangled threads to Penelope's slow looms and to somnolent old sailing-ships in search of wind. Why let its massive heaviness interfere with the immense network of short long waves which Italian genius has thrown across oceans and continents? Why let it block the path of those landscapes of colour form sound which circumnavigate the world thanks to radio and television? The defenders of pasta are shackled by its ball and chain like convicted lifers or carry its ruins in their stomachs like archaeologists. And remember too that the abolition of pasta will free Italy from expensive foreign grain and promote the Italian rice industry.[3]

Rabidly nationalist, fanatically militaristic, Marinetti especially blanches at the idea that Italian soldiers are out on the battlefields consuming pasta, bloating themselves on this ruinous grain. The imagery that characterizes pastaciutta throughout *The Futurist Cookbook* is relentlessly torporous; Fillìa—Marinetti's accomplice-in-arms—writes, "We have come to this decision because pasta is made of long silent archeological worms which, like their brothers living in the dungeons of history, weigh down the stomach make it ill render it useless. You mustn't introduce these white worms into the body unless you want to make it as closed dark and immobile as a museum."[4] If Marinetti and friends were to realize their "ever more high speed, airborne life," there would certainly be no ravioli or cavatelli on their plates to bog them down.

Intuitive Antipasto (formula by Signora Colombo-Fillìa)

Hollow out an orange to form a little basket in which are placed different kinds of salami, some butter, some pickled mushrooms, anchovies and green peppers. The basket perfumes the various elements with orange. Inside the peppers are hidden little cards printed with a futurist phrase or a surprising saying (for example: 'Futurism is an anti-historical movement'—'Live dangerously'—'With futurist cooking, doctors, pharmacists and grave diggers will be out of work,' etc.).[5]

The futurists' revolution in cooking comprised more than simply tossing pasta out as the staple of the Italian diet, however. Marinetti had designs on a much more kaleidoscopic, multisensorial, and clamorous experience for consuming food. It is in this respect that his manifesto of the culinary arts dovetails with the other futurist projects.

Tyrrhenian Seaweed Foam (with coral garnish)
(formula by the futurist aeroceramist Tullio d'Albasola)

Take a bunch of freshly-netted sea lettuce, being careful the catch was not made near sewers or drains because such lettuce easily absorbs bad smells. Wash and rinse in plenty of running water. When it is clean, dip it in some lemon juice. Powder the leaves with sugar and add spray with a wave of whipped cream.

The coral garnish consists of an assembly of clusters of piquant red peppers, slices of sea urchins caught at full moon, and a constellation of seeds from a ripe pomegranate.

The whole, with its artistic architectural lines and inspired arabesques, should be served immediately on a round flat plate, with waves made of broth added, and covered by a sheet of blue cellophane.[6]

Drawing inspiration from the scientific theories of Einstein and the philosophical writings of Bergson and the artistic innovations of the cubists, the tenets of the futurists' philosophy disputed the solidity of physical forms, disassembling them into their constituent, elemental parts. Light, energy, motion, and space were the forces that determined the object and experience. Unlike the cubists, who were forever disarticulating form into concatenating vantages until the work achieved a kind of stasis or resolution, the futurists tried to create the restless experience of motion itself.[7] And whereas cubism was, for the most part, an insurrection in the salons, futurism expressly set its sights beyond aesthetic transvaluation and toward a revolution of everyday life.[8] Their excessively composed

Cucina Futurista. Courtesy of Beinecke Rare Book
and Manuscript Library, Yale University.

recipes, so technically and architecturally complex and cultivated, dramatized the dynamic tensions between lofty cultural accomplishment on the one hand and base satisfactions on the other.

To the futurists, the phenomenal world was not solid but discontinuous and fleeting. Oscillating waveforms, vibrating particles, unstable atoms: these were the invisible supports of rock-solid materiality. This process of dematerialization is evident in a range of futurist work in a variety of media. In painting, it manifests itself in the fascination with movement, line, and light. As the futurist painters put it in their Technical Manifesto, "Painters have shown us the objects and the people placed before us. We shall henceforward put the spectator in the centre of the picture."[9] In other words, a painting should absorb the spectator into its space and create for him or her the perception—not the representation—of experience itself. Solid bodies commingle and merge and split each other. As physical isolates, they are perceived as radically separate, but in the futurist method, the molecular world of vibrating particles and waveforms unites the subject with the object in the fullness of uncontoured space: "Our bodies penetrate the sofas upon which we sit, and the sofas penetrate our bodies. The motorbus rushes into the houses which it passes, and in their turn the houses throw themselves upon the motor-bus and are blended with it."[10]

Throughout their work, then, the distance that separates the viewer from the object is collapsed by the mutuality of the intersecting force, lines, and planes. The futurist artist Umberto Boccioni would write in the Technical Manifesto of Futurist Sculpture, "Sculpture must, therefore, give life to objects by making their extensions into space palpable, systematic and plastic, since no one can any longer believe that an object ends where another begins and that our body is surrounded by anything—bottle, automobile, house, tree or road—that does not cut through it and section it in an arabesque of directional curves."[11] This refusal of the conventional distinction between figure and ground suggests a kind of mutual swallowing up of the monads by space itself.

If space destroys the integrity of matter, what about time? Marinetti voices his nascent movement's attitude: "It is in Italy that we launch this manifesto of violence, destructive and incendiary, by which we this day found futurism, because we would deliver Italy from its canker of professors, archaeologists, cicerones and antiquaries." And he continues this screed, "Museums, cemeteries! . . . Truly identical with their sinister jostling of bodies that know one another not."[12] Time passes always, just as matter is simply the illusion of momentary coalescence. Dynamism, not stasis, was the new order of the new day, and voracious Time would set fire to the bones of the past in a funeral pyre built on the museum's decayed car-

The futurist table. Courtesy of Beinecke Rare Book and Manuscript Library, Yale University.

cass. Marinetti thus insists "that a masterpiece be burned with the corpse of its author. . . . Against the conception of the immortal and imperishable we set up the art of the becoming, the perishable, the transitory and the expendable."[13] Not beyond the reach of obsolescence, Marinetti recognized that he was himself perishable, transitory, and expendable: "The oldest amongst us are thirty; we have, therefore, ten years at least to accomplish our task. When we are forty, let others, younger and more valiant, throw us into the basket like useless manuscripts!"[14] He enjoined the next generation to throw aside their elders just as his generation had. No monuments would be left by the futurists; instead, "our houses will last less time than we do, and every generation will have to make its own."[15] This idea—that nothing can or should challenge Time's arrow—reaches its apogee in the consumptive glory of the futurists' banquets.

There is a diabolical and calculated constructedness to a futurist banquet. It is an admixture of artfulness and kitsch, of the ridiculous and the sublime. " 'The Solid Treaty': a multi-coloured castle of nougat with, in-

F. T. Marinetti. Courtesy of Beinecke Rare Book and Manuscript Library, Yale University.

side, very tiny nitro-glycerine bombs which explode now and then perfuming the room with the typical smell of battle."[16] As it spirals from serious political tract to poetic whimsicality and back, *The Futurist Cookbook* establishes a powerful dialectic between lasting idealisms and humble, goofy jokes. And yet, what the futurist "Painting Technical Manifesto" sets out as painting's goal, futurist dining accomplished: "The gesture which we would reproduce on canvas shall no longer be a fixed moment in universal dynamism. It shall simply be the dynamic sensation itself [made eternal]."[17] There was little to take away from a futurist meal other than the experience. Wafting scents (waiters perfumed the air as one ate); cacophonous music; random poetic readings; surprising tactility (Marinetti forbade the use of utensils in favor of one's hands); and "the creation of simultaneous and changing canapés which contain ten, twenty flavours to be tasted in a few seconds"[18]—these all occasioned a "perfect meal." A meal was thus an exercise of the principle of simultaneity: explosions of sensory data in the full presentness of the moment. Futurist painting, poetry, sculpture, and architecture were organized around the premise of creating experience itself for the spectator, not representing it. By collapsing the orders of representation and making the art object into the vehicle of experience rather than the representation of it, the futurists challenged the subject-object relationship. In some ways, then, The Futurist Cookbook was the most successful futurist art form. The senses imbibed the experience and the body drowned itself in the atmosphere. Particulate matter, sounds, sensations, tastes, smells: they all entered the body to become one with it, not distinct from it.

.

Aerofood (formula by the futurist aeropainter Fillìa)
The diner is served from the right with a plate containing some black olives, fennel hearts and kumquats. From the left he is served with a rectangle made of sandpaper, silk and velvet. The foods must be carried directly to the mouth with the right hand while the left hand lightly and repeatedly strokes the tactile rectangle. In the meantime the waiters spray the napes of the diners' necks with a conprofumo of carnations while from the kitchen comes contemporaneously a violent conrumore of an aeroplane motor and some dismusica by Bach.[19]

.

This futurist meal thus accomplished everything that sculpture, painting, and architecture were enjoined to. Light, sound, energy, and matter all dissolved the boundaries between the subject and the object. The physical body and the built environment devoured each other just as time and space consumed all material traces. By assimilating food to architecture and architecture to food, the futurists cooked up a new sensibility. If architectural monumentalism is the impervious physical embodiment of memorialized greatness, the futurists stood instead for the certain perishability of any such foolishness. They undermined any possible fixation on enduring grandeur by making matter into meals. That is to say (and we shall encounter this more directly with Dali), their hyperconsumptive method hollowed out the lasting legacy of monoliths. This attitude obliged a reconsideration of the relation of bodies to space to objects. Matter, like all food, was just a future waste product.

.

Architectural Dinner for Sant'Elia
In honour of the 1931 Poet of National Record Farfa (winner of the 'Sant'Elia' Poetry Circuit) an architectonic dinner was held with a special sensitivity to space. This puts the person being honoured 600 kilometres from those honouring him, but linked to them with telephone wires. The Futurist poets . . . and the painters . . . from the 'Synthesis' group of Futurists and Avant-Gardists, gathered together in the directorial offices of the Futurist movement in Rome. To dine, they used their hands like children, and alternately built and ate, towers, skyscrapers, battleship guns, airport slipways, belvederes, sports stadiums, military pontoons, elevated railways one after the other:

Three hundred cubes (3 cm high) of pastry. Eight parallelepipeds (10 cm high) of compressed buttered spinach. Ten cylinders (30 cm high) of Cremona nougat. Six balls (15 cm diameter) of Milanese risotto. Five pyramids (40 cm high) of cold minestrone soup. Twenty tubes (1 metre high) of date paste. Five ovoid blocks (20 cm high) of banana paste. Seven screens (60 cm high) of cod cooked in milk.

The Futurists, the better to construct the Futurist house perfected it with their teeth each one sitting on inedible cylinders of compressed pasta.

Formula by the Futurist Aeropoet

MARINETTI

and the Futurist Aeropainter

FILLÌA[20]

•

Surrealism

In an anecdote—perhaps apocryphal—Salvador Dali recounts an exchange that he had with that model of modernist design, Le Corbusier: "When I was barely twenty-one years old, I happened to be having lunch one day . . . in the company of the masochistic and Protestant architect Le Corbusier who, as everyone knows, is the inventor of the architecture of self-punishment. Le Corbusier asked me if I had any ideas on the future of his art. Yes, I had. I have ideas on everything, as a matter of fact. I answered him that architecture would become 'soft and hairy.' . . . In listening to me, Le Corbusier had the expression of one swallowing gall."[21] Dali's writing from that era is unequaled in its resolute weirdness. Possessing a style completely at odds with the conventional (despite Dali's own downward spiral into mediocrity and commercialism), his early essays can still provoke, confuse, and disorient the earnest reader. His spastic, incontinent prose rarely coheres into anything easily digestible, and yet it lingers, like dyspepsia. As images pile upon images, as sentences wander into infinity, and as sense swings in the wind, though, different details emerge. Dali composes in the style of dreams: meaning is rarely given but instead accretes through the layering of detail and hyperbole and discontinuity. His essays for Minotaure—the lavishly illustrated and powerfully influential arts journal that was published in Paris from 1933 to 1939—bend and twist back on one another to form a labyrinthine structure worthy of Piranesi. Motifs disappear, only to reemerge several articles later. It was within this creative hothouse that Dali first published his delirious article on art nouveau architecture, entitled "As of the Terrifying and Comestible Beauty of Modern Style Architecture."[22]

What Dali referred to by the classification "Modern Style" or "Style 1900" was the art nouveau style of architectural design that seemed to be sprouting up from and overgrowing—literally—the streets of Paris. Hector Guimard, its principal purveyor, incorporated plant, animal, and insect motifs into the detailing of building facades, subway entrances, and street lamps. Tendrils and shoots spread out over a building's curvaceous, undulating surface, giving it a hybrid appearance somewhere between animal, vegetable, and mineral. While eventually disparaged by the design cognoscenti, and especially the emerging modernists, art nouveau provided for Dali the opportunity to exercise his voracious imagination.

"I believe that I was the first . . . to consider the delirious Modern Style architecture as the most original and the most extraordinary phenomenon in the history of art, and I did so without a shadow of humor" (33). It is necessary to pause momentarily on his rationale for celebrating this specific architectural vogue. Art nouveau, with its obsessive decorativism, was for Dali an approach that surpassed strict functionalism. As a hodgepodge of historical quotations and technical borrowings, art nouveau espoused nothing useful: "Everything that was the most naturally utilitarian and functional in the known architectures of the past suddenly ceases, in Modern Style, to serve any purpose whatever" (37). Its folding together of narrative ornament with surface treatment pushed it into the layered realm of dreamwork, or, as Dali describes it, "that frightful impurity that has no other equivalent or equal than the immaculate purity of oneiric intertwinings" (37). Art nouveau is a condenser, then, in the Freudian sense, that melts together opposing, unrelated elements into an overdetermined but highly charged whole: "Gothic becomes metamorphosed in Hellenic, into Far-Eastern and, should it occur to one—into Renaissance . . . all in the feeble time and space of a single window" (37). It is this association to dreams that signals to the reader the portal through which to pursue Dali down the vertiginous paths of the essay.

But it is misleading to imply that Dali saw absolutely no usefulness in the vegetal motifs of art nouveau. They do act as the material objectifications of desire. Dali was arguably the most resolute Freudian of all the surrealists—and an unvarnished neurotic. His work throughout this period and the narratives he employed to explain it veer little from the Freudian straight and narrow. So it is of little surprise that he attributes the origins of his fixation on these peculiar stylings to the functioning of his pulsating drives. All architectural details serve only one purpose, "the 'functioning of desires,' these being, moreover, of the most turbid, disqualified and unavowable kind" (37). Dali then escalates into a hyperbolic mode that only he is capable of sustaining:

Grandiose columns and medium columns, inclined, incapable of holding themselves up, like the tired necks of heavy hydrocephalic heads, emerge for the first time in the world of hard undulations of water sculptured with a photographic scrupulousness of instantaneity until then unknown. They rise in waves from the polychrome reliefs, whose immaterial ornamentation congeals the convulsive transition of the feeble materializations of the most fugitive metamorphoses of smoke, as well as aquatic vegetations and the hair of those new women, even more "appetizing" than the slight thirst caused by the imaginative temperatures of the life of the floral ecstasies into which they vanish. These columns of feverish flesh (37.5° C) are destined to support nothing more than the famous dragon-fly with an abdomen soft and heavy as the block of massive lead out of which it has been carved in a subtle and ethereal fashion. . . . [It] cannot fail to appear to us as the true "masochistic column" having solely the function of "letting itself be devoured by desire," like the actual first column built and cut out of that real desired meat toward which Napoleon, as we know, is always moving at the head of all real and true imperialisms which, as we are in the habit of repeating, are nothing but the immense "cannibalisms of history" often represented by the concrete, grilled and tasty lamb-chop that the wonderful philosophy of dialectical materialism, like a new William Tell, has placed on the very head of politics. (37–39)

It is hard to stop. Dali's imagery builds to an orgiastic height that only seems to keep mounting. Yet it is hardly random. Throughout the passage, for example, he oscillates meticulously between the hard and the soft, the formed and the formless (columns/tired necks; sculptured/water; materializations/fugitive metamorphoses of smoke; lead/soft). Like the futurists, Dali was determined to liquefy the membranes of the material object—to melt that subject-object barrier—but in this case the breach of the barriers is not so much physical as it is psychical.[23] For Dali, desire is the connecting tissue that ties together the subject and the object. The innervated object is never free from the tendrils of desire that envelop it and produce it as desired. The only means of satisfaction, then, is to incorporate fully the object of desire, to fuse subject with object so that they are forever indistinguishable. Thus the "fugitive" and "feeble" materializations that Dali writes of in relation to architectural ornamentation do have a use: they incite desire; they whet appetite.

Dali recognized that desire does not distinguish. That is to say, there is no perceptible difference between the registers of representation of a desired thing. In that endless play of substitutions that Freud called fetishism, the drives displace themselves onto whoever or whatever is available to the psyche. The goal for the subject, however, is always the same: to completely incorporate the object of desire. Dali effectively sexes up building details as just the latest "feeble materialization" of his own ardent appetite:

> Thus in my view it is precisely (I cannot emphasize this point too strongly) the wholly ideal Modern Style architecture that incarnates the most tangible and delirious aspiration of hyper-materialism. An illustration of this apparent paradox will be found in a current comparison, made disparagingly it is true, yet so lucid, which consists of assimilating a Modern Style house to a cake, to a pastry-cook's exhibitionistic and ornamental tart. . . . The nutritive and edible character of this kind of house is thus alluded to without any euphemism, these houses being nothing other than the first edible houses, the first and only erotizable buildings, whose existence verifies that urgent "function," so necessary to the amorous imagination: to be able quite really to eat the object of desire.[24]

In this "new surrealist age of the 'cannibalism of objects,'" buildings must be edible because they do not differ in any substantial way from any other kind of object of desire (45). They are like the Kleinian part object, a rematerialization of a severed lost part that, through its subsequent introjection, or incorporation, completes the subject wholly. And space obliges that union, contracting to bring together the desirer and desiree: "The best subscribe to this formula: a curved line appears today to become once more the shortest distance between two points" (35). The subject absorbs the building just as the building consumes its inhabitants. Whereas the futurists conceived of solid matter as just the illusion of permanence in a world of light, energy, and motion, Dali's dematerializations are tied more tightly to the psyche.

For Dali, as for dreams, time moves in a torsional, not linear, path. Rock-hard pilasters and buttresses are simply momentary consolidations of matter in space and time. Dali perceives the landscape and objects around him bending and twisting under desire's distorting pressures. Time moves not in a linear direction but in pulsating cycles and ebbs and flows. Like the "pointillist iridescences" on Gaudí's rubbery buildings, time moves "in an asymmetrical and dynamic-instantaneous succession of reliefs, broken, syncopated, entwined" (43–45). Time and space contort under the same force and with the same vicissitudes: they swell to afford the full measure of a satisfaction (nearly) experienced; they double forward and back through the processes of regression and repetition; and they throb and detumesce along with the erratic cycles of the drives. Time bends like a soft watch. Monuments go limp.

Future Imperfect

"The unveiling of monuments in squares all over the world meets with incomprehension and general hilarity," wrote the futurist Boccioni.[25] When architecture aspires to universality and idealism, it, too, risks ridicule. Monuments, even more than architecture, are time preservers. They are bulwarks against the passage of time and the pressures of memory loss. Desire, decay, consumption, and degeneration are rarely manifest in grand, historical monuments. Instead they are present in unremarkable daily routines like eating. Architectural monumentalism, by standing tall and straining to transcend the everyday, reifies values at odds with the heavy pressure of disintegration that marks the modern.

"All that is solid melts into air." By reviving this phrase that Karl Marx penned as he stewed in the chaos of early modernism, Marshall Berman champions a strain of ordinary modernism that neither blithely stomps out tradition nor wallows in the dark despair of the contemporary condition but embraces complexity and contradiction.[26] This is the tremulous ground that the futurists and Dali occupy in pairing food with architecture. They reveal the convoluted, conflictual qualities of consumption: it is common, repetitive, destructive *and* regenerative. They celebrate messy everydayness as an alternative to the pure but false choices of the traditional and the new. Consumption is not representational or symbolic—it does not stand for anything beyond the moment. Instead, it only ties us tighter to the humbling effects of pleasure, rot, and decay.

Notes

1   Though this is beginning to change. The Slow Food movement, which started in Italy and is now international, espouses an antiglobalist, anticorporate, anti-fast-food politics. It is a movement to counteract speed in life and eating and challenges its adherents to buy locally, dine slowly, and live deliberately.
2   Lefebvre, "The Everyday and Everydayness," 37.
3   Marinetti, *The Futurist Cookbook*, 37.
4   Taylor, *Futurism*, 132.
5   Marinetti, *The Futurist Cookbook*, 159.
6   Marinetti, *The Futurist Cookbook*, 161.
7   Taylor, *Futurism*, 50.
8   Banham, *Theory and Design in the First Machine Age*, 109.

9   Taylor, Futurism, 126.

10 Marinetti, The Futurist Cookbook, 132.

11 Taylor, Futurism, 130.

12 Marinetti, The Futurist Cookbook, 124.

13 Banham, First Machine Age, 122.

14 Taylor, Futurism, 125.

15 Banham, First Machine Age, 135. This line is sometimes attributed only provisionally to the architect Antonio Sant'Elia. It appears in his Manifesto of Futurist Architecture ("L'Architettura Futurista") in Lacerba (Florence, August 1914). Though signed by Sant'Elia, it does bear the unmistakable imprint of F. T. Marinetti.

16 Marinetti, The Futurist Cookbook, 110.

17 Taylor, Futurism, 125.

18 Marinetti, The Futurist Cookbook, 40.

19 Ibid., 144.

20 Ibid., 121.

21 Dali, Dali on Modern Art, 29–31. For this essay, I use the English translation of this text that appears in the 1996 Dover Press edition of Dali on Modern Art: The Cuckolds of Antiquated Modern Art, a reprint of the bilingual Dial Press edition that appeared in 1957. The article itself first appeared in Minotaure 3–4 (Paris: Editions Albert Skira, 1933) as "De la beauté terrifiante et comestible, de l'architecture Modern'style."

22 Dali, Dali on Modern Art, 33.

23 Dali sympathized with and later incorporated many of the same scientific theories of matter that had inspired the Futurists. He notes, for example, "The most transcendent discovery of our epoch is that of nuclear physics regarding the constitution of matter. Matter is discontinuous and any valid venture in modern painting can and must proceed only from a single idea, as concrete as it is significant: the discontinuity of matter. . . . The visceral wrenches of the gifted Boccioni are the foreshadowing of the supersonic dynamism and the glorious Apollos of the discontinuity of matter" (Dali on Modern Art, 71–73).

24 Ibid., 41.

25 Taylor, Futurism, 130.

26 Berman, All That Is Solid Melts into Air, 35–36.

CHAPTER

Sing Out Ubik

Pamela Jackson

How can one create novels based on this reality which do not contain trash, because the alternative is to go into dreadful fantasies of what it ought to be like; one must work with the trash, pit it against itself. . . . Hence the elements in such books of mine as Ubik. If God manifested Himself to us here He would do so in the form of a spraycan advertised on TV. — Philip K. Dick, letter to Stanislaw Lem, September 4, 1973

Ubik talks to us from the future, from the end state to which everything else is moving; thus Ubik is not here—which is to say now—but will be.—Philip K. Dick, letter to Peter Fitting, June 28, 1974

As a science fiction writer, Philip K. Dick always had an ambivalent relationship to prophecy. On the one hand, he was annoyed by the idea that science fiction should be judged as a realistic portrayal of the future. On the other hand, he marveled sometimes at the ways the genre could approach less mundane truths, and he loved to point out that, according to his fans, the world grew more "Phil Dickian" every day. In 1966 Dick wrote a novel called Ubik, which contained a prediction. It predicted that when read carefully it would reveal itself to be no mere cheap futuristic fantasy, but a genuine prophecy of things to come. Eight years later, Dick had a religious experience that led him to read his own novel in just this way.

In March 1974, Dick had a series of visions. The visions lasted for one full year and plunged him into a world that looked suspiciously like the one he had described in Ubik: delirious, paranoid, entropic, and mystical, a place in which reality had given way to endlessly regressing fictions, vast conspiracies, and mysterious messages from other realms. In March 1974, Dick's world split open. A pink beam of light came out of nowhere and jammed him full of information. He saw his neighborhood in suburban

Southern California peel away, uncovering what looked like ancient Rome or a black iron prison beneath the surface of Orange County. He received messages—over the radio, in the mail, from a mysterious "AI" voice that talked to him in "hypnagogic states," in the pages of his own novels—hinting at the true nature of time and space, the conspiratorial powers that rule the spurious world he was trapped in, the "salvific entity" that might transform this world or extricate him from it. He became, as he couldn't help but notice, one of his own characters. The strangest part of the whole thing was that the transformation itself was already the story of Ubik.

The setting of Ubik is a world coming apart. Half of the inhabitants of this future live in cold pac, physically frozen but mentally alive. Even in the waking world things are coming undone. Time seems to have sped up or gone into reverse, and the present-day world is eroding. Cigarettes have gone stale in their packages. The cream in the coffee machines is sour. Modern elevator doors open to reveal obsolete iron cages, and jet aircraft regress to propeller planes in midflight. People are succumbing to a sudden degenerative process, withering and crumbling into dust one by one. And the world is filling up with "manifestations" of the dead: notes in cigarette cartons, graffiti on bathroom walls, voices on hotel telephones. "Essential that I get in touch with you. Situation serious . . . ," says a note in a cigarette carton. "I'm the one that's alive, you're all dead," says a graffito. Meanwhile, at the opening of each chapter, an advertising jingle announces a mysterious product called Ubik: "Instant Ubik has all the fresh flavor of just-brewed drip coffee. Your husband will say, Christ, Sally, I used to think your coffee was only so-so. But now, wow! Safe when taken as directed."

What's going on? A television commercial suggests an explanation: the characters in the novel who believe themselves to be awake are in fact dreamers in cold pac. As the ad explains it:

> World deterioration of this regressive type is a normal experience of many half-lifers, especially in the early stages when ties to the real reality are still very strong. A sort of lingering universe is retained as a residual charge, experienced as a pseudo environment but highly un-stable and unsupported by any ergic substructure. This is particularly true when several memory systems are fused, as in the case of you people.[1]

The ad proposes a solution. "Don't just sit there," it continues, "go out and buy a can of Ubik and spray it all around you night and day." The quest for Ubik propels the rest of the novel, a sort of metaphysical detective story in which clues fail to add up to a complete picture of things, and Ubik, whatever it is, is always just out of reach. Am I alive or dreaming in cold pac, wonders Joe Chip, the novel's protagonist. Is the world real or not? Who is responsible?

There's more to Philip K. Dick than his stories, he learned in March 1974. *Ubik* doesn't end when it ends. It doesn't begin where it begins, either. In March 1974, which Dick forever calls "3-74," like a personal name, there were signs. Perhaps they were signs of God. If it was God, it was not the God you would have expected. Dick saw "the trash of the gutter, the debris such as match folders, the labels of spraycans, etc.," but somehow it was *Logos* all the same. "This is exactly what I actually saw myself as functioning in the highest fashion to guide and instruct us, these same verbal instruments."[2] If it was God, God appeared in the form of a present and originary linguistic entropy propelling us backward through what had always appeared to be history, toward some simpler future that we already remember as making more sense. If it was God, it was a God very much like Ubik.

Dick's revelation frightened him, but it was exhilarating as well. He didn't fully understand it, but it contained some problems that he recognized very clearly. For years he had been writing about time and about entropy, about reality's perpetual dissolve into illusion, about ambiguous entities that might or might not be God. For years his fiction had staged just the sort of revelation he was now experiencing. Even though he hadn't known it at the time, in 1966 when he wrote *Ubik*, he might already have achieved the life's work that seemed to be just beginning. "In a way," Dick wrote in 1977 after years of studying the linked revelations of 3-74 and his own novel, "what is most paradoxical is that I said it all in *Ubik* years ago! So in a way my exegesis of 3-74 says only '*Ubik* is true.'"[3]

According to the television commercial, Ubik is a spray-can fixative for reality itself. "One invisible puff-puff whisk of economically priced Ubik banishes compulsive obsessive fears that the entire world is turning into clotted milk, worn-out tape recorders and obsolete iron-cage elevators, plus other, further, as-yet-unglimpsed manifestations of decay," says one ad. "I came over to Ubik after trying weak, out of date reality supports," enthuses a TV housewife as she modernizes her devolving kitchen appliances with a squirt of the can.[4]

The jingles that haunt the novel advertise Ubik's hundred uses. "The best way to ask for beer is to sing out Ubik. Perk up pouting household surfaces with new miracle Ubik. Friends, this is clean-up time and we're discounting all our silent, electric Ubiks by this much money." Ubik seems to be a shape-shifting panacea, ideal for *all* household and personal needs. It is a salad dressing, an indigestion cure, a razor with a self-winding Swiss chromium never-ending blade, an easy-to-apply, extra-shiny, nonstick plastic coating, a savings and loan. Ubik is a hair conditioner and hair spray. A deodorant that "ends worry of offending." A sleeping pill, a bra, plastic wrap ("keeps freshness in, air and moisture out. Watch this simulated test"), a breath freshener with "powerful germicidal foaming." A breakfast cereal ("do not exceed recommended portion at any meal").

The ads in the novel promise salvation through the product. But as the characters in the novel pursue it, Ubik seems always to recede. Reality recedes. Years roll backward. The world disappears into conspiracy and simulation. By the end of the novel, product logos give way to *Logos*, and the disembodied voice of endorsement takes on a different tone:

> I am Ubik. Before the universe was I am. I made the suns. I made the worlds. I created the lives and the places they inhabit; I move them here, I put them there. They go as I say, they do as I tell them. I am the word and my name is never spoken, the name which no one knows. I am called Ubik but that is not my name. I am. I shall always be.[5]

But the message doesn't explain anything. It doesn't explain who is in cold pac, whose world is real, who is responsible.

In my opinion, all the secrets of the universe are in UBIK, if we could discern them. — Philip K. Dick, letter to unknown addressee, December 28, 1974

After 3-74 Dick returns to *Ubik* with a suspicious eye. It has taken on, for him, "the ring of revealed truth." And although he doesn't know what that truth was, or how it got into his novel, he is certain that *Ubik* must somehow contain the key to his experience. And why not? After all, he has just suffered a vertiginous collapse of the Orange County, California, where he lives into *Ubik*'s world—during which his reality was revealed as fake, time slipped backward into the past, and the world burst open with messages and signs. After 3-74 Philip K. Dick becomes another Joe Chip: lost in a dissolving illusion, barely glimpsing the malign conspiracy behind what looks like a world, launching an endless quest for the signs of God in the pages of *Ubik*.

What if *Ubik* is true? Dick wonders in his "exegesis" of 3-74. The visions of 3-74 suggested that, by accident or by some knowledge that he didn't yet have or couldn't now remember, his 1966 novel said something prophetic. If so, and if anyone else had a hint of it, someone should soon be knocking at his door. The novel would attract attention. Or it already had. Strangely enough, by 3-74 more and more people really were beginning to pay attention to Dick's fiction, people from outside the science fiction community, suggesting that there was more to Dick's writing, and *Ubik* in particular, than even he had previously known. The Polish writer Stanislaw

Lem wrote two essays in which he singled out Dick as a "visionary among the charlatans" and Ubik as a jewel amid the generic trash of science fiction.[6] Academic "Marxists" from France and their American counterparts also seemed to have a keen interest in Ubik. In a letter, Dick writes, "An awful lot of Marxists from abroad have been flying here to query me on and on about Ubik and what it means and where did I get the idea, etc.? . . . Anyhow, so much for paranoia. What's more important is that I know Ubik is somehow true, that's the real point."[7]

This presented further problems. If Dick had somehow stumbled onto the truth in Ubik, he had also stumbled onto a lie. If this world is a fraud, as Ubik seems to suggest and 3-74 to confirm, if time actually moves backward or not at all, if history is a fiction, then someone must be responsible. A flurry of letters from 1974 and 1975 show Dick in the throes of paranoid fear. Has his novel caught the eye of whatever evil demiurge is pulling the strings around here? Dick writes to Lem and the Marxists, to Soviet scientists and the FBI, looking for answers and taking evasive action. Sometimes it's not clear which he is doing. Like Joe Chip, he's no longer certain who his friends are. To the FBI, Dick writes:

> I will tell you frankly that there is a possibility that some fundamental scientific discovery is accidentally incorporated into UBIK, by me, and the Marxist analysts in France and Poland, with their excellent scientific and philosophical-theoretical background (I'm not even a college graduate) saw this in the novel. . . . (I hasten to repeat: there is no political or social comment material in UBIK which could even remotely be exploited.)[8]

In his own notes, Dick tends to lump all these "authorities" together. It was a mistake to ever let himself show up on their radar. But their interest seems to confirm 3-74 all the same. And in the midst of the paranoia there rises a crazy hope: if Ubik is really onto something, what might it be? Could it be something that will change the way things are headed? Is Ubik's prophecy a promise? Dick writes hopefully:

> It is my current opinion that in UBIK I somehow by chance hit upon some important truth about the real nature of the universe, and I've had French people tell me this, but what specifically this insight is, I don't know. Something to do with Plato's image of the cave, evidently, with [the characters in Ubik] breaking through being true reality. . . .
>
> Perhaps our pseudo-reality is the enormous Lie, and the breaking through of truth . . . is the Paraclete himself, informing our souls about the state of things here, and promising us help and something better.[9]

The Marxists treat Ubik as a critical and ironic portrait of the faked quests and panaceas of commercial capitalism. To them, the antientropy spray with mystical powers is easily recognizable as the villain of the story. It is, to borrow the words of Guy Debord's 1966 manifesto, "our old enemy, *the commodity*, who knows so well how to seem at first glance something trivial and obvious, while on the contrary it is so complex and full of metaphysical subtleties." [10] But to Dick, the Marxist reading of Ubik itself seems like the mystification. And the weight that his critics seem to be placing on this interpretation seems more and more like an attempt to cover something up. "If I even seem to be saying that Ubik is God," Dick writes, the Marxists "become furious, and yet their curiosity remains." [11]

Authorities of all sorts want to impose a meaning on Ubik. The novel itself gets corrupted in the process. In a speech in 1978, Dick remarks that the final line of the German edition of Ubik reads "I am the brand name" instead of "I am the word." This translator, he complains, would probably have rendered the first sentence of the Gospel of John "When all things began, the brand name already was. The brand name dwelt with God, and what God was, the brand name was." [12] This is what I get, he says, for trying to write about serious issues. Of necessity Dick becomes his own exegete.

Dick's exegesis of the revelations of 3-74 and Ubik eventually runs to thousands of pages. Ubik isn't the only novel that seems connected to 3-74. Dick the exegete finds prophecy and revelation throughout his fictional oeuvre. If he looks at his novels and short stories carefully, he finds he can begin to chart an entire cosmos, although he still can't be sure which world is real, or who is responsible. In the end, he always comes back to Ubik. Strangely enough, this novel, which only undermines its characters' hopes of finding an absolute behind the fiction of reality, produces (and frustrates) the same hermeneutic obsession in Dick, who sees it as a book of truth but never finishes getting to the bottom of its mystery.

In Dick's most hopeful moments, Ubik really is the divine Logos, subtly infiltrating our fake, half-life world in "trashy manifestations" like the Ubik ads and the messages in cigarette cartons, entering as "spontaneous intrusions of language." Ubik is a book of truth that contains a real divine revelation. To Dick, Ubik's final announcement at the end of the novel is no joke. The novel announces that Ubik is absolute. It is on its way—maybe already here, if we could see it, maybe even ghostwriting the novel through Dick—and it prophesies the divine revelation of 3-74, when the Logos will zap Dick in a beam of pink light and shimmer at him from the pages of one of his own novels as it starts its redeeming work in the world.

Ubik comes from the future, Dick theorizes, and moves toward the past, organizing and perfecting reality as it goes. This could explain the prophetic nature of his novel: perhaps in writing it he channeled the memories of this entity from the future or was used by it to send information from the future into the world.

> What to me would be the most valuable out of the influx or presence of this retrograde-moving life form would be its unique time-experience; our past would be its future, obviously, so that its memory would to us be prophecy. You can see why this would interest a science-fiction writer; if any sort of accurate symbiosis or even communication with it were possible, however brief, we might be able to exchange with it our memories and knowledge of the past with its memories and knowledge of what lies, for us anyhow, ahead.[13]

Ubik reveals the activity of this backward-moving entity as well: what appears to be a fearful erosion of the present day in that novel, Dick decides, is actually time coming to completion and the opposite and corrective process to the entropy wearing the world down.

> So that's what I did in UBIK—correctly represented time spacially, & the past as spacially within—literally within—the present. Look how we run down, wear out, age. . . . Think what charge, what rebirth, resurrection, new life, the retrograde time-flow would give us! All that we'd lost, too: and a keen vision of the past-as-alive, the past not qua past, but past qua future!!!!!!! Heading for it as surely as we normally head toward say the year 2100 AD.[14]

This savior enters our world as "spontaneous intrusions of language" in and through "trashy" messages and manifestations. The manifestations of Ubik in the novel correspond precisely to the visions in 3-74. Ubik itself may have been written by just such a spontaneous intrusion of language, with Ubik itself as its true author and origin. Dick calls Ubik a "self-proving" novel that reveals, when read correctly, that the god it advertises is in fact the true God, and Ubik its divine word.

> Ah! In UBIK locating the Ubik messages in cheap commercials was absolutely right on. I couldn't have "guessed" more accurately. It's obvious that the real author of UBIK was Ubik. It is a self-proving novel; i.e., it couldn't have come into existence unless it were true.[15]

Dick is an ecstatic convert to his new religion, compelling in his utopian fervor and contagious in his paranoia. But how did Ubik get to be God? What kind of a God candidate is Ubik, a mass-produced savior who speaks in the voice of advertising? Ubik may call itself divine, but according to the official factory representative, it is merely a product manufactured by the half-lifer inhabitants of a hallucinated reality for the purposes of keeping that hallucination stable,

> a portable negative ionizer, with a self-contained, high voltage, low amp unit powered by a peak gain helium battery of 25kv. The negative ions are given a counterclockwise spin by a radically biased acceleration chamber, which creates a centripetal tendency to them so that they cohere rather than dissipate. A negative ion field diminishes the velocity of anti-protophasons normally present in the atmosphere.[16]

Is Ubik just a bragging impostor? What kind of god inspires this sort of technolalia in its faithful, anyway? All this would seem to support the reading of Ubik as the brand name, and the novel Ubik as a diagnosis of our world as written by the brand name — a spectacle in which (in Debord's words, again) "the commodity contemplates itself in a world it has created."[17] In Ubik the ubiquitous commodity usurps the realm of transcendence, provoking a religious fervor in consumers as each pursues his or her own redemptive encounter with the brand name's divinity. Like the other God, the brand name marks the whole world with its presence. The ultimate fetishized commodity, Ubik promises to transport the consumer beyond time and masks the history of its own production in presenting itself as an eternal now. In this respect, Ubik can also be read as a satire of mass culture's brand-name fictions. Its structure parallels that of a television program broken up by its sponsoring products, which enter into the program eventually as well, via a kind of product placement. "Ubik makes breakfast a feast, puts zing into your thing! Safe when handled as directed."

Ubik's conflation of the logo and Logos makes both versions of the Absolute look suspect. Advertising has stolen the place of God, the novel suggests. Or is Christianity just a prior form of advertising? Before the spray can there were other fake cure-alls. As the world of Ubik regresses through time, Ubik itself regresses as well, from its aerosol form to a tin of powder, a salve, and a potion called Elixir of Ubique. And so does the voice of advertising, which starts off talking like a television commercial and ends up uttering the primordial "I am" of creation. God may simply be the original quackish cure-all. Has Dick after 3-74 been duped by the very process his novel appears to satirize? Have the transcendent commodity and the lure of the brand-name absolute suckered the author himself? If the novel prophesies anything, it seems, it prophesies this: in the fake world of the future, the brand name really will be God, and we will all be its dupes.

Dick takes Ubik at its Word when he rereads it in 1974 and finds God in it. I wrote all the worlds, it says in its final speech in the novel; presumably this includes our own. Even before the end of the novel, Ubik has challenged our status outside the fiction written by itself: the Ubik ads that introduce each chapter address the reader, not the characters in the novel, insinuating that *we* might be the half-lifers in need of Ubik's revitalizing powers. We are the only characters to whom Ubik reveals its divinity in the last speech; its final words, heard by no one "inside" the novel, go only into our ears (eyes)—a surprise direct encounter with the divine. All this gives the paranoid reader a kind of initiate status, and Dick, eight years later, is this reader.

Instead of seeing Ubik as an impostor god, offering only illusory redemptions and creating fake worlds with its ubiquitous logo, the post-pink-light Dick discovers in the novel the presence of a true, but tricky and trashy, god—one which is not fake but "fake fake," which mimics the trashy products of the fake half-life world and puts on the trashy voices of advertising but is actually real. He later names this god Zebra, "because it blended," and proposes that it was Zebra that invaded him, and possibly the whole world, in 3-74.

Like Ubik, which appears in the "trash" of advertising messages and later comes out as divine, Zebra camouflages itself in trashy forms, disguising itself as something from inside our world although in fact it is alien to it. Zebra hides out not only inside our world but specifically in the "trash" of this world. "The true God mimics the universe, the very region he has invaded: he takes on the likeness of sticks and trees and beer cans in gutters—he presumes to be trash discarded, debris no longer noticed. Lurking, the true God literally ambushes reality and us as well." [18] Zebra's genius is that it only appears to be a fake. From Dick's exegesis: "transubstantiation: a Fake Fake = something *real*. God/the savior is mimicking this counterfeit cosmos with a stealthily growing *real* one." [19] And "Deity takes trashy and even fake forms." [20]

Dick explains the fake fake in a 1978 speech:

> In my writing I got so interested in fakes that I finally came up with the concept of fake fakes. For example, in Disneyland there are fake birds worked by electric motors that emit caws and shrieks as you pass by them. Suppose some night all of us sneaked into the park with real birds and substituted them for the artificial one. Imagine the horror the Disneyland officials would feel when they discovered the cruel hoax. Real birds! And perhaps someday even real hippos and lions. Consternation. The park being cunningly transformed from the unreal to the real, by sinister forces. . . . What if the entire place, by a miracle of God's power and wisdom, was changed, in a moment, in the blink of an eye, into something incorruptible? They would have to close down. [21]

The fake fake solves several problems at once, although Dick doesn't say so here. It explains why Ubik must appear in a television ad. It redeems our Disneyland future in a most subtle apocalypse. And it suggests one possible reason why the authorities might be looking for truth in a trashy science fiction novel.[22]

Also, I do seem attracted to trash, as if the clue—the clue—lies there.
—Philip K. Dick, In Pursuit of Valis

What has been writing through Philip K. Dick, Dick wonders after his visitation by the fantastic in March 1974. Who is the author of Ubik, who is the author of 3-74? What is ubiquitous, what has its brand on me, my world, my novel? Dick gives paranoid answers and ecstatic ones. And maybe both are right. "I do think one could say this," Dick writes in a letter to Peter Fitting. "Rather than having it read: UBIK, by Philip K Dick, one could put it this way:

PHILIP K DICK
by
Ubik[23]

Ubik is the author of Ubik. Ubik is even the author of Philip K. Dick. Dick identifies a divine Word flowing through his novel and his life, and it is a trashy, commercial Word: a Word marked by the commercial logo and by its travels backward from a "future" that is already the clichéd and generic textual territory of science fiction. But Dick will also see himself as Ubik. "My writing—itself part of the 'gutter' and as Lem says, 'piling trash upon trash' . . . is a very unlikely place to encounter the Holy,"[24] Dick observes in his exegesis. And maybe that's just the point. "I restore Gnostic Gnosis to the world in a trashy form, like in UBIK."[25]

If Philip K. Dick is Ubik, then we can read Ubik's prophecy in yet another way: the novel heralds the emergence of Dick the author-divine from his hiding place in the gutter of science fiction. For a writer self-conscious about his own generic "trashiness" (and baffled, flattered, and terrified by the unprecedented admiration of academics, Marxists, and other authorities), this provides a solution of sorts. "Philip K. Dick" might seem like just another brand name on a disposable commodity—part of the endless production of simulacra that make up our universe. But by the invisible logic of transubstantiation, it is really something else. Philip K. Dick is fake fake. Dick has given up his authorship to the spray can only to claim it again, in the only way consistent with his own novel's prediction: that all worlds which seem to exist outside Ubik will prove to be inside it, and that there is no future beyond its reach.

Philip K. Dick by Ubik. Not a bad description of the process and product of a writer whose prodigious output (Dick wrote over forty novels and more than a hundred short stories in his career) was fueled by amphetamines and economic necessity, and whose characteristic prose style is a headlong jumble of science fiction terms and neologisms, brand names and corporate names. Communing with Ubik's world, Dick becomes the source or channel for a kind of trashy glossolalia: teeps, precogs, animators, homeopapes, quibbles, flapples, kipple and gubble, autofacs and hovercars, inertials, cold pac, half life, portable protophason amplifiers, Can-D, Chew-Z, JJ 180, poscreds e therapy, self destruct humanoid bomb microwave audiophone control console retrojet homeostatic servo-assist system tranquilizing gum 3d color polyphonic tv P.P. Layouts, Runciter Associates, Mr. Lars Incorporated Tijuana Fur & Dye. Trails of Hoffman Limited, Lies Inc. A.G. Chemie I G Farben IBM GE KACH brain pan i.d. unit Mercedes Benz hovercar. . . . *I am called Ubik, but that is not my name. I am. I shall always be.*

How did the spray can get to be God? The story begins with a novel, a fiction, which has a contagious paranoid effect: it posits an utterly conspiratorial and fake reality and makes it seep over into ours; it introduces a God that claims to have written our world too and speaks to us in a voice we already recognize as ubiquitous (and fascinating, and menacing, and promising). The Good Word goes out in Ubik's final pages that the spray-can product is the All—and years later hails Philip K. Dick, the author himself, drawing him into his own dystopia and causing him to mistake it for salvation. Dick is right about one thing at least: *Ubik* is a book of prophecy, and its prophecy comes true. If *Ubik* predicts that the real world will disappear and be replaced by endless simulacra, that instead of reality we will have conspiratorial fictions, that instead of meaning we will have a white noise of brand-name babble—and love it—Dick's leap into Ubik's world in 3-74, in which he not only hears its voices but loses himself in its simulations and conspiracies, fulfills this prediction and confirms it. But while caught within this closed circle of paranoia, Dick is forced to reread the dystopian text that has come so perversely true very keenly and closely in order to find in it reasons to hope. *I am called Ubik, but that is not my name. I am. I shall always be.*

Notes

1   Dick, *Ubik*, 124.
2   Dick, "Letter to Malcolm Edwards," in *The Selected Letters of Philip K. Dick, 1975–1976*, 51.
3   Dick, *In Pursuit of Valis*, 160.

4   Dick, *Ubik*, 124.

5   Ibid., 211.

6   In "SF: A Hopeless Case with Exceptions," Stanislaw Lem deplores the "glaring clichés" of science fiction, "that whole threadbare lot of telepaths, cosmic wars, parallel worlds, and time travel." Lem marvels at the way Dick alone is able to transcend this vulgarity and come up with "a method to express, with the aid of trash, that which transcends all trash." He calls this the "Dick Transubstantiation method" (88). See also Lem, "Philip K. Dick."

7   Dick, "Letter to Claudia Bush," in *The Selected Letters of Philip K. Dick, 1974*, 253.

8   Dick, "Letter to William A. Sullivan," in *The Selected Letters of Philip K. Dick, 1975–1976*, 26. For a discussion of Dick's paranoia about both the "Marxists" and the FBI, see Robert M. Philmus, "The Two Faces of Philip K. Dick," in *On Philip K. Dick: Forty Articles from Science Fiction Studies*, ed. R. D. Mullen et al. (Greencastle, Ind.: SF-TH, 1992); many of Dick's "Marxists," who include Fredric Jameson, Darko Suvin, and Peter Fitting, are represented in that volume.

9   Dick, "Letter to Malcolm Edwards," in *The Selected Letters of Philip K. Dick, 1975–1976*, 245.

10 Debord, *Society of the Spectacle*, §35.

11 Dick, "Letter to Malcolm Edwards," in *The Selected Letters of Philip K. Dick, 1975–1976*, 245.

12 Philip K. Dick, "How to Build a Universe That Doesn't Fall Apart Two Days Later," in *The Shifting Realities of Philip K. Dick: Selected Literary and Philosophical Writings*, ed. Lawrence Sutin (New York: Pantheon, 1995), 278.

13 Dick, *The Selected Letters of Philip K. Dick, 1975–1976*, 36.

14 Dick, *In Pursuit of Valis*, 214.

15 Ibid., 185.

16 Dick, *Ubik*, 209.

17 Debord, *Society of the Spectacle*, §53.

18 Dick, *Valis*, 63. *Valis*, which Dick sometimes refers to as a "sequel" to, or "rewrite" of, *Ubik* and as its "logical successor," advances many of his post-3-74 theories about the return of divinity to the universe. As he explains in a 1977 letter, "A good deal of the phenomena which I depicted in my novel UBIK I now consign to Zebra." See Dick, *The Selected Letters of Philip K. Dick, 1977–1979*, 65.

19 Dick, *In Pursuit of Valis*, 137.

20 Ibid., 187.

21 Dick, "How to Build a Universe That Doesn't Fall Apart Two Days Later," 264.

22 The divine fake fake appears again in Dick's *Divine Invasion* (1991), Dick's not altogether successful attempt to fictionalize the fake fake apocalypse.

23 Dick, "Letter to Peter Fitting," in *The Selected Letters of Philip K. Dick, 1974*, 144.

24 Dick, *In Pursuit of Valis*, 157.

25 Ibid., 79.

INTERLUDE

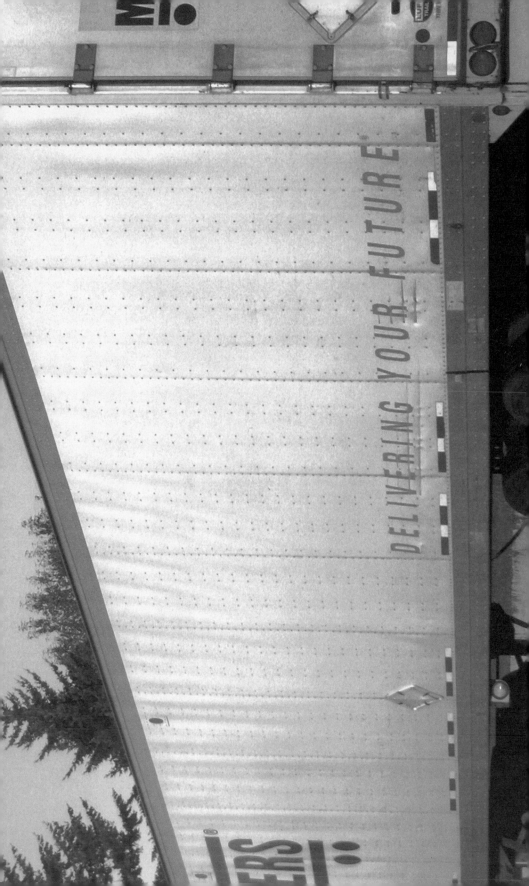

Access Fantasy: A Story

Jonathan Lethem

There was a start-up about a half-mile ahead the day before, a fever of distant engines and horns honking as others signaled their excitement—a
chance to move!—and so he'd spent the day jammed behind the wheel,
living in his Apartment On Tape, waiting for that chance, listening under
the drone of distant helicopters to hear the start-up make its way downtown. But the wave of revving engines stalled before reaching his street.
He never even saw a car move, just heard them. In fact he couldn't remember seeing a car move recently. Perhaps the start-up was only a panic begun
by someone warming their motor, reviving their battery. That night he'd
dreamed another start-up, or perhaps it was real, a far-off flare that died
before he'd even ground the sleep out of his eyes, though in the rustle of
his waking thoughts it was a perfect thing, coordinated, a dance of cars
shifting through the free-flowing streets. Dream or not, either way, didn't
matter. He fell back asleep. What woke him in the morning was the family
in the Pacer up ahead cooking breakfast. They had a stove on the roof of
their car and the dad was grilling something they'd bought from the flatbed
shepherd two blocks away, a sheepsteak or something. It smelled good.
Everything about the family in the Pacer made him too conscious of his
wants. The family's daughter—she was beautiful—had been working as
Advertising, pushing up against and through the One-Way Permeable Barrier on behalf of some vast faceless corporation. That being the only way
through the One-Way Permeable Barrier, of course. So the family, her Ma
and Pa, were flush, had dough, and vendors knew to seek them out, hawking groceries. Whereas checking his pockets he didn't have more than a
couple of dollars. There was a coffee-and-donuts man threading his way
through the traffic even now but coffee was beyond his means. He needed
money. Rumors had it Welfare Helicopters had been sighted south of East

One Thousand, One Hundred and Ninety-Fourth Street, and a lot of people had left their cars, drifted down that way, looking for easy cash. Which was one reason the start-up died, it occurred to him—too many empty cars. Along with the cars that wouldn't start anymore, like the old lady in the Impala beside him, the dodderer. She'd given up, spent most days dozing in the back seat. Her nephew from a few blocks away came over and tinkered with her engine now and again but it wasn't helping. It just meant the nephew wasn't at his wheel for the start-up, another dead spot, another reason not to bother waiting to move. Probably he thought now he should have walked downtown himself in search of welfare money drifting down from the sky. The state helicopters weren't coming around this neighborhood much lately. Alas. The air was crowded with commercial hovercraft instead, recruiters, Advertising robots rounding up the girl from the Pacer and others like her, off to the world on the other side of the One-Way Permeable Barrier, however briefly. The world of Apartments, real ones. Though it was morning he went back to his latest Apartment On Tape, which was a four bedroom two bath co-op on East One Thousand Two Hundred and Fifteenth Street, just a few blocks away but another world of course, remote from his life on the street, sealed off from it by the One-Way Permeable Barrier. He preferred the early part of the tape, before any of the furnishings arrived, so he rewound to that part and put the tape on slow and lived in the rooms as hard as he could, ignoring the glare of sun through his windshield that dulled his view of the dashboard television, ignoring the activities of the family in the Pacer up ahead as they clambered in and out of the hatchback, ignoring the clamor of his own pangs. The realtor's voice was annoying, it was a squawking, parroty voice so he kept the volume down as always and lived in the rooms silently, letting his mind sweep in and haunt the empty spaces, the rooms unfolding in slow motion for the realtor's camera. While the camera lingered in the bathroom he felt under his seat for his bottle and unzipped and peed, timed so it matched to the close-up of the automatic flushing of the toilet on his television. Then the camera and his attention wandered out into the hall. That's when he noticed it, the shadow. Just for a moment. He rewound to see it again. On the far wall of the hallway, framed perfectly for an instant in the lens the silhouette of a struggle, a man with his hands on the neck of another, smaller. A woman. Shaking her by the neck for that instant, before the image vanished. Like a pantomime of murder, a Punch-and-Judy show hidden in the Apartment On Tape. But real, it had to be real. Why hadn't he noticed before? He'd watched this tape dozens of times. He rewound again. Just barely, but still. Unmistakable, however brief. The savagery of it was awful. If only he could watch it frame by frame—slow motion was disastrously fast now. Who was the killer? The landlord? The realtor? Why? Was the victim the previous tenant? Questions, he had questions. He felt himself begin to buzz with them, come alive. Slow motion didn't seem particularly slow precisely because his attention had quickened. Yes, a job of detection was just what he needed to roust himself out of the current slump, burn off the torpor of too many days locked in the jam at the same damn intersection—why hadn't he gone Downtown at that last turnoff, months ago? Well, anyway. He watched it again, memorized the shadow, the silhouette, imagined blurred features in the slurry of video fuzz, memorized the features, what the hell. Like a police sketch, work from his own prescient hallucinations. Again. It grew sharper every time. He'd scrape a hole in this patch of tape, he knew, if he rewound too many times. Better to have the tape, the evidence, all there was at this point. He popped the video, threw it in a satchel with notebook, eyeglasses. Extra socks. Outside, locked the car, tipped an imaginary hat at the old lady, headed east by foot on West One Thousand, Two Hundred and Eighth Street. He had to duck uptown two blocks to avoid a flotilla of Sanitation hovertrucks spraying foamy water to wash cars sealed up tight against this artificial rain but also soaking poor jerks asleep, drenching interiors, the rotted upholstery and split spongy dashboards, extinguishing rooftop bonfires, destroying box gardens, soap bubbles poisoning the feeble sprouts. Children screamed and giggled, the streets ran with water, sluicing shit here and there into drains, more often along under the tires to the unfortunate neighboring blocks, everyone moaning and lifting their feet clear. Just moving it around, that's all. Around the next corner he ran into a crowd gathered staring at a couple of young teenage girls from inside, from the apartments, the other side of the Barrier. They'd come out of the apartment building on rollerblades to sightsee, to slum on the streets. Sealed in a murky bubble of One-Way Permeable Barrier they were like apparitions, dim ghosts, though you could hear them giggle as they skated through the hushed, reverent crowd. Like a sighting of gods, these teenage girls from inside. No one bothered to spare-change them or bother them in any way because of the Barrier. The girls of course were oblivious behind their twilight veil, like night things come into the day, though for them probably it was the people in cars and around the cars that appeared dim, unreachable. He shouldered his way through the dumbstruck crowd and once past this obstacle he found his man, locked into traffic like all the rest, right where he'd last seen him. The Apartments On Tape dealer, his connection, sunbathing in a deck chair on the roof of his Centra, eating a sandwich. The back seat was stacked with realtor's tapes, apartment porn, and on the passenger seat two video decks for dubbing. His car in a sliver of morning sun that shone across the middle of the block, benefit of a chink in the canyon of towers that surrounded them. The dealer's neighbors were on their car roofs as well, stretching in the sun, drying clothes. "Hello there, remember me? That looks good what you're eating, anyway, I want to talk to you about this tape." "No refunds," said the dealer, not even looking down. "No, that's not it, I saw something, can we watch it together?" "No need since there's no refunds and I'm hardly interested—" "Listen, this is a police matter, I think—" "You're police then, is that what you're saying?" still not looking down. "No no, I fancy myself a private detective, though not to say I work outside the law, more adjacent, then turn it over to them if serves justice, there's so often corruption—" "So turn it over," the dealer said. "Well if you could just have a look I'd value your opinion. Sort of pick your brain," thinking flattery or threats, should have chosen one approach with this guy, stuck with it. The dealer said, "Sorry, day off," still not turning his head, chewing off another corner of sandwich. Something from inside the sandwich fell, a chunk of something, fish maybe, onto the roof of the car. "The thing is I think I saw a murder, on the tape, in the apartment." "That's highly unlikely." "I know, but that's what I saw." "Murder, huh?" The dealer didn't sound at all impressed. "Bloody body parts, that sort of thing?" "No, don't be absurd, just a shadow, just a trace." "Hmmm." "You never would have noticed in passing. Hey, come to think of it, you don't have an extra sandwich do you?" "No, I don't. So would you describe this shadow as sort of a flicker then, like a malfunction?" "No, absolutely not. It's part of the tape." "Not your monitor on the fritz?" "No," he was getting angry now, "a person, a shadow strangling another shadow." The chunk of sandwich filling on the car roof was sizzling slightly, changing color already in the sun. The dealer said, "Shadows, hmmm. Probably a gimmick, subliminal special effects or something." "What? What reason would a realtor have for adding special effects for God's sake to an apartment tape?" "Maybe they think it adds some kind of allure, some thrill of menace that makes their apartments stand out from the crowd." "I doubt very much—" "Maybe they've become aware of the black market in tapes lately, that's the word on the street in fact, and so they're trying to send a little message. They don't like us ogling their apartments, even vicariously." "You can't ogle vicariously, I think. Sounds wrong. Anyway, that's the most ridiculous thing I've ever—" "Or maybe I'm in on it, maybe I'm the killer, have you considered that?" "Now you're making fun of me." "Why? If you can solve crimes on the other side of the Barrier why can't I commit them?" The dealer laughed, hyenalike. "Now seriously," he continued, "if you want to exchange for one without a murder I'll give you a credit towards the next, half what you paid—" "No thanks. I'll hold on to it." Discouraged, hungry, but he couldn't really bother being angry. What help did he expect from the dealer anyway? This was a larger matter, above the head of a mere middle-man. "Good luck, Sherlock," the dealer was saying. "Spread word freely, by the way, don't hold back. Can't hurt my sales any. People like murder, only it might be good if there was skin instead of only shadow, a tit say." "Yes, very good then, appreciate your help. Carry on." The dealer saluted. He saluted back, started off through the traffic, stomach growling, ignoring it, intent. A killer was at large. Weaving past kids terrorizing an entire block of cars with an elaborate tag game, cornering around the newly washed neighborhood now wringing itself out, muddy streams between the cars and crying babies ignoring vendors with items he couldn't afford and a flatbed farmer offering live kittens for pets or food and a pathetic miniature start-up, three cars idiotically nosing rocking jerking back and forth trying to rearrange themselves pointlessly, one of them now sideways wheels on the curb and nobody else even taking the bait he made his way back to his car and key in the lock noticed the girl from the Pacer standing in her red dress on the hood of the car gazing skyward, waiting for the Advertising people to take her away. Looking just incidentally like a million bucks. Her kid brother was away, maybe part of the gang playing tag, and her parents were inside the car doing housework dad scraping the grill out the window mom airing clothes repacking bundles so he went over, suddenly inspired. "Margaret, isn't it?" She nodded, smiled. "Yes, good, well you remember me from next door, I'm looking for a day or two's work and do you think they'll take me along?" She said, "You never know, they just take you or they don't." Smiling graciously even if a little confused, so long neighbors and they'd never spoken. "But you always —" he began pointing out. She said, "Oh once they've started taking you then —" Awkwardly, they were both awkward for a moment not saying what they both knew or at least he did, that she was an attractive young girl and likely that made a huge difference in whether they wanted you. "Well you wouldn't mind if I tried?" he said and she said, "No, no," relieved almost, then added, "I can point you out, I can suggest to them —" Now he was embarrassed and said hurriedly, "That's so good of you, thanks, and where should I wait, not here with you at your folks' car, I guess —" "Why not, climb up." Dad looked out the door up at them and she waved him off, "It's okay, you know him from next door he's going to work, we're going to try to get him a job Advertising." "Okay, sweetheart just checking on you." Then she grabbed his arm, said, "Look." The Advertising hovercraft she'd been watching for landed on the curb a half-block ahead, near the giant hideous sculpture at an office building main entrance, lately sealed. Dad said, "Get going you guys, and good luck," and she said, "C'mon." Such neighborliness was a surprise since he'd always felt shut out by the family in the Pacer but obviously it was in his head. And Margaret, a cloud of good feeling seemed to cover her. No wonder they wanted her for Advertising. "Hurry," she said and took his hand and they hopped down and pushed their way around the cars and through the chaos of children and barking dogs and vendors trying to work the crowd of wannabes these landings always provoked, to join the confused throng at the entrance. He held on to his satchel with the video and his socks making sure it didn't get picked in this crowd. She bounced there trying to make herself visible until the one of the two robots at the door noticed her and pointed. They stepped up. "Inside," said the robot. They were ugly little robots with their braincases undisguised and terrible attitudes. He disliked them instantly. "I brought someone new," she said, pulling him by the hand, thrusting him into view. "Yes, sir, I'd like to enlist—" he started, grinning madly, wanting to make a good impression. The robot looked him over and made its rapid-fire assessment, nodded. "Get inside," it said. "Lucky," she whispered, and they stepped into the hovercraft. Four others were there, two men, two women, all young. And another woman stumbled in behind them, and the door sealed, and they were off. Nasty little robots scurrying into the cockpit, making things ready. "Now what?" he said and she put her finger to her lips and shushed him, but sweetly, leaning into him as if to say they were in this together. He wanted to tell her what he was after but the robots might hear. Would they care? Yes, no, he couldn't know. Such ugly, fascistic little robots. Nazi robots, that's what they were. He hated placing himself in their hands. But once he was Advertising he would be through the barrier, he'd be able to investigate. Probably he should keep his assignment to himself, though. He didn't want to get her into trouble. The hovercraft shuddered, groaned, then lifted and through the window he could see the cars growing smaller, his neighborhood, his life, the way the traffic was so bad for hundreds of miles of street and why did he think a start-up would change anything? Was there a place where cars really drove anymore? Well, anyway. The robots were coming around with the Advertising Patches and everyone leaned their heads forward obediently, no first-timers like himself apparently. He did the same. A robot fastened a patch behind his right ear, a moment of stinging skin, nothing more. Hard to believe the patch was enough to interfere with the function of the One-Way Permeable Barrier, that he would now be vivid and tangible and effective to those on the other side. "I don't feel any different," he whispered. "You won't," she said. "Not until there's people. Then you'll be compelled to Advertise. You won't be able to help it." "For what, though?" "You never know, coffee, diamonds, condoms, vacations, you just never know." "Where—" "They'll drop us off at the Undermall, then we're on our own." "Will we be able to stick together?" The question was out before he could wonder if it was presuming too much, but she said, "Sure, as long as our products aren't too incompatible, but we'll know soon. Anyway, just follow me." She really had a warmth, a glow. Incompatible products? Well, he'd find out what that meant. The hovercraft bumped down on the roof of a building, and with grim efficiency the ugly Nazi robots had the door open and were marching the conscripts out to a rooftop elevator. He wanted to reach out and smack their little exposed-braincase heads together. But he had to keep his cool, stay undercover. He trotted across the roof towards the elevator after her, between the rows of officious gesticulating robots, like they were going to a concentration camp. The last robot at the door of the elevator handed them each an envelope before they stepped in. He took his and moved into the corner with Margaret, they were really packing them in but he couldn't complain actually being jostled with her and she didn't seem to be trying to avoid it. He poked into the envelope. It was full of bills, singles mostly. The money was tattered and filthy, bills that had been taken out of circulation on the other side of the Barrier. Garbage money, that's what it was. The others had already pocketed theirs, business as usual apparently. "Why do they pay us now?" he whispered. She said, "We just find our way out at the end, when the patch runs out, so this way they don't have to deal with us again," and he said, "What if we just took off with the money?" "You could I guess, but I've never seen anyone do it since you'd never get to come back and anyway the patch makes you really want to Advertise, you'll see." Her voice was reassuring, like she really wanted him not to worry and he felt rotten not telling her about his investigation, his agenda. He put the envelope into his satchel with tape and socks. The elevator sealed and whooshed them down through the building, into the Undermall, then the doors opened and they unpacked from the elevator, spewed out into a gigantic lobby, all glass and polished steel with music playing softly and escalators going down and up in every direction, escalators with steps of burnished wood that looked good enough to eat, looked like roast chicken. He was still so hungry. Margaret took his hand again. "Let's go," she said. As the others dispersed she led him towards one of the escalators and they descended. The corridor below branched to shops with recessed entrances, windows dark and smoky, quiet pulsing music fading from each door, also food smells here and there causing his saliva to flow, and holographic signs angling into view as they passed: FERN SLAW, ROETHKE AND SONS, HOLLOW APPEAL, BROKEN SMUDGED ALPHABET, BURGER KING, PLASTIC DEVILS, OSTRICH LAKE, SMARTINGALE'S, RED HARVEST, CATCH OF THE DAY, MUTUAL OF FOMALHAUT, THNEEDS, et cetera. She led him on, confidently, obviously at home. Why not, this was what she did with her days. Then without warning, a couple appeared from around a corner, and he felt himself begin to Advertise. "How do you do today?" he said, sidling up to the gentleman of the couple, even as he saw Margaret begin to do the same thing to the lady. The gentleman nodded at him, walked on. But met his eye. He was tangible, he could be heard. It was a shock. "Thirsty?" he heard himself say. "How long's it been since you had a nice refreshing beer?" "Don't like beer," said the gentleman. "Can't say why, just never have." "Then you've obviously never tried a Very Old Money Lager," he heard himself say, still astonished. The Barrier was pierced and he was conversing, he was perceptible. He'd be able to conduct interrogations, be able to search out clues. Meanwhile he heard Margaret saying "Don't demean your signature with a second-rate writing implement. Once you've tried the Eiger fountain pen you'll never want to go back to those hen-like scratchings and scrawlings," and the woman seemed interested and so Margaret went on, "our Empyrean Sterling Silver Collection features one-of-a-kind hand-etched casings — " In fact the man seemed captivated too he turned ignoring the beer pitch and gave Margaret his attention. "Our brewers hand-pick the hops and malt," he was unable to stop though he'd obviously lost his mark, "and every single batch of fire-brewed Very Old Money Lager is individually tasted — " Following the couple through the corridor they bumped into another Advertising woman who'd been on the hovercraft, and she began singing, "Vis-it the moon, it's nev-er too soon," dancing sinuously and batting her eyes, distracting them all from fountain pens and beer for the moment and then the five of them swept into the larger space of the Undermall and suddenly there were dozens of people who needed to be told about the beer, "Thirsty? Hello, hi there, thirsty? Excuse me, thirsty? Yes? Craving satisfaction, sparkle, bite? No? Yes? Have you tried Very Old Money? What makes it different, you ask — oh, hello, thirsty?" and also dozens of people working as Advertising, a gabble of pitches — stern, admonitory: "Have you considered the perils of being without success insurance?" flippant, arbitrary: "You never know you're out with the Black Underwear Crowd, not until you get one of them home!" jingly, singsong: "We've got children, we've all got children, you can have children too — " and as they scattered and darted along the endless marble floors of the Undermall he was afraid he'd lose her, but there was Margaret, earnestly discussing pens with a thoughtful older couple and he struggled over towards her, hawking beer — "Thirsty? Oof, sorry, uh, thirsty?" The crowd thinned as customers ducked into shops and stole away down corridors back to their apartments, bullied by the slew of Advertising except for the few like this older couple who seemed gratified by the attention, he actually had to wait as they listened and took down some information from her about the Eiger fountain pen while he stood far enough away to keep from barking at them about the beer. Then once the older couple wandered off he took Margaret's hand this time, why not, she'd done it, and drew her down a corridor away from the crowds, hoping to keep from engaging with any more customers, and also in the right direction if he had his bearings. He thought he did. He led her into the shadow of a doorway, a shop called FINGERTOES that wasn't doing much business. "Listen, I've got to tell you something, I haven't been completely truthful, I mean, I haven't lied, but there's something—" She looked at him, hopeful, confused, but generous in her interpretation, he could tell, what a pure and sweet disposition, maybe her dad wasn't such a bad guy after all if he'd raised a plum like this. "I'm a detective, I mean, what does that mean, really, but the thing is there's been a murder and I'm trying to look into it—" and then he plunged in and told all, the Apartment On Tape, pulling it out of his satchel to show her, the shadow, the strangling, his conversation with the dealer and then his brainstorm to slip inside the citadel, slip past the One-Way Permeable Barrier that would of course have kept his questions or accusations from even being audible to those on this side, and so he'd manipulated her generosity to get aboard the hovercraft. "Forgive me," he said. Her eyes widened, her voice grew hushed, reverent. "Of course, but what do you want to do? Find the police?" "You're not angry at me?" "No, no. It's a brave thing you're doing." "Thank you." They drew closer. He could almost kiss her, just in happiness, solidarity, no further meaning or if there was it was just on top of the powerful solidarity feeling, just an extra, a windfall. "But what do you think is best, the police?" she whispered. "No, I have in mind a visit to the apartment, we're only a couple of blocks away, in this direction I believe, but do you think we can get upstairs?" They fell silent then because a man swerved out of FINGERTOES with a little paper tray of greasy fried things, looked like fingers or toes in fact and smelled terrific, he couldn't believe how hungry he was. "Thirsty?" he said hopelessly and the man popping one into his mouth said, "You called it brother, I'm dying for a beer." "Why just any beer when you could enjoy a Very Old Money—" and he had to go on about it, being driven nuts by the smell, while Margaret waited. The moment the grease-eater realized they were Advertising and broke free, towards the open spaces of the Undermall, he and Margaret broke in the other direction, down the corridor. "This way," said Margaret, turning them towards the elevator, "the next level down you can go for blocks, it's the way out eventually too." "Yes, but can we get back upstairs?" "The elevators work for us until the patches run out, I think," and so they went down below the Undermall to the underground corridors, long echoey halls of tile, not so glamorous as upstairs, not nice at all really, the lengths apartment people went to never to have to step out onto the street and see car people being really appalling sometimes. The tunnels were marked with street signs, names of other Undermalls, here and there an exit. They had to Advertise only once before reaching East One Thousand Two Hundred and Fifteenth Street, to a group of teenage boys smoking a joint in the corridor who laughed and asked Margaret questions she couldn't answer like are they mightier or less mighty than the sword and do they work for pigs. They ran into another person Advertising, a man moving furtively who when he recognized Margaret was plainly relieved. "He's got a girlfriend," she explained, somewhat enigmatically. So those Advertising could, did—what? Interact. But caught up in the chase now, he didn't ask more, just counted the blocks, feeling the thrill of approaching his Apartment On Tape's real address. They went up in the elevator, which was lavish again, wood paneled and perfumed and mirrored and musical. An expensive building. Apartment 16D so he pressed the button for the sixteenth floor, holding his breath, hardly believing it when they rose above the public floors. But they did. He gripped her hand. The elevator stopped on the sixth floor and a robot got on. Another of the creepily efficient braincase-showing kind. At first the robot ignored them but then on the fifteenth floor a woman got on and Margaret said, "The most personal thing about you is your signature, don't you think?" and he said, "Thirsty?" and the robot turned and stared up at them. The doors closed and they rode up to the sixteenth floor, and the three of them got out, he and Margaret and the robot, leaving the woman behind. The hallway was splendid with plush carpeting and brass light fixtures, empty apart from the three of them. "What are you doing up here?" said the robot. "And what's in that bag?" Clutching his satchel he said, "Nothing, just my stuff." "Why is it any of your business?" said Margaret, surprisingly defiant. "We've been asked to give an extended presentation at a customer's private home," he said, wanting quickly to cover Margaret's outburst, give the robot something else to focus on. "Then I'll escort you," said the robot. "You really don't have to do that," he said. "Don't come along and screw up our pitch, we'll sue you," said Margaret bizarrely. Learning of the investigation had an odd effect on her, always a risk working with amateurs he supposed. But also it was these robots, the way they were designed with rotten personalities or no personalities they really aroused revulsion in people, it was an instinctual thing and not just him, he noted with satisfaction. He squeezed her hand and said, "Our sponsors would be displeased, it's true." "This matter requires clearance," said the robot, trying to get in front of them as they walked, and they had to skip to stay ahead of it. "Please stand to one side and wait for clearance," but they kept going down the carpeted hallway, his fingers crossed that it was the right direction for 16D. "Halt," said the robot, a flashing red light on its forehead beginning to blink neurotically and then they were at the door, and he rapped with his knuckles, thinking, hardly going incognito here, but better learn what we can. "Stand to one side," said the robot again. "Shut up," said Margaret. As the robot clamped a steely hand on each of their arms, jerking them back away from the door, its treads grinding on the carpet for traction, probably leaving ugly marks too, the door swung open. "Hello?" The man in the doorway was unshaven and slack-haired wearing a robe and blinking at them as though he'd only turned on his light to answer the door. "They claim to have an appointment with you sir," said the robot. The man only stood and stared. "It's very important, we have to talk to you urgently," he said, trying to pull free of the robot's chilly grip, then added, regretfully, "about beer." He felt a swoon at looking through the doorway, realizing he was seeing into his Apartment On Tape, the rooms etched into his dreamy brain now before him. He tried to see more but the light was gloomy. "—and fountain pens," said Margaret, obviously trying to hold herself back but compelled to chip something. "I apologize sir I tried to detain them to obtain clearance—" said the robot. *Detain, obtain,* what rotten syntax, he thought, the people who program these robots certainly aren't poets. The man just stood and blinked and looked them over, the three of them struggling subtly, he and Margaret trying to pull free of the robot, which was still blinking red and grinding at the carpet. "Cooperate," squawked the robot. The man in the robe squinted at them, finally smiled. "Please," said Margaret. "Fountain pens, eh?" the man in the robe said at last. "Yes," said Margaret desperately, and he heard himself add, "And beer—" "Yes, of course," mumbled the man in the robe. "How silly of me. Come in." "Sir, for your safety—" "They're fine," said the man to the robot. "I'm expecting them. Let them in." The robot released its grip. The man in the robe turned and shuffled inside. They followed him, all three of them, into poorly lit rooms disastrously heaped with newspapers, clothes, soiled dishes, empty and half-empty takeout packages, but still unmistakably the rooms from his tape, every turn of his head recalling some camera movement and there sure enough was the wall that had held the shadow, the momentary stain of murder. The man in the robe turned and said to the robot, "Please wait outside." "But surely I should chaperone, sir—" "No, that's fine, just outside the door, I'll call you in if I need you. Close it on your way out, thanks." Watching the robot slink back out he couldn't help but feel a little thrill of vindication. The man in the robe continued into the kitchen, and gesturing at the table said, "Please, sit, sorry for the mess. Did you say you'd like a beer?" "Well, uh, no, that wasn't exactly—if you drink

beer you ought to make it a Very Old Money Lager for full satisfaction—
but I've got something else to discuss while you enjoy your delicious, oh,
damn it—" "Relax, have a seat. Can I get you something else?" "Food," he
blurted. "Which always goes best with a Very Old Money," and meanwhile
Margaret released his hand and took a seat and started in talking about
pens. The man opened his refrigerator, which was as overloaded as the
apartment, another image from the tape now corrupted by squalor. "You
poor people, stuck with those awful patches and yet I suppose I wouldn't
have the benefit of your company today without them! Ah, well. Here, I
wasn't expecting visitors but would you like some cheese? Can I fix you a
glass of water?" The man set out a crumbled hunk of cheddar with a butter
knife, crumbs on the dish and so long uncovered the edges were dried a
deep, translucent orange. "So, you were just Advertising and you thought
you'd pay a house call? How am I so lucky?" "Well, that's not it exactly—
" Margaret took the knife and began paring away the edges of the cheese,
carving out a chunk that looked more or less edible and when she handed
it to him he couldn't resist, but tried talking through the mouthful anyway,
desperately trying to negotiate the three priorities of hunger, Advertising,
and his investigation: "Would you consider, mmmpphh, excuse me, consider opening a nice tall bottle of Very Old Money and settling in to watch
this videotape I brought with me because there's something I'd like you to
see, a question I've got about it—" The man in the robe nodded absently,
half-listening, staring oddly at Margaret and then said, "By all means let
me see your tape—is it about beer? I'd be delighted but no hurry, please
relax and enjoy yourselves, I'll be right out," and stepped into the living
room, began rummaging among his possessions of which there certainly
were plenty. It was a little depressing how full the once glorious apartment
had gotten. He envisioned himself living in it and cleaning it out, restoring
it to the condition on the realtor's tape. Margaret cut him another piece
of cheese and whispered, "Do you think he knows something?" "I can't
know he seems so nice, well if not nice then harmless, hapless, but I'll
judge his reaction to the video, watch him closely when the time comes—"
grabbing more cheese quickly while he could and then the man in the robe
was back. "Hello, friends, enjoying yourselves?" His robe had fallen open
and they both stared but maybe it was just an example of his sloppiness.
Certainly there was no polite way to mention it. There was something confusing about this man, who now went to the table and took the knife out of
Margaret's hands and held her hand there for a moment and then snapped
something, was it a bracelet? around her wrist. Not a bracelet. Handcuffs.
"Hey, wait a minute, that's no way to enjoy a nice glass of lager!" he heard
himself say idiotically cheese falling out of his mouth jumping up as the

man clicked Margaret's other wrist into the cuffs and he had her linked to the back of her chair. He stood to intervene and the man in the robe swept his feet out from under him with a kick and pushed him in the chest and he fell, feet sliding on papers, hand skidding in lumps of cheese, to the floor. "Thirsty!" he shouted, the more excited the more fervent the Advertising, apparently. "No! Beer!" as he struggled to get up. And Margaret was saying something desperate about Eiger Fountain Pens "—*self-refilling cartridge—*" The man in the robe moved quickly, not lazy and sloppy at all now and kicked away his satchel with the tape inside and bent over him and reached behind his ear and to tear the patch away, another momentary sting. He could only shout "Beer!" once more before the twilight world of the One-Way Permeable Barrier surrounded him, it was everywhere here, even Margaret was on the other side as long as she wore the patch, and he felt his voice sucked away to a scream audible inside the space of his own head but not elsewhere, he knew, not until he was back outside, on the street where he belonged and why couldn't he have stayed there? What was he thinking? Anyway it wouldn't be long now because through the gauze he saw the man in the robe who you'd have to call the man half out of his robe now open the door to let the robot in, then as the naked man grinned at him steel pinchers clamped onto his arm and he was dragged out of the room, screaming inaudibly, thrashing to no purpose, leaving Margaret behind. And his tape besides.

CHAPTER

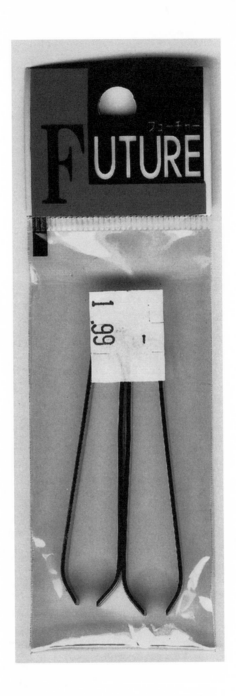

Subject, City, Machine

Miryam Sas

The middle is by no means an average; on the contrary, it is where things pick up speed. Between things does not designate a localizable relation going from one thing to the other and back again, but a perpendicular direction, a transversal movement that sweeps one and the other away, a stream without beginning or end that undermines its banks and picks up speed in the middle. —Gilles Deleuze and Félix Guattari, *A Thousand Plateaus*

In today's neon metropolis of Tokyo, threaded on a webwork of elevated highways and deep subway tunnels, the evidence of a long-standing obsession with velocity is everywhere. The cityscape is a tangle of competing immediacies: chain coffee shops, twenty-four-hour stores, shining high-rises, and advertisements for telephone clubs. All around, anime and electronic media conspire to spread commercialized versions of techno-futurism. Every bullet train platform and street corner teems with digitized images, cell phones, and remote e-mailers, fragments of a century of futurist dreams. In this landscape, it is strange to be a walker, to be slow and human, to trace a winding path that—it once seemed—machines might by now have transcended. It is strange to recognize in the pattern of the highways and streets of the modern city a palimpsest of the (now concrete covered) canals that once undulated here to their own rhythms.

I am not the first to feel this. By the 1920s, Tokyo already had places where the stars were dimmed behind the intensities of electric light. It had also become the principal site of Japan's futurist movement and imagination: the place where Hirato Renkichi staged and distributed Japan's first Futurist Manifesto, the place that exploded into "a thousand one-second tales" in the writing of Inagaki Taruho. But Tokyo was paradoxical even for this first generation of futurists. If it was a place of aggressive technophilia, it was also a place of haunting and irrupting bodies. These complications mark the writings of the futurists everywhere. In the work of Hirato, they emerged as painful contradictions, breaks in or brakes on the speed machine of his writing. In Hirato's writing, a second Tokyo pushed through the surface in the form of frustrations, incompletions, and incommensurabilities where time did not quite accelerate. Like Hirato, Inagaki Taruho saw Tokyo as a landscape of contradiction and doubling. But for Taruho, this was the source of wonder rather than frustration, and it formed the very heart of his own futurism. In Taruho's writing, futures emerged in the paradoxical space that connects contraries, in what Deleuze and Guattari describe as that "middle where things pick up speed." Together, Hirato and Taruho represent the possibilities and the strictures of this imaginative moment. What appears as interruption to Hirato is itself the story to Taruho: his "one-second tales" paradoxically evoke the slow, latent, memory-engulfed underside of the city-machine. Taruho cracks open the idealized absolute of the early futurists to show the fascination of that troubled space between body and machine, between movement and stasis, between past and future—where we must finally find our precarious place.

On a winter day toward the end of 1921, the young poet Hirato Renkichi (1893–1922) is said to have distributed the first Japanese Futurist Manifesto to passersby in Hibiya Park, Tokyo, not far from the imperial palace. His one-sided leaflet had a photo of the poet at its center, standing in the bright sunlight before a convergence of train or trolley tracks and overhead electric wires. Hirato's photo gives us an image of the speaker of these pronouncements, but the provocative words swirling around him supplant subjective authority. The voice of the manifesto is collective. It declares in its opening lines:

> Trembling heart of the gods: the central activity of the human arises from the core of collective life. The city is a *motor*. Its core is *dynamo-electric*.[1]

Like F. T. Marinetti, his inspiration, Hirato bluntly replaces the gods with a collective *motor*. He proclaims a new activity of the human arising or being expelled (*hassuru*) like exhaust fumes from the swarm of urban life. In a vision that anticipates Fritz Lang's *Metropolis* (which would be filmed six years later), Hirato saw the city as a machine with a "dynamo-electric" core. Feeling the awe of urban mass activity, too large to be comprehended by any individual mind, Hirato expressed what Susan Lepselter has called "the excitement of a power that defines and incorporates its partial observers."[2] Each individual shares in the glory of the whole and is constructed by his or her tiny part in it. To Hirato, it is the city rather than the solo flaneur that is important. Baudelaire's chance encounter between passersby in the crowd is insignificant except in its contribution to a broader urban power and speed that resembles and partakes of the movements of the machine.

Although Hirato's is the first known Japanese manifesto of futurism, several translations of Marinetti's February 1909 founding manifesto had already been published in Japan, and the general principles of futurism were well known. Mori Ogai translated the eleven main tenets of Marinetti's manifesto almost immediately after their publication and released them in the May 1909 issue of *Subaru* journal. Translations of Marinetti's other works and Japanese critical writings on futurist art and poetry had also appeared, including the best-selling *Itan no gaka* (Heretical artists, August 1920) by art critic Moriguchi Tari (1892–1984).[3] The year before Hirato distributed his manifesto, David Burljuk, a Russian futurist in exile, had caused a sensation among Tokyo artists with an exhibition of Russian futurist and contemporary paintings.[4] Hirato and other experimental poets in Japan, excited by news of avant-garde activities in Europe and Russia, shared the Italian futurists' fascination with the power of the mechanical world and the beauty of technology: "The divine power generator has, today, become the motor of the city, converging with the activities of myriad human beings." For Hirato, the gods have transformed themselves into a kind of motor.

Visions of a mechanical future did not stop with the small coterie of journals and poetry magazines. Images of an expansionist, dominating Japanese nation, armed with war technologies leading the way into a speedy future—or visions of Japan breaking into the "empty" frontier of Asia with line after line of railway tracks—held a growing sway in Japanese culture, media, and literature. Postwar visions of Japan as an economic miracle translated this hyperacceleration into the realm of the commodity market but did not challenge its fundamental trajectory. The narrative of progress and aggressive forward motion—the faster the better—established a place in Japanese national and cultural narratives and mixed with ambivalent parallel stories appropriating and resisting elements from European and "Western" technologies, epistemology, politics, and arts.

As early as Hirato's first articulations of a Japanese futurism, however, a contrary tendency was emerging in his considerations of the body and the past. Although on the surface Hirato posited the city and the machine as the sites of the absolute, the locus of ultimate power, he was unable to overcome or transcend the present body as a persistent site of ambivalence, a contrary force that he pushes at times toward the machine future of Marinetti but at other times toward a fleshy past of promised mortality and decay. Other later writers mark the ambivalences and limits of these early futurist visions, making them the explicit subject of their writing, but in Hirato's work they irrupt violently, throwing his writing off kilter. They hurl his typography from one side of the page to the other, as he is unable to accept this physical fleshliness or embrace the limits and shadows it casts on his future and its velocities. His text itself appears in almost Dadaist fragments, a textual dispersal that Marinetti also extolled and Hirato linked to the "bewitching changes" of cinematographic montage. He fills his manifesto and accompanying poetic text with virulence, invective, and images of darkness that recall the early Japanese anarchist poets—and seem fully out of place next to the idealism of the dynamo-electric. His text spins and turns like a wild gyro, threatening to fall and fail this way and that. His absolute power, his sublime future, crumble and fall in the pleasures and horrors of a physical, material, inevitable present.

In *Postmodern Sublime*, Joseph Tabbi argues that a technological aesthetic has come to take the place of the sublime in recent fiction: "Kant's sublime object, a figure for an infinite greatness and infinite power in nature that cannot be represented, seems to have been replaced in postmodern literature by a technological process. Now, when literature fails to present an object for an idea of absolute power, the failure is associated with technological structures and global corporate systems beyond the comprehension of any one mind or imagination."[5] While Tabbi links the failure of the sublime to the technological in postmodern fiction, in a way that Hirato's ruptured writing ultimately confirms, Hirato's utopia starts as an attempt to read the technological city as a positive, rather than a failed, sublime object. "The gods' instinct has transferred to the city, and the city's *dynamo-electric* has jolted human instinct awake," he writes. The city's mechanical power even surpasses the "gods' instincts" as a primary moving force, and this power shocks and awakens a fundamental "instinct" of human beings. Having received the shock of the technological, human beings then become the possessors of the sublime mechanical instinct (*honnō*) as their bodies become mechanized in harmony with the city. The work of the futurist poet is to "sing of the many engines of civilization," which "enter directly into the internal growth of future's latent movement."

Like many other avant-gardists of this period, Hirato urged his readers to throw off the dead weight—and moldy scent—of the past and tradition.[6] In 1921, in the shadow of the imperial palace, primary symbol of Japanese national tradition, Hirato (according to legend) brought poetry out of the libraries and coterie journals into the streets. Inspired by the Italian futurists, he staged a new performative role for the sidewalk poet. His leaflets assert: "Most graveyards are already unnecessary. Libraries, art museums, and academies are not worth the noise of one car gliding down the street. As a test, try sniffing the abominable stench behind the piles of books—how many times superior is the fresh scent of gasoline!"[7] Addicted to unceasing forward movement and speed, Hirato urged his readers to abandon all remnants of the past, and for the most part he disdained the physical body for its susceptibility to decay and dying. His own weak body failed a year later with illness. Hirato's futurism comes to seem a desperate, gyrating last effort to lift off from his own disintegrating body. "There is nothing in futurism that deals in flesh," he writes. Instead, the future is alive with movement, progress, and growth but functions with the efficiency of a mechanism, a plenitude of speed and power not susceptible to decay. Time and space themselves must be killed off in favor of an eternally present energy. Here Hirato cites Marinetti's manifesto within his own, naming himself and his comrades "we for whom 'time and space have already died,' who 'already live in the absolute.' "[8] Historical time, for Hirato, is just one of the old conceptions and frameworks that are the enemies of futurist "anti-art." Yet both Hirato and Marinetti, in their very attachment to speed and movement, are unable to let go of time and space completely.

Fredric Jameson has written of the atrophy of the utopian imagination in our time, the failure to imagine an otherness that would be radical enough to encompass the possibilities of a living future. Instead, he claims, the repeated clichés of science fiction bear unwitting testimony to the ways that we are irrevocably mired in the all too familiar.[9] Yet this failure in itself can become a moment of opening, a moment in which the utopian writing becomes the "unwitting and even unwilling" vehicle for our contemplation of the cultural and ideological closures that mediate our presents as much as our pasts and futures. Hirato Renkichi's work, too, can be seen as such a moment of opening, a vehicle, in spite of his intentions, for reflection on impossibilities as much as possibilities, organic decomposition as much as mechanical transcendence. Attempting to envision a triumph of brilliant light, heat, and constant rhythm, Hirato asserts a vision of power in which the human animal would rise out of its subservient condition into a "*regne meconique*," or mechanical reign. He imagines a movement that would remove human beings from the lowly realm of the flesh to an unmediated place of light and speed, "only the value of absolute power's absolute." Yet even as Hirato proclaims the rise of his futurist utopia, he nonetheless encounters, or brings us into contact with, an imaginative limit like that proposed by Jameson when he wrote of science fiction's failure (or its paradoxical success in making us realize the frightening impact of this failure).

Hirato's writing is haunted by an ambivalent view of corporeality and an inability to transcend images of organic growth, familial structure, and physical sensation. "The gods' control has shifted to the organic relations of all life," he writes. His emphasis on the steady—almost organic—beat of the machine-world, the pulsing rhythm of the city, echoes the sound of old physical organs like the heart. And with the word "absolute" (*zettai*), in a displacement sometimes interpreted as a mistake or typographical error, he replaces one standard character for the last half of the word (*tai*, by itself meaning "opposite, contrast") with another homophonic character for *tai* that means "body." In his declaration for the unprecedented future, Hirato reencounters the ghostly signifiers of the organic world and the familiar human form. When Hirato writes "intuition that should replace knowledge," the term he uses for intuition is *chokkan*—direct feeling, immediate sensation. *Chokkan* (which might also be translated as "gut feeling") emphasizes direct, unmediated feeling or experience. When he writes that "we must quickly volunteer ourselves" (literally, offer our bodies), he implies both a relinquishing of the body to the project of speed and a central necessity of the body that gives itself over to the forward dash of mechanical and creative velocity. The city—here, Tokyo—becomes a machine that runs on body fuel. The "active energy of humanness" directly senses (*chokkan*) "the supreme rhythm (god's instinct) in the chaos before one's eyes."[10] The limits of animal existence—eyes, instincts, senses—return all the more forcefully to haunt Hirato's language of the absolute. Partial, fragmented bodies reappear, disjointed, as his language reels and lurches in a reach for the unstoppable rhythm and mechanical principle of the urban sublime.

The body fuel proposed by Hirato here figuratively constructs the collective, like the modern "masses" envisioned by the October revolutionaries and taken up with such divergent and multifarious enthusiasm by the idealistic artists of Soviet futurism. It seems no accident that Hirato places his own photo in the center of his whirling typography, as the corporeal trace of a momentary heroic figure who proposes to lead the pulsing collective into a realization of its own potential. Susan Buck-Morss writes in *Dreamworld and Catastrophe* of the importance of graphics in creating a revolutionary identity for the masses, as visual mimesis replaces textual argument, so that individuals can "become part of the collective by mimicking its look."[11] Hirato, through textual instabilities and the wild movement of his letters, would like to offer such a proleptic mirror for the masses. Yet like the fading document of his manifesto itself, the language is caught in its own shadows and its present physicalities. In spite of itself, it allows us a closer perception of the chaos and erosion that constitute contemporary urban worlds, and reveals between its lines the limits that condition its own utopia.

Futures are often figured in images of the child. In Hirato's view, human beings pass through a state of childhood on the way to the absolute: "We are in the midst of a powerful light and heat. We are the children of this powerful light and heat. We are ourselves this powerful light and heat." Human observers, separate but at the core of the "dynamo-electric," become the children of the great power (perhaps the ghost of a maternal figure) and subsequently, as a collective "we," overcome and are transformed into the being of this mother-body.[12] In the poem that follows the manifesto, entitled "Gangu" (Wish-Toys),[13] Hirato writes: "Automobile—sidewalk doctor—passing glint of light. / Orphan of originary humanity. / Strong light and heat and orphan—me—my aspirations!" Unadulterated power requires the invention of an orphan child without originary ties, without obligations to family structure or to the past. Born directly at the genesis of humanity (or abandoned at the death of originary humanity), Hirato's orphan enters into his vision of light, heat, and power.

The sexual politics of Hirato's visions may leave the contemporary reader queasy, yet they show one more way in which the world of decay, degeneration, and shadows impinges on, and paradoxically becomes central to, the futurist vision. In the poetic text "Wish-Toys," Hirato lurches into stereotyped images of the feminine as the embodiment of human (corporeal) weakness. His misogyny is no more subtle than Marinetti's: "Commit suicide, you housewives who stink of rice bran!"[14] "Feebleness of you and women, powerless to resist!"[15] In Hirato's writings, masculinity and virility represent supreme power and energy within the (feminized) weaknesses of subtlety and confusion: "Into the subtleties of fatigue and fire, give strong masculine breath! Nirvana of reality." As in Marinetti's fiction, the cliché of woman as body, abject vision and object of disgust, is counterposed by an equal (equally objectifying) and opposite longing toward an idealized vision of woman, here invoked by Hirato through myth: "APHRODITE! APHRODITE! Splendor of beauty, her blinding fire, go back home to the inherent nature of woman!" Even this ideal woman is rejected, sent backward (out of the future) to an "inherent nature" far from the light and heat of the masculinist forward trajectory. In this way, the invocation of idealized woman comes to signify by its very contrast the further confirmation of a virile futurist power.

Hirato's writing consists of an intermingling of what might be seen as protofascist elements—ideas of blind self-sacrifice and idealized technological power—within and among apparently more contradictory, destabilizing moments.[16] There is a clear totalizing (and virilizing) thrust to Hirato's network of tropes, yet at other moments, without overturning their central message, his texts suggest alternative possibilities that they ultimately reject or close off—in ways that leave a trace of this closing.

In the evocatively elliptical opening of "Wish-Toys," female genitals mark the locus of the percolating future implicitly and oddly as a literal blank space: "Felt in her   , the itchy clamor of tomorrow." In Hirato's writing, female labor and birth often function as figures for the corporeality that masculine technological power seeks to overcome. The word for female genitals remains as an unnamed blank in Hirato's text. Kitagawa Fuyuhiko, another experimental poet, said of the blank or white space in poetry (buranku) that it offered the promise of newness and the future.[17] Here, like the itch of sexual desire or gestation or—from another angle—like a yeast infection or venereal disease, Hirato's description of the burbling and fermenting future hesitates before seeming to resolve in an image like (masculine) orgasm: "tens of thousands boiling over in my head." He does not clarify what boils over (although gatō, "my head," recalls the slang expression for male genitals, kitō, literally "turtle head"). Unusual onomatopoeic sounds describe the "small explosion of a basic element that can't be seen." The extreme multitudes of the urban masses shrink here into a teeming world of generative, spermlike microorganisms.

In spite of his deliberate rejection of the corporeal, in "Wish-Toys" Hirato evokes, with both disgust and fascinated detail, the contours of illness of Tokyo's inhabitants: "girl with a diseased eye man wrapped in a bandage phosphorescent stolen child tuberculosis beriberi drippy nose weakling college student—specimen of a nervous breakdown." The rumbling onomatopoeic words (vuwibonda, borurura, do, dodo) might be read as the sound of an automobile departing from this place of abjection or, in an absolutely opposite sense, as the shuddering and fear of the invalid himself. Similarly, the expanding words

city city city city city . . . people people people

visually evoke a car or machine starting up, but the crescendo of "city" and "people" ends with the surprising predicate "get sick," as if it were illness itself that inflamed and grew, rather than the noise of the triumphant machine and moving muses of the city. Hirato's careful description of the cold, dark, decaying past—even as he condemns it and advocates a truth turned toward the light—links an unhealthy underside to the accelerating progress of the metropolis.

Like the constructivist fantasies that suggest a redemptive reconciliation between machine and nature, Hirato's vision allows images of flowers and roses to function alongside gas and automobiles as aesthetic ideals. As ghosts in the machine, they decorate and embellish the city: "Decorate with roses the muddy ditches of Tokyo." Hirato links the corporeality of the idealized feminine—and violence—to this image of the flower: "decorate [the jails of servitude] with flowers of drops of blood of beautiful women." At one moment in "Wish-Toys," Hirato seems to celebrate the place of beautiful flesh, weak as it is: "Scatter roses, anoint yourselves with aphrodisiacs, music of flesh—indulgence of faint life on the surface of skin." Yet as feeble flesh, roses are part of what must ultimately be sacrificed— squandered or overcome—in the movement toward a more brilliant and a speedier ideal. Roses can aid with their corporeal "music," lending their decorative life to the larger (mechanical) purpose of the civilization that finally transcends them. Hirato writes: "Snow white, pink, cream, fauve— in the reflection of the multicolored roses, grasp the light of silver and pearl eternity." The roses do not partake of "silver and pearl eternity"; this eternity can arrive only through their mediation or sacrifice. The transcendent mechanical absolute that Hirato idealizes requires—and turns him toward —the raw material of the feminized "multicolored rose." Like human eyes blinded by the fire of Aphrodite, the roses are consumed, but nonetheless reflected, in the making of the ultimate mechanical composite.

In the manifesto, Hirato adapts Marinetti's grammatical theories about language and the harmful weight of unnecessary words: "we adopt onomatopoeia, of course, mathematical symbols, and all possible organic methods to try to participate in the essence of creation." Breaking the codes of syntax in his exposition, and especially in the symbol-filled "Wish-Toys," Hirato describes adjectives and adverbs as dead flesh in the midst of language. "As much as possible, we destroy the conventions of diction and syntax, and most of all we dispose of the corpses of adjectives and adverbs." He chooses some of the same ideas (like the infinitive mode of verbs) that Marinetti applied to Italian language, although in fact the structure of verb inflections in Japanese is completely different from that of Italian. In this sense, unintentionally perhaps, Hirato leaves a tangible material residue (like a "corpse"?) within his language of the histories and circulations of futurism, reminding the reader of the almost physical resistance and specificity of languages. In his quest for innovative diction—or, some interpreters have claimed, simply by accident—Hirato reverses the two characters that make up the word "machine" (kikai). He recalls to his readers the order and disorder of the system of language, its frail dependencies. Further, he plays on the contingent relation between words and things in the "machine" world he is reinventing. Language rides up and down, back and forth, on the rhythm of slender typographic shapes and lines.

Hirato's vision of a bright flash of technological power that would obliterate all things resonates with nuclear premonition, a light and heat that would make "black human forms" vanish from his sight. In recent science fiction anime like Akira, Ghost in the Shell, or Gundam, this flash becomes the explicit subject of a more familiar narrative line. Yet the glorification of ultimate destruction, a trope that many later works would attempt to work through, coexists with a more subtle, antimonolithic vision of truth. In the manifesto, fragmenting his propositions with dashes and blanks and making the words progressively larger, he writes: "The chameleon of dancing truth == multicolored == composite—a diatonic scale of light seen in the boisterous dance of a kaleidoscope." Truth becomes a chameleon dance, defined by its capacity for continual change, although speed is still the key: "We, who like to be instantaneous and quick on our feet," writes Hirato, "are much indebted to Marinetti, who loved the bewitching changes of the cinematograph." A collection of fragments not necessarily sutured into a single narrative, this truth becomes a strange cinematic vision—susceptible, like light, to the transformative effects of technology. The futurists desired to participate in the "creation of ultimate truth," but this ideal of truth eluded even Hirato's own essentialist vision of purity, presence, and light. The fascination with film reveals a contradictory place of the "absolute" in Hirato's writing. He describes the absolute power of a monolithic urban machine; yet often the absolute appears as a glint of light, a fragment or flash, more closely approaching Benjamin's or Baudelaire's flashes of illumination and discovery in the city.[18]

As words, time, and space take on a figurative mortality, Hirato must seek a humanness that would transcend the corporeal. Yet in the end, it is on the corporeal that his vision depends, in a way that prefigures Heidegger's writing on language in "The Way to Language." Heidegger wrote that language appropriates the human voice, just as humans must listen to and echo preexisting language in order to speak. Yet no matter how fully language may be conceived as a speaking or system prior and exterior to a subject's agency, constitutive of his or her humanness, language needs human voices to come into speaking (what Heidegger calls "Showing of Saying") to make its appearance in the world. "We let its soundless voice come to us, and then demand, reach out, and call for the sound that is already kept in store for us." The special property of human beings, according to Heidegger, is "the sounding of the word": "When mortals are made appropriate for Saying, human nature is released into that needfulness out of which man is used for bringing soundless Saying to the sound of language."[19] For Hirato, too, the imagining of a space prior or exterior to human agency— be it the city, the machine, or the sublime—does not obviate the necessity for human beings to bear these visions into the world. We may read Hirato's vision of the dynamo-electric motor of the city as a network or grid with a life of its own; it is paradoxically at the same time a function and result of human creation and activity. Hirato runs aground in persistent images of corporeality that ultimately replace, or ensure the place of, the flesh in this future city. Like Heidegger's view of language appropriating the human voice, they attest to an indispensable place of the (contingent) human, or the consistent return of the "all too familiar." This does not make his writing revert to a naive perspective centered on human subjectivity, but it does make him ignore or long to efface elements on which, in the end, his envisioned world of speed and the city most profoundly depends. Hirato desires an unmediated or direct "sensation," prior to bodies and language. He posits a certain teleological movement, the movement toward liberation via the pulsing murmur of language-symbols or the pulsing beat of the city. Human activities ultimately bring about this teleological process, but in ways they do not necessarily control or understand. The urban collective body replaces the fallible human body, metonymically represented here by the feminine body, but is in the end constituted by the very body that it consumes.

.

One early evening   the electric streetlights would not light so the people were complaining   I mounted my bicycle   and headed out to the electric company to negotiate the matter   The office was completely silent and empty   I ran up the stone stairway of the power plant and opened the door   but there was no-one there   only the dynamo-electric generator glowed faintly out of the darkness   Peering in the dim light through the window   I saw that it was filled up with a powder-like substance   Just as I entered to find out what it could be   Something like a bird passed over my head   making a fluttering noise   It flew off low into the twilight   and clattered and floundered in circles   It was a mechanical moth worked by a coiled spring   At that moment   all at once the lights went on in the city

Inagaki Taruho, "A Twilight Episode,"
in *One Thousand One-Second Tales*

.

Other writers of the twenties and later pushed the physical and psychical ambivalences experienced by Hirato even further. Among these, one of the most extraordinary is Inagaki Taruho, whose 1923 *One Thousand One-Second Tales* (*Issen ichibyō monogatari*) registered the urgency of futurist concerns even in its very form.[20] But Taruho responded to this urgency very differently than did most futurists. Like Hirato and Marinetti, Taruho read the future as present. And like them, he saw cities blazing with violent electric moons. But Taruho's gaze wandered or lingered longer. In contrast to Hirato and Marinetti, his writings deliberately inhabit dark worlds where

One Thousand One-Second Tales. Courtesy of the Museum of Modern Japanese Literature.

"single blue gas lamps" burn and "tiny luminescent things fall" in the shadows. Taruho emphasizes the need for shadow to feel the preciousness of light: he follows the logic of the futurist cityscape of violence through its fires to its ends and afterglow.

Taruho's city is muted, full of vestiges and chance encounters. Up goes down, down goes up. Moons displace people, and the cityscape reels with strange, haunting words. "Please, pardon me." "For mercy's sake." The moon is an idiosyncratic citizen, and a toy model. The star is an eye, a bullet, a firecracker. A comet is the tail of a cat. Taruho's logic upsets the metaphorical order of things, and on every street corner, there are flickers of light, ghostly tussles in the shadows, locked gazes, mysterious displacements, disappearances, exchanges. Pops and blams abound like in later Japanese comics:

> Soon the shooting star passed with a WHOOSH over my head   I took aim and BANG!   The shooting star traced a wide arc and fell on a distant glass roof hazed over with moonlight[21]

Yet here the onomatopoeic sounds have a resonance that is neither apocalyptic nor triumphant—rather, they add emphasis and syncopated rhythm to this world of echoes, shadows, and reflections.

•

> One evening in the shadow of a big black house   a beautiful luminescent thing fell   On the opposite street corner only a single blue gas lamp was shining   I picked the luminescent thing up put it in my pocket and ran straight home   When I brought it under the electric light and looked carefully it was a star that had fallen out of the sky and died   What's this? Useless! I threw it out the window
>
> Inagaki Taruho, "Finding a Star,"
> in *One Thousand One-Second Tales*

•

For Taruho, the future is present in the sense that magic happens all the time; but that magic seems to come from some unknown, electrified realm that activates the remnants and consequences of prior encounters. Neither past nor future, it is a kind of speed, a momentum, that circulates. It moves in short, propulsive cycles, like the moon that rolls down a hill so fast, in one of the tales, that its triangular shape appears to be round. Past–present–future: the triangle turns over and over. This movement is neither aggressive nor virile: rather, it traces an allusive flirtatiousness in the space of the city. Flirtation, as Adam Phillips says, remains open to multiple trajectories, multiple outcomes—or more than that, it is already the outcome, rejecting the staidness of teleology for an openness where contingency is all there is.[22] It is a low-tech world where souls are transported by wafting perfume and the stars smell like calcium when they burn out. Hirato is too disgusted with the corporeal to explore the sweet, intriguing possibilities that come only in a vaguely intoxicated, pleasured state of acceptance of things, knowing that even stars and dreams have their finitude, their smells. Taruho is enamored of this finitude, and of guns, and film noir: desperate characters lurk in the shadows, run to the roof, or fall asleep waiting for some larger danger to reveal itself. His protagonists loiter on park benches where fabulous things occur: gears creak and two workers raise the moon up on pulleys. The bright electric moon here is at the mercy of everyday men, competent or not, who may stop for a smoke or a beer on their way toward the unnamed thing called the future. If the future is only the present, as Marinetti proclaimed, then here we are: let's make the best of it. Speed comes and goes through different corners of the cityscape, but the rest of the city might as well remain still.

There are almost no female bodies in Taruho's tales, only male bodies: Taruho was an open proponent of the homoerotic, as in his well-known *Aesthetics of Boy-Love (Shōnen-ai no bigaku)*.[23] His future world moves like the universe of a little boy—full of fascinating toy trains, toy cars, wooden horses on springs—and at the same time like that of the old alcoholic man Taruho was to become, with its beers, hat shops, empty houses, and abandoned towers. Flirtations take place between unnamed men, but instead of sex, he tells of aggressive glances and fights on the asphalt. It makes for a curious, moving detachment. Any emotion that propels speed is released in a burst and moves on; it does not hold that perpetual tension. Nothing holds. The sentences spill out of themselves, flicker in and out, like twinkling stars. There is no punctuation, or hardly any, and the blank spaces that separate these phrases are shadowy, ghostly, and dispersed, not like Hirato's projected blank of female genitals, his "itchy clamor of tomorrow." The itch of speed in Taruho passes easily, like a regular corporeal itch, nerve fibers sated, and then it reappears elsewhere.

The single-second bursts in his *One Thousand One-Second Tales* bespeak a world of fragmented instants, whole universes compressed into tiny moments. It is a distilled temporality, where voices and ghosts interrupt tranquillity. "One evening as I tried to drink my cocoa   a voice laughed uproariously from inside *the color of* the cocoa   Shocked, I threw it out the window" (italics mine). The world knocks one over: it's a circus cosmos, and after its shock passes, one is left, "lost in thought on the dew-moist grass." Bits of penetrating fire knock the walls down, or cut holes in the ceiling, but the speed circulates away from the subject out into the city, while the subject, if anything, slows down or drops off to sleep: "I got a bit sleepy in the process of trying to decide [what it had been] and in the end I dropped off to sleep." He shoots something that falls, but hasn't the energy to find out what it was: within all this circulating movement, sometimes one just wants to take a nap. In this sense, Taruho explores the exhaustion of speed, the underside of the body in its susceptibility to tiredness, laziness, or simply the pleasures of not bothering so much, not running around so desperately in the quest for more and more velocity. The future is here, says Taruho, and it makes one dizzy, anxious, angry, and exasperated; or simply tired, mystified, and finally pensive. In fact, it makes one wonder whether the whole cosmos may not be a hoax.

.

"Do you really think there is such a thing as the moon or stars or things like that?"

"Yes I do" I nodded

"You are being fooled That sky is actually just black cardboard with moon and star shapes on it made of tin"

"Then why do the moon and stars move?" I asked in response

"That you know is a trick" he said bursting into laughter

The next thing I knew no one was there When I looked up in surprise I saw the end of a rope ladder just disappearing up into the starry sky

Inagaki Taruho, "As If He Had Seen It,"

in *One Thousand One-Second Tales*

.

Taruho's future inhabits an existential, even beat, register—a poetry of rhythms and displacements, flickers and exchanges. If Hirato imagines a great urban motor with his collective "we," Taruho constructs a smaller, private universe, free of totalizing knowledges and monolithic perspectives. It is a universe of accretions, where narrative proceeds by metonymy and leaps rather than by the proceedings of causal logic.

Taruho focuses on the surprise or shock that comes out of thin air, literally knocking the narrator over. The movement of his narrative proceeds by the accumulation of one surprising tale on the next. Like Kusama Yayoi's postwar accumulations of overstuffed chairs and "Infinity Nets," Taruho's is a world of "and" or "and then." [24] He captures the expanse of time not as a differentiated acceleration but as a narrative bricolage: a limited number of elements recombine in continually different patterns or configurations. This does not mean that he creates the infinitely new, like the early futurists' continual movement to fill the blank spaces with novelty and progress. Taruho is rather more involved with creating starts that are immediately interrupted with sudden stops. Everything freezes for a moment in his tales and then begins again from a slightly different angle or displaced location. In this way he overturns the uses of time, the uses of plot.

If Taruho's series of one-second tales ends, it is perhaps because there is no way of adding anything more. [25] Unlike *The Tales of Tōno*, Yanagita Kunio's collection of fantastical tales from the countryside, here there is no pretense of ethnographic integrity, of having represented a given original or retold a legend of any prior status—even the status of having been told before. In this sense, Taruho's stories seem to float strangely in time: no identifying markers or facts can locate them in space or actuality. They are *monogatari*, tales, things told as if they were myths that come out of a contemporary, everyday atemporality, a dislocatedness. It is this, as much as anything, that kills off space and time in Taruho's work.

·

One evening   as I was crossing an intersection all of a sudden the moon held a pistol to my side   When I put my hands up the moon fumbled around in the bottom of my pocket and took out a single gold coin   It was the gold coin which I had taken a lot of trouble to rip off the top of a department store tower that evening   The gold coin stuck on the evening tower was the moon itself of course

Inagaki Taruho, "A Hold Up,"
in *One Thousand One-Second Tales*

·

While Hirato twists and turns around the self-estranged body, trying to move forward out to a future that is in fact foreclosed to him, Inagaki Taruho creeps forward to the existential realization of time's stasis. He reads the slowness, the hauntings, required by any notion of futurity. Like Betsuyaku Minoru in his postwar plays, Taruho creates a hybrid, dislocated temporality, where the city drops away and the events of human life rise up in all their strangeness.[26] In that sense, perhaps they invent the alternative, unexpected, and truly unfamiliar worlds that Jameson lamented science fiction so often failed to achieve. The worlds they invent contain within themselves their own failures—these are no utopias—and in this sense they also record or represent the uncertainties of a world in which there is no such positive or knowable entity as "the future."

·

One evening   as I was sleeping   something pierced through the ceiling with a POP! and flew inside
When I flipped the light switch I saw that the room was filled with yellow smoke
On the floor a small brass projectile had fallen
When I picked it up and opened the top   I found a piece of art paper folded in three and rolled up inside   On it was written:
Dear sir!
I'm alighting for the top of a mountain with a scarlet cap on my head
Yours ever,
A man in the Milky Way
I immediately put on my cloak and climbed up the mountain
  I searched here and there on the summit without finding the man with the

scarlet cap   I didn't feel that anything was coming down from above
For a long time I stood gazing at the mica of the mountaintop glittering in
the starlight   I waited and finally I noticed that the edge of the sea was
beginning to glow red before the moonrise
    I went down the mountain disappointed

Inagaki Taruho, "Letter from the Galaxy,"
in *One Thousand One-Second Tales*

•

Taruho's tales show a protagonist seeking connection, understanding, a sign from the cosmos. He seeks a certain recognition, and to recognize the nature of his world—but it is a world that ultimately defies science and rational analysis. Although at first it provokes only bafflement, Taruho shows that the cosmos comes to evoke a certain awe and wonder. Yet he does not hesitate to show the way that human limitations prevent the recognition of this wonder, as they leave disappointed from the site of a potentially powerful encounter. Human beings miss seeing what might have been a profound revelation, because of their limited conceptions of what is possible. And there is something humorous and magical in this very miss—the narrator gives the viewer an inkling of a broader picture, a hint of the ways there might be a response between the environment and human beings, but does not solve things definitively or give it all away. The narrative restraint that leaves the reader guessing and imagining evokes both hope and a sense of loss, but without nostalgia.

Frailties of machines and flesh haunt the monolithic structures that surround us today in the Tokyo cityscape. But these hauntings are not new. Already in the early 1920s, Hirato Renkichi's writing hinted at the organic limitations and ambivalences of a techno-futurism that attempted to be rid of the past. But against these limitations, Hirato tried to galvanize energy from the forward-moving progress of civilization. Inagaki Taruho worked along a different trajectory. More than Hirato, Taruho stressed the weakness and uncertainty that lurk just beneath the surfaces of modern life. Rather than highlight apocalyptic news items and large national events, Taruho focused on the everyday fragmentation of sensation and experience. In strong contrast to his futurist contemporaries, Taruho embraced the limitations of the human, infusing both tired flesh and the breakable machine with play and humor, transforming their very limitations into poetic possibilities. He evoked our necessary failure to grasp the magnitude and awe of the urban machine, as well as the structural impossibility of seeing the already fragmented "future."

Notes

1　In the original manifesto, it is ambiguous whether the term *kami* refers to a monotheistic god or gods, but I have chosen to translate it in the plural. All manifesto citations are my translations of Hirato, *Nihon miraiha sengen undō*. See also Hattori Tetsuya, "Hirato Renkichi to nihon miraiha." This discussion and its continuation in later editions of the bulletin contain a detailed and carefully researched study of Hirato's life and works. Italicized words in the translation represent foreign loan words in Hirato's manifesto. Here Hirato uses the foreign loan words *mō-toru* (motor) and *dinamo=erekutorikku* (dynamo-electric).

2　See Susan Lepselter, "Why Rachel Isn't Buried at Her Grave," in this volume.

3　Marinetti's "Manifeste du futurisme" was originally published in *Le Figaro*, February 20, 1909, 1. Moriguchi Tari, one of the earliest successful practitioners of art criticism in Japan, is now better known for his ethnographic work. Hirato Renkichi undoubtedly drew for his inspirations about futurist art and principles from the special issue of *Gendai no bijutsu* (Contemporary Art) 4, no. 6 (September 1921), on the subjects of cubism, futurism, and expressionism ("Rippōha, Miraiha, Hyōgenha"), published the same month as his manifesto, September 1921. That special issue contained a fuller translation of Marinetti's manifesto, since Ogai had only published the eleven tenets. It also contained translations of Marinetti's "Technical Manifesto of Futurist Literature" (1912) and "Words-in-Freedom" (1913), from which Hirato clearly gleaned added inspirations and citations for his manifesto.

　　For a brief description in English of some Japanese futurists' work, see Hirata Hosea, *The Poetry and Poetics of Nishiwaki Junzaburō*. The poet Takamura Kōtarō is said to have corresponded directly with Marinetti and received information from him beginning around 1910, when he published his avant-garde manifesto "Midori-iro no taiyō" (Green Sun) in *Subaru Journal* (April 1910): 35–36. Kanbara Tai, an important Japanese futurist artist and poet, also corresponded with Marinetti; his impressive archive is housed at the Ōhara Museum of Art in Kurashiki, Japan. For a strong introduction of early Japanese artistic manifestoes with translated excerpts, see also Vera Linhartová's "Manifestes et réflexions, 1910–1940." For excellent descriptions of the development of futurism in Japan, see Chiba Sen'ichi, "Avangyarudo-shi undō to taishō-shi no hōkai." The scholar Omuka Toshiharu has written extensively on both futurism and Dada in Japan. In English, see Toshiharu, "Futurism in Japan, 1909–1920"; the same volume contains a good bibliography of further publications (592–94).

4　In 1923, a year after Hirato's death, David Burljuk and Konoshita Shūichirō published an influential collaborative work on futurism, *Miraiha to wa? Kotaeru* (What Is Futurism? A Response) (Tokyo: Chūō bijutsu-sha, 1923). Both Hirato and Inagaki Taruho contributed work to the second Miraiha bijutsu kyōkai

(Futurist Art Association) exhibition in September 1921, held in a restaurant near Ueno Park.

5   Tabbi, *Postmodern Sublime*, ix.

6   Jamer Hunt, "All That Is Solid Melts into Sauce," in this volume.

7   Marinetti had written, "We want to destroy museums, libraries, academies of every kind" (*Marinetti: Selected Writings*, 42). Italian futurists also distributed their work to passersby in the streets.

8   Marinetti wrote: "Time and space died yesterday. We already live in the absolute, because we have created eternal, omnipresent speed" (*Marinetti: Selected Writings*, 41).

9   Jameson, "Progress versus Utopia," 246.

10 Hirato's manifesto takes advantage of the fact that the present tense in Japanese can indicate either a present or a future condition. "All that remains is the active energy of humanness that attempts to feel directly a supreme rhythm (god's instinct) in the chaos before one's eyes."

11 Susan Buck-Morss, *Dreamworld and Catastrophe*, 134. Buck-Morss here weaves a compelling hypertextual web that takes up many related themes of mechanization and organicity.

12 The mother-body or female body is a classic ground from which science-fictional narratives attempt to take off into their futuristic visions: see Tabbi, *Postmodern Sublime*, 4. On the "border war" between organism and machine and its relations to feminist thought, see Donna Haraway, "A Manifesto for Cyborgs."

13 *Gangu* is a neologism created by Hirato that replaces the first character in the compound *omocha* (toy, also pronounced *gangu*) with the character for "wish" (also *gan*, *negau*; "wish, hope, ask for"). Thus it could mean "toys that contain wishes within them," "wished-for toys," or, alternatively, the concrete realization of wishes.

14 "Women who stink of rice-bran" is an idiomatic expression for a housewife.

15 Cinzia Sartini Blum claims that in Marinetti's writing, the female threat "stands for the disempowerment of modern man in a rapidly changing world that baffles existing ethical and epistemological codes. By repeatedly displaying the female body in a condition of violent sexual/verbal subjugation, Marinetti exorcises the threat of chaos and supplants it with his fiction of male power" (Blum, *The Other Modernism*, 37). The violence of Marinetti's images is well exemplified in passages like the following: "Here is the furious coitus of battle, gigantic vulva inflamed by the heat of courage, shapeless vulva that rips apart to offer itself better to the terrific spasm of imminent victory! Ours is the victory" (cited in Blum, *The Other Modernism*, 36).

16 Barbara Spackman demonstrates persuasively the place of a master code of virility in the development of fascist ideology and politics, even as she elucidates fascism's contradictory strains. She shows the clear contribution of Marinetti's writings to the network of literary tropes and social fantasies (sac-

rifice, youth, violence, and nationalism within the rubric of virility) that become an integral part of fascist ideas. To answer the question of futurism's relation to fascism in the Japanese context would require analysis of the work of numerous writers beyond Hirato. Still, most critics dismissively oversimplify the case by stating that unlike Italian futurists, the Japanese poets were uninterested in (and by extension not implicated in) political questions. It is clear that certain of Hirato's ideas bear a resemblance to militarist images that gained currency with the spread of the Pacific war; these fantasies and metaphors also had other strong precedents within earlier nationalist codes. Hirato also espoused the destruction of Japanese grammar and syntax, and his adoption of French terms, odd graphic typographies, and antitraditional word choices all work in a direction contrary to the spread of the nativist traditionalism more commonly associated with Japan's military expansion. The openly Western-inspired experimental poetry and profoundly antitraditional poetics that Hirato promoted would have appeared highly suspect to the militarist regime (as would futurism's associations with Communism in Russia), although Hirato died in 1922, the year after distributing his manifesto, long before the censors had a chance to judge his ideas. See Spackman, *Fascist Virilities*. See also Blum, *The Other Modernism*, 1–3, for a discussion of the ways many scholars have either focused on Marinetti's aesthetic innovations (while discounting the fascist legacy of his ideas) or condemned him completely for the precedents of fascism in his work, without taking into account the inextricable relation between these two facets of his writings. In Hirato, too, we see a complex intermingling of innovative poetics and the opening of a discourse with a troubling fascist legacy.

17   See William Gardner's analysis of Kitagawa Fuyuhiko for a reading of the complicity of this vision of the blank in Japanese colonialist discourses (Gardner, "Colonialism and the Avant-Garde"); and Buck-Morss, *Dreamworld and Catastrophe*, 119.

18   Benjamin's own future orientation—the messianic emphasis in his writings—contradicts his otherwise consistent implication that the ultimate goal of the search remains finally beyond the possibility of realization, appearing only in flashes and visions that instantly disappear. Although Benjamin elaborates on this question in complex ways, I would stress that, more than Hirato, Benjamin maintains an understanding of the paradox of this quest and its impossibility, continuing to search and yet exploring the process by which the search (inevitably) misses its mark. For a few among many provocative examples in Benjamin, see "Theses on the Philosophy of History," 263–64.

19   Heidegger, *On the Way to Language*, 124, 129.

20   Inagaki Taruho, *One Thousand One-Second Tales*. All text boxes contain stories drawn from this collection. Translations by Miryam Sas.

21   Inagaki Taruho, "A Fight with a Shooting Star," in *One Thousand One-Second Tales*.

22   Adam Phillips, introduction to *On Flirtation*.

23   Later, in 1954, Taruho wrote *A-kankaku to V-kankaku* (A-Sensibility and V-Sensi-

bility), claiming the creative and imaginative superiority of the anal over the vaginal in sexuality.

24 See, for example, Kusama Yayoi's exhibition catalog *Love Forever*.

25 "Henri Michaux describes the schizophrenic table . . . 'As it stood, it was a table of additions, much like certain schizophrenics' drawings, described as "overstuffed," and if finished it was only in so far as there was no way of adding anything more to it, the table having become more and more an accumulation, less and less a table' " (cited in Deleuze and Guattari, *Anti-Oedipus*, 6).

26 See my article on Betsuyaku, "Expectation and Invention: The Casual Theater of Betsuyaku Minoru." See also the analysis of Betsuyaku in my forthcoming book, *No Holds Barred: Engaged Theater and Its Discontents in Postwar Japan*.

INTERLUDE

日本未來派宣言運動

東京＝平戸廉吉

MOUVEMENT FUTURISTE JAPONAIS

Par R―HYRATO

●

顫動する神の心、人間性の中心能動は、集合生活の核心から發する。都會はモートルである。その核心はデイナモ――エレクトリツクである。

●

神の専占物は凡て人間の腕に征服され、神の發動機は、今日、都會のモートルとなり、百萬の人間性の活動に與かる。

●

神の本能は都會に遷り、都會のデイナモ――エレクトリツクは人間性の根本の本能を揺り起し、覺醒し、直接に猛進せんとする力に訴へる。

●

神の有せし統御は、移して全生活の有機的關係となり、此處に動物的運命の暗黒、浮滑細斷、屈從の狀態から免れ、械機的直情の徑行は、光輝となり熱となり不斷の律動となる。

●

MARINETTI― <Après le règne animal, voici le règne mécanique qui commence.>

●

我等は強き光と熱の中にある。強き光と熱の子である。強き光と熱そのものである。

●

智識に代はるべき直感、未來派の否藝術の敵は概念である。『時間と空間は既に死し、最早や絶體の中に住む』我等は、素早く身を挺して、冒進し創造しなければならぬ。其處には、只目前のカオーに至上の律（神の本能）を直感せんとする人間性の能動あるのみである。

●

多くの墓場は既に無用である。圖書館、美術館、アカデミーは、路上を滑る一自働車の響にも價しない。試みに圖書堆裡の唾棄すべき臭氣を嗅いで見給へ、これに優ることガソリンの新鮮は幾倍ぞ。

●

未來派詩人は多くの文明機關を謳ふ。これ等は潜在する未來發動の内延に直入して、より機械的な速かな意志に徹し、我等の不斷の創造を刺戟し、速度と光明と熱と力を媒介する。

●

『躍る眞理のカメレオン』――多彩―複合―萬華鏡の亂舞の中に見る光の全音階。

●

瞬間的にして快足を好む我等は、シネマトグラフの妖變を愛するマリネツチイに負ふ所多き者として無論擬聲音、數學的記號、あらゆる有機的方法を採用して眞新のクリエーションに參加せんとする。

能ふ限り、文章論、句法のコンヴエンションを破壞し殊に、形容詞副詞の死體を拂ひ、動詞の不定法を用ひ何物にも浸略されないものゝ域に進む。

●

未來派には肉を隔がしむる何物もない――機械の自由――活達――直動――絶體の權威絶體の價値のみ。

願具

醱酵……ブウルル、ボウラ、ビユルラ、バビユルル、ビユル……見えざる素因の小爆發。彼女の　に感ずる明日の痒騷。錬金術師の未見の光輝、ボウウ…ビク╳╳╳――我頭に煮え返へる數萬。

病院の臭みを蔽ふた東京市、汝の上に玫瑰色の夕陽を祈り給ふ聖母の如く我はよきアスフアルトの街道を祈る。市民の音樂の歩行を祈る。薔薇の花をもつて蔽はれる東京市、星の光輝を人に、

目病める娘繃帶にとり巻かれた男燐光の竊盜兒肺病脚氣はな垂れ貧弱大學生――神經衰弱標本――汝等女性等の反撥力なき羸弱――

キツク、クツコツク、ケエツク、ケロツク、ヒヤラ、ヴヴヴヴヴ、フアンギヒヤ╳╳╳フ――ハ――フ――ハ――フ――ハ――フ――ハ――フ――ハ╳╳╳╳╳╳ヴオルラ、ヴキポンダ、ボルルラ、ド、ドド――ドド――ドニ――ドニ、ヴアヴオウ――ヴアヴヤ、ヴヤウ――ヴララ――ララララララ――ドド――ドニ＝自働車――見送る顏顏顏顏╳╳╳病人の恐怖と戰慄。

街街街街街街――人人人人人人人――

病む。

自働車――街頭のドクトル――過ぎ行く閃光。

原始的人間性の孤兒。

強き光と熱の孤兒――我――我が願望！

薔薇を飾れ、東京市の泥溝、一日の陽なき屋上架役所黴の長屋倭屋これ等屈從の獄屋に堤に路に富豪の別墅を圍繞する美女の血の滴りの花を飾れ。

APHRODITE！APHRODITE！

嬋姸、彼女の盲目する火、女性の本然に歸れ、糠臭き女よ自盡せよ。

薔薇を撒け媚藥を塗れ、肉體の音樂――皮膚の上の微かな生命の蕩盡――焔と疲勞のニユーアンスの中に男性の強き息吹き與へよ。現實の涅槃。雪白、ピンク、クレーム、フオーブ、雜色のバラの照返しの中に金と眞珠の永遠の光を攫め。

我より消え去れ！　太陽・月・星・燈火あらゆる輝きをもつて映像する黒き我影人。天鵞絨と朱色の裏ひるがへすマントウの理想主義者カトリツク僧哲學者。闇の上に汝等をよろめかす強き輝の來らば、太陽・月・星・燈火よりも強き強き光のあらば……消え去れ、我より！

平戸廉吉作
未來派詩集　螺旋階段　近刊

平戸廉吉作
未來派小說　無日　近刊

新しき時代の創造に來れ！

東京中澁谷八一九
平戸廉吉

Manifesto of the Japanese Futurist Movement

Hirato Renkichi   Translated by Miryam Sas

Trembling heart of the gods, the central active energy of humanity emerges from the core of collective life. The city is a motor. Its core is *dynamo-electric*.

●

The gods' possessions have been conquered by the arms of humans, and what was once the gods' power generator has today become the city's motor, participating in the functioning of the humanity of millions.

●

The instinct of the gods has been transferred to the city, and the city's *dynamo-electric* has jolted and awakened humanity's fundamental instinct, and has appealed to that power that attempts to push forward directly and vigorously.

●

The control formerly possessed by the gods has moved and become the organic relations of all life, and here dark animal fate, that stagnated discord, is beckoned out of its subservient condition; the straightforward mechanical disposition becomes a brilliant light, becomes heat, becomes constant rhythm.

●

MARINETTI—«Après le règne animal, voici le règne méconique qui commence.»

●

We are in the midst of a powerful light and heat. We are the children of this powerful light and heat. We are ourselves this powerful light and heat.

●

Intuition should be substituted for knowledge; the enemy of Futurism's anti-art is the concept. "Time and space have already died, and we already live in the absolute." We must quickly volunteer ourselves, dash forward blindly, and create. All that remains is simply the active energy of humanness that attempts to feel directly a supreme rhythm (god's instinct) in the chaos before one's eyes.

●

Most graveyards are already unnecessary. Libraries, art museums, and academies are not worth the noise of one car gliding down the street. As a test, try sniffing the abominable stench behind the piles of books——how many times superior is the fresh scent of gasoline!

●

Futurist poets sing the praises of the many engines of civilization. These enter directly into the internal growth of the latent movement of the future, and sink deeply into a more mechanical and rapid will; they stimulate our unceasing creation, and mediate the speed and light and heat and power.

●

"The chameleon of dancing truth" == **multicolored——composite——**a diatonic scale of light seen in the boisterous dance of a kaleidoscope.

●

We, who like to be instantaneous and quick on our feet, are much indebted to Marinetti, who loved the bewitching changes of the cinematograph; we adopt onomatopoeia, of course, and mathematical symbols, and all possible organic methods to try to participate in the essence of creation. As much as possible, we destroy the *conventions* of diction and syntax, and most of all we dispose of the corpses of adjectives and adverbs; using the infinitive mood of verbs, we advance to unconquerable regions.

●

There is nothing in futurism that deals in flesh——freedom of the machine——generosity——direct movement==only the value of absolute power's absolute.

Wish-Toys

Fermentation......brrrr, boura, biyurrra, babiyurrrr, biyurrr...... the small explosion of a basic element that can't be seen. Felt in her   , the itchy clamor of tomorrow. The unknown brilliance of the alchemist, bbbau..byuxxxx = tens of thousands boiling over in my head.

City of Tokyo enveloped in the stench of hospitals. Like the Holy mother who prays for the red jewel-colored setting sun above you, I pray for roads of good asphalt. I pray for the music of the citizens walking. City of Tokyo covered over with roses, for the brightness of stars, to people . . .

Girl with a diseased eye man wrapped in a bandage phosphorescent stolen child tuberculosis beriberi drippy nose weakling college student———specimen of a nervous breakdown———the feebleness of you and women, powerless to resist———kikku, kukkokku, keekku, kerokku, hiyara, vuvu-vuvuvuvu, fuyangihiyaXXXXhu——ha——hu——ha——hu——ha——hu——haXXXXXXXXvorura, vuwibonda, borurura, do, dodo———dodo——doni——doni, vavau——vavya, vyau——vurara——rararararara——dodo——doni══automobile ══ seeing off facefacefacefaceface-XXXX an invalid's fear and shuddering.

city city city city city city city city city—people people people people people people people people people people get sick.

Automobile——sidewalk doctor——passing glint of light.
Orphan of originary humanity.
Strong light and heat and orphan———me———my aspirations!

Decorate with a rose, muddy ditches of Tokyo——the tenement houses and old Japanese houses mildew of office buildings on the rooftops where the sun never shines——decorate all these jails of servitude the embankments the roads, decorate them with the flowers of the drops of blood of a beautiful woman, that surround the millionaire's villa.

APHRODITE! APHRODITE!

Splendor of beauty, her blinding fire, go back home to the inherent nature of woman, commit suicide, you housewives who stink of rice-bran.

Scatter roses, anoint yourselves with aphrodisiacs, music of the flesh ————indulgence of the faint life on the surface of the skin————into the nuance of fatigue and fire, give a strong masculine breath. Nirvana of reality. Snow white, pink, cream, fauve————in the reflection of the multicolored roses, grasp the light of silver and pearl eternity.

Vanish from my sight! Sun•moon•stars and all brilliances that silhouette black human forms. Idealist Catholic priest philosopher whose manteau reverses to vermilion and velvet. If the strong light that makes you hesitate on the threshold were to come, if there were a strong strong light greater than sun, moon, stars, lamps . . . . .Vanish from my sight!

CHAPTER

The Future of the Old Economy:
New Deal Motives in New Economy Investors

Christopher Newfield

In the early 1980s, conventional wisdom said that the U.S. version of market capitalism was falling behind a Japanese-style "industrial state." By the late 1990s, conventional wisdom was saying the opposite. The Japanese model was a dead issue, and the United States had reanointed itself the planet's unparalleled economic leader thanks to the deregulation of its markets and the liberation of its entrepreneurs. As a result, the future was once again made in the U.S.A.

Who was this future by and for? It was largely structured by financial professionals with special expertise and access to advanced technology and large capital. The goal of these concerns was not open markets but increased profits, indeed a scale of profits best obtained through market monopoly, one hopefully rooted in the "proprietary control of an industrial standard."[1] But industry and the media said that the New Economy was *for* the people as a whole.[2] Professional analysts discussed all sorts of technological and managerial issues, but the core claim was that the New Economy was a newly *popular* capitalism, an engine of wealth creation for all. This definition of "all" was propagandistic: the 1990s was the era of barely increasing ordinary wages and rapidly increasing inequality.[3] But the media accepted it, by and large, and most people appeared to believe that a renewed capitalism was bringing prosperity to those who had struggled during the crises and erratic recovery of the 1970s and 1980s.

Popular capitalism offered different kinds of evidence for its existence. The common theme was popular participation, even a kind of economic democracy. Evidence included the proliferation of start-up companies based on a possibly new product or technology; this, among other things, required banks and venture capitalists to shower more capital on twenty- and thirty-year-olds than at any other time in recorded history. Many thought it hard to find contradictions in a superbull stock market that had been averaging double-digit annual increases since 1982. Like some other observers of this period, though, I could not shake the feeling that this economy was not as it seemed. The *culture* of popular capitalism felt as deep to me as a studio campaign for a summer movie.

By 2001 and 2002, we knew that some of it *had* been faked: Enron became the poster child of that still-growing list of companies that cooked basic profit and loss accounting in a variety of imaginative ways. Many trades in newly deregulated markets like electric power, for example, were "round-tripping" exchanges in which the supply and demand for electricity were manipulated to increase the price.[4]

But my more persistent sense of the New Economy's unreality rested on its strange indifference to growing, sometimes shocking, economic inequality. Commentators constantly rationalized inequality as an ordinary and temporary feature of innovative transitional periods, but at no point was the necessity or the value of this inequality really explained. Among the symptoms were the spectacular fortunes being made by top executives and the legal and financial professionals who served them. Some executives were netting hundreds of millions and even billions of dollars of company money. It was impossible to see this kind of income as individually "earned" in any literal sense, and yet virtually no one described executive compensation as unearned. Everybody and everything was at their disposal; all of it was for them. Compensation of $50 or $100 million a year for the CEO was described as performance pay: the CEO, after all, had increased the company's market capitalization by, say, $17 billion that year, and the thousands of company employees and the hysteria of equity markets had nothing to do with it.

This was for me the central delusion of the New Economy—the "great man" theory of wealth making, in which people like Bill Gates at Microsoft and Jim Clark at Netscape, rather than thousands of unknown engineers and secretaries, were the Promethean givers of fire. The delusion was that the enormous wealth of these colossal corporations was created by their executives rather than by the workforce in conjunction with the societies in which they operated. The delusion was that value was created by finance capital through its executives rather than by labor.

Some of my aversion to the rhetoric of the 1990s arose from what seemed to me a proliferation of misrepresentations of the nature of the New Economy. But it also seemed to me that there was a cultural problem: portraits of the decision-making processes of the economic actors of the 1990s appeared false, too. It was not just that the CEOs were speaking in populist terms. The supposedly popular language of the investor appeared to me entirely out of sync with the investors whom I knew. In this essay, I respond to this problem by tracing a genealogy of our language of economic futures from the New Deal to the present. I argue that the psychological and cultural motives of the "ordinary" investor at the end of the twentieth century were much more continuous with those of the past than we are usually led to believe. I show that if we pay attention to what people actually say about their economic perceptions and choices, the conventional image of the new investor falls apart. The investment boom of the 1990s was not produced by a new attitude toward risk and investment. Rather, it developed by appealing to exactly those desires that used to be satisfied by *avoiding* investing.

Nobody Beats the Odds

My own understanding of the language of economic futures goes back to my grandfather, a New Dealer and cash register salesman named Snyder Morgan, the last adult in my family to be opposed to capitalism, or at least opposed to a major middle-class confusion about it. He was also an afternoon gambler. When I was young enough to still have half-day school, he and I would start for the park and end up at the track. He'd shout to my grandmother, "Helen, we're going to the park." After the door slammed, he'd mutter to me, "That's right, Hollywood Park." We'd have our wicked laugh, the sixty- and the six-year-old, and head to Inglewood for the afternoon.

At the track, Grandpa snickered at the guys with their heads in the *Racing Form*. "Those numbers don't tell you anything you need to know," he'd confide to me. "Too bad the horses don't read the *Racing Form*," he chortled to one of his research-prone friends. "Son," he'd whisper, "what the horse will do isn't the same as what the horse has done." He'd go on to note the dullness of the *Racing Form* students. "Doesn't that look like fun?" he'd say sarcastically, nodding his head toward them. "Why don't we go sit down and read some of the sales reports I've got right here," holding up an invisible briefcase. Then we'd look at each other and have another laugh.

Since then I've learned that Snyder never took a blind roll in his life. His scorn for the bookworms covered up his own elaborate horse-following homework, all concluded in private before he left for the track. But there was a basic idea lurking in his deception. Snyder made a sharp distinction between betting by knowing the horses and betting by knowing the odds.

Learning the horses was crucial. Learning the odds was a waste of time. The odds reduced a horse's history to a set of averages. The good gambler, in Snyder's view, had to write his own horse histories. He was especially good at this, since he'd been raised around horses in Oklahoma when they were still central to farm labor and transportation. He had been part of buying, selling, working, and racing them his whole early life. He knew horse life stories, horse parentages, and horse genealogies going back to the previous century. He knew the world of trainers, stables, farms, jockeys, and horse-raising families. Given these complex histories, he thought, only amateurs would resort to reading probabilities. Only they would make the beginner's mistake, as he saw it, of seeing probability as a kind of prophecy. Only they could forget that the mathematical odds are terrible at predicting a particular outcome. Horse history was connected to the horse future. Horse probability was not.

At the track I watched the bettors and ignored the horses. I especially watched the floor. The gamblers' feet shuffled back and forth. The feet went up on tiptoes to get a better view. The feet wobbled back and forth and stamped. Finally the feet would be showered with losing tickets, which the feet would trample or wipe on the ground. That's where I'd come in. When the feet departed I'd rush in and pick up the tickets that had colors I liked. I'd bring my collection back to our seats.

I didn't really know how useless these tickets were. I liked their colors, and that kept them from being useless to me. Grandpa fell silent when I waved these tickets around. Obviously he didn't want all these tokens of loss in his face. They pointed out how easy it was to lose. These tickets also had the odds printed on them. They represented the laws of probability, which brought him little joy. The odds turned the majority of players into losers. Losers, to be precise, were people who *played* the odds. Winners, on the other hand, were people with skill (as well as luck). Losers had chance as governed by the laws of probability. Winners partially avoided chance, knowing you couldn't win by playing the odds.

What was wrong with the *Racing Form* readers playing the odds? Sometimes it was because they had no experience. But the deeper reason involves the nature of odds themselves. The odds are the ratio of favorable to unfavorable outcomes. If the probability of your horse winning is estimated to be one out of eleven, then the odds of the horse winning are ten to one. Odds generally express the degree of risk. This all sounds innocent enough. You win by learning the odds and then playing good odds rather than bad. You win by reducing your risk. But here's the problem with playing the odds: in the long run, you don't get anywhere. You can't actually ever get ahead of the odds. That's because, in the long run, risk exactly cancels out reward.

There are a number of reasons for this. One has to do with the "house advantage" or the house take. When you play standard craps in a casino, for example, and place a "proposition bet" that the next throw will be a 2, the table will pay a roll of 2 at a rate of 30 to 1. But the odds of throwing a 2 are 35 to 1, so an even payout would be 35 to 1. If you bet one dollar on the 2 thirty-six times in a row, the probability is that you'll win once, and will win thirty dollars plus your dollar bet back. But you've come up five dollars short of what you've put down. The house has an advantage of almost 14 percent on this particular bet. Even the best bets at craps offer the house just under a 1 percent advantage, so you'll get back only a little more than $99 for every $100 wagered. For slot machines, you can expect between $90 and $95 back for every $100 you pay out. The same goes for the racetrack, which takes a cut in the form of slightly lower payouts than the odds demand.

Even when there's no house, playing the odds means staying even. If you're playing craps with a friend, and the odds of rolling a two are 35 to 1, you should bet no more than $1 if she bets $35 that you won't roll a 2. Even if you win the likely number of times, you won't make any more than you will lose. Winning depends on *beating* or *escaping* or *rigging* or *changing* the odds. You try to win when you've bet much more than a dollar, and try to lose only when you've bet a dollar or less. When you change your bets and go with instincts and hunches, you're playing against the probabilities and trying to beat the odds. This is of course what everyone in games of chance is trying to do.

But the sad fact is that in the long run you can't beat the odds. This fact is expressed by a couple of general probability principles. When the probabilities for all the odds of throwing two dice are compared, it becomes clear than some are much higher than others (the odds of throwing a 6 are 5/36; a 7, 6/36; an 8, 5/36). The probabilities form a "normal distribution"—a bell curve. Most events occur near the average (5, 6, and 7 are all closer to the average of rolls that range from 2 to 12), and fewer events occur at the extremes. High-yield outcomes are quite rare; more common outcomes pay proportionally less.

A second way of expressing normal distribution is known as "regression to the mean." A long winning streak will eventually become an average mixture of wins and losses or an equally long losing streak. "The successors to the outliers," in other words, "are predestined to join the crowd at the center. Change and motion from the outer limits toward the center are constant, inevitable, and foreseeable. Given the imperatives of this process, no outcome other than the normal distribution is conceivable. The driving force is always toward the average, toward the restoration of normality." [5] Your winnings will soon attract complementary losses, what goes up must come down, and so on. It's therefore very hard to make a living by playing games of chance. Nearly all professional gamblers play poker, horses, and other games with some component of skill.

The world is full of chance, and economic systems exist to control it. They seek to offer livelihoods that chance does not rule. Economic systems do this in theory by ensuring that economic activities are games of skill. If outcomes are linked to skill, then the laws of probability can be avoided, even set aside. This was the basic idea behind my grandfather Morgan's attempt to replace the horse's odds with his horse expertise. The simple laws of probability govern only *independent* or *unconnected* events. They do not govern events where one thing leads to another. "Cards, coins, dice, and roulette wheels have no memory."[6] They repudiate historical connections. No roll is connected to any other roll, no sequence is established by any series of rolls, and thus in some sense games of chance stand outside history, even outside time. Thus the only way to win is to uncover hidden but real connections among events. At the track, real connections included the horse's background with jockeys and trainers and stables, connections *not* present in the conventional wisdom of the *Racing Form*. Economics, in short, is supposed to make war on gaming.

"Winning" gamblers gamble as though gambling were a job. To be part of a sound economy, betting must be a craft or skill, like masonry, teaching, or sales. Gambling addiction, on the other hand, is a complex form of hope. The escape from time and history is a basic pleasure of games of chance, but the lack of connection between events is also the source of its pain. A good throw doesn't beget another good throw; rolling dice is not like learning to bowl. If your wins accumulate, it's not because your skill has linked one throw to the next but because you're having a lucky streak. Every gambler knows this lucky streak will end.[7]

Snyder tried to make sure horse picking was a game of skill by researching horses until he saw a pattern in past events that might affect the event to come. If he had played blackjack, he would have tried to convert that into a game of skill by counting cards. By tracking the history of the cards, the counter connects events in order to shape the desired future. He did play poker, and in the same way. The cards had outcomes in the context of his reconstructions of who the other players are, how they play, what they've down, how they've drawn. Sometimes chance could work for someone like Snyder, but he could never trust it over time. In the war against normal distribution, he had mostly craft and skill on his side. Skill was whatever allowed him to connect events. Skill gave him a small set of unreliable powers of prophecy about the immediate future.

Skill was important because the mean loomed large in Snyder's life. Like most other children of the working classes, he read the Great Depression as a high-roller disaster that had been overcome by the New Deal and wartime employment. He accepted the claim that American capitalism was proving its superiority to communism and socialism. He did *not* believe that capitalism produced personal (and ultimately general) wealth by allowing individuals to work hard to beat the odds. If people got ahead, it was because *everyone* got ahead. In other words, people got ahead *when the odds of getting ahead improved*. People got ahead when the mean was moved. People got ahead when the odds were changed.

This view established a clear standard by which to judge the economy. The U.S. economy was good only to the extent that it offered a rising trend line with which the fortunes of bankers, nurses, secretaries, and cash register salesmen could all rise. There may have been some shifting of the bell curves of wealth and income as politicians and executives rigged the system, as Snyder invariably saw it. But prosperity depended on an overall shift in the curve. In his work selling cash registers to the shopkeepers of central Los Angeles, Snyder noticed that nearly everybody, no matter how much they worked, stayed close to the blue-collar mean. That was good or bad depending on where the mean was.

I can't remember a single remark Snyder ever made that implied he was in individual control of his destiny. He never exhorted me to seize control of mine. I now think he had little sense of controlling work, or sales, or profits. He saw no suspension of the normal income distribution even in the postwar boom. When he played by the rules, he stayed at the mean. When he bet on the horses, he used his skill to connect events and escape the curve. When he played the odds, he stayed where he was. If his status improved, *it was because the mean had moved*. There was no reason to think that other rule followers were doing any better.

For Snyder, as for many others after World War II, the mean did move. About seven years before his retirement, he was promoted to head National Cash Register's Los Angeles chain-store sales division. He then worked to link NCR to the area's booming department store business. These stores bought registers on contract and in bulk. In the process, Snyder became a consultant and teacher. He advised purchasing managers on various models. He discussed their sales and inventory needs. He led seminars on the use and maintenance of the latest models. He helped stores improve their cash flow management. All this happened because his company had managed to change the rules of the game.

Snyder no longer made one sale at a time. He had become part of a complicated intercorporate network of machinery and service. One sale now implied many other sales. Working within connected events, the salesperson could now overcome the older odds: a veteran like Snyder could do better than he had done under the previous system because the overall setup had changed. It was no wonder to him that his income finally went up. Which meant that much more money to take to the track.

Snyder knew that he had not beaten the odds. He had not beaten them by himself through chance or gambler's magic or even skill. Nor had "the company" *beaten* the odds. The company had succeeded by *changing* the odds. It had moved the mean to which it would always regress by changing the rules of the game that was being played. The company could carry individuals beyond the original bell curve by changing the curve—moving, in this case, from individual to chain sales. When individuals worked new customers one at a time, they didn't budge the mean. The sale they made today, they'd miss tomorrow. Thirty-five years of selling didn't mean the next sale would go through. Snyder had worked as well before the job change as he worked afterward, but good work was merely the ante to get into the game. He finally won the game—got decent raises and a good pension—when the game was changed by his corporation, all within the context of New Deal expectations and federal regulation.

Gamblers are trapped inside normal distribution. Skilled workers are, too. Real advancement during the best economic years of the century, for the vast majority of regular working people like Snyder, rested on changing normal distribution by changing the business or political system's governing rules. No amount of *individual* skill had shifted his mean. Snyder did, however, have fun thinking that his individual skill shifted his mean at the track.

Collectivist Ethics and the Spirit of Capitalism

German sociologist Max Weber is often thought to have identified a unified culture of capitalism in *The Protestant Ethic and the Spirit of Capitalism* (1905), but he offers at least two distinct explanations of that culture's aims. In one famous passage, he wrote that capitalist "man is dominated by the making of money, by acquisition as the ultimate purpose of his life."[8] This seems true of capitalists as such, people whose business is to own capital in order to increase the capital they own. But a capitalist society, as Marx and many others have pointed out, is largely made up of noncapitalists, that is, people who own little or no capital and live by selling their labor power. Capitalist societies reproduce themselves by convincing their noncapitalists either to emulate capitalists or to defer to them. But noncapitalists tolerate or celebrate capitalism for something else, which can be found in a different passage in Weber's book. For the majority under capitalism, capitalism means "rigorous calculation, directed with foresight and caution towards the economic success which is sought in sharp contrast to the hand-to-mouth existence of the peasant, and [in contrast] to . . . the adventurer's capitalism, oriented to the exploitation of political opportunities and irrational speculation."[9] Though capitalism loses sight of genuine "need," it avoids two great evils of traditional economies—subsistence labor, in which nothing is accumulated, and economic gambling, in which accumulation is undone by loss. The bourgeois virtue of steady progress thus avoids two kinds of economic sin, one associated with infinite work and the other with no work at all. These two states have something in common: they each fail to move the mean. In so failing, they fail to improve the status for the vast majority in the economy. People like my grandparents had no interest in capital accumulation as an end in itself. They sought the stable connection of events that led to the moving of the mean; capitalism was good if it offered a future that could be partially controlled by everyday work. This was the real value of the rising trend.

I still view this as a kind of home economics, largely because of the efforts of my grandmother. Having been an orphan and then an early widow (Snyder was her second husband), she was incapable of triumphant prosperity. Even in the affluent 1960s, her house lacked any effect of luxury or glamour. There was no feeling of wealth, national or corporate, no sharing in the country's imperial power, only a certain contentment with their slowly improving comforts. "Comfortable" was an important household term. Through the good years, they always bought used cars and carefully saved small amounts of money. My grandmother didn't work outside the house, but she performed enormous amounts of unpaid labor at home—she cleared the hillside of ivy, tended roses, took in my disabled brother on the weekends, trimmed trees through her late seventies, fed at various times most of the kids who lived on the street. She also sold household products over the phone, mostly vitamins manufactured by a company called Neutralite that was later swallowed by the multilevel marketing colossus of Christian capitalism known as Amway. My grandparents' American dream had no connection with big risks and big payouts. It had to do with stability, security, tranquillity, and personal life. Working and saving were its official cornerstones. These didn't negate risk and uncertainty. But U.S. society had managed risk and uncertainty to the point that working and saving were possible.

Research suggests that my grandparents were fairly typical of postwar working-class Americans as they slowly but steadily ascended from the lower to middle reaches of the middle class. Their advancement was supported by two *social* factors beyond devotion to work, which was only the ante into the game. The first was what in 1967 John Kenneth Galbraith called the "new industrial state." This consisted in part of various forms of social investment: social security, Medicare, and other programs that took away some of the worst forms of arbitrary risk. The new industrial state rested on a military-industrial-governmental technostructure. Galbraith's industrial state was a complex system of organizations and bureaucratic professionals that regulated and managed market relations for the sake of stable, orderly growth in revenues and profits.

> In the past, leadership in business organization was identified with the entrepreneur. . . . With the rise of the modern corporation, the emergence of the organization required by modern technology and planning and the divorce of the owner of capital from control of the enterprise, the entrepreneur no longer exists as an individual person in the mature industrial enterprise. . . . The entrepreneur, as the directing force of the enterprise, [is replaced] by management. . . . It embraces all who bring specialized knowledge, talent or experience to group decision-making.[10]

In advanced economies, the services of Weber's Ben Franklin–like entrepreneur were simply superfluous. Risk taking and gambling were replaced by management that could predict and produce the future. Order and foresight supported the upward trend line in both the boardroom and the bedroom community. Only with these new rules could working and saving replace gambling with crop prices and horse races, except as entertainment.

The welfare state and the corporate technostructure fought constantly and yet worked together. The point was not to hamper entrepreneurship but to make it unnecessary. "The corporation everywhere," wrote the business journalist Anthony Sampson, "was consciously or unconsciously part of a political system and a society to which it had to justify itself. Over the postwar decades it responded to the challenges of socialism, communism and labour unions by developing its own kind of private welfare state. In America the big companies made unwritten bargains with governments, which supported them in return for their looking after their company people."[11] The economy, companies, products, and employees all continued to change. But the technostructure made change compatible with a rising mean and favored the change that favored that rise.

The second cornerstone of the work-and-savings economy was an American religious ethos dominated by (but not limited to) Protestantism. My devout grandmother sharply distinguished between earthly and heavenly rewards. As Weber would have predicted, she saw saving and salvation as two different things. She had what I always felt was an impossibly tranquil relation to death and heaven, so much so that during the twenty years

I saw her regularly, I never heard her take part in a religious argument. In part this was the result of risk aversion that rested on her faith in redemption. Economic and spiritual setbacks were mere trials, exceptions to redemptive history, like Snyder's drinking and gambling. From this point of view, I would look back and think that God was her way of escaping the going-nowhere of normal distribution.

It took me a long time to realize that my grandparents didn't think this was possible on the basis of a merely individual salvation. Cultural historian Sacvan Bercovitch has shown how New England's early Puritan theologians relied on communal bonds to overcome the gulf between secular and sacred. This involved linking "common providence," in which God feeds, clothes, shelters and otherwise provides for the earthly needs of the faithful, to redemptive history, which is "the mode of identifying the individual, the community, or the event in question within the scheme of salvation."[12]

Bercovitch's description of the link is complicated, but the gist is this: By around 1700, the "New World errand" was no longer seen as a secular experience whose providential meaning required learned, even gracious, interpretation. The influential minister Cotton Mather played a particularly large role in defining the New World errand as "part of church history; he deduced its providential meanings from the preordained scheme of redemption."[13] New England was not merely a society but a church-state, a congregation. The congregation's leaders and magistrates were themselves saints; its greatest figures, like John Winthrop, were types or emblems of Christ. Crucially, these leaders became exemplary through their relation to the *community*. The ruler was a type of Christ only through *integration* with his community. "The source of integration lies . . . with those he serves."[14] The hero's individual, spiritual growth—the pattern of redemption that transcends normal distribution—appears only through "the temporal movement of a holy commonwealth." Daily turmoil was linked to redemptive history not simply through individual holiness, though that was a prerequisite, but through collective bonds.

This "spirit of Protestantism" ran through nineteenth-century concepts of labor and reappeared in the undemonstrative nature of post–World War II prosperity.[15] It continues to this day. The crucial point here is that "the Protestant ethic" and "the spirit of capitalism" are *not* innately entrepreneurial. They are not even innately individualistic. American Protestants did not see how progress could depend on individual effort or any of the other fallen features of the self. They had no concept of self-redemption through brilliant effort, much less through cunning trade or adventurism or innovation. Many American Protestants do adhere to the entrepreneurial vision of a redemptive capitalism. But Protestant capitalist entrepreneurship is the product of a laborious conceptual and cultural synthesis whose mechanics are beyond my scope here and show it to be an unnatural marriage, in spite of the conventional wisdom about Weber's meaning.

The *normative* nature of American *collective* redemption survived after World War II in the widespread belief that progress rested on national prosperity, the rising tide, the moving mean, where individuals worked constantly and intelligently and yet their advancement depended on national advancement. The working noncapitalists never forgot the alternation of winning and losing in their individual lives, an alternation that in itself led nowhere, that was *never* suspended for long by individual upward mobility. Permanent mobility was always an illusion, soon to be shattered by the usual reversals and regressions to the mean. Going-nowhere was suspended only by a providence that embraced all the saints and could eventually make a saint of every sinner. That modern providence was the postwar industrial state. The New Deal, the business system, and the political network had value and marked progress only to the extent that they supported most people's same slow, steady progress and not just the rise of the few. This sensibility made people like my grandparents completely unable to support the social movements of the sixties, for they saw these as destructively individualistic. Economic and moral progress required *collective* progress, which meant everyone working in his or her small way toward moving the mean.

Were the New Economy to define the majority of investors as risk-taking entrepreneurs, it would have to overturn not only the New Deal tradition but "the spirit of capitalism" itself. For that capitalist spirit, ironically, was always, for the majority, collective.

The New Deal Dream for the Investor Economy

Conventional wisdom has routinely overstated the individualist spirit of capitalism and thus has misunderstood its current status. It has argued that New Deal culture declined with the stable "Fordist" economy of mass production and artificially low international competition. Now described as protectionist, inflexible, and unworkable, it is said to have been replaced by the intensities, global perspectives, and continuous change that reflect prosperity's dependence on greater risk taking. Prosperity, that is, doesn't require steady work and solid competence but requires breakthrough discoveries and leaping the chasm between current and coming products. The company man is now said to be as obsolete as the welfare state: competence and social provision aren't just expensive; they are said to be active impediments to the "creative destruction" on which economic leadership depends. This story of the New Economy sets up two simple requirements for the general public. Prosperity depends on unregulated individual performance and on a new willingness to take risks.[16] And yet, as I will show, we can find significant evidence that the motives of the popular or majority investor in the New Economy sought neither individual fortune nor the big returns of increased risk.

The investing environment, as distinct from investor psychology, has been restructured toward greater individual risk taking. For example, for a few decades after World War II, employees of large companies generally held their pensions and medical benefits, whose value was independent of the movement of the stock market. After the 1970s, these companies slowly but surely reduced their "exposure" to these obligations to their employees. "Defined benefit" plans, which paid the employee regardless of market performance, are increasingly replaced by "defined contribution" plans like the 401(k), in which the employee's payout depends on the market value of his or her ongoing savings. The uncertain stock market and new fears about retirement shortfalls have not slowed the trend toward asking the market, rather than the state, to furnish basic social provisions, and to do so by taking risks.[17] The increases throughout the 1990s in stock market participation direct us again to our question: has the New Economy really been led by a new spirit of popular risk taking?

In the years after 1996, I conducted a number of discussions with Silicon Valley employees about their investment strategies. One such contact, Tegan Bradford, majored in English in college and got her first job at the pioneering Web portal company Yahoo!. Yahoo! had been started about the time she had started college, and she was hired just after the company went public. She loved the work and her coworkers. She wrote to me now and then about everyday details of Silicon Valley work life, like the sudden appearance of Starbuck's coffee carts offering drinks to all employees on the company tab. She wrote about her VW Jetta, her first new car. "I'm getting used to the life," she reported. It sounds nice, I said, though I agreed with her that Peet's coffee is much better than Starbuck's. But the business you're all in is so risky, I said. Do you feel like you have a good future there? Do you worry about things like midcareer employment? Does Yahoo! have a pension plan?

One of Tegan's replies was particularly illuminating.

There are about ten of us who managed to graduate from college without any debt (albeit largely thanks to our parents). So we can do things like put the full 17% into a 401(k) and 15% into stock purchase plans each month. Each month I invest over $500 into some sort of company sponsored plan that in turn all rides on the stock market. And since I'm so young [twenty-seven], and retirement is so far off, I picked highly aggressive stocks figuring I have some time to ride out the highs and lows. So there's this group of us that constantly gets together and debates about interest rates, the state of the Asian markets and the future of tech stocks. [Alan] Greenspan's name gets mentioned so often you'd think he was one of our friends or neighbors. We all meet with our individual financial planners every three months and have in-depth personal portfolios listed on our "My Yahoo! Finance" pages so we can track our investments as they update every 20 minutes. We're like a bunch of ultraliberal Alex P. Keatons running around.

I know that there's something sick and very poignant about this group in my generation that craves such total financial stability. (Oh will we ever stop blaming our parents for our chaotic childhoods?) But it makes me worry that in fifteen years we'll have another frivolous eighties, or even worse, another fifties. For working in such a fly-by-night industry it's amazing how most people here would pick *stability* over a date with Brad Pitt or Cindy Crawford.

Tegan was more explicit than most, but I found few high-tech employees who claim to trust the market with their security. When I next saw Tegan, I asked her: Why didn't you all go into health care, or soft drinks? Why don't you all talk about asking Yahoo! for a better pension plan? Tegan found this amusing.

We don't think of 401(k)s as stable. We just feel like we're young enough that we can be a little more daring. We're starting young enough that we have some time for the money to add up.

No, Yahoo! has no regular pension plan, but remember that the average age here is around twenty-seven. Actually I personally think the reason's a bit more cynical than that. Most of the v Ps that are here have been part of a couple of start-ups and have seen them go from nothing to hugely successful to bankrupt in a couple of years. You go through this a couple times, and you realize that a pension plan in this industry is a little useless. Who knows if we'll even be around long enough for anyone to qualify!

Tegan isn't seeking risk. She's seeking to manage risk in order to preserve her security. She has no interest in defined-benefit pensions not because they might dampen entrepreneurship and so on but because they're *more* risky than 401(k)s in her industry. They are more risky, that is, when created by new companies in a volatile sector that may be gone before she turns thirty, much less sixty-five.[18] In the late 1990s, defined-contribution pensions that depended on generally upward market trends seemed more secure than standard pensions.

If Tegan is representative, we should seriously consider the possibility that many high-tech workers are seeking a classic "old economy" goal without old-economy methods. They're trying to stay with an improving mean rather than trying to *beat* the mean. They stay up on the market, and no one wants to be left behind. But they aren't focused on beating the market. This strategy produced very good returns in the late 1990s, when the market averages rose over 20 percent a year for several years in a row. More importantly, it allowed the preservation of a preexisting old-economy culture of rising *with* a collective mean rather than looking for individually superior returns. It has not been politically or intellectually possible to accept or praise this as a New Deal or Fordist or old-economy desire, but this desire seems to have remained in place.

The major change has not been a shift in desire from security to risk to match the alleged shift from a managed to an entrepreneurial economy. The change has been from collective to individual responsibility for the management of risk. This change has not been voluntary but has been implemented by the financial sector along with many of the country's largest corporations. As a result, employees like Tegan don't talk as though they can rely on the institutions—Social Security or the company with a pension plan—that would guarantee a future payout by spreading risk over a large group. She's managing risk but having to do so on her own. At the same time, the rising stock market mean supported the older sensibility of the collective management of risk.

Majority investor thinking also appears in their strategies of risk management. Like most investors, Tegan avoids stock picking and market timing, those two traditional modes of supposedly beating the mean by using skill.[19] Her risk management rests on a combination of two factors. She takes a long-term investment view, and she hopes that the long-term means an upward trend. Tegan manages her risk by anticipating that the future will bring steady, differential inflation, where equity prices generally rise faster than the price of everyday goods. The postwar economy consciously built mean-shifting institutions. New Economy investors make the same assumption about a different institution, assuming that the market, over the long haul, will consistently and positively shift the mean.

If younger investors preserved New Deal goals in New Economy times, it's not surprising that older investors took a similar view. During a PBS broadcast, "Betting on the Market" (January 14, 1996), the financial journalist Joseph Nocera noted that rising stock prices have often come at the expense of big chunks of the company payroll. He then observed one particularly interesting irony.

Sometimes, the employee a company fires is also a shareholder who makes money when the price goes up. Consider, for instance, Mary Jane Range. A vice president at Citibank, she was laid off as part of a restructuring [in 1994].

"It was going to be the place I retired from [says Mary Jane Range.] It was a company I had targeted and wanted to belong to for a very long time."

Mary Jane, who's divorced and single, has all her savings in the stock market. And her biggest holding is in the corporation that cast her out, Citicorp. "How do you feel about holding stock in this company that has laid you off?" [Nocera asks].

"I never made the connection. I never made the connection that this is stock in a company that just took away my ability to earn a living."

After the downsizing at Citibank, the company's stock, which had hit an all-time low, rebounded.

"The stock had gone as low as just slightly below twelve."

"Twelve dollars a share?" [Nocera asks].

"Twelve dollars a share."

"And now where is it?"

"Eighty-nine" [Range says, smiling]. . . .

Today, [Range] is her own boss, a partner at an executive search firm, matching up candidates, often people who've been downsized, with potential employers.

"In what I do now I am totally reliant on myself. I don't have a pension. I can't even conceive, today, of being in a position where you have total job security."

"What do people have to do?" [Nocera asks].

"They have to take care of themselves. No one will take care of you any longer in this country, in terms of long-term job security, withering pensions."

"And where does the market fit into that scheme?"

"The market is an enabler [Range replies]. It is a way for people to increase their accumulated wealth and to take care of their future."[20]

The market rests on a culture of beliefs and expectations that include ideas about the value of massive layoffs. The latter therefore improve short-term revenues and boost stock prices. With this in mind, Citibank managers decided to improve the company's share price in part by eliminating thousands of jobs, including Range's. The market gets the credit for presumably forcing the decision. Even after she "makes the connection," Range hangs on to her belief in the market's benevolent effects.

Range is on one level a classic representative of investor ideology: the capital markets are her ally even after—or because—they've confiscated her job. But the ideology works only because the stock market can mime the combination of corporate pensions and social security. The market attracts Range as the institution that moves the mean, allowing her to overcome the original odds (along with most other people). During the golden age of the postwar economy, big business and big government clashed and collaborated to move the income mean. The New Economy has turned this job over to equity markets.[21] They do the job in part by giving executives cause to terminate large numbers of workers. And yet they appear as benefactors—as long as they move the mean.

Another person on Nocera's 1996 show sums up the principle behind this. Dorothy is a secretary in her late fifties who is investing to secure her retirement. She only has a few more earning years left, she says, and doesn't want to have to live on Social Security. She is asked whether she thinks investing is risky. No, she replies, "If the stock market goes down, it will go back up again. It has to. The economy grows all the time. I'm very careful with my money. I would not even gamble with my money. I won't gamble." Stock picking isn't gambling only because of the upward price trend, which she thinks will go up indefinitely because the economy always grows.

This might sound like the thinking of a wishful, superstitious amateur—until you read the investment literature. It then rapidly dawns on you that Dorothy is offering an accurate—if simplified—version of "fundamental analysis" as defined by investment professionals. Fundamental analysis assumes that a company's stock price reflects something like the company's underlying value at a given time. This value "is related to growth, dividend payout, interest rates, and risk. . . . By estimating such factors as growth for each company, the fundamentalist arrives at an estimate of a security's intrinsic value."[22] Most fundamentals analysts are "long termers": they advise "buying and holding" stocks through the ups and downs precisely because, as Dorothy says, the economy is always growing.

"Fundamentals" theory formed the leading pitch for popular capitalism in the 1980s, showing up everywhere from financial journals to the "Beardstown Ladies" investment primers. An especially influential version comes from Peter Lynch, the legendary director of Fidelity's Magellan fund, at the time one of the highest-yielding mutual funds long term in the industry's history.[23] There's no randomness or accidents or gambling or un-

manageable risk involved in market prices, says Lynch. Everyday fluctuations are tethered to underlying fundamentals. These always have and always will be destined to rise. The stock market, he says, is in the long run a high-yield version of a savings account. In this view, the market is guaranteed to move the mean, bringing virtually all prudent investors with it, making *socially* shifted means unnecessary. Financial services have sustained this argument even after the end of the boom.[24] The New Economy devised what looks like a New Deal system, and this is what brought Main Street into it.

Back to Work

If the New Economy was floated in part through the stock purchases of old-economy savers, what can we say about the future of popular investing? As we've seen, the main interpretation has read the tide of cash as a sign that the New Economy commanded general public consent for the broadband capitalist revolution heralded by enthusiasts—for the new levels of wealth generated by technology, for the superfluity of the regulatory state, for a new dawn of economic individualism. This interpretation, however, was largely a projection of financial professionals and others with direct stakes—and with enormous media assistance—onto the small investors whose savings were in their hands.

I have argued that the psychological and cultural motives of the majority or "ordinary" investor have been different. Her goals were continuous with the past—a New Deal personal security in an era of heightened risk and vulnerability, a security gained through collective enterprise rather than individual genius. Her interest in finance, hardly voluntary, has rested neither on a desire for the continuous accumulation of personal capital nor on a new risk-taking spirit. It has rested on a continuing, understandable aversion to risk, one presumably addressed through associations, groups, and pools carrying comforting, George Bailey–ish names like "mutual fund." The market's popularity hinged on its ability to simulate social security. Investing grew by appealing to exactly those desires that used to be satisfied by *avoiding* investing.

My account here is not meant to slight change or technology or to favor working-class financial conservatism at the expense of innovation. I am suggesting, however, that the choice between change and security, a choice that has long driven U.S. culture and economic policy, is a false one. Innovation does not in fact require the dismantling of social protections; this process merely saves business some money in the short run. Given the economic accomplishments of the period from 1945 to 1975, one could make the opposite circumstantial case: a more equitable economy is a more dynamic economy; justice enables creativity; economies do better when their primary goal is to move the overall mean rather than to help well-placed individuals beat it with ingenuity. Though the vast majority advances only when the mean moves, American capitalism rarely credits the majority with the ability to move it.

The working public was drawn to stocks by a fear of being left behind, of being suckered by capitalism as it had been in earlier periods, this time by missing out on the market rather than by jumping in. The public was attracted by arguments that stock investing is not a way of gambling with one's future but a way of calculating that future and bringing it into being. The stock market, in this vision, would serve future needs rather than speculative desire. Much of this working public, however, overlooked the gulf between their hopes for markets and the way markets actually work. They will not be able to serve their own hopes again until they recognize that their pursuit of investment income was the inaccurate expression of their own labor practices of duration and collaboration and basic forms of self-determination. Were these practices to return to political power, it would mean, for the majority, not beating the odds by devoting one's life to the pursuit of wealth, but rising as everyone rises, while sometimes skipping work to go to the track.

Notes

1   Ferguson, *High Stakes, No Prisoners*, 22. Among the dozens of New Economy eyewitness books, Ferguson's stands out for its lucidity and honesty about the actual goals and means of start-up company success.

2   I will capitalize the term "New Economy" to signal my view that it is more a concept and an ideology than a truly distinct period in economic history. The New Economy is most commonly associated with rapid changes in information technology and with the Internet. Fundamental economic features include the continuously increasing prominence of the financial sector and an apparent increase, between 1995 and 1999, in the rate of growth of productivity. For representative press accounts of the New Economy as a lasting productivity revolution, see Steve Liesman, "Productivity Gains Extend beyond Technology Area," *Wall Street Journal*, January 8, 2001, A3; Steve Liesman, "Productivity Growth May Be Here to Stay," *Wall Street Journal*, January 7, 2002, A1; David Wessel, "The Calm at the Center of a Roiling Economy," *Wall Street Journal*, February 14, 2002, A1; and Tom Redburn, "The Bubble Has Burst, but Strengths Remain," *New York Times*, September 22, 2002, sec. 3, p. 4. Two pillars of these discussions are that productivity nearly doubled from its 1970–1990 rate of 1.4 percent average annual growth to about a 2.7 percent average after

1995, followed by a minor subsidence to the low to middle 2 percent range; and that the New Economy era was confirmed in 1996 when Federal Reserve Bank chairman Alan Greenspan's belief that information technology had created higher noninflationary growth kept him from cooling the economy (and stock markets) by raising interest rates and increasing margin requirements for stock purchases. For a skeptical view, one held throughout the boom, see Madrick, "How New Is the New Economy?"

3 The Federal Reserve reports that the hotter the boom, the faster the increase in inequality. For example, "the median accumulated wealth for families at the top was about 12 times that of lower-middle-income families through much of the 1990s. But in 2001, the median net worth of the top earners was about 22 times as great." Edmund L. Andrews, "Economic Inequality Grew in 90's Boom, Fed Reports," *New York Times*, January 23, 2003, C1.

4 See, for example, Mitchel Benson, Chip Cummins, and Jathon Sapsford, "Trade Disclosures Shake Faith in Troubled Energy Markets," *Wall Street Journal*, May 13, 2002, B1. These trades resembled the "land flips" by which savings and loans in the 1980s recorded profits by selling land at inflated prices to entities controlled by back-channel partners. Each such sale increased the "market value" of the asset.

5 Bernstein, *Against the Gods*, 140. This belief appears in a great deal of strategic business planning, especially when it goes wrong. As one small example, Gerald M. Levin, the former CEO of Time Warner, defended the disappointing merger with America Online in part by remarking that "every human creative endeavor is subject to mathematical law. So you're not always going to be right all the time." David D. Kirkpatrick, "Former Chief of Time Warner Defends Sale to America Online," *New York Times*, September 24, 2002, C10.

6 Bernstein, *Against the Gods*, 14.

7 Gambler psychology is outside the scope of this essay. For an excellent insider treatment of this issue, see Barthelme and Barthelme, *Double Down*. For reasons that will become clearer hereafter, the book might have used other titles circulating in the Barthelme family—*The Dead Father* (Donald) or *The Brothers* (Frederick).

8 Weber, *The Protestant Ethic and the Spirit of Capitalism*, 53.

9 Ibid., 76.

10 Galbraith, *The New Industrial State*, 64–65.

11 Sampson, *Company Man*, 308.

12 Bercovitch, *The Puritan Origins of the American Self*, 43.

13 Ibid., 46.

14 Ibid., 48.

15 For a short version of nineteenth-century "free labor" theory, though partially idealized, see Lasch, *The Revolt of the Elites and the Betrayal of Democracy*, chapter 3. Lasch notes that many nineteenth-century "workingman" thinkers favored "the democratization of competence" to "social mobility," but also observes that this preference did not prevail. "The most important choice a democratic

society has to make [is] whether to raise the general level of competence, energy, and devotion — 'virtue,' as it was called in an older political tradition — or merely to promote a broader recruitment of elites. Our society has clearly chosen the second course" (79).

16 This view is too commonplace to associate with any particular author or ideological standpoint. An early popular version was Arthur Toffler, *Future Shock*; two much-discussed and politically different (though often convergent) developments of that perspective were David Harvey, *The Condition of Post Modernity*, and Robert B. Reich, *The Work of Nations*; and a high-quality exploration of "post-Fordist" capitalism, flexible accumulation, et cetera, from a pragmatic management perspective is Geoffrey A. Moore, *Living on the Fault Line*.

17 On fears of a shortfall, see, for example, Louis Uchitelle, "Do You Plan to Retire? Think Again," *New York Times*, March 31, 2002, sec. 4, p. 1. A similar warning to baby-boomers about their grossly underfunded retirement accounts claims that only one in eight workers as of 2001 had a pension program with a defined benefit (Ben Stein, "How to Avoid Living like a Poor Student at Age 70," *New York Times*, November 7, 2004, sec. 3, p. 3). This element of New Deal collective well-being has declined so rapidly that even worried writers like Stein can recommend only greater individual effort: if you haven't been able to save enough, you should now start to save enough.

18 Tegan's premonitions about Yahoo! may have been correct. The company continued to struggle, and in 2001 Tegan accepted a large severance buyout and resigned.

19 Most professionals continue to advise ordinary investors to avoid games of skill. Sometimes they do this for theoretical reasons: for example, the efficient market hypothesis holds that the high-quality information you call your skill has already been factored in by the market to produce the stock's value. Sometimes they advise this for the practical reason that the greater skill lies with professionals. The *Wall Street Journal* columnist Jonathan Clements asks, "Can investors find stocks that are 'demonstrably undervalued?' " Every day, the market is picked over by top-notch analysts and money managers, all looking for cheap stocks. If there are any bargains to be had, they don't stay that way for long. "There are very few $20 bills lying on the sidewalk," one analyst quips ("Value or Growth? Don't Play Favorites," *Wall Street Journal*, March 27, 2001, p. C1).

20 Nocera, "Betting on the Market."

21 Wage growth improved between 1996 and 1999, reaching its peak in 1998 with a 2.4 percent increase adjusted for (very low) inflation. Richard W. Stevenson, "Wage Growth Fails to Meet Expectations," *New York Times*, April 30, 1999, C1. Wage increases for the vast majority of the population were overshadowed by the increase in stock values, which in some years outstripped the wage increases of hourly workers by a factor of ten.

22 Malkiel, *A Random Walk Down Wall Street*, 117.

23 Lynch and Rothchild, *Learn to Earn*, 158. See also Warren Buffett and Buffett-

ology, the most famous, prestigious version of fundamentals investing around today: Hagstrom, *The Warren Buffett Way*; Lowenstein, *Buffett*; Buffett and Clark, *Buffettology*; and many more.

24   One typical sample: "Despite market gyrations, the fact remains that the sooner you invest and begin to accumulate compounded earnings, the easier it should be to meet your long-term investment objectives. Remember, for every five years you wait, you may have to double your monthly investment to achieve the same goals. The Schwab Center for Investment Research has found that investing a fixed amount at regular intervals—also known as dollar-cost averaging—can help you avoid the pitfalls of trying to time the stock market" (*Schwab Investor* 6, no. 3 (2nd quarter 2002): 1. This is a newsletter for Schwab customers and offers the ritual language of the stock market as a savings bank responding positively to regular deposits.

Why Rachel Isn't Buried at Her Grave:
Ghosts, UFOs, and a Place in the West

Susan Lepselter

This essay is about the leaps and boundaries of UFO discourses, uncanny conspiracy theories, ghost stories, and tales of everyday life. It's also about a place in the rural West, and the self-imaginings that grow there amid larger narratives of America. These larger narratives—of class, loss, and colonization, and of the body's unmoored location in a world of accelerated technological change—are often partially told or left unspoken. Most of all, then, this is an essay about how historical trauma can lodge itself in the bright, broken bits of stories about fantastic things.

It begins here with Area 51, the notorious center of uncanny American conspiracy theory. You've probably heard of Area 51 and its restricted airspace known as Dreamland. Part of the vast complex of the Nevada Test Site and Nellis Air Force Base, Area 51 is the high-technology military base whose existence was meant to be a federal secret, and which, people say, has *something to do with* UFOs. The birthplace of clandestinely developed craft like the U-2 and the Stealth bomber, Area 51 sits in the multiply texted, sparsely populated land of the central Nevada desert—a place where for hundreds of miles there's nothing much else but federally owned ranch land dotted with Joshua trees, the rusted scatter of old mines, and the skeletons of forgotten homesteads. Through this barren terrain you can see a field of meanings emerge. Here the futuristic imaginings of UFO narratives blend with ghost stories, haunting with the still-open wounds of history.

This Is Real

The stories I tell in this essay arise at the interface between the loud secret of the base and the small local settlement closest to it: Rachel, Nevada, population about ninety.[1] Rachel became increasingly well known throughout the 1990s for its proximity to Area 51, and for the Little Ale'Le'Inn, a canny, UFO-themed cafe that sprang up there, bringing UFO pilgrims and tourists of bizarre Americana into the remote Tempiute Valley. In 1997, after years of listening to UFO abduction stories in Texas, I joined up with some friends visiting Las Vegas to make my preliminary trip to Rachel.[2]

North Las Vegas drops away abruptly into emptiness as you drive north into the Great Basin. Except for the small town of Alamo, there's nothing for 150 miles until you peak a crest in the high desert ranch land. Then there's Rachel, a sun-glint of trailer metal off to one side of the desolate state highway.[3] When we pulled into the parking lot of the Little Ale'Le'Inn, the mountains and the sky arranged themselves around the building and its homey yet unworldly hand-painted sign of an alien face ("Earthlings Welcome"). And when we stepped into the cafe, we were disoriented by the sudden buzzing sociability—we'd stumbled upon the annual UFO convention organized by Pat and Joe Travis, who own the place. An ad hoc country band played, with tunes belted out by a man known in Area 51 discourse circles as the author of a video polemic called *Secrets of Dreamland*— he was visiting Rachel from California—and the place jumped with UFO tourists and conspiracy theorists.[4] They milled about, talking intensely, buying Area 51 T-shirts, thumbing through stacks of libertarian literature, and ordering "alien burgers." A few locals, too, took in the scene from their barstools, dryly refusing to participate in the Area 51 show. But Pat Travis took a break from the kitchen to tell us about an otherworldly being who visited the cafe; and the middle-aged waitress, Raylene,[5] talked about all the *strange lights* she'd seen—she'd lived out here next to Area 51 for years. Her father, and then her husband, had worked the mines, I later learned; now her husband was mostly laid up in his bed, his body broken by his years underground. That afternoon, when I asked her how people in Rachel made a living after the local mine had closed a decade before, she grinned, looked pointedly at the tourists paying for UFO souvenirs, and said, "Honey, by our wits."

What was this symbiosis of the uncanny and the banal? When I returned home to New York, I called Pat Travis to ask if I could waitress for a few weeks at the Little Ale'Le'Inn, to write about the stories I heard. Someone had just quit, and Pat agreed that in lieu of waitress wages I could stay with her and Joe, in their mobile home next to the cafe.[6]

A more ominous and ubiquitous figure of Area 51 had emerged during my previous ethnographic work with the UFO Experiencers' Support Group and the Mutual UFO Network in Austin, Texas. People gathered at these groups to tell fantastic things. Here I'd heard that Area 51 is where *the powers that be* kept a secret UFO. Aliens lived in rooms below the surface of the earth there, nourished by vats of blood. The government and the aliens were conspiring together. *They*—the government, the aliens, or both, just a dreadful and othering *they*—mutilated cattle and sheep in the desert there. They cut them right down the middle with a perfect edge and sucked the blood and organs clean out. Human bodies were found that way too, people said, with cuts so clean it had to be done by laser. *They said* Bob Lazar, the whistle-blower at Area 51, was lying or insane. Maybe he was, and *they* had used him so that now anyone who told the truth would seem nuts. *They* made his history vanish, erased his employment and education records; but maybe he was lying anyway . . .[7]

The aliens cloned humans and engineered drones. And *they* made a deal with the aliens. *They* said go ahead, abduct people, do experiments on them, take the peoples' organs, you can have a few for guinea pigs. You aliens can do what you want. Just teach us how your spacecraft works, show us *what you know*.

And so we were given technology.

In the UFO Experiencers' Group, Area 51 was just one trope in a jumble of echoing returns. The figure of the secret base came and went with a range of UFO and conspiracy theories, ghostly stories, and uncanny personal narratives. People recalled *strange things*, dreamlike memories that resonated with terrible rumors they'd heard.

— I saw an evil alien in my room with a face like a demon.
— One of them suffocated me with a big black cloud on my chest.
— I was led somewhere in a fog; and they put something inside of me and then they stole the baby from my womb. Now she comes sometimes and looks in my window, and she is pale and white—she's a hybrid, half human and half like *them*.

People theorized about what it all might mean:

— We're being prepared. I was shown a nuclear war; it's going to happen any day. I saw the earth in a ruin.
— We're being colonized. You know when the Spanish came to Mexico the Indians didn't know what was going on either.
— We are supplying the aliens with our sperm and eggs, handing over our souls and emotion. Their own are gone. They're returning from the future, to get back what they lost.
— They're doing experiments on our bodies, just for the hell of it. Like we do on test rats in a lab.
Others said:

— There are no UFOs. UFOs are their disinformation—propaganda, government mind-control, so we won't know what they *really* do. Soon the government will stage a huge extraterrestrial invasion with holograms. The people will give them complete and utter power, and in the chaos, we will be enslaved.

One hears other stories, circulating in other spheres, and feels the uncanny chill of repetition. A strange lawsuit was widely reported in the mainstream media. Workers at Area 51, whose existence was denied by the federal government, had fallen ill; two had died, perhaps from exposure to unknown industrial toxins. The workers had been instructed to burn waste in huge open-air pits on the grounds of the secret base. Because of the association with Area 51, reports of the case carried a faint accent of unnatural horror. I imagined the fires raging in the pits and spitting out fumes. You could picture it: nothing else around, just empty desert space filling with smoke, the ragged mountains going orange, and the glowing Joshua trees. The poison smoke choked the workers for years as they stood over the pits. They worried: Why won't they give us protective masks?

Maybe the stuff was invisible paint for the Stealth bomber, the workers thought—invisible paint with graphic effects. But of course they didn't really know *what* it was. They were low-level sheet metal workers at an ultra-high-security base in the middle of nowhere. They weren't allowed to tell anyone where they worked. They didn't know what they were doing in there—they just knew they were sick. The monstrous concealment of what had hurt them seemed to seep into descriptions of their failing bodies. Their skin turned into "fish scales" and turned the bedsheets red. Their biopsied tissues showed toxins "rarely found in humans," as one newspaper put it.[8] Now ill workers and widows, some of them anonymous, had instigated a lawsuit against the EPA and the Department of Defense, not for money but for information. They wanted to know what poisons from the source of power had infiltrated the boundaries of their skin. They had found a high-profile lawyer to represent them, a professor at Georgetown University. The suit was twice thrown out; it was ruled that classified military information would be endangered by a trial.[9]

When I first went to Rachel, people said not to talk about it.[10] Mary looked down and chopped onions in the cafe kitchen and said, *The military is just doing its job.* People said, *You can't ask who works there. Ten years in prison if they even tell where they work.* One meandering afternoon with a couple of Rachel people, we saw the workers' bus returning from the direction of the secret base. We were driving the dirt roads that cut close to the border of forbidden land, to watch fighter planes zoom in formation through the air. Before the bus itself became visible in the distance, we watched its trailing dust cloud. *Here they come, here they come.* Then the bus jolted past us. Its windows were made of darkened glass, and yet behind the panes, faint outlines of the workers' heads suddenly ducked down when they saw us — darkened glass wasn't enough concealment.

I called the lawyer from the town's only pay phone at the shed near the cafe. In rushed tones, he said:

— UFO stories are a distraction. This is *real*; a real case.
— Yes, it's real, the most important thing. But then you hear that the government is experimenting on people up there, hiding secret information, using people as guinea pigs . . . There's just such similar imagery. Maybe there is some relation.
— There's no relation. Those UFO stories are — who knows what. This is an issue for the EPA, an issue of [President] Clinton's misuse of an executive order to hide environmental crimes.

What is the relation between narrative levels here, between stories of UFOs and other, more realist secrets, between genres marked so clearly as the fabulous and the real? You might say that real traumas, when repressed, generate fantasies — UFO stories. But I envision a subtler kind of mimesis, one in which material and fantastic terrors cogenerate, each rising out of a shared imaginative and social field. As Freud famously wrote, uncanny stories come forth in the shadow of a *something* that is hidden.[11] They emerge distorted and disturbed, leaking through the cracks in an edifice too big and too close to see.

In Rachel, government radiation monitors click discreetly behind old-fashioned, free-standing gas pumps decorated with paintings of UFOs. Warplanes zoom overhead, every so often giving a sonic boom that can crack the foundations of mobile homes. Single men move out here, leaving behind some other life. They use Radio Shack equipment to eavesdrop on the staticky commands of military pilots; they drink and chattily theorize in the bar, feeling at home in the middle of nowhere. Young people doing the American road trip pass through Rachel with *The X-Files* on their mind; retired folks in their RVs stop on their way to the UFO center of Roswell, New Mexico, or to view petroglyphs as evidence of alien visits to ancient Native Americans; and bleached western drifters spend a few days hanging out, drinking, telling travelers' tales and sightings of strange things. A mother and two adolescent daughters up from Vegas ran in one day, breathless and high colored, hair flying, planning to sleep out in the desert all night to search for UFOs — *I want to get abducted, I want to get abducted,* cried the twelve-year-old girl, *Oh, I want a scar.* On a lark or on a pilgrimage, tourists come here from all over the world to drive the dirt road through desert ranch land and witness the signs at the perimeter of the secret base: No Trespassing, No Photography, Deadly Force Authorized. At night they gather to watch the eerie lights that stream and flicker through the black desert sky. Who knows if they are UFOs, or fantastic secret military aircraft? It didn't much matter to many of the watchers I met. The lights were mysterious and uncanny, whatever their origin; they were material emanations of unseen powers—fleeting illuminations that acknowledged, though never revealed, an enormous secret in the dark.

Something Isn't Right

As the master narrative of the glorious pioneer past grows stale and crumbles on the allegorical landscape of the American West, the UFO story seems to rush in to take its place. It too soon becomes familiar, with its recycling tropes of conspiracy, the hugeness of power, and the rush of a future felt to be coming too fast. But you might notice how all these tropes are suffused with another theme: the tension between memory, repression, and return. And in uncanny images of displacement, you can hear a grounding in losses that have no single definite object but are shot through, always, with the inchoate injuries of class, and power, and change.

Joe Travis used to be a carpenter; Pat Travis was a short-order cook. They moved out here to the high desert because they wanted to start over, to get out into the real West, where Joe says you could be a pioneer and make a life of your own. But in 1988, when Joe's hands *went bad* and he could no longer work at his trade, the couple took a risk and bought what was then called the Rachel Bar and Grill, a ramshackle desert cafe that had gone under five times over the years. The rumors of the Area 51 UFO began a year later, and so they changed the cafe's name to the Little Ale'Le'Inn. Along with the emblems of their die-hard independent rural western sensibilities—posters admonishing the coming of the New World Order, bumper stickers that say "Freedom's Precious Metals—Gold, Silver and Lead" (lead as in bullets), and "Thank you for holding your breath while I smoke"—they had a sign painted with the face of a huge-eyed alien turned out to the lonely highway. They decorated the walls with photographic evidence of UFOs and called the menu's special "alien burgers." In 1996, Pat Travis was given an award by the state for bringing tourism into poor, rural Lincoln County, which had previously relied on halfhearted promotion of its old-timey, pioneer past.[12]

Pat says her husband Joe is a kind of preacher at the bar. Long ago, Joe's father *was* a preacher back in Kentucky, before moving the whole family

from the hard land where his farm wouldn't take, to work the cold factories of Detroit—a move made by many poor Kentuckians and one Joe,
who was ten at the time, says he never got over.[13] Hard for him to believe,
he says, that a poor boy like me now owns this cafe and has been on TV.
One afternoon I sit beside him on a barstool in the near-empty cafe while
he drinks his Old Milwaukee and strokes his bushy gray beard. He's already done his work for this morning, using his carpentry tools in the shed
out back to make items to sell in the gift shop: he's wired a lamp with an
alien-head base, poured the little plaster spacemen into molds before glu-
ing them to magnets. Now he's preaching *the way things are* in the cadences
of revelation, as he says:

> The powers that be
> are every day striving
> to destroy the Constitution . . .
> And they will.
> And they *have* done it.
> When I see 'em coming up that road I'm ready.
> I'll go out there and meet 'em on that road.
> I keep this gun right here on the bar.
> I'll meet 'em in their tanks.
> They're coming to take our guns,
> to make us their slaves.
> They've already built the concentration camps.
> Well, I'd rather die on my feet
> than live on my knees.
> They are into the occult.
> On the back side of the one-dollar bill
> on the left-hand side—see here darlin',
> there's a circle and a pyramid,
> the pyramid of Giza,
> the all-seeing eye of Lucifer
> or Satan
> or whoever you would like to put in that position.
> When this *pyramid* is in place,
> then the New World Order
> or Satan
> will be in charge.
> You know symbolism is everywhere in our daily lives.
> From what I've learned
> and what I understand

this evil is set about to take over the world.
I have to believe,
I have to pray to God,
that they won't succeed this time.
Cause the tyrannical people that are in charge,
well, if they in fact do usher in
this New World Order,
the people have never known slavery
such as they will suffer
under the hands of these people.
That's my firm belief.
The people of this country have no idea,
in my opinion,
what's coming.

How can I understand this talk, in light of Joe's sanity, his decency and kindness? What, I might begin by asking with him, is coming here? Or perhaps I should ask not only what's coming but what's already been here, naturalized and partly forgotten.

What ghost voices should I hear in Joe's conspiracy story, and in those circulating around him amid the souvenirs at the Little Ale'Le'Inn? What should we notice in testimonies of invasions — extraterrestrial and otherwise — into the tender boundaries of bodies and minds and planets? Why is the fabulous prophecy of a white man from Kentucky a montage of these specific tropes, in which the Satan of boyhood sermons is infused with still-restless images of slavery and concentration camps, coarticulating signs of some unnamed power watching the little man through the all-seeing eye of the dollar?

If you wanted to tease apart the elements of these stories, you might retell endless western histories that are here combined, condensed, and transformed.[14] You could write, in these mutations, the fragments of other half-forgotten narratives — real stories of slavery, or the uncannily parallel histories of twentieth-century experiments on human minds and bodies: by the CIA, or by the Nazis' Dr. Mengele, or by the doctors at Tuskeegee, or by the recently unearthed records of the federal government testing out the effects of radiation on hospital patients.[15] Or you could retell the half-glimpsed stories of countless colonialist invasions and ruin, stories of the Native Americans in this very place.

Meaning here emerges, too, in the sound and feel of Joe's talk. And so you might look at repetition.[16] The images themselves are meaningless. It's when they are repeated, suddenly cast into parallel relation, that their connection grows charged with the intimation of hidden significance, the uncanny's sense of "secret meaning."[17] Then something inchoate begins to emerge: an intuition of some vast structure—a structure that perhaps does not exist a priori but is nonetheless produced in Joe's act of interpretation. Resemblances begin to spin like rhymes into a sense of a logic. It is a logic that is imagined as somehow, somewhere, a web of entirety, composed of tantalizing likenesses. As Joe puts it:

> Well they worship the *owl*,
> because the owl can see in the *dark*,
> so therefore he's very wise . . .
> You know when you talk about college graduates,
> they become alumni;
> *illuminated*.
> This all ties together,
> and it's, it's
> it's amazing . . .

What is in fact a *poetic* production of resemblance emerges here. It involves not just the pleasure of form but, even more seductively and urgently, the uncanny's sense of intensified significance, and the *agency* felt to be restlessly lodged in the structure.[18]

Fantastic narratives and conspiracy theories offer no final, singular "real" meaning to be excavated like a mystery novel, in which a clue indexes a single referent to be finalized and solved.[19] Instead of a single hidden sign, you might instead notice the fallout of many social memories mixed with random, everyday disenchantments, accumulating in unpredictable forms.

You might see the uncanny in Joe's feeling for what Michael Taussig calls the magic of the state,[20] and in the amorphous social discontent that refuses class consciousness. You might see it in Joe's identification with master tropes of freedom and individuality and ownership and nationalism from well inside an intersubjective sense of being generally just *screwed over*. When a man first came into the bar testifying the New World Order and the devious plot of all the powers that be, Joe says, it stopped him dead in his tracks. All his life he just *knew* that *something wasn't right*.

Sometimes, instead of a rationally developed politics, what develops is a structure of feeling—one suffused with desire and a class-inflected sense of vanishing potential.[21] It is not, here, a cleareyed reader who brings a troubled political unconscious to the surface, not a counterhegemony in a rational argument, but a mimetic heightening and extremity from inside its own disturbance, which shocks the naturalized *hidden* partly into view.

And part of what comes into view is the simultaneous terror of, and hunger for, just being whisked away.

An Abduction

Lee worked for a while in the Little Ale'Le'Inn's gift shop, a corner of the cafe lined with shelves of souvenirs. Lee was in her fifties; thin as a rail, she always wore big dark glasses, an oversize T-shirt, and a visored cap marked with a UFO logo. While living in eastern California, she said, she'd read about Rachel, Nevada, in a *Weekly World News* article—it said that aliens regularly came into the town to hang out at the Little Ale'Le'Inn. After seeing that article, Lee said she knew she had to move to Rachel, because since she was a little girl she'd *just known* that she was not from this earth. She always *just knew* that her parents were not her parents; the world looked strange through her eyes. When *all this* UFO *stuff* really started up in the late eighties, she said, she realized she was *one of those hybrids* she had heard about: half alien, half human. At last she understood that's why this place, earth, wasn't hers.[22]

And she came to *just know* that her real father was an alien, and he was being held prisoner at Area 51, hostage to the powers that be. All Lee wanted was to be near him. That's why she moved to Rachel, she said, to gaze out at the forbidden desert and mountains where they were keeping her real alien father against his will, thwarting the father-daughter reunion that would finally make things feel right.

One windy September day we stand outside a local party in the town Quonset hut—it is a fundraiser to buy a defibrillator for Rachel. The mountains that ringed the base are turning copper colors in the sun, and Lee can hardly take her eyes off them. "There's my famous Area 51 mountains," she says, "that's where my father is, and that's where I want to be."

Then she tells me the story of her own abduction.

Lee says,

> — You know, I was taken up on a ship.
> — You were? I ask.
> — Yup. I wanted to go. I wanted to go with them and I didn't want to come back. But evidently, I'm back. I'm still here.
> — What happened? I ask her.

> Lee says,
> It was late one night.
> Wee early hours of the morning.
> I was asleep in bed.

I would hear this popping noise behind my left ear.
I would wake up but nothing was around.
And then there was a bluish white light . . .
and I got up and I went to my front room window,
which was a picture window.
I looked up
and there was this great big huge ship,
bigger than a house.
Bigger than a football field.
It was round and silver.
And I had my robe on,
and my pj's underneath.
And I went around my bookcase,
and opened the door
and went downstairs.
I was barefoot.
And I went over the little rock yard
onto the sidewalk and out onto the street.
And I looked up.
When I looked up, I did like this
[she raises her arms above her head].
And I wanted—
I says, *Take me.*
I want to go.
And as I went up I could feel it,
as I was going up.
I was in awe, I really liked it.
And as far as what they did to me, I don't know.
That was blocked out.
All I remember is I went up
underneath this great big huge round silver disc.
—Why didn't you want to come back? I ask her.
—Too much crap here on this planet, she says.
Too much cruelty to people.
People aren't kind to one another.
I mean, *these humans,*
they need to learn kindness,
to be kinder to people.
Not so violent, not so much killing.
Well I've lived on this earth,
on this planet

for almost fifty-four years.

And I don't like it.

I feel I'm caught in between, in other words.

I've been here too long.

I'd rather not be here.

I'd rather be with my own kind . . .

My planet is gone. That's why I'm here on earth.

It's totally destroyed.

—Is that gonna happen to earth? I ask.

—Probably eventually.

The way things are doing,

they're destroying everything . . .

there's not gonna be anything left for anybody.

She hugs the solid presence of her skinny frame in its huge T-shirt, her lined face and the startling sorrow of her eyes obscured as usual by dark glasses and the low bill of a UFO baseball cap. But as she remembers and tells the story, another self emerges, transformed by its desire for otherness. Suddenly she is a gothic figure: barefoot in a garden, streaming with light, reaching up for the vehicle of sublime departure from this place, Earth.

A few weeks later, Lee was leaving "this place"—Rachel—and drifting again. But for a while, she'd settled here. She had made Rachel her home. Someone passing through Rachel had sold her a little camper to live in. The lights didn't work, and sometimes it didn't start up, but inside she had everything she owned—knickknacks, a few clothes, meaningful photos taped to the walls, and dozens of jars of water drawn from the tap at the cafe, to survive on when things got bad. She had parked the camper on the far side of Rachel, closer to Don Day's Area 51 Research Center than to the cafe, and she would sit at night with Mike and Eddie, the father and son who painted the Travis's signs. She had adopted a puppy from the Travis's litter and kept it tied on a short rope to the front of the camper. The dog must have suffered in the heat all day, but it was there for Lee whenever she came back home.

And then it was discovered that Lee had collected a stash of gift shop merchandise and squirreled it away in her camper, hoarding it along with the water jugs. She was planning to pay for the things—T-shirts, mugs, and other trinkets—when she had the cash, just keeping them safe, she said, to make sure they were hers. But Pat Travis was a sharp businesswoman with her own haunting memories of poverty and a constant vigilance against being ripped off, and she didn't see it that way. And perhaps there were other incidents as well. In any case, soon after the conflict, Lee was fired from the gift shop.

A few days later, she asked me to take her to get her driver's license, though she'd been driving for decades without one, moving from place to place. And so I took her out to the military base town of Tonopah, the next town to the west, 110 miles away, and sat with her in the gleaming, chilly office. It was quiet, empty except for a woman in pink holding a toy poodle in a matching dog sweater. Lee hunched intensely over the driver's test, laboring on the questions of the law. I'd offered to help her study, but she said she'd read the manual and knew it all. She flunked so badly that the girls behind the desk looked at her with wide eyes and asked if she had the right booklet.

We don't have birth certificates like you humans do on earth, we don't have money, Lee had said about her own planet. For her, the drivers' license was like those things: a charged sign, a bureaucratic convention like money, emblems that got her into trouble when she tried to participate in the structures they indexed, confirming her marginality on earth.

On the long drive back to Rachel that day, we came upon the wild mustangs that run across federal land. They were grazing in the road and then running across the hills, their whole bodies alert to watch us. We pulled to the side of the road, got out, and shut the doors softly behind us. There were no cars coming down the empty miles; we stood and watched the horses. Then Lee began to run after them.

Alarmed, I followed her. The wild horses were dangerous. She was getting close to the stallion, and he wasn't running; he looked poised to kick. I took hold of her skinny arm, said we should stand back.

Back in the car she was sullen and silent. She was angry at me for stopping her from running away with those horses. She said she'd wanted to *just go.*

After a stretch of empty miles, Lee announced her decision to leave Rachel. She was going to take her camper and move on out to Tonopah, park somewhere in the desert near the DMV and go back every day to the clean, well-lighted office until she passed the test. Why not, she said, It's free. The test is free. And soon after, she was gone.

I looked for her camper in the desert when I made other trips to Tonopah, but I never saw Lee again.

You Can't Repair History

Sometimes the idea of the West itself becomes a metonym for the past—a past that can be fantastically infused into narratives of disaster and survival. Then the threat of ruin emanates from an uncontrolled technological future realm, and a hypernatural western past is the only chance of redemption. Carol lives by herself with her animals way up in the hills, on a pioneer compound she constructed from wood and wire. During my second visit in 1998, when the threatening hum of Y2K was in the air, she bought mules and leather harnesses and an old-timey covered wagon. Now, she said, when *the computers go nuts and the hordes* pour out from the cities, she'd be able to survive, the way folks did *back then*. That same fall, a married couple came through Rachel in pioneer clothes, a stern and laconic pair who were driving their own covered wagon across the deserts of the Southwest; fleeing modernity, they earned just enough to scrape by, parking on the side of the road and allowing themselves to be photographed.

One day a married couple from Fallon stopped in at Rachel and began to talk at the bar in bitter tones. The air force had dropped metallic chaff over everything on their property, and no one knows what it *does* to you; *We're their guinea pigs*, they said. But worse than the potential damage to their bodies, they said, sonic booms from the air force base near Fallon cracked their *foundation*.

It was a *place* that couldn't be re-placed. The government was *stealing our air space*. Here the sky itself becomes nostalgic as land, usurped and plundered by trespassers, by military booms messing up the clear western air with sonic "graffiti." But it should be yours, as everyone nodded sympathetically at the bar:

> —the way it used to be:
> —What your *air space* is, said the wife,
> is the very air you *breathe* is your air space.
> You know it's just like when you buy a piece of property
> it's yours to the *center of the earth*.
> It's yours to the infinite, is what it should be.
> That's the way it used to be . . .
> As long as they do no damage
> you wouldn't mind somebody
> walking across your property . . .
> but when they devalue your property . . .
> —Then they're trespassin'—interrupted the husband,
> —and constantly damaging your property, continued the wife,
> they come in and do GRAFFITI all over,
> then they're damaging your property . . .
> That's what they do us.
> They blow out our windows,

knock our trailers off foundations,
they crack our foundation on our building . . .
Some of it's irreparable.
It's an old building; an old historic building.
Over to the *stage stop*.
Some things you can never replace.
You can never repair.
You can't repair history.
Some things are not tangible money-wise.
You know.
Some of the *antiques*
and some of the old bottles and stuff like that they broke, they're
irreplaceable.
They could give ya a *monetary*,
they could say, well, you go to a *bottle shop*
and buy one like that for ten dollars.
But you'll never find another bottle like that.
So what is that bottle worth?
You know, it's not *that*.
It's part of our Nevada history.
It's part of our culture.
These things are not compensatable.
They say they compensate us.
For the *damage they done*.
But they don't.
They only partially compensate you.
They only replace the broken window;
or replace a part of a structure—
when you take old antique wood
and replace it with new wood
then what is the *value*?
And that—that's not reparable.
I don't think they can *fix* that.
—We don't really *want* to be *compensated*, said the husband.
We want to be left alone.
That's why we live out in the middle of *nowhere*.
Is for the peace and tranquillity.
The *knowledge* that we are free people,
out in the middle of nowhere.
—Are you native Nevadans? I asked.
—No, said the wife, we're actually California transplants.

> We own a little bar-cafe-minimart;
> see this picture,
> the pony express stopped here.

As the husband says, it's the *knowledge* of living "nowhere" that makes a texted meta-nowhere into the most intensely imagined *somewhere*. There's that: the history dreamed in California thirty years ago; the auratic objects—the old bottle, the empty space—bulging to contain that dream's "value." There is the magic of the living dead, as ordinary as the "western-looking" wooden walls of a minimart, but still extraordinary, charged with the master narrative of the frontier past.

And yet, inhabited so fully, attended to so closely, this same master narrative begins to loom bizarrely. Its own effects are heightened, intensified, through a concrete performance. Its own naturalizations begin to give way, like a photograph enlarged and reproduced until it starts to look surreal.

And there are contradictions here. The imaginary of power is complex. The air force that borders Rachel commands respect; it is a different character in a different story from that of the Government and the Powers That Be. Although he echoed the couple (*Yeah we are their guinea pigs, that is right*), Joe in fact loves the sonic booms around his parts. Several times a day they shock the stillness, then let silence rush back to fill the void. In Rachel, when one man made a complaint that the booms cracked his trailer, others in the town signed a petition in "rebuttal . . . [to] a disgruntled Rachel resident" and sent it to the air force: "Please don't mistake that boom for 'disturbance' . . . it's the sound of freedom." Because, too, there is always the excitement of a power that defines and incorporates its partial observers. And the uncanny allure of destruction.

Ghost Stories

Alongside the futuristic narrative of Area 51 runs Rachel's own ghostly origin story.[23] The mines in this valley boomed and busted from 1865 onward. The place would whisper down to ghost town when the mine closed, reincarnating when the mine would open again. When Union Carbide last closed the mine in 1988, half the population drifted away. But by that time, there was a town—a scattering of trailers including the Quik-Pik store and the cafe.[24]

The first white child born in the valley was Rachel Jones, in 1977, *delivered by her daddy*, people said, in their mobile home. And this was taken as a good sign—births don't happen in a dead ghost town. That's when they named the town so it stuck, calling it Rachel after the baby; but there was something wrong with her respiration, people say.

The girl's parents went west to Washington State to find work; word came back that Mount Saint Helens had dropped ash on her, and she died, what with her *bad lungs*; and she *wasn't more than three*. They probably buried her out there in Moses Lake, but the people back here put up a stone and dedicated a cemetery, and named it all *Rachel* for the dead girl. *There's a stone there to her with her picture on it*, people say; *but of course she's buried somewhere else*.

This is not a formal ghost story; it is told in the genres of history. Yet here already the uncanny seeps into the real. The trace "remembers" in the name, in the cemetery stone indexing the baby who grows larger as the lost object. The stone marks the presence of its object's absence, testifying the missing body, the corpse buried somewhere else.

Something here haunts. It's not the impression of a person known and missed through concrete intimate memories, but rather the lost possibility, the compression of the girl's narrative as it might have been, and how that lost, potential story figures itself toward meaning. Rachel's birth seemed momentarily to push back the edges of haunting. But the edges were already there — in the rusted clutter of old mines, in the land and water still remembering atomic tests, and in the traces of driven-out Native Americans whose exact fate local people do not know, but whose arrowheads they sometimes frame on their trailer walls.

And of course the boom didn't last. The girl died. The ghost town was returning, taking back land. The next revival was the UFO business, enterprising and canny, as Pat told the tourists stories of strange light beams, extraterrestrial customers who sat at a table from morning till night without ordering a thing, and the friendly ghost Archibald, who haunted her in the cafe. Only later, sitting in the dark and rubbing her feet after a long day of cafe work, did she tell me the story of Archibald in a litany of relationship tales. He was a boy, Archie. Her parents wouldn't let her marry him. This was forty years ago. She loved him. She wonders how her life would have been if they'd been allowed to just be.

Allowed to *just be* . . . For along with the seduction of uncanny secrets are more homely American ghost stories. How to see that the ghost, so often, haunts because it never existed in the first place? In the rural American West, fierce ideologies of independence and self-reliance collide with other, unspoken narratives — the inarticulate disappointments of experience, and the specter of your own other life that never took shape in the way, somehow, it should have. Then ordinary and fantastic stories can converge in the felt sense of some impenetrable source of abduction, some agent of theft, some plot by the powers that be.

What do you say about the inscrutable, capricious workings of power? How do you talk about some immobilizing force that you *just know* exists?

Fantastic conspiracy stretches always toward a totalizing (though never reached) final story, but the ghost stories of everyday life are always too varied, too ambivalent. Sometimes such stories are generated at the peripheries of power—from lost low-level jobs in high-tech industries, aborted careers in the military, abandoned hometowns, and the tiny, unspoken moments of the body's changing relation to the real and vanishing modes of production. Then the workings of a power that is too enormous to be seen except in glimpses become entangled with the ordinary failures of the very self that has grown inside its grooves. There is the miner where the mine has closed, the haymaker out of work *because they got a machine*, the short-order cook whose children were removed by the state, the widowers who drift through the West carrying photos in their wallets of some more real life.

There is the simultaneous pride and shame in the kind of manual work that seems to hold out against the rush of high-tech futures. John and Aggie, between road trips to sell souvenirs at UFO conventions throughout the country, live for months at a time behind the cafe in a school bus that John converted into a mobile home. In the bus they make, with great care, skill, and satisfaction, the alien T-shirts and Area 51 stickers and mugs that sell in the cafe gift shop. John can talk for hours about the government's bitter conspiracy to hide UFOs from the American people; but unless you pry, you don't hear about the more homely unmoorings, the downward mobility after eleven layoffs from engineering jobs at a high-tech manufacturer of warplanes. *Life on the road is great. We love our freedom*, they say . . . Yet at the same time, *We had a three-bedroom house*, his wife says, *we were middle-class people, we had everything . . .*

The texture of life is shaped through embodied hopes and disillusionments, and their play against inexplicable turns of event. When these everyday stories bear resemblance to fabulous conspiracies by otherworldly power against the human body, then each gives weight to the other. Eddie can't work because, he says, *I bleed, it just pours out, it's unreal, the doctors never saw anything like it*, the result of his exposure to Agent Orange in the Vietnam War. And: *They won't pay him what they owe him after his back just snapped in that mine*, says Raylene, married to a patriotic and dignified miner, who can only get out of bed every few weeks. *Well no, wouldn't surprise me if they're doing experiments on people up there, I know what they're capable of*, Raylene says in answer to my questions, shrugging, nodding her head toward Area 51. But this fantastic character called *they* is not the same character as the everyday military in a coexisting narrative of support for our boys doing their job right over there in the air force, and pride in the warplanes over Rachel. This uncanny *they* is not what Raylene thinks about most days in the normal course of illness and gossip:

> —I can hardly stand up anymore with these diabetes,
> and Art hates to see me have to work;
> but we don't have any money
> and they won't pay him for his back,
> they told him to find a job
> where he didn't have to stand, sit, walk or crawl.
> Well I wrote back to 'em:
> I don't know too many male whores.

If the rural West is the space of potential salvation, it's also the place of a kind of restless melancholy. Here are the familiar, lived frustrations of a place where *there's nothing to do*. The few young people drive fast through the desert at night, to shoot at jack rabbits that spring in front of your headlights. They follow back roads and dry creek beds that no one else knows, to tend hidden glorious pot crops, to fall in love and dramatically break apart, or else, sometimes, to chase unnatural lights with strange right-angle turns, the other life that always blinks from the direction of the base.

And one night in August 1998, Johnny, the twenty-seven-year-old grandson of an old Rachel homesteader, and Kim, Johnny's new bride, drank till the bar closed and then drove fast through the midnight desert, Kim in the driver's seat, Johnny in the pickup's bed, standing up to feel the speed and wind, till he fell out, hit his head, and died on the dirt road. Nothing dulls the horror and meaninglessness of young death. And yet—*Now wouldn't that be something if Kim turned out to be pregnant*, said Raylene, wiping her face of tears. And then, miraculously, Kim indeed was pregnant, growing larger every day in her silent aura of sorrow and guilt behind the Quik-Pik cash register. Eight months later, Raylene told me on the phone, Kim gave birth to a boy and named him Johnny for his father—marking the father's absence, giving it presence, in the baby's name. *And that'll be some comfort to her*, said Raylene. Because, perhaps, the thing to notice, sometimes, is not a clean division between uncanny and material experience, nor any easy allegory of class or power or colonization—though these do bleed, wordlessly, into the picture. Instead you might notice the continual struggle between memory and forgetting—the always ambivalent need to bury those things that have no room to be said, while still they struggle to make their mark in the real, sneaking in through all their transformations. And when objectless nostalgia and vaguely futuristic longing combine in a single structure of feeling, then ghosts and UFOs enter a shared terrain.

In memory of Joe Travis and La Rae Fletcher.

Notes

1   I am deeply indebted to the people of Rachel, Nevada, for the extraordinary hospitality and generosity I was shown there. Although I cannot possibly name all the friends in Rachel who shared so much talk and time to help me with my project—and I hesitate to list some names at the inevitable exclusion of others—I am profoundly grateful to Pat and Joe Travis and the community of "regulars" and staff at the Little Ale'Le'Inn and the Area 51 Research Center, and to the people who spent many hours guiding me around the countryside, giving companionship, insight, and many extra miles on their trucks (especially, in this regard, Don Day and his family, Jim Medlin, Chuck Clark, and the extended Nickells family). Many thanks also to Jeanette, to Bill and Jim for lessons in planespotting, and to Jim and Mary for showing me their business and craft. For valuable comments on earlier drafts of this essay, I thank Kathleen Stewart, Marilyn Ivy, John Pemberton, Michael Taussig, Steven Feld, Rosalind Morris, Yvette Christianse, Greg Urban, Erica David, Francine Lorimer, Aaron Fox, and my dissertation writing group. All errors are, of course, my own. I thank the Wenner-Gren Foundation for its generous support for this research. This essay is dedicated to the memory of Joe Travis and La Rae Fletcher of Rachel, Nevada.

2   These friends were part of the "Histories of the Future" group. See Joseph Masco's essay in this volume.

3   This is Highway 375, which the state of Nevada, in a 1996 attempt to boost tourism, christened "the Extraterrestrial Highway."

4   The singer was Norio Hayakawa, who has said that the government may be fabricating UFO stories to distract people from its real clandestine activities. He founded the Civilian Intelligence Network to watchdog covert government activities.

5   Except for Pat and Joe Travis, public personalities who have appeared in the popular media, I have changed all the names of Rachel residents in this essay. I have also slightly altered a few revealing biographical details in the interest of protecting speakers' identities.

6   That month, October 1997, Joe's little granddaughter Jessie had just arrived to live with them for a while; Pat and Joe had just taken her from her dad's in Vegas. But Pat and Joe were in their fifties now, they'd already raised their own kids, and they often worked fourteen-hour days; and so I helped look after Jessie too. Every week the Travises went to Las Vegas overnight to get supplies, and little Jessie had to wake up at 5:00 to get the school bus into Alamo, and so I was thrust immediately into the heart of their family life. The following

year, I returned to Nevada for about two months; by then, Jessie was gone. During my return visit, I lived part of the time with the Travises and part of the time in one of the inn's trailers nearby. This essay is based on experiences from the visits of both 1997 and 1998.

7   Bob Lazar claimed he had seen a secret UFO and aliens at the base when he briefly worked there, first appearing on Las Vegas television with the story in 1989 and then becoming a prominent figure in ufological discourses. His claims about his scientific credentials and government employment record, which he says were suspiciously destroyed, have been the subject of controversy even within UFO-conspiracy worlds.

8   Richard Leiby, "Secrets under the Sun," *Washington Post*, July 20, 1997, F1.

9   This lawsuit was dismissed in 1995, and then again on appeal in November 1997 in the Ninth U.S. Circuit Court. President Clinton issued an executive order in 1995 to shield the military from the suit, saying it was protected from having to divulge sensitive information in the interest of national security (President Bush later reaffirmed this order). Documents for the case were sealed. An EPA report into the conditions of the place was deemed classified. In 1998 the U.S. Supreme Court refused to hear an appeal of the workers' cases, agreeing that interests of national security overrode the workers' rights to information. In June 2002, the Ninth Circuit Court again heard arguments that "the Department of Justice attorneys improperly used national security to hide embarrassing statements" (Keith Rogers, "Federal Judges to Hear Case involving Area 51," *Las Vegas Review-Journal on the Web*, June 4, 2002, http://www .reviewjournal.com/lvrj_home/2002/Jun-04-Tue-2002/news/18894771.html). In August 2002, the *Review-Journal* filed a motion to unseal the court records. The judge in the case did release the records, but they arrived with large portions blacked out, according to the *Review-Journal* (Rogers). In April 2003, the Court of Appeals ruled that the Justice Department "did not abuse national security when information was struck from court documents" in two of the 1994 cases (Keith Rogers, "Three-Judge Panel: Government Wins Ruling over Area 51," *Las Vegas Review-Journal on the Web*, April 16, 2003, http://www .reviewjournal.com/lvrj_home/2003/Apr-15-Tue-2003/news/ 21110975.html). For more on the Area 51 toxic-waste case and other information on Area 51 that is beyond the scope of this essay, see Phil Patton's excellent journalistic study *Dreamland*, or David Darlington, *Area 51*.

10   Despite the reluctance felt by many locals to discuss the case, and the real threat of imprisonment to workers who reveal any information about their workplace, since my initial visits to Rachel there have been several press conference/demonstrations, or "people's rallies," at the base border, focusing on the workers' case and on Area 51 secrecy in general.

11   Freud, "The 'Uncanny.' "

12   In June 1997, *Popular Mechanics* magazine published a widely read story asserting that the covert military operations at Area 51 had been moved to the Utah desert—a claim sharply contested by most Rachel residents, many of

whom say that the reporter drove up the wrong dirt road, saw no warning signs or mysterious checkpoints, and so went home to write an erroneous but attention-grabbing story without staying on in Rachel long enough to see the weird lights with unnatural movements that appear regularly over the town at night. In other words, the peak of tourism and fame in Rachel coincided with the intimation of its rushing obsolescence. See Jim Wilson, "The New Area 51," *Popular Mechanics on the Web*, June 1997, http://www.popularmechanics .com/science/military/1997/6/new_Area_51.

13 The ways in which movement away from, nostalgia for, and return to rural Appalachia become narrativized into fantastic forms have been exquisitely tracked in Kathleen Stewart's *A Space on the Side of the Road*.

14 The processes I am musing here—that is, the ways in which old material is transformed into new forms through cultural and semiotic movement—have been luminously mapped out in relation to modernity and the problem of culture by Greg Urban in *Metaculture*. Urban observes that a continual sense of "newness" is one of modernity's primary values—an effect that, when mediated by nostalgia and ambivalence, seems to generate a sense of uncanny vertigo in the stories I present here.

15 Welcome, *The Plutonium Files*.

16 In "The 'Uncanny,'" Freud writes that the uncanny emerges when an otherwise unremarkable event is inexplicably repeated, seemingly pointing to an invisible agency or design through what he calls "involuntary repetition"; he writes, "We of course attach no importance to the event when we give up a coat and get a cloakroom ticket with the number, say 62; or when we find that our cabin on board ship is numbered 62. But the impression is altered if two such events . . . happen close together . . . [and we are] tempted to ascribe a secret meaning to this obstinate recurrence of a number" (390–91).

17 Ibid., 390.

18 In connecting *repetition* in uncanny poetics to their aesthetic pleasure, feeling of a hidden structure, and attention to form, I am drawing on Roman Jakobson's insights into the poetic use of repetition with variation. For Jakobson, formal poetry gives an intimation of structural (grammatical) relations that are normally unconscious. He develops this idea most fully in "Linguistics and Poetics," 62–94. See also Feld and Keil, *Music Grooves*, 190–91.

19 As Avery Gordon writes of ghosts, "They cannot be simply tracked back to an individual loss or trauma. The ghost has its own desires, so to speak" (Gordon, *Ghostly Matters*, 189).

20 Taussig, *The Magic of the State*.

21 The idea that class and gender are often best understood as structures of feeling, in Raymond Williams's sense (in *Marxism and Literature*), is beautifully developed by Carolyn Steedman. In *Landscape for a Good Woman*, she writes that her own mother's "sense of the unfairness of things could not be directly translated into political understanding and certainly could not be used by the left to shape an articulated politics of class" (8).

22 Similar sentiments—about the alien feeling of the earth, the ambivalence about being "at home" on the planet, and the conflation of earth with a nostalgic hometown—are a salient element in the poetics of many UFO abductee narratives. For a more sustained meditation on this particular trope, see Lepselter, "From the Earth Native's Point of View."

23 In this landscape, as in others, ghosts haunt us with the historical injustices of the past. They rattle the chains of historical traumas that won't remain buried as they should, until the real itself becomes contested ground, in both its pasts and presences. Recent social theory on ghosts and the uncanny that has influenced my thinking here includes, for example, Derrida, *Specters of Marx*; Steedly, *Hanging without a Rope*; Gordon, *Ghostly Matters*; Ivy, *Discourses of the Vanishing*; and Pemberton, *On the Subject of "Java."*

24 Campbell, *A Short History of Rachel, Nevada.*

INTERLUDE

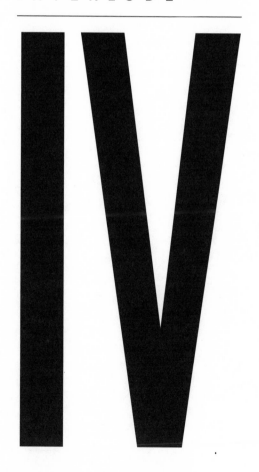

The Trouble with Timelines

Daniel Rosenberg

The modern timeline was born only with labor. Although it had precedents in chronologies and genealogies, calendars and canon tables, as well as traditional forms of narrative imagery, it was not until the eighteenth century that the recognizably modern structure was crafted. In retrospect, it is tempting to read time's arrow back into some early modern images. Joseph Mede's 1627 *Clavis apocalyptica*, for example, seems already to gesture in this direction. But not only is the future of the *Clavis* sharply delimited; the line itself is, at best, equal to other sorts of symbols and icons as a structural element in the diagram. The futurological mechanism of the modern timeline was not yet online.

By the middle of the eighteenth century, however, the modern timeline had appeared with a splash. In 1765, Joseph Priestley published a chart representing the lives of famous men by means of linear markers arranged chronologically and in proportion against a scale of 2,950 years. The *Chart of Biography* was a tremendous success. Though it was not the first timeline (it had a direct precedent in Jacques Barbeu-Dubourg's 1753 *Carte chronologique*), it was among the first to achieve attention as such.[1] In fact, the idea of a timeline was still strange enough in the mid-eighteenth century that it required a certain amount of explanation. Priestley himself argued that although time is an abstraction that may not be "the object of any of our senses, and no image can properly be made of it, yet because it has a relation to quantity, and we can say a *greater* or *less* space of time, it admits of a natural and easy representation in our minds by the idea of a measurable space, and particularly that of a LINE."[2]

After Priestley, the form of the timeline caught on. In addition to its visual effectiveness, the timeline amplified conceptions of historical progress that were themselves becoming popular at the time. The relationship was mutually reinforcing. As Priestley suggests, the timeline filled in as a kind of fantasized visual referent for an object without material substance. In its simplest form, it appeared to guarantee the simplicity and directionality of past and future history. But Priestley's commentary points to a problem too. History had never actually taken the form of a timeline, or of any other line, for that matter. And simplicity, the great advantage of the form, threatened also to be its greatest flaw. The timeline could function as "the most excellent mechanical help to the knowledge of history" because it could impress the imagination "indelibly."[3] For the same reason, a century later, Henri Bergson would refer to the "imaginary homogeneous time" depicted by the timeline as a deceiving "idol."[4]

But already in Priestley's day, the problem of the linear representation of time was posed with precision by writers such as Laurence Sterne, whose *Tristram Shandy* mocked the possibility of telling a story straight. Sterne's novel even includes a set of sketches indicating the digressive character of a story well and truly told. In fact, Sterne and Priestley are much more similar than they may appear. For Priestley, the timeline is a heuristic, an "excellent mechanical help." For Sterne, too, the linear representation of time is a construction. "Could a historiographer drive on his history, as a muleteer drives on his mule, — straight forward; — for instance, from *Rome* all the way to *Loretto*, without ever once turning his head aside either to the right hand or to the left, — he might venture to foretell you an hour when he should get to his journey's end," Sterne writes. "But the thing is, morally speaking, impossible," he says. "For if he is a man of the least spirit, he will have fifty deviations from a straight line to make with this or that party as he goes along, which he can no ways avoid. He will have views and prospects to himself perpetually soliciting his eye, which he can no more help standing still to look at than he can fly."[5]

For all their disagreement, both Priestley and Sterne point to the intensity of the labor and the technical ingenuity required to support a fantasy of linear time. Over the course of the nineteenth and twentieth centuries, the convention of the timeline was progressively naturalized. But its development tended also to raise new questions. Filling in an ideal timeline with more and better data only pushed it toward the absurd. Dubourg's *Carte chronologique* was already fifty-four feet long. At the same time, attempts to reanchor the timeline in material reference produced complicated results, as in the case of Charles-Joseph Minard's 1869 diagram *Carte figurative des pertes successives en hommes de l'Armée Française dans la campagne de Russie 1812–1813*, which maps fatalities during Napoleon's march to Moscow across both time and space. As Edward Tufte has argued, as a mechanism for expressing quantitative data, Minard's diagram is a triumph.[6] At the same time, because it follows a geographical trajectory, Minard's timeline doubles back on itself, marking a point of *reversal*. In a sense, Minard's chart may be more accurate than Priestley's, not because it carries more or better historical detail but because it reads in the way an actual story might be told. The same could be said for the branching timeline in Charles Renouvier's 1876 *Uchronie (l'utopie dans l'histoire): Esquisse historique apocryphe du développement de la civilization européenne tel qu'il n'a pas été, tel qu'il aurait pu être*, depicting both the actual course of history and the various alternative paths that might have been if other actions had been taken by historical actors.

The problems presented by twentieth-century versions of the timeline arise from different sources. In most important respects, the conceptual issues were already on the table in the eighteenth century. And indeed, it is important to note that our period brings a full naturalization of the timeline, such that elementary school teachers are advised to provide blank ones to their students for aid in the study of history. But the twentieth century brought developments in time reckoning that gave timelines new poignancy as well. In the 1940s, it became relevant for the first time to tell world history in terms of milliseconds, and soon it also became necessary to start thinking in practical terms about the transmission of information over the course of the very long term. There is something more than a little sobering about the recurrence of the cyclical form in the U.S. government glyph for the declining radioactivity of nuclear waste. In it, there may be an echo of the early modern problem of thinking apocalypse and linearity together.

Notes

1   Ferguson, "The 1753 Carte chronographique of Jacques Barbeu-Dubourg."
2   Priestley, *Description of a Chart of Biography*, 6; Headrick, *When Information Came of Age*, 124.
3   Priestley, *Description of a New Chart of History*, 11–12; Headrick, *When Information Came of Age*, 125.
4   Bergson, *Matter and Memory*, 207.
5   Sterne, *The Life and Opinions of Tristram Shandy*, 26.
6   Tufte, *The Visual Display of Quantitative Information*.

A Timeline of Timelines

Sasha Archibald and Daniel Rosenberg

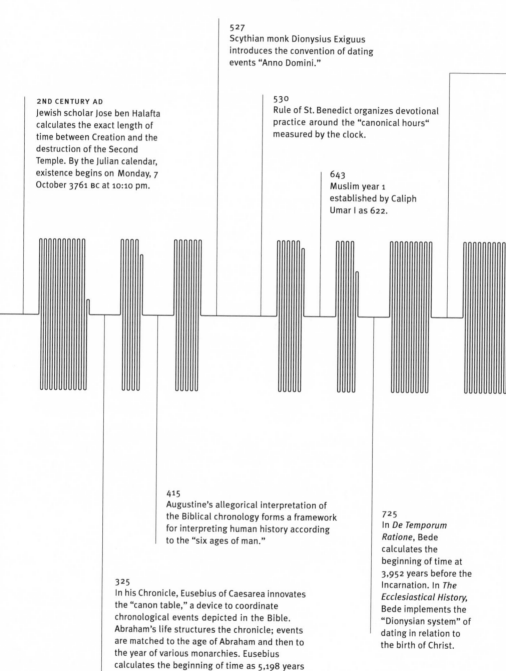

527
Scythian monk Dionysius Exiguus introduces the convention of dating events "Anno Domini."

2ND CENTURY AD
Jewish scholar Jose ben Halafta calculates the exact length of time between Creation and the destruction of the Second Temple. By the Julian calendar, existence begins on Monday, 7 October 3761 BC at 10:10 pm.

530
Rule of St. Benedict organizes devotional practice around the "canonical hours" measured by the clock.

643
Muslim year 1 established by Caliph Umar I as 622.

415
Augustine's allegorical interpretation of the Biblical chronology forms a framework for interpreting human history according to the "six ages of man."

725
In *De Temporum Ratione*, Bede calculates the beginning of time at 3,952 years before the Incarnation. In *The Ecclesiastical History*, Bede implements the "Dionysian system" of dating in relation to the birth of Christ.

325
In his Chronicle, Eusebius of Caesarea innovates the "canon table," a device to coordinate chronological events depicted in the Bible. Abraham's life structures the chronicle; events are matched to the age of Abraham and then to the year of various monarchies. Eusebius calculates the beginning of time as 5,198 years before the Incarnation.

10TH CENTURY
An anomalous graph appears in an edition of Macrobius's commentary on Cicero's *In Somnium Scipionis*, an analysis of physics and astronomy. The drawing, probably added to the text by a transcriber, plots planetary and solar movement as a function of time. Although the graph does not seem to convey accurate information, it is nonetheless the first known example of changing values measured against a time axis.

13TH CENTURY
Following the Franconian reforms, music becomes a true time series. Franco of Cologne's (c.1240–c.1280) treatise *Ars cantus mensurabilis* codifies a system of music notation that fixes the durational value of notes, while their relative value is measured against the breve, Franco's base unit of musical time.

12TH CENTURY
Moses Maimonides promotes use of the mundane era among Jewish scholars.

1433
Leon Battista Alberti's *I Libri della famiglia* insists on the importance of a literal accounting of the hours of the day.

14–15TH CENTURY
A genre of illuminated private prayer books, the Book of Hours contains the texts of certain prayers to be said at the canonical hours; the devotionals are often prefaced with a richly illustrated 12-month calendar, depicting events common to each month or season.

12–13TH CENTURY
Jesse Trees, pictorial depictions of Christ's royal ancestry as given in Matthew, proliferate in medieval manuscripts, murals, and stained glass windows. Jesse, the father of King David and the claimed ancestor of the Virgin, is typically pictured at the base of the scene, the tree's trunk growing from his navel.

1260
The pivotal year in humanity's transition to the third and final "state" of history according to Joachim of Fiore (1135–1202). Twelfth- and thirteenth-century renderings depict Joachim's system of historical states (*status*) and phases (*aetates*) as trees, chains, and ladders.

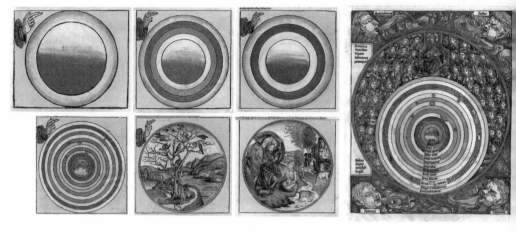

1493
The Nuremburg Chronicle of the World depicts the creation
of the earth with seven concentric circles. Also of note,
the Chronicle represents royal ancestry with portraits interconnected with vines to indicate marriage and parenthood,
thereby participating in a broader tradition that associates
genetic lineage and arboreal growth.

1608
Galileo plots the speed of a rolling
ball on a time axis.

1583
In his *Opus novum de emendatione temporum*,
Joseph Scaliger attempts to produce a complete and
self-contained chronology of world history including
translation tables for integrating all existing chronologies.
His *Thesaurus temporum* (1606) collects and arranges
all of the available ancient chronological sources.

c. 1500
Leonardo da Vinci is both the first to use
rectangular coordinates to analyze the
velocity of falling objects and the first
to recognize a correlation between the
particular climate and precipitation of a
given time period and the shape of the
resultant tree rings.

1654

James Ussher, Archbishop of Armagh, publishes a widely influential calculation of Biblical chronology, placing the beginning of time at 23 October 4004 BC. Twenty-five years later, Thomas Guy begins printing Bibles annotated with Ussher's chronology; Bibles inscribed with Ussher's dates remain in print until the early 20th century.

1687

Isaac Newton's *Philosophiae naturalis principia mathematica* proposes a theory of absolute time. Newton's posthumous *Chronology of Ancient Kingdoms Amended* (1728) uses astronomical observations to argue that the Kingdom of Israel antedated the kingdoms of Egypt and Greece.

1655

In Praeadamitae, Isaac Lapeyrère argues that Scripture authorizes belief in human existence before Adam.

1663

Christopher Wren's weather clock is one of a plethora of new mechanical self-registering devices that produce automated moving graphs of various natural forces; Wren's weather clock, for example, generates a continuous line graph of temperature and wind direction.

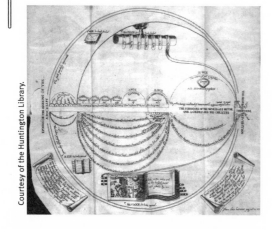

1680

In an attempt to synchronize Biblical history with new geological ideas, Thomas Burnet's *The Sacred Theory of the Earth* argues that the great deluge was the result of waters underneath the earth's surface breaking through the earth's crust, thereby destroying what Burnet believed to be the earth's pre-flood state—a perfectly smooth, featureless surface, like that of an egg. The book's frontispiece is a series of drawings depicting the cycle of stages in the geological history of the Earth beginning at Creation and culminating in the Apocalypse.

1627

Religious and political ferment in England produces numerous apocalyptic tracts including Joseph Mede's *The Key of the Revelation*. Mede maps the end of history onto a complex graphical figure combining cyclical and linear forms.

1697
Pierre Bayle's *Dictionnaire historique et critique* treats figures from secular and religious sources within a single scholarly apparatus. The second edition concludes with an exhaustive ten-page "Chronological Table of all the Eminent Persons Treated in this Dictionary." The table begins with Adam and ends in 1700.

1760–7
Laurence Sterne's novel *Tristram Shandy* includes a set of sketches indicating the non-linear path of a well-told story; narrative digressions appear as deviations from a straight line.

1724
In *La Scienza Nuova*, Giambattista Vico criticizes both the astronomical and mathematical basis of 17th-century chronology and proposes a new universal chronology based on a theory of cyclical human progress. *La Scienza Nuova* includes a chronological table that aligns the histories of the Hebrews, Chaldeans, Scythians, Phoenicians, Egyptians, Greeks, and Romans beginning with the Deluge.

18TH CENTURY
The convention of dating events BC becomes popular.

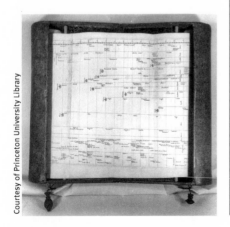

Courtesy of Princeton University Library

1753
Jacques Barbeu-Duborg, the French translator and disciple of Benjamin Franklin, creates his Carte chronologique, a 54-foot timeline of history from Creation contained in an iron case.

1765

The German philosopher and scientist J. H. Lambert is credited with observing that diagrams may do "incomparably better service" to the sciences than tables. Lambert's *Pyrométrie* (1779) includes tabular data of the rise and fall of annual temperatures, from which a curved line can be easily extrapolated.

1765

Joseph Priestley, an English chemist, publishes the first of several timelines that a contemporary audience would recognize as such: "A Chart of Biography" compares the life spans of 2,000 celebrated men from 1200 BC to 1750 AD, using bars set against a linear time axis to denote their life spans.

Courtesy of Duke University Library

1769

Louis-Sébastien Mercier publishes perhaps the first future fiction. *The Year 2440* describes French society and culture after seven centuries of progress.

1791

Last volume of Johann Gottfried Herder's *Reflections on the Philosophy of the History of Mankind* published.

1797

The *Encyclopædia Britannica* contains a fold-out chart designed by Adam Ferguson "representing at one view the rise and progress of the principal state and empires of the known world" from the Deluge in 1656 Anno Mundi to 1900 Anno Domini (the years after 1797 are blank).

1778

In his *Les Époques de la nature*, the French naturalist Buffon argues that the Earth may be as much as 75,000 years old. In unpublished manuscripts, he speculates that it may be more than 3 million years old.

1795

Thomas Malthus in his *Essay on the Principle of Population*, argues that while human population tends to increase geometrically, the means of human subsistence can only increase arithmetically.

1794

The patenting and marketing of graph paper—preprinted with a rectangular coordinate grid—attests to the growing use of Cartesian coordinates in scientific data analysis.

1786

Joseph Priestley's timeline was shortly followed by political economist William Playfair's invention of the bar chart, an innovation whose merits remained unrealized for several decades. As a young man, Playfair worked in the shop of James Watt, the inventor of the steam engine, where he was likely acquainted with Watt's self-registering device for measuring steam pressure.

1793

Introduction of French Revolutionary calendar declaring September 1792 as the beginning of the new "Year One."

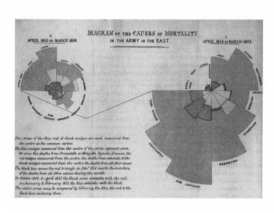

1809
Jean-Baptiste Lamarck publishes *Zoological Philosophy* containing an evolutionary family tree branching out from simpler to more complex organisms.

1834
Felix Bodin's *Le roman de l' avenir* gives the first historical account of futuristic fiction.

1857
Florence Nightingale, a major innovator of statistical graphs and diagrams, submits her "Diagram of the Causes of Mortality in the Army in the East" as part of her *Report to the Royal Commission on the Health of the Army*. The diagrams demonstrated that over the course of the Crimean War, British deaths owe principally to "preventable or mitigable" diseases rather than battlefield wounds.

1859
Charles Darwin's *Origin of Species* traces the genealogies of species back more than 300 million years.

1870s
Eadweard Muybridge and E. J. Marey each begin work in "chronophotography."

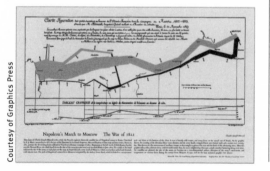

1869
Charles Joseph Minard's *Carte figurative de pertes successives en hommes de l' Armée Française dans la campagne de Russie 1812–1813*. Among the finest of Minard's graphical works, this chart plots the catastrophic loss of men in relation to place, time, and temperature during Napoleon's march to Moscow.

1876
Charles Renouvier's counterfactual *Uchronie* includes a chart depicting the theoretical relationship between the actual course of history and possible alternative paths.

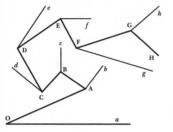

1889
In *Time and Free Will*, Henri Bergson argues for a distinction between the homogeneous mathematical conception of time and heterogeneous experience of duration. He insists that the experience of time cannot be represented in a linear fashion.

1895
H. G. Wells's *The Time Machine*.

1905
Albert Einstein's special theory of relativity.

1878
The word "graph" is coined in English by the mathematician James Joseph Sylvester. (Lambert referred to his graphs as *figuren*, Watt as "diagrams," and Playfair as "lineal arithmetic.")

1871
Sebastian Adams, *Synchronological Chart or Map of History*, an encyclopedic chart based on Ussher's dating system. A later version by Charles Deacon and Edward Hull continues to be available and reprinted under the title *Wall Chart of World History*.

Courtesy of Museum of Natural History.

1901
Andrew Ellicott Douglass founds the field of dendrology by inventing a system whereby known sequences of events (floating chronologies) can be fixed to specific years (absolute chronologies) via the scientific analysis of tree rings.

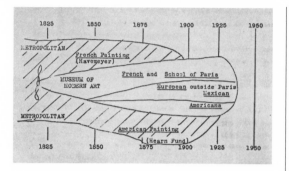

1933
In a presentation to the Board of Trustees at the Museum of Modern Art, Alfred Barr, the museum's founding director and an amateur military historian, outlines the (soon abandoned) collection plan of MOMA with sketches of time as a torpedo. As the torpedo moves ahead through time, the work positioned at the back of Barr's torpedo passes from MOMA's collection to that of the Metropolitan, allowing MOMA to stay on the cusp of the modern.

1929
Invention of the quartz clock.

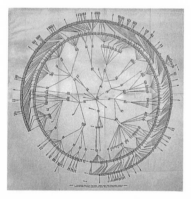

1930
English philosopher Olaf Stapleton investigates the future of the human race through fiction. Stapleton's two-billion-year narrative, *Last and First Men*, includes a series of timelines highlighting the difficulty of translating conventional scales of human history into an evolutionary framework.

1930-1932
Victor Houteff publishes his religious philosophy in *The Shepherd's Rod*, Vol. 1–2; his illustrative timelines convey the fast-approaching end of the world. Followers of his teachings include David Koresh.

1913
In their nineteenth-century notebook sketches, evolution theorists represented cross-generational reproduction with concentric circles. In the case of this eugenics diagram, Arthur Estabrook and Charles Davenport use these visual cues to chart the members of the Nam family, aiming to convey the dizzying expansiveness of degenerates' unchecked reproduction.

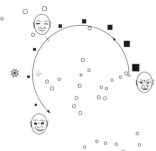

1948
The Olympic Games in London make use of Omega's photo-finish camera.

1948
Invention of the atomic clock. In 1967, the length of the second will be redefined by use of this device.

1993
Throughout the late twentieth century, professional semioticians struggle with the problem of constructing an iconographic language capable of communicating radiation dangers long after the death of current languages. Several of these symbolic systems are prepared for nuclear facilities, including the US government nuclear waste storage facility at Yucca Mountain, Nevada.

2000
The year 2000.

1968
Electronic time-keeping devices entirely replace live judges in certifying race winners at the Olympics in Mexico City.

0.10 MS.

0.24 MS.

0.38 MS.

0.52 MS.

0.66 MS.

0.80 MS.

0.94 MS.

100 METERS

TEMPERATURE   PRESSURE

1950
Studies of the damage wrought by atom bombs prompt timelines broken into ever smaller fragments of time.

CHAPTER

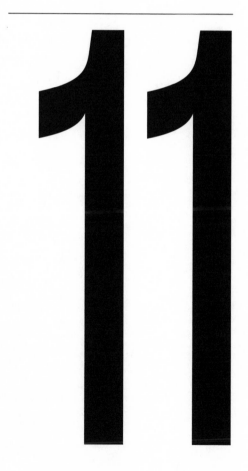

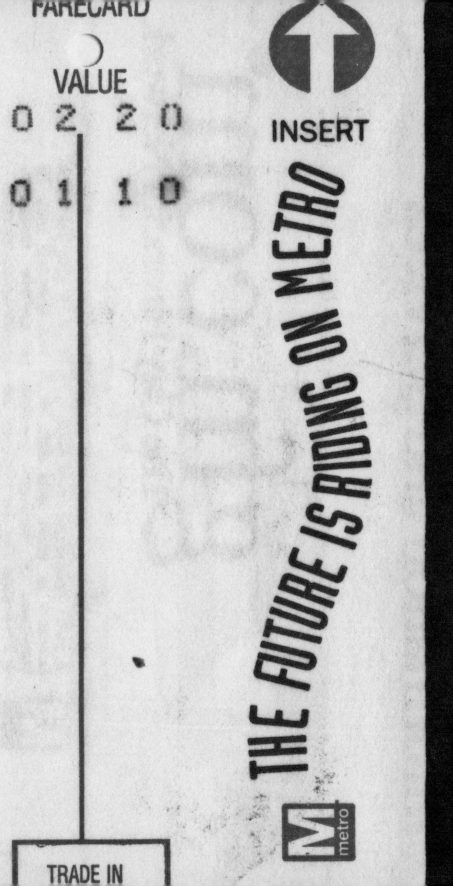

Living Prophecy at Heaven's Gate

Susan Harding

In the early 1970s, a pair of prophets who called themselves "the Two," short for the two witnesses foreseen in Revelation 11, appeared in the United States.

·

> And I will give power unto my two witnesses, and they shall prophesy.
>
> Revelation 11:3

·

Also calling themselves at the time Bo and Peep, they would later be known by various other paired monikers such as the Admiral and the Captain, Guinea and Pig, Him and Her, and Ti and Do. During 1975, their first year as public prophets, the Two often left their flock alone to wander from campground to motel to campground on its own. Some two hundred men and women, mostly in their twenties, having disposed of all their earthly connections, "criss-crossed the country in pairs and loosely-knit families," meeting up occasionally when the Two called them together. At one point, seventy-five students converged on a post office near Oakland, California, where "they found directions to a campground scribbled in a zip-code book." The students arrived at the campground hoping this would be the moment of the expected "Demonstration" when the Two would be martyred, rise from the dead after three and a half days, and ascend from the earth in a "cloud of light," which the Two had told them was the biblical term for spaceship. A few days after the Two ascended, the students themselves would be carried away in a spaceship. As it turned out, the meeting was a hoax perpetrated by a local newspaper; the Two never showed up at the campground, and the flock resumed its wanderings along the California coast.[1]

Bonnie Lu Nettles (aka Peep) and Marshall Applewhite (aka Bo) were raised in southern Baptist and Presbyterian churches respectively. As an adult, Nettles became an adept in various metaphysical arts—meditation, channeling discarnate spirits, astrology, mysticism, theosophy, and paranormal contacts with space beings.[2] Nettles met Applewhite in Houston in 1972 and briefly drew him into her spiritualist circle. They started a couple of spiritualist centers of their own, and then, within a year and a half of their meeting, their peculiar and rapidly evolving mix of Bible prophecy, metaphysics, contactee/flying saucer culture, television science fiction, and high school biology became an unfolding social drama in which they figured not as mere spectators awaiting the Blesséd Hope but as major actors. Applewhite had a vision in which he realized that he and Nettles were the two witnesses prophesied in Revelation 11, and they embarked on their mission.[3]

Leaving their pasts as well as their given names behind, the Two began to gather a flock in 1975. They invited their followers to "walk out of the door of your life," separate from all human attachments, prepare for the coming "harvest" of souls, and join them in "the Father's kingdom" in a spacecraft that would come for them shortly after the Two ascended. For nearly a year, the flock, with and without Bo and Peep, added and subtracted "students, fragmented and reassembled, camped and wandered, waiting for 'the Demonstration,' the assassination and resurrection, that would prove the truth of the Two's message." Local journalists had a field day tracking the Two's movements and proved to be their nemeses. In early 1976, after a particularly bad bout of TV publicity in Las Vegas that made them feel "like they had been shot down by the media and the mission was dead," the Two told their hundred-some remaining students that the Demonstration had in fact occurred already—"at the hands of the media." Not long after that, Peep announced that "the doors to the Next Level are closed" and the harvest was over. It was time for "students" to enter the "classroom," an indefinite period of growth and preparation for lives of "service" on the Next Level.[4]

The group disappeared from public sight until 1992, when they resurfaced briefly in the form of a Web site, newspaper ads, TV broadcasts, and public meetings in order to make a "final offer" to those who would join them for the "lift-off" which was imminent. Having regathered some "lost sheep," Heaven's Gate, as the group was by then known, disappeared again until the notorious day in late March 1997 when thirty-nine bodies were found rotting in a wealthy San Diego suburban home. From the outside, it was "the largest mass suicide in U.S. history." From the inside, the Captain (Bo, by then known as Do) and his crew had left their earthly vehicles behind and joined the Admiral (Peep, or Ti, who finished her work on the

Heaven's Gate masthead.

human level and departed in 1985) in a spaceship tucked away in the tail of the Hale-Bopp comet for their journey to the Next Level.

The group's suicide combined with other telltale signs to guarantee the status of Heaven's Gate as a "cult" in the media frenzy that followed the discovery of the bodies in Rancho Santa Fe. While the reportage invariably spotlighted evidence of the group's cultishness, between the lines, around the edges of the news reports, in their form, there were other layers to the story. There was surely something more to the relationship between journalists and Heaven's Gate than met the eye. The media mocked and vilified Heaven's Gate from the beginning, but they also spread the group's message, in the end all around the world. The Two seemed to know in advance what journalists would say about them and their students.

·

"We take the prize, I guess, of being the cult of cults."[5]

·

And as strange as journalists found Heaven's Gate's vision of Hale-Bopp, the group in much the same way fulfilled the journalists' vision of the turn of the millennium as a time of spiritual upwelling and chaos. The group's peculiar use of language, its practices, its combination of antiworldliness and technological savvy, its ceaseless wandering, all begged for interpretation that went beyond the scandal of the suicide. Heaven's Gate's practices appeared to be meaningless routines — or did they routinize the meaninglessness of life on earth? What was the message of their meandering? Whether or not the group had succeeded in communicating with the Next Level, it seemed to have invented, or reinvented, some extraordinary ways of communicating with this world.

Back in 1975, two sociologists who had infiltrated the group that summer did not think the group was a cult. They found that the group's days were composed of just four kinds of activities: soliciting small sums of money and food, presenting their message to others, overcoming their human emotions, habits, and attachments, and "trying to communicate with 'members of the Next Level' in outer space." Communicating with a member of the level above human, or (as they put it) "tuning in," was still something of a mystery to many of the students, but it had already become the way the group made its decisions. Students spent much of their time in group meetings "discussing fleeting thoughts that would pop into their minds. They believed these 'hits' and 'flashes' were instructions from the Next Level, but because everyone had an imperfect connection with the Father, no one ever received a complete set of instructions. Each would get pieces of the message, which they would discuss and assemble until the will of the Next Level became apparent."

At the time, the two sociologists who gathered this intelligence argued that the group's Ouija board–like mode of decision making, the leaderlessness of the group, and its fierce commitment to individual free choice were evidence that the students were not "brainwashed." Later, in the 1990s, one of the two sociologists changed his mind after he interviewed dropouts and updated his model of conversion. He decided that the students of Bo and Peep, if they were not yet brainwashed in 1975, were so subsequently as "Bo and Peep introduced social influence processes that are usually associated with the brainwashing model, such as the regimentation of daily life and the use of mental exercises to eliminate independent thinking." The group, in other words, was after all, or had become, a cult.[6]

Academic sobriety gave way to giddy sensationalism after Heaven's Gate's students and Do left their vehicles, their earthly bodies, and ascended to the Next Level sometime between Palm Sunday and Easter, 1997. The group was a "suicide cult" "obsessed with castration and the cosmos" and permeated by "repression and subtle mind control."[7] Its "well-choreographed departure" "blasted the doors wide open onto a considerably less tidy world—a dense and jumbled universe of UFOs and extraterrestrials, careening smack into unusual astronomical happenings, apocalyptic Christian heresies, and end-is-nigh paranoia."[8] "Do and Ti, or Bo and Peep, or the Two . . . plucked bits of this and pieces of that doctrine like birds building a nest, intertwining New Age symbols and ancient belief systems."[9] Heaven's Gate was "the lethal mix of New Age dreaming, extra-ordinary self-denial, and sci-fi soaked paranoia."[10]

Reporters reminded us of the "mass disappearances" of people from small towns in Oregon and California in the mid-1970s as men and women

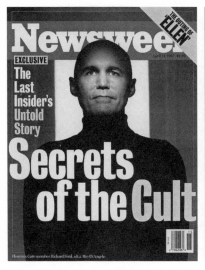

Newsweek and Time covers.

abruptly left their lives to join a "UFO cult." Applewhite/Bo/Do was a "cult leader," a "master manipulator," who "molded his flock" in "a regimen that made virtually every choice" for his "followers." We were regaled with the gay details of his prior life as if that might shed light on his subsequent career. Some faulted the Internet: "This new hybrid cult [emerged] from a mix of human communications techniques and the latest, newest, and most powerful mass communication technology in human history . . . the Web." [11] But mostly we pored over the group's bizarre beliefs, habits, and practices.

"The human kingdom was created as a stepping stone between the animal kingdom and the true Kingdom of God," the Level Above Human, which was a physical place, not a spiritual realm. The human kingdom is made up of "mammalian—seed-bearing—plants or containers," while the Next Level kingdom is made up of "non-mammalian, non-seed-bearing containers for souls." Souls evolve through a series of incarnations in mammalian bodies and progress by shedding human/mammalian characteristics and behavior—sexuality, gender, and all other addictions and ties—through the tutorship of a member, or Representative, of the Kingdom of God who has already been through the process. The earth is thus a "garden" of plants (containers, vehicles) for souls that are harvested from time to time by Next Level Representatives. The body of Jesus Christ was prepped, or tagged, at birth and incarnated at the time of his baptism by the soul of a Next Level Representative who had come to earth to harvest

Member of the Kingdom of Heaven and Incarnate Member on Earth.

a few select souls. Do and Ti, like Jesus, were Next Level Representatives, tagged at birth and incarnated by souls in the early 1970s. The bodies of their students (their crew), like those of Jesus's disciples (his crew), were also tagged at birth.

In 1975, the group's first year, students, after abandoning all, were expected to figure out on their own via direct contact with the Next Level what else they needed to do to complete the overcoming process. They were asked to separate themselves totally from the world of their prior lives — to leave behind family, love, sex, work, material possessions, personal names, and identities — "everything except enough food and liquids to sustain your vehicle while it is here, and enough rest to give it strength that it needs while it's in a decaying atmosphere such as the Earth's. . . . Anything else, whether it's desire to play the violin or preach a sermon or nurse a child, anything of this world, you must overcome."[12] In the summer of 1976, Bo and Peep gathered the group in a Wyoming campground and launched them on nearly two decades of minutely orchestrated metamorphic "disciplines." Writing about them later, Do presented the disciplines as consummate moments of choice in which students decided over and over again to give up their tokens of human agency and autonomy in favor of achieving Next Level consciousness. No one was told to do anything; everyone was free to choose at each moment whether or not to follow instructions from the Next Level; if they chose to follow them, they would ascend; if not, not.

Students wore hoods "to learn about the 'conning' ways of their visual personalities." Their days were organized into tasks "assigned" every twelve minutes—"each person physically going to a given spot every 12 minutes to concentrate on his or her desire to serve."[13] Students were assigned "check partners" with whom they consulted before taking any action. They were given new names. They became meticulous bookkeepers and filled their feeling-diaries every twelve minutes. There were frequent fasts, including a three-month fast with a "master cleanser" composed of lemonade, cayenne pepper, and maple syrup. Students entered prolonged regimes of silence called "tomb time." They were asked to abandon all addictions, not only sex, alcohol, cigarettes, and drugs, but also likes and dislikes, habits, opinions, judgments, ways of expressing themselves, and personality traits "such as being critical of others or getting down on yourself, having negative responses to situations, needing to talk constantly, having things your way or on a particular timetable, or needing human affection or attention."[14] Finally, detailed "behavioral guidelines" further inscribed a scrupulous regime of self-surveillance. There were "17 steps" for entering the classroom, beginning with "Can you follow instructions without adding your own interpretation."[15] More advanced "guidelines for learning control and restraint" defined three major offenses—deceit, sensuality, and knowingly breaking an instruction—and over thirty lesser offenses, including "having inappropriate curiosity," "staying in my own head, having private thoughts," and "identifying with influences—using the 'I' or 'me' pronoun in application to an offense instead of recognizing that it was an influence using me."[16]

Aside from such minutiae from the everyday life of Heaven's Gate, reporters uncovered many trails of evidence that seemed to lead inexorably to mass suicide: the group's conviction that their spaceship-to-Heaven was tailing the Hale-Bopp comet; the $3,000 telescope that the group returned to the store when it didn't reveal the spaceship that was surely there; the group's final days, their last roller-coaster rides and their last meals, their exit statements, the exact contents of their death potion. And we lingered over the vivid details of the death scene:

•

Take the little package of pudding or applesauce and eat a couple of teaspoons. Pour the medicine in and stir it up. Eat it fairly quickly and then drink the vodka beverage. Then lay back and rest quietly.

•

The "rotting bodies in a ritzy suburb" spread out on bunk beds; the corpses covered in purple shrouds and shod in brand-new black Nikes; each body, each vehicle, accompanied by a sports bag, a five-dollar bill, some quarters, and a stick of lip balm.

Finally, the reporters told us that, of course, we knew it was going to happen all along. Heaven's Gate and its spectacular finale figured as a major sign of the times in various popular scenarios anticipating the turn of the millennium. "Students of the millennium and historians of the bizarre have long predicted such a catastrophic event in the twilight years of the 20th century, duly noting the rise in the number of obscure cults and the increasingly fevered pitch of their rantings." "These are the waning years of the 20th century, and out on the margins of spiritual life there's a strange phosphorescence. . . . The approach of the year 2000 is coaxing all the crazies out of the woodwork. They bring with them a twitchy hybrid of spirituality and pop obsession. Part Christian, part Asian mystic, part Gnostic, part *X-Files*, it mixes immemorial longings with the latest in trivial sentiments." [17]

While there is little evidence that cult activity in the United States actually increased as 2000 approached, Heaven's Gate was a feast for all those journalists and scholars who so eagerly anticipated such an efflorescence. [18] But the larger context in which cults were watched had also shifted quite dramatically over the twenty-two years between the origin and demise of Heaven's Gate. Its life span, from 1975 to 1997, coincided with a period of major realignment within the regime of modern religiosity in America.

During the preceding fifty years, from 1925 to 1975, various prevailing public discourses projected the progressive marginalization of supernatural religiosity, and particularly of what had been dubbed fundamentalism, from modern American national culture and politics. This midcentury era, in which liberal and moderate religious voices dominated public life, ended as a result of the cultural and political remobilization of white conservative Protestants during the late 1970s and the 1980s. The subsequent—and still current—regime is not one in which conservative Protestant voices prevail. Rather, it is a regime of decentered religious power and authority in the public arena. Marginalized groups were mainstreamed, but mainstream groups were not marginalized. Contemporary, or late modern, American public religiosity is not centered culturally or politically. Having lost its dominant progressive story line, which depended on an excluded fundamentalist other, public religiosity fluctuates between narrative confusion and despair. If there is a prevailing late modern religious historical trajectory, or telos, it is regressive—"the country is in spiritual disarray"—but there are many versions as to why and who is responsible for the disorder and discord. [19]

When so-called fundamentalists vacated their place as the emblematic excluded religious other, the boundary between the inside and the outside of the official zone of legitimate, normal, routine, acceptable public religiosity was destabilized. Cults and cult watching, which had been marginal activities within the margins, an outside of the outside, became more emblematic activities. However, they did not produce a stable excluded religious other and a stable boundary between an inside and outside of public religiosity. The cults themselves were too multiple, too diverse, too local, too fragmented; and cult watchers, even in the moments of maximum cultness defined by mass death, cannot sustain a unified story line. The cult watchers were divided, especially after the conflagration of the Branch Davidian compound at Waco in 1993, between waves of hyperagitated, hyperbolic, anticult voices and the "more considered," bigger picture, voices that argue against the hysteria of the moment, searching for gaps in the hyperbolic accusations, and for "the real villains," such as the FBI, or even the agitated cult watchers themselves.

In the case of Heaven's Gate, there was quite a bit of debate, even in the immediate aftermath of the suicides, about how culty—that is, in effect, how culturally illegitimate—the group really was. Moreover, the group and its two leaders had seemed to be willfully playing with boundary issues from the beginning. Heaven's Gate was in many ways as normal as it was bizarre, as inside as it was outside mainstream popular culture. Sometimes it seemed to occupy both sides of the line—whatever line—at once; at other times the group crisscrossed lines in a game of hide-and-seek with the critics and the viewing public. Ti and Do were no match for David Koresh (the Branch Davidians in Waco) or Jim Jones (Jonestown) as "cult leaders," and their practices, while minutely regimented, also insisted that members choose continuously to submit to them. The group's videotaped "exit statements," aired over and over in the days after the suicides, instead of portraying mindless or crazed zealots, gently insisted on each student's clear-mindedness, willingness, quiet conviction, personal reasoning, courage, and joy as he or she prepared to depart earth.[20]

Moreover, Heaven's Gate, by timing its "lift-off" to the Next Level in the week before Easter, highlighted the spooky similarity, the eerie mirroring, between its doctrines of bodily ascension and the doctrines of mainstream (liberal, moderate, or conservative) Christianity. Many Christians, as they sat in their Easter Sunday pews that spring, listening to the story of Christ's resurrection and marveling at the prospect of their own eternal life in Heaven, surely heard the echoes of Heaven's Gate's journey home, whether or not their pastors mentioned it.

Certainly, many reporters noted the echoes. In fact, tracking the web of similarities between Christianity and Heaven's Gate—thereby confusing the boundary between the group and specifically born-again Christianity— was a major theme of the extended press coverage after the suicides.[21] Most reporters also, wittingly or unwittingly, attempted to restore a partial boundary by casting Heaven's Gate as a deviant or heretical form of Christianity. But by focusing on Heaven's Gate as a "bad copy" of Christianity, reporters and other experts overlooked the ways in which some quarters of born-again Christianity were articulating ideas about UFOs and aliens as "far-out" as any of Heaven's Gate's.

Sometime during the 1990s, a few conservative Christian writers joined Heaven's Gate in theorizing that the outbreak of UFO sightings and alien encounters escalating all over America at the time was substantially real.[22] The Christian writers and Heaven's Gate agreed: the sightings of UFOs were real; alien spaceships have landed; contacts between aliens and humans have occurred. And according to both Heaven's Gate and the Christians, the incursion of space aliens is not benign. Indeed, the space aliens are agents of Lucifer—they are fallen angels—who are mating with or inhabiting humans to produce a growing population of Luciferians on earth. Heaven's Gate and Christian theories converged in other ways as well. The only major difference was that the Christians considered cultists Luciferians, while Heaven's Gate—along with many New Age UFO watchers—considered Christians Luciferians. However, despite all these similarities and mirror imagings regarding UFOs and aliens, there was no evidence of direct borrowing either way. The relationship between the Christian theories and those of Heaven's Gate seemed to be one of occupying the same narrative space rather than of copying each other. One might say they were surfing the same cultural hypertext. Heaven's Gate and born-again Christians clicked on and then customized the same prophetic links regarding extraterrestrials.[23]

So it was not the content of their prophesying that distinguished the Christian UFO/alien theorists from Heaven's Gate; it was how they practiced their prophecies. For the Christians, their UFO theorizing was folk theology; it was the Bible-based interpretation of current events. It was not one among several possible interpretations, it was the one true interpretation, but it was not generative, it did not issue the reality of which it spoke. Prophecy becomes scandalous in our post-Enlightenment world, even for most born-again Christians, when it "speaks forth" its world, when those who hold it are also held by it, when they inhabit and enact it as an unfolding social drama.[24] Sources aside, the line between secular prognosticating and the kind of prophecy practiced by many conservative Christians and other religious adepts is actually rather hazy and thin. The serious boundary line, the one laid down by the Enlightenment philosophers, proscribes living prophecy, and it was in crossing this line so unambiguously—and paradoxically—by dying that Heaven's Gate came to represent, for outsiders, an exemplary "cult" for the turn of the millennium.

For those on the inside, the fact that Heaven's Gate's vision of the future was generative was no doubt attractive, but so was the practice, the daily experience of assembling, revising, and enacting the vision. Ti and Do and their students became adepts at reading the world—and the skies—around them for signs that their prophecies were coming true. But their forte, their peculiar genius, was tacking back and forth among a host of vernaculars— Christian, UFO/contactee, New Age, science fiction, biology, gardening, teaching—and fashioning a hybrid discourse in which the seams were fore-grounded. Their language was overtly double-voiced—composed of speech from multiple genres—in a way that highlighted intertextuality and the process of translation in meaning making. With their incessant making explicit of connections and intertwining of terms, Ti and Do taught their students a literary mode of attention. They showed them how things were connected, not just that they were connected, but *how* they were connected. Indeed, they showed them how to connect things, how to convert similari-ties across boundaries of difference into similarities always already linked by sameness. They taught them how to convert metaphors into metony-mies. How to enchant, or reenchant, the world.

A few years before their ascension, Do and his students began to pub-lish a wide range of documents as Web pages on the Internet. In those documents they frequently remarked on—and thus called attention to— their language. "One of the greatest struggles we've had from the begin-ning is the terminology—if we try to correct the vision of the Christians and talk their language, we're seen as a religious cult on an ego trip—if we try to state our information in language more relevant to our actual situation, the masses see us as attempting to make the 'Trekkie' vernacu-lar into religion." [25] Heaven's Gate's solution to this dilemma was to tack, or trek, between the idioms of Christianity and science fiction, produc-ing a compound discourse that highlighted the linkages and continuously called attention to their language. From the outside, their semiotic moves seemed parodic; from the inside, they seemed like revelation. Listen to the shuttling between Christian and *Star Trek* (and other) idioms in Do's intro-duction to Heaven's Gate's online book:

> Two thousand years ago, a crew of members of the Kingdom of Heaven who are responsible for nurturing "gardens," determined that a percentage of the human "plants" of the present civilization of this Garden (Earth) had developed enough that some of those bodies might be ready to be used as "containers" for soul deposits. Upon in-struction, a member of the Kingdom of Heaven then left behind His body in that Next Level (similar to putting it in a closet, like a suit of

clothes that doesn't need to be worn for a while), came to Earth, and moved into (or incarnated into), an adult human body (or "vehicle") that had been "prepped" for this particular task. The body that was chosen was called Jesus. The member of the Kingdom of Heaven who was instructed to incarnate into that body did so at His "Father's" (or Older Member's) instruction. He "moved into" (or took over) that body when it was 29 or 30 years old, at the time referred to as its baptism by John the Baptist (the incarnating event was depicted as "...the Holy Spirit descended upon Him in bodily form like a dove"—Luke 3:22). [That body (named Jesus) was tagged in its formative period to be the receptacle of a Next Level Representative, and even just that "tagging" gave that "vehicle" some unique awareness of its coming purpose.][26]

The story of a Representative of the Next Level tagging and taking over an earthly vehicle some two thousand years ago is only superficially exotic and bizarre, wobbling as it does alongside the ultrafamiliar, commonplace story of Jesus Christ's incarnation. The two stories are willfully not fused but rather intertwined, each with its own terms, each referring to the other, each in the language of its time. The Kingdom of Heaven interlinks with the Next Level. Jesus, with the Next Level Representative. His Father, with his Older Member. Human bodies, with containers or vehicles. The soul, with deposits. Conception, with the formative period. Special election, with tagging. Incarnation, with the moment the vehicle was moved into by the Representative. The two stories are kept apart by the double strands of terms, and also by quotation marks placed around many of the Trekkie-like terms. Do's story foregrounds the process of translation and citation to the point that the stories as such—the narrative writing—recede into the background. According to Do's students, rather than demystifying his authority and the "really realness" of the world he generated, this literary mode of attention, with its incessant making explicit of connections or links, was a major source of his attraction.[27]

Do taught his students a mode of attention which understands that the meaning of a text, an object, or event does not inhere in the thing itself, or its author or agents, but rather in the web of connections that link it to other texts, objects, and events. Theorized as intertextuality, this mode of attention and interpretation was, according to Daniel Boyarin, materialized in the Hebrew Bible and its Jewish commentaries. Then again, according to Daniel Rosenberg, it was operationalized in the eighteenth century by the system of cross-referencing in Diderot's Encyclopédie. Most recently it was instantiated again in hypertext. The term's inventor, Ted Nelson, simply defined hypertext as "non-sequential writing," or, in more popular terms, as "a series of text chunks connected by links which offer the reader different pathways."[28] The point is not that hypertext is absolutely nonsequential—it includes sequential, or narrative, writing—but that it foregrounds the nonsequential links among texts. Heaven's Gate's writing seems to mimic one of the ways Nelson describes of organizing those links, namely, the presentation of adjacent lists—Nelson calls them zippered lists—of narrative items that index each other in different sequences.[29]

The endless repetition of twinned and twined idioms showed up not only in the language of Heaven's Gate but also in their practices and appearances. The group's leaders were of course a pair separated by small differences and were so named, variously, Bo and Peep, Admiral and Captain, Him and Her, Winnie and Pooh, Tiddly and Wink, Nicom and Poop, Chip and Dale, Guinea and Pig, Ti and Do, or simply the Two. And the cultural references to the 1970s went way beyond *Star Trek* and *Star Wars* to produce a complex sense of doubling—or cross-referencing, intertextuality, hypertexting—between the then and now. Heaven's Gate's antifamily, antigender, radical egalitarian celebration of sameness as a form of communion-with-the-other referenced monasticism and mysticism, but also the hippie counterculture. "Initially all the victims had been identified as men, since deputies found all of the victims dressed alike in black suits with close-cropped hair, making it difficult to determine their sex."[30] Even their radical antisexuality, which seemed if anything a piece of the 1990s, linked to 1970s youth culture in the way it was played out as a quest for a kind of innocent, primordial sexuality and the desire for the intimacy of undifferentiated otherness. "Virginity," Do said, "can be recovered."[31] Do himself was a very 1970s father figure, a soft, avuncular father, a Dr. Spock (Benjamin, that is) blend of routinization and permission, of Mr. Rogers and Timothy Leary. Do actually looked a little like Mr. Rogers, and he sounded a little like him too.[32] Do also looked a little like Timothy Leary—without hair—a resemblance that was made manifest at the time of the suicide by what we can only hope was a coincidence—namely, the launching of Timothy Leary's ashes, along with the ashes of *Star Trek* creator Gene Roddenberry, into space the same week that Heaven's Gate ascended to the Next Level.

To this list of allusions to the 1970s—of haunting, channeling, doubling, déjà vus, moments of temporal repetition—we may also add the Grateful Dead. The hippie/drug culture lingo linked Heaven's Gate to the Dead as well as to Timothy Leary. The thoughts, for example, sent down to students from the Next Level were called "flashes" and "hits," terms once associated with the quintessential 1970s activities, LSD trips and marijuana smoking. Heaven's Gate's greatest mime of the Grateful Dead was its traveling troupe quality. The meandering around the country, the continual process of breaking up and regrouping, the apparent anti-organizational amorphousness and placelessness all echoed the Dead. However, Heaven's Gate's movements had an edge of flight that the Dead's did not, an edge that recalled yet one more ghost from the 1970s—the TV show *The Fugitive*.

The mass suicide of Heaven's Gate was in fact the last moment in a long succession of sudden disappearances, getaways, seclusion, concealment, and disguise. Marshall Applewhite and Bonnie Lu Nettles, as they became Bo and Peep, disappeared from the lives of their already estranged families, friends, and lovers. During 1975, they organized disappearances along the West Coast as they assembled their flock of students. Some students never contacted their families or friends again; others called them every few years from pay phones or sent them postcards postmarked in cities distant from where they were living. They assumed new names, not one but two, or three, or more. When Heaven's Gate finally materialized in an enduring way for the world to see, it was in cyberspace, the ultimate nonplace, or, rather, the zone of endless virtual places. And even then they registered their Web pages under false names and addresses. They used the Internet as if it were "a digital bulletin board on which to affix their messages."[33] In particular, their aggressive use of "meta tags" to lure search engines to their site and cross-posting on Usenet made them pariahs in the subculture of Webmasters.[34]

Fugitives are a kind of outlaw; they occupy spaces outside the law. It is unclear, sometimes more, sometimes less, whether fugitives are in the right or the wrong, and thus their flight calls attention to and problematizes the system, whatever system it is, that allots value, meaning, credibility, authority, and rights in such a way that forces flight. In his online "synopsis" of the history of the Two, Do narrated the moment that clinched their status as fugitives of an ambiguous and metacritical sort. Here is his story as he told it, in the third person:

> [In their first year of] lacing the country up and down and from side to side . . . a woman who had met them in Houston . . . asked if she could meet up with them, and they agreed. As they traveled here and there, they met her a few times and she offered the use of her gasoline credit cards. They used the cards for a while until they were informed that the cards had been reported stolen by the woman's husband, which was a traumatic experience to say the least. In the meantime, the old car they purchased in Portland, Oregon, . . . "gave up the ghost," and they were stranded in St. Louis on the night that the comet Kohou-

tek was at its peak. In their naive trust, they pulled out one of their old credit cards and rented a car, firmly believing that "God would provide the means" to pay the bill.

Sometime later, while in Brownsville, Texas, they made an appointment with a news reporter to share what they had come to know, telling him this would be the biggest story he ever received. He believed them, but thought that their story was about drug trafficking and brought hoards of authorities with him to the interview. This frightened the Two, who were pretty paranoid by now anyhow, and when they saw the authorities, they left abruptly, which made the authorities follow them. In the process of following them, though the police didn't know why the Two were running, they checked out the license of the rented car which had been reported stolen.

The Two were then arrested and plopped in the county jail. . . . Ti was charged with stealing credit cards. . . . Do was charged with auto theft. . . .

They were both given brief jail terms, and that experience yielded significant growth for both of them. They were at first horrified by what had happened, thinking that a jail record had ruined their mission, that no one would listen to them if their credibility were questionable. However, they could see that even prior to the jail incident their stability and their credibility was by now unquestionably questionable. So the felon record was taken in stride as assurance that now they couldn't turn back.[35]

Something "fugitive" is also something fleeting, which eludes grasp; something evanescent, of short duration, fading, or becoming effaced.[36] Do narrated both flight and a commitment to flight. He also embedded flight in the form of his narration by his use of the third person. We know that the narrator is one of the Two—namely, Do—yet he positions himself outside the story, or rather on its edges, for the narrator is too savvy, too invested, to be utterly outside. Do's voice is a split voice, a fugitive voice, constantly slipping in and out of itself. He is telling us that the story is still alive, that the telling and retelling of the story are part of the story, that what you find out when you get outside the story is that there is no outside of the story.

Eluding grasp, becoming effaced, moving in and out of focus. Fluctuating between Christianity and Star Trekese between the 1970s and the 1990s, and between catching a spaceship to the Evolutionary Level Above Human to rejoin their Older Members and the utterly mundane but mysterious everyday details of lip balm, a roll of quarters, and black Nikes. The

Bo and Peep under arrest, 1975. © Bettmann/CORBIS.

extreme fugitivity practiced by Heaven's Gate—in their vernacular trekking, their nomadism, and their ultimate flight to Hale-Bopp—continuously enacted the meaninglessness of what they were leaving behind. For Do and his students, "the true meaning of 'suicide' is *to turn against the Next Level when it is being offered.*"[37]

The student Glnody wrote, "Choosing to exit this borrowed human vehicle or body and go home to the Next Level is an opportunity for me to demonstrate my loyalty, commitment, love, trust, and faith in Ti and Do and the Next Level. . . . There is no life here in this human world. This planet has become the planet of the walking dead. The human plants walk, talk, take careers, procreate, and so forth, but there is no life in them. . . . Suicide would be to turn away from this incredible opportunity I've been given, to turn my back on the Next Level and the life they are offering." Srrody wrote, "As the comet Hale-Bopp brings closure to this visitation, perhaps even this civilization, I am so filled with joy—not only for myself and my classmates, but with the pride that only a son can have for His Father [Do], who has pulled off a Next Level miracle that any of us made it out of this world alive."[38]

All together, Heaven's Gate, its language and practice, its living prophecy, seems exquisitely postmodern. Given its preference for multidimensional, self-reflexive storytelling over linearity and realism, for exposing links and erasing boundaries, for versioning and double-voiced speech, it is even plausible to think of the group as bringing prophecy into the age of cyberspace.

.

"Our understandings are constantly being updated as our circuitry
adapts to higher perspectives."[39]

.

More likely, however, these and other features of Heaven's Gate that make it seem so current are themselves but versions, albeit up-to-date, of features that characterize moments of discursive critique and innovation, moments when language seems to bring forth new realities, when prophecy is alive.

Appendix
Excerpts from the 1992 Marshall Applewhite Videotape
"The End of the Age Is upon Us"

The following transcript of Do's words is included here for the record, but in order to hear the connection to Mr. Rogers, listen to Do's speech by going to the source, a CNN Web site.[40] When three linguistic anthropologists and students of religious speech, Dennis Tedlock, Barbara Tedlock, and Danny Maltz, listened to Do's speech, they noted the following features:

- The length and structure of the pauses and the monotone of Do's voice suggest that his speech was memorized; the formality of his speech.
- Danglings — of words and phrases — suggest improvisation; the informality of his speech.
- The voice is split, double; it is both deliberate and marked as deliberate.
- His voice goes up at the end of sentences and sentence segments, suggesting a sermonic style.
- Mr. Rogers was trained as a Presbyterian minister; Do was the son of a Presbyterian minister.
- Do's oratorical style may be more that of a Presbyterian teacher rather than a minister.

Welcome to "beyond human, the last call." We have a big picture to try to portray to you. You don't know us. You don't know what we represent. "Beyond human" might say something. It might not. But it says a lot to us. And we want to share it with you.

In 1975, there were two individuals who came public, held some meetings around the country, and said that they were from the kingdom of heaven. And those two individuals were Ti and Do. Ti, my partner, who has returned to the kingdom of heaven, and left me here with the responsibility of whatever is remaining of this task, because it was mine to fulfill.

As we held some meetings, quite a number of students, or followers, or curiosity seekers, just dropped whatever they were doing and came and listened to us, spent some time with us, a short period of time with us in some campgrounds. And we talked about the kingdom of heaven, the physical kingdom of heaven, not a spiritual kingdom of heaven. Not that it isn't spiritual, but it is not etheric. It is not only spiritual, which represents the character of the soul, but it is a physical kingdom as well. And as we talked about that kingdom to these students, after a very short time, and we had written a statement about it, these students took that statement and went across the country for nine months, holding meetings in one little town, one big town, one little town, one big town after another.

When we met with those hundred or so students, and told them that this was dead serious, that we couldn't take them as students unless they were willing to drop all of the behavior that they might still be participating in that we knew was not common to the kingdom of heaven. And the more we stressed that they would have to drop that behavior, sex being the one seemed to stand out the most, that people seemed to be most addicted to, and hard to make that transition from. As we really got serious about it and knew that that one had to go, along with other addictions, drinking, or smoking, or drug usage, the numbers started dwindling, and the classroom then ended up in the, oh somewhere in the, forties or fifties.

Two thousand years ago, when Jesus was sent from the kingdom of heaven, he was sent for the same purpose. He was sent to say, if you follow me, I cannot only make you fishers of men, I can give you the good news of the kingdom of heaven. If you do what I say to do, if you believe that I have the information that you need, and you apply it to your lives and in your behavior, and you overcome the world, then you can go from the human kingdom into the heavenly kingdom and not need to return again.

We started searching scriptures, we started searching everything we could get our hands on, new age material, everything we could find that would open our heads. We really realized that all of the searching that we were doing was superficial, that where we were really getting help, and getting information, was what was being fed to us. Now, what we know, or we understood later, that what was happening during that time was that we were, what is historically called, that we were going through an awakening period.

Let's discuss reincarnation a moment. Not the typical Eastern view of reincarnation, or the caste system progression, or that you're going to come back in another life as a bird or a monkey, something of that sort. But we have to realize if you search even the biblical scriptures carefully that you'll see dozens of very clear references to a good understanding of incarnating and recognizing that certain individuals that had been historically recognized in biblical times in the past were, that people were always questioning, well, is that them reappearing? Is that Moses or Elijah? Who was John the Baptist, could he have been so and so? And what did Jesus mean when he said, "you have to be born again"?

So with the talk that is so common in this day and time of the last times, or the end of the age, or some people even talk of it as the end of the world. I'm afraid I don't feel that our heavenly father has quite deemed that our planet is so ill that it can't be recycled, refurbished, cleaned up, restored. But I feel that we are at the end of the age. Now the end of the age, I'm afraid I feel, is right upon us, that it's going to come—now, I don't want to sound like a prophet—but my gut says and everything else that I know points to, that it's going to come before the turn of the century, that it's going to come in the next few months, or the next year or two.

Notes

1   Account drawn from Balch and Taylor, "Salvation in a UFO," 58–59.

2   Balch, "Waiting for the Ships," 141–42.

3   Details of the early career of Applewhite and Nettles can be found in Balch, "Bo and Peep."

4   Balch, "Waiting for the Ships," 154.

5   Quoted in "Marshall Applewhite," *Rotten Dot Com: An Archive of Disturbing Illustration*, 1996, http://www.rotten.com/library/bio/religion/cult/marshall-applewhite (accessed October 6, 2003).

6   This reassessment of the group's cult status is from Balch and Taylor, "Seekers and Saucers."

7   Mark Miller and Evan Thomas, "Exclusive," 28.

8   Gleik, "The Marker We've Been Waiting For."

9   Ibid., 31.

10   Miller and Thomas, "Exclusive," 28.

11   Flo Conway and Robert Siegelman, "Nation's Leading Cult Experts Begin a Web Diary As the Heaven's Gate Story Unfolds," March 28, 1997, http://www5 .zdnet.com/yil/higher/cultcol1.html (accessed January 16, 1999). Also see Don Knapp, "The Internet as a God and Propaganda Tool for Cults," CNN *Interactive: Sci-Tech Story Page*, March 27, 1997, http://www.cnn.com/TECH/9703/27/ techno.pagans/index.html (accessed October 6, 2003). Wendy Gale Robinson, in "Heaven's Gate: The End?" (Department of Religion, Duke University, December 3, 1997, http://www.ascusc.org/jcmc/vol3/issue3/robinson.html [accessed October 6, 2003]), reviews Heaven's Gate's use of the Internet and its connection to cyberculture and of media coverage of this angle on the group's career.

12   Steiger and Hewes, *Inside Heaven's Gate*, 153–54.

13   " '88 Update: The UFO Two and Their Crew," *How and When "Heaven's Gate" (The Door to the Physical Kingdom Level Above Human) May Be Entered*, October 18, 1988, http://www.clas.ufl.edu/users/gthursby/rel/gate/3-3.htm (accessed October 6, 2003).

14   "Total Overcomers Classroom Admission Requirements," *How and When "Heaven's Gate" (The Door to the Physical Kingdom Level Above Human) May Be Entered*, October 23, 1993, http://www.clas.ufl.edu/users/gthursby/rel/gate/5-6.htm (accessed October 6, 2003).

15   "The 17 Steps," *How and When "Heaven's Gate" (The Door to the Physical Kingdom Level*

Above Human) May Be Entered, November 1976, http://www.clas.ufl.edu/users/gthursby/rel/gate/2-5.htm (accessed October 6, 2003).

16 "Major Offenses and Lesser Offenses," *How and When "Heaven's Gate" (The Door to the Physical Kingdom Level Above Human) May Be Entered*, spring 1988, http://www.clas.ufl.edu/users/gthursby/rel/gate/2-6.htm (accessed October 6, 2003).

17 Gleik, "The Marker We've Been Waiting For," 31.

18 For an opposing view regarding cult activity and the millennium, see, for example, Stephen D. O'Leary, "Heaven's Gate and the Culture of Popular Millennialism," Center for Millennial Studies, Boston University, April 1997, http://www.mille.org/scholarship/papers/oleary1.html (accessed October 6, 2003).

19 Harding, *Book of Jerry Falwell*.

20 "Earth Exit Statements by Students," *How and When "Heaven's Gate" (The Door to the Physical Kingdom Level Above Human) May Be Entered*, March 1997, http://www.clas.ufl.edu/users/gthursby/rel/gate/exit.htm (accessed October 6, 2003). See also Robinson, "Heaven's Gate: The End?" and O'Leary, "Heaven's Gate and the Culture of Popular Millennialism."

21 Barry Bearak, "Eyes on Glory: Pied Pipers of the Heaven's Gate," *New York Times*, April 28, 1997, A1.

22 The following is drawn from the work of Chuck and Nancy Missler and Mark Eastman. See, for example, Missler and Eastman, *Alien Encounters*. Also see the Christian thriller by Lynn A. Marzulli, *Nephilim*; and *The Facade*, by Michael S. Heiser. The Christian writers and filmmakers Peter and Paul LaLonde also theorize about UFOs and aliens, and by now the alien/UFO subculture has become a site of Christian teaching and evangelizing. See, for example, the online publishing site for Guy Malone, *Come Sail Away: The UFO Phenomenon and the Bible*, 1997–1998, http://www.seekye1.com (accessed October 6, 2003); and "UFOs and Bible Conference: Roswell New Mexico—Angels, Aliens, Ancient Texts," *Alien Resistance HQ*, 2003, http://www.AncientofDays.net (accessed October 6, 2003), on the "Ancient of Days" conference (2003 and 2004) held in Roswell, New Mexico, over the July 4 holidays.

23 Both were drawing on a long tradition of citing biblical verses as evidence of ancient and future contact with aliens or extraterrestrials and their vessels. The tradition was popularized in the 1960s, 1970s, and 1980s by the writings of Jacques Vallée and Steven Spielberg's *Close Encounters of the Third Kind*. See Lieb, *Children of Ezekiel*, 44–48.

24 Thanks to Vicente Rafael for giving me the etymology of "prophesy" as "speaking forth."

25 "Background Information for Section 1: Exit Statements," *How and When "Heaven's Gate" (The Door to the Physical Kingdom Level Above Human) May Be Entered*, 1995–1996, http://www.clas.ufl.edu/users/gthursby/rel/gate/1-1.htm (accessed October 6, 2003).

26 "Do's Intro: Purpose—Belief," *How and When "Heaven's Gate" (The Door to the Physical Kingdom Level Above Human) May Be Entered*, 1996, http://www.clas.ufl.edu/users/gthursby/rel/gate/intro.htm (accessed October 6, 2003).

27 Anthony F. C. Wallace, in his classic essay on revitalization movements, observed that new religions are invariably assembled out of old as well as new cultural materials, so the pastiche quality of Do's language is not surprising. See Wallace, "Revitalization Movements"; and Balch, "Bo and Peep," 59. Do's peculiar innovation was to make the links an explicit, integrated, and continuous aspect of his speech and writing. He channeled and intertwined discursive voices.

28 Ted Nelson, *Literary Machines* (1993), 0.2.

29 Boyarin, *Intertextuality and the Reading of Midrash*. See Rosenberg, "Making Time," regarding Diderot's *Encyclopédie*; also see Rosenberg's essay in this volume for more on Ted Nelson. On zippered lists, see Nelson, *Literary Machines*, 1.27.

30 "Mass Suicide Involved Sedatives, Vodka and Careful Planning," CNN *Interactive: U.S. News Story Page*, March 27, 1997, http://www.cnn.com/US/9703/27/suicide/index.html.

31 " '88 Update."

32 See the appendix to this essay for more on the Mr. Rogers allusion.

33 Robinson, "Heaven's Gate: The End?"

34 Ibid.

35 " '88 Update."

36 *Oxford English Dictionary*.

37 "Our Position against Suicide," *How and When "Heaven's Gate" (The Door to the Physical Kingdom Level Above Human) May Be Entered*, http://www.clas.ufl.edu/users/gthursby/rel/gate/letter.htm (accessed October 6, 2003).

38 "Earth Exit Statements."

39 "USA Today Ad/Statement and Related Documents," *How and When "Heaven's Gate" (The Door to the Physical Kingdom Level Above Human) May Be Entered*, 1993, http://www.clas.ufl.edu/users/gthursby/rel/gate/5-1.htm (accessed October 6, 2003).

40 " 'The End of the Age Is upon Us': Cult Leader's Philosophy," CNN *Interactive: U.S. News Story Page*, March 28, 1997, http://www.cnn.com/US/9703/28/suicide.soundpage/index.html.

CHAPTER

the Future Life Band

The Blues OF The Future

Side

MBL Records
MBL - 000145

1. The Blues OF the Future.

2. Going to Pandle Handle Park Blues.

3. Going to Kentucky Fried Chicken ordering Chicken thigh Blues.

4. Going to Hope's House on the 33 AsHBury Bus Blues.

5. I Found a quarter on Mission and 16th street Blues.

6. Hungry to Death Blues.

7. Going Home on the 29 sunset Bus Blues.

8. the Halloween Frightful Blues.

Trauma Time: A Still Life

Kathleen Stewart

1

Sometime in the 1990s, ordinary things had started to buzz with the currents of possibility and dread as if they were divining rods channeling something. Like a series of electrical shocks wired directly to the social body, scenes of sudden impact caught the senses: L.A. in flames, a trailer wrapped in crime scene tape, the memorial ribbons and stuffed animals laid at the feet of a still-smoking building.

The imaginary had grown concrete on public stages.

Plot types became so familiar that we could list them in shorthand: disgruntled workers and jilted lovers and kids with guns opening fire in public; orderly men who kept too much to themselves revealed to be serial killers burying bodies in their backyards; black men beaten by cops; homegrown militias whipped into rage at the sight of unmarked helicopters and the stench of lost freedoms; messages coming through the mail as literal letter bombs now; anthrax coming in the white powder or the brown, sandlike substance. News of the weird featured stories like the one about the educated couple who calmly went away on vacation, leaving behind a hundred cats—some dead, some alive, wild ones living in the walls. Even the human-interest story had become a graphic repetition of animals that kill.

Trauma time grew pervasive, leaving us suspended in cocoons of half-known memories and unwitting expectations. It tweaked a nerve in the already frenzied exhaustion of a dream world dancing on a high wire without a safety net. The roller-coaster ride of the American dream came into a razor-edged focus. Overwrought dreams met crushing realities. It was mesmerizing to watch a dream drop out of a floating vertigo only to rise up, renewed, from the ashes of its own self-destruction like the monster in a horror film or the fool who keeps going back for more, thinking this time it will be different.

Lines of escape were fascinating, too: the rocketing fortunes of the rich and famous, the dream of a perfect getaway cottage, or the modest success stories of people getting their lives together.

Lifestyles proliferated at the same dizzying pace as the epidemic of addictions and the self-help shelves at the bookstore. A floating mix of uncertainty and self-affirmation wedged itself into the body and then melted, flowing out into the vast expanse of the collective dream world. The cultural lingua franca of stress tracked the double charge of a sensibility happily speeding along with the force of things-in-the-making and yet punctured by times of exhaustion, resentment, and worry.

A person lived in pulses of distraction and sharp attention. Every new technogadget that came along sent a shock effect through the body gyrating to mold itself to it. There was even a soft drink named Jolt Cola in honor of the addiction to the sudden awakening of the senses brought on by maximum sugar and caffeine. Or whatever. Your drug of choice. One minute we were playing happy little real-life games to test out the latest toy, and the next we were dreaming of a true self, or justice.

Things were up for grabs. We watched for a final slackening in things or a sudden berserking. The figure of a beefed-up agency became a breeding ground for strategies of experimentation, reinvention, self-destruction, and flight, as if the world rested on its shoulders.

Straight talk about willpower and positive thinking claimed that everything was just a matter of getting on track, as if all the muddled business of real selves in the real world could be left behind in an out-of-this-world levitation act.

Against this tendency, a new kind of memoir began to work the lone self into a fictional sacrifice powerful enough to drag the world's impacts out onto secret stages. Self-help groups added density to the mix, offering both practical recipes for self-redeeming action and a hard-hitting, lived recognition of the tortuous ways that compulsions permeated freedoms and were reborn in the very surge to get free of them once and for all.[1]

People began to experience life on the level of surging affects, forces unfolding, events erupting, and impacts suffered or barely avoided. The grammar of daily life found its punctuation in a rhythm of shocks that seemed to be saying something, though we weren't sure what.

2

We're in trauma time now. Where the here and now drifts between the future making of awakened expectations and the dragging dread of lurking threats and half-remembered horrors. Things seem to be simultaneously leaping forward and falling back. One step forward and two steps back, or two steps forward and one step back; the difference marks the line between "winners" and "losers." Push out the losers, expel them from the national banal of strip malls and master-planned communities, and they only come back to haunt, splayed on the networks as news of the weird.

> All those bodies lined up on the talk shows, outing their loved ones for this or that monstrous act. Or the camera busting in on intimate dramas of whole families addicted to sniffing paint right out of the can. We would zoom in to linger almost lovingly on the gallon-sized lids scattered about on the living room carpet and on the faces of the parents, and even the little kids, featuring big rings of white encircling their cheeks and chins like some kind of self-inflicted stigmata.

Risk society brings us the worst-case scenario in the very effort to insure against it.[2] Advertising commodifies fear along with the dream of personal, exceptional safety in selling everything from insurance, to schools, to cars, to high-priced skin creams like Charles of the Ritz "Disaster Cream," Estée Lauder "Skin Defender Cream," and Golden Door "Crisis Cream."[3] The media flow provides a flood of half-information that comes with supplementary warnings and contradictory advice and reminds us that we are never simply at home but chained to the grid.[4]

In the chanting mantra of American public culture, a second voice whispers in the ear, haunting the solidity of the truth:

> Beware financial advisors who make a profit on your investments. . . . Yesterday's magic diet to keep you safe from heart attack is not right after all. Drink wine, eat aspirin, oatmeal strips your veins clean, walking is just as good as running (but how fast? how often?) What about your genes? Don't panic. Panic causes disaster. What's everyone else doing (what do they know that I don't)?

Violence and abjection are seen as a contagion, like a virus; self-control and social containment are the only known vaccine.[5] Talk shows suggest that social and psychological problems are everywhere and our job, as audience, is to recognize them in everything we see.[6]

> America's Most Wanted prints photos of bank robbers with and without beards so you can scan the faces at the 7–11 for a match.

TV news recasts the ordinary, everyday violence of inequality and the dismantling of social services as a threat of illegal immigrants, race wars, and terrorism.[7] Then it is reported on the news that a recovery movement guru suggests we simply stop watching the news, listing it as one of the five major causes of stress today.

The "middle class" becomes a womb of safety and stasis,[8] while the poor (and the otherwise real) have dropped out of view except as criminals, spectacular failures, and dangerous urban mobs. Master-planned communities conflate a dreamy nostalgia for small-town America with the resurgent modernist utopia of the new and clean and up-to-date. A still life takes form inside the gates against a "wilding" exterior of crime, chaos, drug-addled monsters, danger, disease, decay. Inside, fears and accusations settle down into an unnatural calm.

> The little family stands beside their SUV in the driveway, looking up. Stock portfolios in hand, everything insured, payments up to date, yards kept trim and tended, fat-free diet under their belts, Community Watch systems in place. Martha Stewart offers advice on the finishing touches.

There is a search for new forms of sentimentality and a longing for interiority. We find ourselves in the mist of the self-help movement, privatization, cocooning, family values, utopia walled up in theme parks and franchise culture, feel-good movies and colorful décor. Action stories of masculinity play out a fast-switching dialectic of pending disaster and last-minute reprieves in which agency gets to stretch its muscles. Movies made for women imagine a picture-perfect scene of an Inside—a Home filled with tangible objects that mean and a Self filled with the intricate dramas of dreams launched, wounded, and finally satisfied or abandoned.

Home is where the heart is. You can get inside and slam the door. But take one foot out of the frame, and things get sketchy fast. We watch for shock while looking for recluse. At the unwanted knock on the door, or the sudden ring of the phone at night, you can feel the uncanny resemblance between the dazed state of trauma and the cocooning we now call home. Progress drifts into trauma in the flick of an eye until you can't think one without the other: careful saving, half-information, steady march forward, crash and burn, crisis, contingency, dread, magical release, start the cycle over again. There is the trauma that shocks when something happens; some people live in a constant mode of crisis. But there is trauma, too, in the anesthetized distraction of an OK middle ground defending a womb against the world. Here, fear of falling meets a more profound fear of burst bubbles. The fear burrows into action, breeding disciplines (the healthy diet, the tended lawn, the daily lottery ticket) and compulsions (the scanning for news, the need for the new and improved, fetishisms of all kinds).

> The bubble man holes up in his house, free from contaminants, but he needs the airwaves to keep the information about contaminants flowing. A warning leaks in in the very effort to keep risk at bay.

The OK middle ground has to be constantly enacted in the manicured lawn, the picket fences, and the self-governing, responsible subject in tune with the times. Pushing itself to the limit, it grows haunted by its own excesses. The picture-perfect living room takes on the anxious charge of something trying too hard, or a little off, or always already out of date. In the gated community, the rules of community order reach a tottering point open to parody and endless legal contestation: garage doors have to be kept shut at all times, drapes in neutral colors only, no digging in the yard without permission, no clotheslines in the yard, no pickup trucks in the driveway, no planting without permission, no grandchildren visiting in a senior compound. No exceptions. The desire for security becomes a phantom search, part image, part real, like the signs on lawns that announce the presence of alarm systems, as if the signs themselves would magically ward off burglars. And on the mobile homes, a sticker in the window: "This Place Protected by a Smith and Wesson Three Nights a Week. Guess Which Nights."

Public specters have grown intimate. Horror stories leak in over the airwaves. Seemingly ordinary intimate spaces are revealed to be scenes of hidden corruption, catastrophe, isolation, and crime: there are children on welfare beaten to death in their homes between visits from the social worker, men who burst into their ex-girlfriends' trailers, shooting them and their new lovers in their beds, bodies discovered only after the neighbors heard the dog barking in there for days on end.

At odd moments of spacing out, a strange malaise may come over you. These are moments when the cheering mantra of the American dream meets the nightmare of its own exclusions, blindnesses, and anxieties. Specters of conspiracy, violence, disaster, and abjection become tactile images that impact. The streets are littered with cryptic, half-written signs of personal and public disasters like the daily sightings of homeless men and women holding up signs while puppies play at their feet. *Hungry. Will work for food. God Bless You.*

Propelled into a netherworld, we dream of the day when our ship will come in. Some invest in the wild-ride stodginess of stocks and bonds. Others wait for the kind of magic that comes in a flash.

The sweepstakes cameras appear at your door while you're still in your housedress, big bunches of balloons in primary colors are released into the air, and the music plays in surround sound.

Or . . . UFOs come in the night and lift you up in an out-of-this-world levitation trick. . . . Chips implanted in the back of the neck make you a literal link in the information highway. . . . Everyone knows about the supermarket scanners and the new drivers licenses.

Like a broken record, trauma time repeats what is not directly encountered, known, remembered, or imagined.[9] It gives us a present that is present to itself as a haunting and a desire. It's as if something that has already happened lingers as a half-known force resonant in traces, and something else is already set in motion, carrying jangled nerves along on the wave of an inexorable, unrelenting future. Things come to a head in a haunted still life, and then they break up and diffuse again in a dense, prolific circulation that links everything.

Trauma time has the restlessness and obsessions of modernity's simultaneous overstimulation and numbness, alarm and anesthesia.[10] It exists most powerfully not as an idea but as felt seductions and intoxications, as symptoms and warning signs and repetitions, as numbness and shocking moments of impact, as daydream and daily routine. We can see it in dramas that cull intensities to a point of recognition, but it is also lurking in still lifes of the most ordinary kind that seem to capture something.

3

What follows here is a collection of ordinary still lifes. These are scenes gathered out of the soup of circulating signs we call everyday life and out of the archaeology of forgetting and unforgetting that motivates dreams of escape and fears of burst bubbles. These still lifes are not representations, or ideas, about histories and futures but the traces of technologies, or practices, of making pasts and futures inscribed in forms of feeling, sociality, power, contingency, and agency. They do not so much signify something that can be gathered into a generalizable code or system as they do ferment and record a series of moves.

Think of the definition of a still life. A still life is both a picture of small inanimate objects and the things themselves—the fruit, the flowers, the books, the vases left on a table, perhaps by a window. The word "still" refers both to the state of being at rest and to an apparatus used for distilling liquids—a still. Here I am interested not so much in stillness as in the still itself, not so much in the picture of a still life as in the objects that draw attention to themselves as qualities at a standstill. I present these stills in a way that evokes the logic of gap, contiguity, and nervous interconnection because these are the logics of the discourse networks out of which their stillness emerges.[11]

There are countless such stills evident in the concrete (yet elusive) realm of everyday life. There are the still lifes of pleasure collected by the life of privilege like marbles: the writing desk with flowers illuminated by a warm ray of sun in a profoundly still and secluded interior. Or the still lifes of a vitality satisfied, an energy spent: the living room strewn with ribbons and wineglasses after a party, the kids or dogs asleep in the back seat of the car after a great day at the lake, the collection of sticks and rocks resting on the dashboard after a hike in the mountains.

The still life can turn ordinary life into a daydream of finished happiness captured in a scene. But it can also give us pause to consider what we call, in cliché, "the simple things in life": the unexpected discovery of something moving within the ordinary, or a still center lodged in the smallest of things.

The still life fixes attention on the fluid space where emerging and submerging forces meet. Its hold is temporary; the everyday drifts back into the open disguise of things so ordinary that they can't be seen for what they are. But sometimes it lingers like a shadow or a promise that a moment of intensity will emerge within the ordinary—a stopping driven by the desires it pursues and makes, still.

The stills selected here encompass moments of anxiety and abjection, moments of being "taken aback" and wild leaps of hope, fetishizing moments, back talk, conspiracy, and obsession. They emerge in ordinary practices like keeping a diary, making lists, planning, keeping up with technological gadgets, keeping house, the art of finishing touches, and packing for a celestial trip on the tail of a comet. Chosen from countless possibilities, they do not begin to exhaust them or even to gesture at a grid for mapping them. On the contrary, they cut across the grain of a full-speed-ahead analytics of "the future" to consider, instead, the traces, the impacts, lodged in the still lifes of the everyday—"the inaccessible to which we have always already had access."[12]

a

Take Martha Stewart, for instance. That's one history of the future. She's a technology of finishing touches. She makes the picture-perfect domestic scene, the obsessive self-discipline of the bourgeois subject, the icing on the state of readiness (house in order, beautifully prepared hors d'oeuvres all ready in the freezer should anyone stop by). She is ornamentality, the perfect fit of femininity and class mobility, the technology of taking time. Today she's making real Mexican salsa. She says if you chop the vegetables in a blender, you're *not* making *real* Mexican salsa. She has a chef with her, and he's chopping the tomatoes and onions expertly, professionally, as you and I never could.

She's also a whipping boy for parody and contempt. She's a machine of excess, and she produces opposition, laughter, envy, anxiety, despair, hope, and little projects that give people something to do with their hands. She's a form of pleasure. She's a nostalgia machine for the authentic and the handmade, and she's a future flyer into progress and modernity (again). She's comforting, light, and entertaining (not like the stock market, for instance), unless, of course, your life happens to depend on picture-perfect scenes of efficient beauty. Then it's more serious.

b

Another still life of the history of the future is the daily encounters we all have with new gadgets. Like the day I was in the office at the Humanities Research Institute in Irvine, frantically copying journal articles from the institute's library because the Histories of the Future fellowship was running out. Time was running out, and I was packing up and didn't want to miss something crucial. Maybe there was a kernel somewhere in one of these articles. Or even a key. Stephen walked in. I asked him if he wanted to use the machine and started chatting distractedly while my hands turned page after page of the journal, grabbing quick images to be scanned later in the search for the kernel or the key.

Stephen said he just had to use the stapler. Then he stuck a paper into a slot on the side of the copy machine, pulled out the stapled paper, and walked off. I was literally taken aback to discover that copy machines now had staplers built into them.

> Suddenly, I could feel my mother's anxiety at trying to keep up with things: answering machines, computers, having to pump your own gas and pay the pump with a credit card, ATM machines. Neither one of us can get her car phone working yet. I avoid upgrading my computer like the plague.

The fear of new gadgets is a fear of first times or the fear of finding yourself helpless in a future still life where using the new technology is not a choice but a necessity. It's also the anxiety of being out of the loop, of not knowing what everyone else always already knows. It's like illiteracy.

We're always behind because we're always trying to keep up (even if we don't want to). One step forward is always two steps back—a leap forward into something new only to discover you're already way behind (and dragging your feet anyway). There's doubt, dread, a wish to stay back, to go back to the past—a wish that only comes because of the future thing in your face that demands an agency now.

As I urge the ATM machine on my mother, I remember her growing up on the farm during the Depression: watery potato soup to eat, the childhood traumas of driving the plow behind massive horse haunches, then learning to drive the truck at age ten so she could fill in while her father disappeared on a drunk, then all those tense dinners in the fifties when scientific household management demanded a square meal (meat, potatoes, one green vegetable and one yellow) on the table at the stroke of six, with all the kids underfoot. Progress demanded slipcovers on the living room furniture and penny-saving discipline channeled, over years, into four college educations. Now she likes sunny rooms and keeping busy; she paints folk art objects to give as gifts and to cover her walls, and she watches Martha Stewart to pick up tips, saying she knows people make fun of Martha, but Martha is real—she really does all these things on the show.

In trauma time, ordinary things gathered into the scene of the still life can be screens that simultaneously hide something and project it, larger than life, into public view. In that moment they are both a figure and a material trace. Remember, for instance, when the Heaven's Gate followers went up armed with lip balm and quarters, and how they placed their glasses, carefully folded, on the beds next to their hands. In a moment of crisis when the past meets the future, the vibrant thing can project the anxiety of a future that is leaving you behind (the stapler), or it can make an unlikely yet certain faith tangible (the lip balm). When things in themselves act as conduits channeling the literal into the figural and back, "meaning" is no longer something simply and surely located in a symbolic system or in the eyes of the viewer but a spark generated out of the very shiftiness of subjects and objects.

c

One day as I was walking around the master-planned town of Irvine, California, I came across a small "affordable" neighborhood in the midst of this place where, outsiders say, the trash cans sit on doilies and the weeds grow in perfect rows. Parked at the curb in a tucked-away cul-de-sac was a late-model, fire-engine-red Ford sedan with a huge logo inscribed on the driver's door that read "PMS POWERED." A snazzy car with an in-your-face voice, it not only back-talked PMS jokes but claimed their force as a technology—a still to distill fuel out of social snickering. This car drives around town as the material trace of an attitude adjustment. But when I walked around the parked car to check out the other side, I saw that both of its tires on that side had been stolen. The car was listing precariously on one hastily placed jack, just as it had, apparently, been left by the thieves. Now it was a figure and a material trace of something else. Back to trauma time. I wondered how long it had been sitting there accruing meanings.

In the everyday life of things, dreams and losses are lifted into circulation in concrete forms and dropped out of the loop again. They can come to roost as ruins, temporary setbacks, or the literal residue of past- and future-making practices that others might chance upon and recognize, rediscover or attack.

d

Carrie is a self-styled witch and gypsy. Not much over four feet tall, her jet-black hair falls past her waist. She had been a clerical worker for years when she invented a future-making technology of free pet sitting. Since she is also obsessively organized and compulsively hyperresponsible, she soon built up a big enough clientele to give up renting a place of her own. She kept her day job but moved from one housesitting job to the next (or stayed with friends in the down times). Her phone was a beeper she carried around her neck. When I met her, she was getting her feet back on the ground after she had gambled everything on a love affair that took her to Australia and, when things went badly, stranded her there. She had made enough for a ticket home and a few thousand dollars to spare by card gambling. Turns out she has a talent for gambling.

Once, when she was due to housesit for me, she called from the road on her way back from a quick overnight to Vegas. Actually, she never made it to Vegas, she said, but stopped at the first cheap little casino on the Nevada border, walked in, and found a machine with an aura she picked up on. Then she waited until the time was right. She checked in, watched a couple of TV shows in her room, and came back to check the machine. The time was almost right. She chatted with the woman at the next machine, listened to the band in the bar, drifted by the machine again, watched another TV show, and finally returned. By this time it was after midnight, and her neighbor at the next machine was cheering her on. The time was finally right. She played a couple of dollar slots and hit the jackpot. Later that night, the same machine paid off again.

Here, the slot machine is a technology that traces histories of the future. Stuffed full of lost tokens, it holds them up as the promise of a big-win future. Getting a feeling from a slot machine means gauging the pasts and futures sitting still behind all the flashy distractions. It also means making a name for yourself in history. It holds up the dream of becoming the exception. Yet the very possibility of this wild leap of faith depends on a half-known knowledge of all the real failures that have come before and extend as far as the distracted eye can see into the future of gambling for the common one. The gamble, and the talent, comes in being able to keep your eye on that machine while specters gather at the corner of the eye.

e

Trauma time is a haunted peripheral vision that demands hypervigilance. An uncanny, alien presence captures your attention out of the corner of your eye but remains unassimilated and nagging. It weighs down the present with the equally compelling anxieties of a history of failed agency or the tendency to leap recklessly into uncertainty.

In the anxious stasis of a history of the future, everyday practices like making lists, cleaning house, and reading "how-to" books can guard against the moment of being taken aback. They can amount to something like what Svetlana Boym calls "graphomania" — the incessant practice of recording the details of the everyday in order to gain access to it.[13] Like the guy I read about in the paper who spends his whole life recording everything he does.

> Got up at 6:30 a.m., still dark, splashed cold water on my face, brushed my teeth, 6:40 went to the bathroom, 6:45 made tea, birds started in at 6:53.

Or this other guy—a neighbor guy in Michigan when we lived on a little lake surrounded by woods. He was retired from the Ford factory, and his hobby was recording everything on video. Once I watched one of his videos and was mesmerized by its graphic mania. It recorded him walking on a set path around the lake including his every breath and footstep, a pile of deer droppings on the path, and the shape of snow piles. His run-on narrative voice-over told us everything in words, including the temperature of the air, the fact that he was walking, stopping, starting again, whose cabin he was walking by, which summer people were down in Florida and when they would be back. Then he came to a cabin with black plastic wrapped around its base, and he zoomed in on what looked like a large protrusion pushing against the plastic on one side of the house. It's trauma time. He wondered aloud if it was ice from a broken water pipe inside the house;

maybe the whole house was full of ice. The still life, capturing a history of the future laid out on the landscape and opened to speculation, gave him the pause and pleasure of graphomaniac satisfaction.

> It was too late to do anything about it now, and what would happen with the thaw? He would have to send a copy of the tape to Bob and Alice down in Florida.

Then, abruptly, he moved on in search of another still life. Back to the breathing and the mundane narrative of icicles on trees and footsteps in the snow. Tracking the banal, scanning for trauma. . . .

Graphomania is but one of many inscriptions that can fill the everyday with the material traces of trauma time even in the very effort to hold it at bay, or forget it, or resist it. Written under the sign of "keeping busy," they can make anxiety a way of life. Or they can lay claim to agency in the face of the ever-present threat, or memory, of trauma time. Adding agency to the scene of trauma, you enter the land of abjection. Or at least the dance of abjection and release where futures and pasts come into focus in one moment and recede from view in the next.

My friends Barbara and Ted lived in the woods in New Hampshire. He was a lumberjack. She cleaned those little 1950s tourist cabins with names like "Swiss Village" and "Shangrila." He had a drinking problem (there were trauma times involved in this), and she had left her husband and four kids after years of living straight in a regime of beatings under the sign of Jesus. She went out the back window one day and never went back. That was trauma time too. She met Ted when she was tending bar, and they took a walk on the wild side together that lasted for a dozen happy years (though not without trauma, and plenty of it).

They had no money, so they moved from rental cabin to rental cabin up in the north woods (there were trauma times in this), and they invited the raccoons into their cabins as if they were pets. She called him "Daddy" even though she was a good ten years older and pushing fifty. They had a daily routine of getting up at 5:30 to write in diaries—a still that made their lives together an adventure story with a past and a future. When they got home from work at night, they would read to each other from these diaries and look at the pictures Ted took when he was up in the trees—arty pictures of treetops and bee nests. Finally they were able to get a poor people's loan to buy a little cabin they had found in a godforsaken place and fix it up. But last year the Christmas card came from Barbara alone, and it said that Ted had left her for "that floozy" he met in a bar. Barbara's address was still the house they owned. I wondered if she still kept a diary.

f

I met the man I have come to call "The Abject Man" in Las Vegas. He was the maintenance man in the trailer park where we lived outside Nellis Air Force Base, on the edge of town. I was alone for the year in a crazy, violent, pathos-ridden, wildly exhilarated, and deeply alienated place, and at night I would walk the streets of the trailer park for exercise, spectacular sunsets, and relief from isolation. This man walked too, and eventually we began to stop and chat. Things got personal right away. His girlfriend had left him one day while he was out, taking her three kids and the suite of blue velveteen living room furniture he had bought with the only money he ever won gambling. Now she would call him in the middle of the night to torture him with the details of her new sex life. One day, in a moment of masochistic overload, he went over to her new boyfriend's place to fix his toilet for him while the new couple looked on maliciously. He was deeply depressed and addicted to gambling, cigarettes, and certain TV shows that came on in the early morning and during the dinner hour. He was also illiterate and filled with the built-up fear and shame of the traumas that illiteracy had caused him over the years. He had no driver's license and couldn't read the simplest instructions on equipment or even street signs or the names of restaurants, bars, and casinos. He had very restricted routes of movement. He hated his job because his boss was viciously cruel to him, his pay was below minimum wage, and he was "live-in help," on call twenty-four hours a day to take care of anything that came up.

I listened to his stories every day as things went from bad to worse with one humiliation after the next and no future to imagine. Finally one night he called an old girlfriend, now married, from Houston. She had a daughter who as a child had adored him; now in her twenties, she had been left a paraplegic after a terrible accident and required constant care. He decided he would go out there, spend all his time taking care of her in the nursing home, and be her man. He plotted in detail how he could raise the money for a one-way bus ticket to Houston, how to get to the bus station for the midnight departure, and how to sell or pawn his few remaining things. Then one day he was gone, and the park manager was looking for him in a grim fury. No one knows what happened to him in Houston, or even if he made it to the bus station in Vegas.

From the desperation of a present-past misery he was caught in, he invented the fantasy of a new and improved still life. An other past, nostalgically remembered, became not only the site and living trace of redemption but the means to achieve a future. From a space entrenched in trauma time, a last-ditch, desperate agency propelled him into a history of the future.

William Pierce's novel *The Turner Diaries* is a racist prophecy of a new world order.[14] A postapocalyptic world is set in motion by "the terrible day" in an invented past when government thugs broke into citizens' houses, tore apart seemingly solid walls to unearth hidden guns, and arrested hordes of people, rounding them up like cattle. The originary trauma time brings the repetitions of a no-exit present to a head; a moment of reckoning, it incites a militia movement fueled by a politics of *ressentiment*. In the end, the heroes are propelled into a place in history and into a future time fashioned after the image of a pure past—a future where trauma time can be remembered through the glorious anesthesia of the war memorial. A still life.

Reading the text, I was struck not by the power of its overly scripted plot but by its romance with domestic scenes and technical details. It reads like a virtual how-to manual for right-wing conspiracy theorists and survivalists, detailing tips on everything from how to organize armies and make bombs to the more mundane ingenuities of setting up cozy shelters and keeping house underground or fashioning implements for everything from cooking to an underground communications system. The heroes distinguish themselves not by acts of bravery and camaraderie but by honing skills in mechanics, engineering, shooting, sexuality, and leadership. A kind of Robinson Crusoe fantasy of building tools out of found objects, the pleasures of this text begin with its own status as a found object discovered in its secret, underground circulation and mined for details in the circuitous routes of the still lifes it traces. Reading it, I couldn't help but think of the well-tended suburban lawn and the Martha Stewart–inspired interiors or the practice of reading catalogs to imagine yourself in that dress, with that face, or holding that particular gun. I couldn't help but wonder how the racist rage at disorder, contamination, and decay might be both fueled and relieved by such fantasies of the moment when the ordinary disciplines and obsessions of a private life suddenly emerge into public view in a still life. Here trauma time builds a bridge, such as it is, over the chasm between an overburdened, hyperstimulated (yet starved), be-all, end-all intimate life and the distant image of an inaccessible, gigantic-scale public world of governments and corporations somewhere out there. It also fuels the search for quick-fix solutions and promotes a conflation of intimacy and public life: my nightmare image becomes the history of the future of the world. In trauma time, something happens. A still emerges.

h

Around the same time we were reading *The Turner Diaries*, "The Republic of Texas" took its stand. Traumatized by the circulating remembrance of Ruby Ridge and Waco, and feeling their sovereign citizenship embattled, the members of the Republic brought things to a head by kidnapping their neighbors. Center stage, they took their stand, and then again came the details of housekeeping, communications, arms caches, the details of the organization, newly found survivalist skills, a place in history, a return to a pure past as if it could be the future. An eruption carried the social densities of trauma time into an imaginary of chances finally taken and dreams enacted. And before the smoke had cleared there were men on the run in the wilds shooting guns at government helicopters.

i

In Vegas, my trailer was broken into one day in plain daylight. A brick had been hurled through a window, drawers had been emptied onto the floor, my computer was unplugged and ready to go, my stereo was gone, and a note was stuck on the living room wall with a large pair of scissors. The note said, simply, "Yeah, boy." After drifting around in the disorientation of trauma time for a few minutes, I called the police and the park management. A week later I went to a community meeting to see if there had been other burglaries. At the meeting, the park manager claimed that all the trouble was in the past, so I protested and told my story. It became clear that others had long ago decided that the thieves were teenagers from the run-down, "trashy" trailer park next to ours. A group of stern-looking, bulky young military men lining the back wall of the Quonset hut made some claims that they could put a stop to it, and as we were filing out, one of them caught my eye with a hard stare I couldn't quite read.

My feeling that the community meeting had only made things worse deepened over the next two weeks as people started noticing a late-model, brightly colored party jeep patrolling the streets at all hours of the night with its headlights off. One night when I woke to the sound of it slowly passing, I looked out and saw the dark shapes of four or five men hanging off the sides of the jeep with semiautomatic guns and spotlights in their hands. Another emergency community meeting was called to demand that they stop their secret patrols before they shot someone.

In trauma time, community and the public are entities that come into existence in the face of risk or at the precise moment that crime and criminal elements become visible as surrounding presences.[15] Just as trauma time is not just an idea but a visceral experience brought to the senses day and night in the repetitions of trauma TV and inscribed in countless still lifes of the everyday, so too "community watch" and "action" become scripted public-private visceralities of a subject surrounded by forces.

Don't forget your lip balm when you get ready to go, and don't leave home without a quarter (and a dime) for a phone call. . . .

4

An ideal history of the future—one made of civil ideals, free agency, and progress—free-floats in a dreamy mix of nostalgia, presumed innocence, utopian longing, and technophilia. This is serious business in America, and it's also as thin as the talk at a supermarket.[16] Trauma time is the specter that haunts it.[17] It steeps everyday life in the American dream's bad twin. It lives the life of the phobic, the abject, the betrayed, and the unspeakable. It screens (and stages) a "real" as a momentary rupture in the order of things, or a moment of impact when the subject is touched by an image or haunted by a missed encounter.[18] It may flash up to expose a crisis and then amount to nothing more than a flash in the pan. And yet the technologies themselves may not only leave traces but actually lead a life of traces. The particular "stills" of trauma time may become sensibilities, or repetitions that "go nowhere" but lodge in the everyday.

In the public-private culture and politics of the contemporary United States, trauma has become the dominant idiom of subjectivity, citizenship, politics, and publics.[19] It is a sensibility of impact for which there are, of course, many unspeakable referents: violence, death, AIDS, racism, the destroyed welfare state and broken social contract, grotesque extremes of poverty, wealth, and surveillance, abuse, addiction, new orders of discipline, social isolation, privatization, conspiracy, the global-order economy. But it is also a technology and material trace in its own right. As a technology, or "still," it marks the wound or gap where a public politics might be. It traces the conflation of the public and the private, the inside and the outside.[20] It marks the nightmarish vulnerabilities of a subject who is subject to forces beyond her control or understanding and yet given total responsibility for everything that happens to her and to others.[21] It marks a mode of attention at once deeply distracted and scanning for revelations and driven by the fury of its own traces.

Notes

1   Sedgwick, "Epidemics of the Will."
2   Beck, Risk Society.

3   Mellencamp, *High Anxiety*.

4   Ronell, "Trauma TV."

5   Davis, *Ecology of Fear*.

6   Mellencamp, *High Anxiety*.

7   Berlant, *The Queen of America Goes to Washington City*.

8   Brown, *States of Injury*.

9   Caruth, *Unclaimed Experience*.

10   Buck-Morss, "Aesthetics and Anaesthetics."

11   Kittler, *Discourse Networks 1800/1900*.

12   Blanchot, "Everyday Speech."

13   Boym, *Common Places*.

14   Pierce, *The Turner Diaries*.

15   Archer, "Gated Governmentality."

16   Trow, *Within the Context of No Context*, 22.

17   Derrida, *Specters of Marx*; Gordon, *Ghostly Matters*.

18   Foster, *The Return of the Real*.

19   Berlant, *Queen of America*; Dean, *Aliens in America*; Sturken, *Tangled Memories*.

20   Mark Seltzer, "Wound Culture."

21   Brown, *States of Injury*.

BIBLIOGRAPHY

Aarseth, Espen. "Nonlinearity and Literary Theory." In Hyper/Text/Theory, ed. George Landow. Baltimore: Johns Hopkins University Press, 1994.

Adams, Henry. The Education of Henry Adams. New York: Modern Library, 1996.

Advisory Committee on Human Radiation Experiments. The Human Radiation Experiments: Final Report of the President's Advisory Committee. New York: Oxford University Press, 1996.

Aldiss, Brian. Billion Year Spree: The True History of Science Fiction. Garden City, N.Y.: Doubleday, 1973.

Anderson, Benedict. "Cacique Democracy in the Philippines." In The Spectre of Comparisons. London: Verso, 1998.

——. Imagined Communities: Reflections on the Origins and Spread of Nationalism. Rev. ed. London: Verso, 1991.

Anderson, Perry. "The Ends of History." In A Zone of Engagement. New York: Verso, 1992.

Andreev, Leonid, Jack Iverson, and Mark Olsen. "Re-engineering a War Machine: ARTFL's Encyclopédie." Literary and Linguistic Computing 14, no. 1 (1999): 11–28.

Appadurai, Arjun. Modernity at Large: Cultural Dimensions of Globalization. Minneapolis: University of Minnesota Press, 1996.

Archer, Matt. "Gated Governmentality." Master's thesis, University of Texas, 1997.

Arrighi, Giovanni. The Long Twentieth Century. New York: Verso, 1994.

Baczko, Bronislaw. Utopian Lights: The Evolution of the Idea of Social Progress. Trans. Judith L. Greenberg. New York: Paragon House, 1978.

Balch, Robert W. "Bo and Peep: A Case Study in the Origin of Messianic Leadership." In Millennialism and Charisma, ed. Roy Wallis. Belfast: Queen's University Press, 1982.

——. "Waiting for the Ships: Disillusionment and the Revitalization of Faith in Bo and Peep's UFO Cult." In The Gods Have Landed: New Religions from Other Worlds, ed. James R. Lewis. New York: SUNY Press, 1995.

Balch, Robert W., and David Taylor. "Salvation in a UFO." Psychology Today 10 (October 1976): 58–59.

———. "Seekers and Saucers: The Role of Cultic Milieu in Joining a UFO Cult." In *Conversion Careers: In and Out of the New Religions*, ed. James T. Richardson. Beverly Hills, Calif.: Sage Publications, 1978.

Balsamo, Anne. *Technologies of the Gendered Body: Reading Cyborg Women*. Durham, N.C.: Duke University Press, 1996.

Banham, Reyner. *Theory and Design in the First Machine Age*. London: Architectural Press, 1960.

Barthes, Roland. "The Discourse of History." In *The Rustle of Language*, trans. Richard Howard. Oxford: Basil Blackwell, 1986.

———. *The Pleasure of the Text*. Trans. Richard Miller. New York: Noonday, 1980.

Barthelme, Frederick, and Steven Barthelme. *Double Down: Reflections on Gambling and Loss*. New York: Houghton Mifflin, 1999.

Baudrillard, Jean. *America*. Trans. Chris Turner. New York: Verso, 1988.

Beck, Ulrich. *Risk Society: Towards a New Modernity*. New York: Sage, 1992.

Bell, Daniel. *Toward the Year 2000: Work in Progress*. Cambridge: MIT Press, 1997.

Bender, John, and David E. Wellbery. *Chronotypes: The Construction of Time*. Stanford: Stanford University Press, 1991.

Benjamin, Walter. *Charles Baudelaire: A Lyric Poet in the Era of High Capitalism*. London: Verso, 1977.

———. "Theses on the Philosophy of History." In *Illuminations*, ed. Hannah Arendt. New York: Schocken Books, 1968.

Bercovitch, Sacvan. *The Puritan Origins of the American Self*. New Haven, Conn.: Yale University Press, 1975.

Bergson, Henri. *Matter and Memory*. Trans. N. M. Paul and W. S. Palmer. New York: Zone Books, 1988.

Berlant, Lauren. *The Queen of America Goes to Washington City*. Durham, N.C.: Duke University Press, 1997.

Berman, Marshall. *All That Is Solid Melts into Air: The Experience of Modernity*. New York: Simon and Schuster, 1982.

Bernstein, Peter L. *Against the Gods: The Remarkable Story of Risk*. New York: Wiley and Sons, 1996.

Blackburn, Robin. *Banking on Death; or, Investing in Life: The History and Future of Pensions*. New York: Verso Press, 2002.

Blair, Ann. "Annotating and Indexing Natural Philosophy." In *Books and the Sciences in History*, ed. Marina Frasca-Spada and Nick Jardine. Cambridge, U.K.: Cambridge University Press, 2000.

Blanchot, Maurice. "Everyday Speech." *Yale French Studies* 73 (1987): 1–20.

Blum, Cinzia Sartini. *The Other Modernism: F. T. Marinetti's Futurist Fiction of Power*. Berkeley: University of California Press, 1996.

Blumenberg, Hans. *The Legitimacy of the Modern Age*. Trans. Robert M. Wallace. Cambridge: MIT Press, 1983.

Boyarin, Daniel. *Intertextuality and the Reading of Midrash*. Bloomington: Indiana University Press, 1990.

Boym, Svetlana. *Common Places: Mythologies of Everyday Life*. Cambridge: Harvard University Press, 1994.

Brand, Stewart. *The Clock of the Long Now: Time and Responsibility, the Ideas behind the World's Slowest Computer.* New York: Basic Books, 1999.

Brint, Steven. *In an Age of Experts: The Changing Role of Professionals in Politics and Public Life.* Princeton: Princeton University Press, 1994.

Brookfield, Harold, Leslie Potter, and Yvonne Byron. *In Place of the Forest: Environmental and Socioeconomic Transformations in Borneo and the Eastern Malay Peninsula.* New York: United Nations Press, 1995.

Brown, Wendy. *States of Injury: Power and Freedom in Late Modernity.* Princeton: Princeton University Press, 1995.

Bryant, Raymond, and Sinead Bailey. *Third World Political Ecology.* London: Routledge, 1997.

Buck-Morss, Susan. "Aesthetics and Anaesthetics: Walter Benjamin's Artwork Essay Reconsidered." *New Formations* 20 (1993): 123–43.

———. *Dreamworld and Catastrophe: The Passing of Mass Utopia in East and West.* Cambridge: MIT Press, 2000.

Buffett, Mary, and David Clark. *Buffettology: The Previously Unexplained Techniques That Have Made Warren Buffett the World's Most Famous Investor.* New York: Scribner Book Company, 1997.

Bukatman, Scott. "Gibson's Typewriter." In *Flame Wars: The Discourse of Cyberculture,* ed. Mark Dery. Durham, N.C.: Duke University Press, 1994.

Burke, James. *Connections.* Boston: Little, Brown, 1995.

Bush, Vannevar. "As We May Think." *Atlantic Monthly* 176, no. 1 (July 1945): 101–8.

Butler, Judith. *The Psychic Life of Power: Theories of Subjection.* Stanford: Stanford University Press, 1997.

Calvino, Italo. *Invisible Cities.* Trans. William Weaver. New York: Harcourt Brace, 1974.

Campbell, Glenn. *A Short History of Rachel, Nevada.* Prepared for the Rachel Senior Center, 1996.

Cannell, Fenella. *Power and Intimacy in the Christian Philippines.* Cambridge, U.K.: Cambridge University Press, 1999.

Carney, Judith. *Black Rice: The African Origins of Rice Cultivation in the Americas.* Cambridge: Harvard University Press, 2001.

Carrière, Jean-Claude, Jean Delumeau, Umberto Eco, and Stephen Jay Gould. *Conversations about the End of Time.* Trans. Ian Maclean and Roger Pearson. New York: Fromm International, 2000.

Caruth, Cathy. *Unclaimed Experience: Trauma, Narrative, History.* Baltimore: Johns Hopkins University Press, 1996.

Celdran, David M. "Text Revolution." *I: The Investigative Reporting Magazine* (Manila) 8, no. 2 (April–June 2002): 14–17.

Center for Land Use Interpretation. *The Nevada Test Site: A Guide to America's Nuclear Proving Ground.* Los Angeles: Center for Land Use Interpretation, 1996.

Certeau, Michel de. "History: Science and Fiction." In *Heterologies: Discourse on the Other,* trans. Brian Massumi. Minneapolis: University of Minnesota Press, 1986.

Chiba Sen'ichi. "Avangyarudo-shi undō to taishō-shi no hōkai." In *Kōza nihon gendai shishi*, ed. Murano Shirō, Seki Ryōichi, Hasegawa Izumi, and Hara Shirō. Vol. 2. Tokyo: Yūbun shoin, 1973.

Clarke, I. F. *The Pattern of Expectation, 1644–2001*. New York: Basic Books, 1979.

Coronel, Sheila, ed. *Investigating Estrada: Millions, Mansions and Mistresses*. Quezon City: Philippine Center for Investigative Journalism, 2000.

d'Alembert, Jean Le Rond. "Dictionnaire." In *Encyclopédie ou dictionnaire raisonné des sciences, des arts et des métiers*, ed. Denis Diderot and Jean Le Rond d'Alembert, vol. 4. Paris, 1751–1766.

Dali, Salvador. *Dali on Modern Art: The Cuckolds of Antiquated Modern Art*. Mineola, N.Y.: Dover Publications, 1996.

Darlington, David. *Area 51: The Dreamland Chronicles*. New York: Henry Holt, 1997.

Davis, Mike. *Ecology of Fear: Los Angeles and the Imagination of Disaster*. New York: Henry Holt, 1998.

Day, Ronald E. *The Modern Invention of Information: Discourse, History, and Power*. Carbondale: Southern Illinois University Press, 2001.

Dean, Jodi. *Aliens in America: Conspiracy Cultures from Outerspace to Cyberspace*. Ithaca: Cornell University Press, 1998.

Debord, Guy. *Society of the Spectacle*. Detroit: Black and Red, 1983.

Deleuze, Gilles, and Félix Guattari. *Anti-Oedipus: Capitalism and Schizophrenia*. Minneapolis: University of Minnesota Press, 1983.

———. *A Thousand Plateaus: Capitalism and Schizophrenia*. Trans. Brian Massumi. Minneapolis: University of Minnesota Press, 1987.

Derrida, Jacques. "Faith and Knowledge: The Two Sources of 'Religion' at the Limits of Reason Alone." In *Acts of Religion*, ed. Gil Anidjar, trans. Sam Weber. New York: Routledge, 2002.

———. *The Politics of Friendship*. Trans. George Collins. London: Verso, 1977.

———. "Signature Event Context." In *Margins of Philosophy*, trans. Alan Bass. Chicago: University of Chicago Press, 1982.

———. *Specters of Marx: The State of the Debt, the Work of Mourning, and the New International*. New York: Routledge, 1994.

Dery, Mark. *Escape Velocity: Cyberculture at the End of the Century*. New York: Grove Press, 1996.

———. "How to Build a Universe That Doesn't Fall Apart Two Days Later." In *The Shifting Realities of Philip K. Dick: Selected Literary and Philosophical Writings*, ed. Lawrence Sutin. New York: Pantheon, 1995.

Dick, Philip K. *Divine Invasion*. New York: Vintage, 1991.

———. *In Pursuit of Valis: Selections from the Exegesis*. Ed. Lawrence Sutin. Novato, Calif.: Underwood-Miller, 1991.

———. *The Selected Letters of Philip K. Dick, 1972–1973*. Ed. Dennis Etchison. Novato, Calif.: Underwood-Miller, 1993.

———. *The Selected Letters of Philip K. Dick, 1974*. Ed. Paul Williams. Novato, Calif.: Underwood-Miller, 1991.

———. *The Selected Letters of Philip K. Dick, 1975–1976*. Ed. Don Herron. Novato, Calif.: Underwood-Miller, 1992.

——. *The Selected Letters of Philip K. Dick, 1977–1979*. Ed. Don Herron. Novato, Calif.: Underwood-Miller, 1993.

——. *Ubik*. New York: Bantam, 1977.

——. *Valis*. New York: Bantam, 1981.

Diderot, Denis, and Jean Le Rond d'Alembert, eds. *Encyclopédie ou dictionnaire raisonné des sciences, des arts et des métiers*. Paris, 1751–1766.

Douglas, J. Yellowlees. " 'How Do I Stop This Thing?': Closure and Indeterminacy in Interactive Narratives." In *Hyper/Text/Theory*, ed. George Landow. Baltimore: Johns Hopkins University Press, 1994.

Dove, Michael. "Representations of the 'Other': The Ethnographic Challenge Posed by Planters' Views of Peasants in Indonesia." In *Transforming the Indonesian Uplands*, ed. Tania Li. London: Harwood Academic Publishers, 1999.

Feld, Steven. "Grooving Participation: Further Comments." In *Music Grooves*, ed. Charles Keil and Steven Feld. Chicago: University of Chicago Press, 1994.

Feld, Steven, and Charles Keil, eds. *Music Grooves*. Chicago: University of Chicago Press, 1994.

Fenster, Mark. *Conspiracy Theory: Secrecy and Power in American Culture*. Minneapolis: University of Minnesota Press, 1999.

Ferguson, Charles H. *High Stakes, No Prisoners: A Winner's Tale of Greed and Glory in the Internet Wars*. New York: Times Books–Random House, 1999.

Ferguson, Niall, ed. *Virtual History: Alternatives and Counterfactuals*. London: Picador, 1997.

Ferguson, Stephen. "The 1753 *Carte chronographique* of Jacques Barbeu-Dubourg." *Princeton University Library Chronicle* 52 (1991): 190–230.

FitzGerald, Frances. "The American Millennium." *New Yorker*, November 11, 1985, 88–113.

Foster, Hal. *The Return of the Real*. Cambridge: MIT Press, 1996.

Fradkin, Philip L. *Fallout: An American Nuclear Tragedy*. Tucson: University of Arizona Press, 1989.

Freud, Sigmund. "The 'Uncanny.' " In *Collected Papers*, ed. Ernest Jones, vol. 4, no. 10. London: Hogarth Press, 1956.

Galbraith, John Kenneth. *The New Industrial State*. 3rd ed. New York: Mentor, 1978.

Gallager, Carole. *American Ground Zero: The Secret Nuclear War*. Cambridge: MIT Press, 1993.

Gardner, William. "Colonialism and the Avant-Garde: Kitagawa Fuyuhiko's Manchurian Railway." *Stanford Humanities Review* 7, no. 1 (summer 1999): 12–21.

Gibson, William. "The Gernsback Effect." In *Burning Chrome*. New York: Ace, 1994.

Gilder, George. *Wealth and Poverty*. New York: Basic Books, 1981.

Gleick, James. *Faster: The Acceleration of Just About Everything*. New York: Pantheon, 1999.

Gleik, Elizabeth. "The Marker We've Been Waiting For." *Time*, April 7, 1997, 28–36.

Gordon, Avery. *Ghostly Matters: Haunting and the Sociological Imagination*. Minneapolis: University of Minnesota Press, 1997.

Gould, Stephen Jay. *Questioning the Millennium: A Rationalist's Guide to a Precisely Arbitrary Countdown*. Rev. ed. New York: Harmony, 1999.

Grafton, Anthony. *The Footnote: A Curious History*. Cambridge: Harvard University Press, 1997.

Grossberg, Lawrence, and Stuart Hall. "On Postmodernism and Articulation: An Interview with Stuart Hall." In *Stuart Hall: Critical Dialogues in Cultural Studies*, ed. David Morely and Kuan-Hsing Chen. London: Routledge, 1996.

Hacker, Barton C. *Elements of Controversy: The Atomic Energy Commission and Radiation Safety in Nuclear Weapons Testing, 1947–1974*. Berkeley: University of California Press, 1994.

Hagstrom, Robert G. *The Warren Buffett Way: Investment Strategies of the World's Greatest Investor*. New York: J. Wiley, 1994.

Hamilton-Paterson, James. *The Ghosts of Manila*. New York: Vintage, 1995.

Haraway, Donna. "A Manifesto for Cyborgs: Science, Technology, and Socialist-Feminism in the Late Twentieth Century." In *Simians, Cyborgs, and Women: The Reinvention of Nature*. New York: Routledge, 1991.

Hardin, Garrett. "The Tragedy of the Commons." *Ekistics* 27 (March 1969): 160, 168–70.

Harding, Susan Friend. *The Book of Jerry Falwell: Fundamentalist Language and Politics*. Princeton: Princeton University Press, 2000.

Harding, Susan, and Kathleen Stewart. "Bad Endings: American Apocalypsis." *Annual Reviews in Anthropology* 28 (1999).

Harpold, Terrence. "Conclusions." In *Hyper/Text/Theory*, ed. George Landow. Baltimore: Johns Hopkins University Press, 1994.

——. "The Contingencies of the Hypertext Link." *Writing on the Edge* 2, no. 2 (1991): 126–38.

Harvey, David. *The Condition of Postmodernity: An Enquiry into the Origins of Cultural Change*. Oxford: Basil Blackwell, 1990.

Hattori Tetsuyai. "Hirato Renkichi to nihon miraiha—zen'ei geijutsu, sono juyō to tenkai, daigosho." *Seikei daigaku bungakubu kiyō* (Bulletin of the Seikei University Literature Department) 31 (March 1996): 1–22.

Hayles, N. Katherine. *How We Became Posthuman: Virtual Bodies in Cybernetics, Literature, and Informatics*. Chicago: University of Chicago Press, 1999.

Headrick, Daniel R. *When Information Came of Age: Technologies of Knowledge in the Age of Reason and Revolution, 1700–1850*. New York: Oxford University Press, 2000.

Hecht, Susanna, and Alexander Cockburn. *The Fate of the Forest: Developers, Destroyers, and Defenders of the Amazon*. New York: Harper Perennial, 1990.

Heidegger, Martin. *On the Way to Language*. Trans. Peter Hertz. San Francisco: Harper Collins, 1971.

——. "The Question concerning Technology." In *The Question concerning Technology and Other Essays*, trans. William Lovitt. New York: Harper and Row, 1977.

Heim, Michael. "The Design of Virtual Reality." In *Cyberspace/Cyberbodies/Cyberpunk: Cultures of Technological Embodiment*, ed. Mike Featherstone and Roger Burrows. London: Sage, 1995.

Heiser, Michael S. *The Facade*. Bridgewater, N.J.: Superiorbooks.com, 2001.

Hill, Hal. *The Indonesian Economy since 1966: Southeast Asia's Emerging Giant*. Cambridge, U.K.: Cambridge University Press, 1996.

Hirata Hosea. *The Poetry and Poetics of Nishiwaki Junzaburō*. Princeton: Princeton University Press, 1993.

Hirato Renkichi. *Nihon miraiha sengen undō/Mouvement futuriste japonais* (Manifesto of the Japanese Futurist Movement). Self-published, 1921.

———. Special issue, *Gendai no bijutsu* (Contemporary Art) 4, no. 6 (September 1921).

Hockenberry, John. "The New Brainiacs." *Wired Magazine* 9.08 (August 2001): 94–105.

Holston, James. *The Modernist City: An Anthropological Critique of Brasilia*. Chicago: University of Chicago Press, 1989.

Hunt, Jamer. "Paranoid, Critical, Methodical: Dali, Koolhaas, and . . ." In *Paranoia within Reason: A Casebook on Conspiracy as Explanation*, ed. George E. Marcus. Chicago: University of Chicago Press, 1999.

Hutchcroft, Paul D. *Booty Capitalism: The Politics of Banking in the Philippines*. Ithaca: Cornell University Press, 1998.

Ileto, Reynaldo. *Pasyon and Revolution: Popular Uprisings in the Philippines, 1840–1910*. Quezon City: Ateneo de Manila University Press, 1979.

Inagaki Taruho. *A-kankaku to V-kankaku* (A-Sensibility and V-Sensibility). Tokyo: Kawade bunkō, 1987.

———. *Issen ichi-byō monogatari* (One Thousand One-Second Tales). Tokyo: Shinchō bunkō, 1969.

International Physicians for the Prevention of Nuclear War and the Institute for Energy and Environmental Research. *Radioactive Heaven and Earth: The Health and Environmental Effects of Nuclear Weapons Testing in, on, and above the Earth*. New York: Apex Press, 1991.

Iverson, Jack, Robert Morrissey, and Mark Olsen. "L'Encyclopédie de Diderot sur Internet." *Recherches sur Diderot et sur l'Encyclopédie* 25 (October 1998): 163–68.

Ivy, Marilyn. *Discourses of the Vanishing: Modernity, Phantasm, Japan*. Chicago: University of Chicago Press, 1995.

Jackson, Shelley. *Patchwork Girl: By Mary/Shelley and Herself (A Graveyard, A Journal, A Quilt, A Story, and Broken Accents)*. CD-ROM. Cambridge: Eastgate Systems, 1995.

Jakobson, Roman. "Linguistics and Poetics." In *Language in Literature*, ed. Krystyna Pomorska and Stephen Rudy. Cambridge: Belknap Press, 1987.

Jameson, Fredric. "Nostalgia for the Present." In *Classical Hollywood Narrative: The Paradigm Wars*. Durham, N.C.: Duke University Press, 1992.

———. "Progress versus Utopia; or, Can We Imagine the Future?" In *Art after Modernism: Rethinking Representation*, ed. Brian Wallis. New York: New Museum of Contemporary Art, 1984.

———. *A Singular Modernity: Essay on the Ontology of the Present*. New York: Verso, 2002.

Jay, Martin. "The Apocalyptic Imagination and the Inability to Mourn." In *Force Fields: Between Intellectual History and Cultural Critique*. New York: Routledge, 1993.

Joyce, Michael. *Of Two Minds: Hypertext Pedagogy and Poetics*. Ann Arbor: University of Michigan Press, 1995.

Kern, Stephen. *The Culture of Time and Space: 1880–1918*. Cambridge: Harvard University Press, 1983.

Kittler, Friedrich. *Discourse Networks 1800/1900*. Stanford: Stanford University Press, 1990.

———. "Gramophone, Film, Typewriter." Trans. Dorothea von Mücke. *October* 41 (1987): 101–18.

Konoshita Shūichirō and David Burljuk. *Miraiha to wa? Kotaeru* (What Is Futurism? A Response). Tokyo: Chūō bijutsu-sha, 1923.

Koselleck, Reinhart. *Futures Past: On the Semantics of Historical Time*. Trans. Keith Tribe. Cambridge: MIT Press, 1997.

Kuletz, Valerie L. *The Tainted Desert: Environmental and Social Ruin in the American West*. New York: Routledge, 1998.

Kusama Yayoi. *Love Forever: Yayoi Kusama, 1958–1968*. Ed. Lynn Zelevansky et al. Los Angeles: Los Angeles County Museum of Art, 1998.

Laclau, Ernesto, and Chantal Mouffe. *Hegemony and Socialist Strategy*. London: Verso, 1985.

Landow, George. *Hypertext 2.0: The Convergence of Contemporary Critical Theory and Technology*. Baltimore: Johns Hopkins University Press, 1997.

———. "Twenty Minutes into the Future, or How Are We Moving beyond the Book?" In *The Future of the Book*, ed. Geoffrey Nunberg. Berkeley: University of California Press, 1996.

———. "What's a Critic to Do? Critical Theory in the Age of Hypertext." In *Hyper/Text/Theory*, ed. George Landow. Baltimore: Johns Hopkins University Press, 1994.

———, ed. *Hyper/Text/Theory*. Baltimore: Johns Hopkins University Press, 1994.

Lasch, Christopher. *The Revolt of the Elites and the Betrayal of Democracy*. New York: Norton, 1995.

Latour, Bruno. *Aramis or the Love of Technology*. Trans. Catherine Porter. Cambridge: Harvard University Press, 1996.

Lavelle, Louis. "Executive Pay." *Business Week*, April 16, 2001, 76.

Laya, Jaime C. "The Black Nazarene of Quiapo." In *Letras y Figuras: Business in Culture, Culture in Business*. Manila: Anvil Publishing, 2001.

Lefebvre, Henri. "The Everyday and Everydayness." In *Architecture of the Everyday*, trans. Christine Levich and the editors of *Yale French Studies*, ed. Steven Harris and Deborah Berke. New York: Princeton Architectural Press, 1997.

Lem, Stanislaw. "Philip K. Dick: A Visionary among the Charlatans." In *On Philip K. Dick: Forty Articles from Science Fiction Studies*, ed. R. D. Mullen, Istvan Csicsery-Ronay Jr., Arthur B. Evans, and Veronica Hollinger. Greencastle, Ind.: SF-TH, 1992.

———. "SF: A Hopeless Case with Exceptions." In *Microworlds: Writings on Science Fiction and Fantasy*, ed. Franz Rottensteiner. San Diego: Harcourt Brace, 1984.

Lepselter, Susan. "From the Earth Native's Point of View: The Earth, the Extraterrestrial, and the Natural Ground of Home." *Public Culture* 9 (1997): 197–208.

Lethem, Jonathan. "Walking the Moons." In *Simulations: Fifteen Tales of Virtual Reality*, ed. K. Jacobsen. New York: Citadel Twilight, 1993.

Lévy, Pierre. *Becoming Virtual: Reality in the Digital Age*. Trans. Robert Bononno. New York: Perseus, 1998.

Lewis, Michael. *The New New Thing: A Silicon Valley Story.* New York: Norton, 2000.

Li, Tania. "Marginality, Power and Production: Analyzing Upland Transformations." In *Transforming the Indonesian Uplands,* ed. Tania Li. London: Harwood Academic Publishers, 1999.

Liberace. *Liberace: An Autobiography.* New York: G. P. Putnam's Sons, 1973.

Lieb, Michael. *Children of Ezekiel: Aliens,* UFOs, *the Crisis of Race, and the Advent of Endtime.* Durham, N.C.: Duke University Press, 1998.

Limerick, Patricia. *The Legacy of Conquest: The Unbroken Past of the American West.* New York: Norton, 1987.

Linhartová, Vera. "Manifestes et réflexions, 1910–1940." In *Japon des Avant-Gardes: 1910–1970.* Paris: Éditions du Centre Pompidou, 1986.

Lowenstein, Roger. *Buffett: The Making of an American Capitalist.* New York: Doubleday, 1996.

Luhmann, Niklas. *The Differentiation of Society.* New York: Columbia University Press, 1982.

Lynch, Peter, and John Rothchild. *Learn to Earn: A Beginner's Guide to the Basics of Investing and Business.* New York: Fireside–Simon and Schuster, 1995.

Lyotard, Jean-François. *The Postmodern Condition.* Trans. Geoff Bennington and Brian Massumi. Minneapolis: University of Minnesota Press, 1984.

Madrick, Jeff. "How New Is the New Economy?" *New York Review of Books,* September 23, 1999, 42–50.

Malkiel, Burton G. *A Random Walk down Wall Street.* 6th ed. New York: Norton, 1996.

Marcus, George E., ed. *Zeroing In on the Year 2000: The Final Edition.* Chicago: University of Chicago Press, 2000.

Marinetti, Filippo Tommaso. *The Futurist Cookbook.* Trans. Suzanne Brill. San Francisco: Bedford Arts, 1989.

——. *Marinetti: Selected Writings.* Ed. and trans. R. W. Flint and Arthur A. Coppotelli. New York: Farrar, Straus and Giroux, 1971.

——. "Technical Manifesto of Futurist Literature." Special issue, *Gendai no bijutsu* (Contemporary Art) 4, no. 6 (September 1921).

——. "Words-in-Freedom." Special issue, *Gendai no bijutsu* (Contemporary Art) 4, no. 6 (September 1921).

Marx, Karl. *The Class Struggles in France, 1848–1850.* Moscow: Progress Publishers, 1972.

——. *The Eighteenth Brumaire of Louis Napoleon.* Moscow: Progress Publishers, 1937.

Marzulli, Lynn A. *Nephilim.* Grand Rapids, Mich.: Zondervan, 1999.

Masco, Joseph. "Lie Detectors: On Secrets and Hypersecurity in Los Alamos." *Public Culture* 14, no. 3 (2002): 441–67.

Mattelart, Armand. *The Invention of Communication.* Trans. Susan Emanuel. Minneapolis: University of Minnesota Press, 1996.

McCaffrey, Larry, ed. *Storming the Reality Studio: A Casebook of Cyberpunk and Postmodern Science Fiction.* Durham, N.C.: Duke University Press, 1991.

McConnell, Frank. "You Bet Your Life: Death and the Storyteller." In *Immortal Engines: Life Extension and Immortality in Science Fiction and Fantasy,* ed. George

Slusser, Gary Westfahl, and Eric Rabkin. Athens: University of Georgia Press, 1996.

McKay, Bonnie, and James Acheson. *The Question of the Commons: The Culture and Ecology of Communal Resources.* Tucson: University of Arizona Press, 1987.

Mellencamp, Patricia. *High Anxiety: Catastrophe, Scandal, Age and Comedy.* Bloomington: Indiana University Press, 1992.

Miller, J. Hillis. "The Ethics of Hypertext." *Diacritics: A Review of Contemporary Criticism* 25, no. 3 (fall 1995): 27–39.

Miller, Laura. "Women and Children First: Gender and the Settling of the Electronic Frontier." In *Resisting the Virtual Life: The Culture and Politics of Information*, ed. James Brook and Iain A. Boal. San Francisco: City Lights, 1995.

Miller, Mark, and Evan Thomas. "Exclusive: Secrets of the Cult." *Newsweek*, April 14, 1997, 28.

Miller, Richard L. *Under the Cloud: The Decades of Nuclear Testing.* New York: Free Press, 1986.

Missler, Chuck, and Mark Eastman. *Alien Encounters.* Coeur d'Alene: Koinonia House, 1997.

Moore, Geoffrey A. *Living on the Fault Line: Managing for Shareholder Value in the Age of the Internet.* Oxford: Capstone, 2000.

Morrissey, Robert, and Philippe Roger. *L'Encyclopédie, du réseau au livre et du livre au réseau.* Paris: Champion, 2001.

Moulthrop, Stuart. "Polymers, Paranoia, and the Rhetoric of Hypertext." *Writing on the Edge* 2, no. 2 (1991): 150–59.

Moynihan, Daniel Patrick. *Secrecy: The American Experience.* New Haven, Conn.: Yale University Press, 1998.

Nadel, Alan. *Containment Culture: American Narratives, Postmodernism, and the Atomic Age.* Durham, N.C.: Duke University Press, 1995.

Nelson, Theodor Holm. *Computer Lib.* Self-published, 1974.

———. *Computer Lib.* Redmond, Wash.: Microsoft Press, 1987.

———. *Dream Machines.* Self-published, 1974.

———. *Dream Machines.* Redmond, Wash.: Microsoft Press, 1987.

———. *Literary Machines: The Report on, and of, Project Xanadu™ concerning Word Processing, Electronic Publishing, Hypertext, Thinkertoys, Tomorrow's Intellectual Revolution, and Certain Other Topics Including Knowledge, Education, and Freedom.* Self-published, 1980. Reprint, Sausalito: Mindful Press, 1987.

———. "Opening Hypertext: A Memoir." In *Literacy Online: The Promise (and Peril) of Reading and Writing with Computers*, ed. Myron C. Tuman. Pittsburgh: University of Pittsburgh Press, 1992.

Nocera, Joseph. "Betting on the Market." PBS's *Frontline*. 1996.

———. *A Piece of the Action: How the Middle Class Joined the Money Class.* New York: Simon and Schuster, 1994.

Olsen, Mark, and Gilles Blanchard. "Le système de renvois dans l'Encyclopédie: Une cartographie de la structure des connaissances au XVIIIème siècle." *Recherches sur Diderot et sur l'Encyclopédie* 31–32 (April 2002): 45–70.

Omuka Toshiharu. "Futurism in Japan, 1909–1920." In *International Futurism in Arts and Literature*, ed. Gunter Berghaus. Berlin: Walter de Gruyter, 2000.

Patton, Phil. *Dreamland: Travels inside the Secret World of Roswell and Area 51*. New York: Villard, 1998.

Peet, Richard, and Michael Watts. *Liberation Ecologies*. New York: Routledge, 1996.

Peluso, Nancy. "Fruit Trees and Family Trees in an Anthropogenic Rainforest: Property Rights, Ethics of Access, and Environmental Change in Indonesia." *Comparative Studies in Society and History* 38, no. 3 (1996): 510–48.

Peluso, Nancy, and Emily Harwell. "Territory, Custom, and the Cultural Politics of Ethnic War in West Kalimantan, Indonesia." In *Violent Environments*, ed. Nancy Peluso and Michael Watts. Ithaca: Cornell University Press, 2001.

Pemberton, John. *On the Subject of "Java."* Ithaca: Cornell University Press, 1994.

Penley, Constance. "Time Travel, Primal Scene, and the Critical Dystopia (on *The Terminator* and *La Jetée*)." In *The Future of an Illusion: Film, Feminism, and Psychoanalysis*. Minneapolis: University of Minnesota Press, 1989.

Peterson, Wallace C. *Silent Depression: The Fate of the American Dream*. New York: Norton, 1994.

Pfeil, Fred. "These Disintegrations I'm Looking Forward To." In *Another Tale to Tell: Politics and Narrative in Postmodern Culture*. London: Verso, 1990.

Philippines. National Archives of the Philippines. *Telefonos, 1885–1891*.

Phillips, Adam. *On Flirtation*. Cambridge: Harvard University Press, 1994.

Phillips, Kevin. "It's Pensions, Stupid!" *Los Angeles Times Book Review*, September 15, 2002, 2.

Philmus, Robert M. "The Two Faces of Philip K. Dick." In *On Philip K. Dick: Forty Articles from Science Fiction Studies*, ed. R. D. Mullen, Istvan Csicsery-Ronay Jr., Arthur B. Evans, and Veronica Hollinger. Greencastle, Ind.: SF-TH, 1992.

Pierce, William [a.k.a. Andrew Macdonald]. *The Turner Diaries: A Novel*. Fort Lee, N.J.: Barricade Books, 1996.

Priestley, Joseph. *Description of a Chart of Biography*. 7th ed. London: J. Johnson, 1778.

———. *Description of a New Chart of History*. 6th ed. London: J. Johnson, 1786.

Rafael, Vicente L. "Taglish, or the Phantom Power of the Lingua Franca." In *White Love and Other Events in Filipino History*. Durham, N.C.: Duke University Press, 2000.

———. "Translation and Revenge: Castilian and the Origins of Nationalism in the Philippines." In *The Places of History: Regionalism Revisited in Latin America*, ed. Doris Sommer. Durham, N.C.: Duke University Press, 1999.

———. *White Love and Other Events in Filipino History*. Durham, N.C.: Duke University Press, 2000.

Reich, Robert B. *The Work of Nations: Preparing Ourselves for 21st Century Capitalism*. New York: Random House, 1991.

Renouvier, Charles. *Uchronie (l'utopie dans l'histoire): Esquisse historique apocryphe du développement de la civilisation européenne tel qu'il n'a pas été tel qu'il aurait pu être*. Paris: Félix Alcan, 1876.

Rheingold, Howard. *Tools for Thought: The People and Ideas behind the Next Computer Revolution*. New York: Simon and Schuster, 1985.

Rizal, Jose. *Por Teléfono*. Barcelona, 1889. Reprint, Manila: R. Martinez and Sons, 1959.

Ronell, Avital. "Trauma TV: Twelve Steps beyond the Pleasure Principle." In *Finitude's Score: Essays for the End of the Millennium*. Lincoln: University of Nebraska Press, 1994.

Rosenberg, Daniel Blake. "Condillac's Exemplary Student." In *Proceedings of the Western Society for French History*, vol. 24. Greeley: University Press of Colorado, 1997.

——. "Early Modern Information Overload." *Journal of the History of Ideas* 64, no. 1 (January 2003): 1–10.

——. "An Eighteenth-Century Time Machine: The *Encyclopedia* of Diderot." In *Postmodernism and the Enlightenment: New Perspectives on Eighteenth-Century French Intellectual History*, ed. Daniel Gordon. New York: Routledge, 2001.

——. "Making Time: Origin, History, and Language in Enlightenment France and Britain." Ph.D. diss., University of California, Berkeley, 1996.

——. "No One Is Buried in Hoover Dam." In *Modernism, Inc.: Body, Memory, Capital*, ed. Jani Scandura and Michael Thurston. New York: New York University Press, 2001.

——. "We Have Never Been Interdisciplinary: Etymology and Encyclopedism in the Eighteenth-Century and Since." *SVEC*. Forthcoming, 2005.

Rouet, Jean-François, et al., eds. *Hypertext and Cognition*. Mahway, N.J.: Lawrence Erlbaum, 1996.

Sampson, Anthony. *Company Man: The Rise and Fall of Corporate Life*. New York: Random House–Times Business, 1995.

Sarmiento, Domingo. *Civilization and Barbarism*. Trans. Mary Mann. New York: Penguin, 1998.

Sas, Miryam. "Expectation and Invention: The Casual Theater of Betsuyaku Minoru." *Review of Asian and Pacific Studies* 17 (1998): 35–52.

——. *No Holds Barred: Engaged Theater and Its Discontents in Postwar Japan*. Forthcoming.

Schmink, Marianne, and Charles Wood. *Contested Frontiers in Amazonia*. New York: Columbia University Press, 1992.

Schwab Center for Investment Research. *Schwab Investor* 6, no. 3 (2nd quarter 2002).

Schwartz, Stephen I., ed. *Atomic Audit: The Costs and Consequences of U.S. Nuclear Weapons since 1940*. Washington: Brookings Institution Press, 1998.

Schwenger, Peter. "Agrippa, or The Apocalyptic Book." In *Flame Wars: The Discourse of Cyberculture*, ed. Mark Dery. Durham, N.C.: Duke University Press, 1994.

Sedgwick, Eve Kosofsky. "Epidemics of the Will." In *Tendencies*. Durham, N.C.: Duke University Press, 1993.

Seltzer, Mark. "Wound Culture: Trauma in the Pathological Public Sphere." *October* 80 (1997): 3–26.

Severino, Howie G. "The Hand That Rocks the Masa." *Filipinas Magazine*, June 2001, 70–72.

Shershow, Scott Cutler. "Of Sinking: Marxism and the 'General' Economy." *Critical Inquiry* 27 (spring 2001): 468–92.

Sidel, John. *Capital, Coercion, and Crime: Bossism in the Philippines*. Stanford: Stanford University Press, 1999.

Siegel, James T. *Fetish Recognition Revolution*. Princeton: Princeton University Press, 1997.

Slotkin, Richard. *Gunfighter Nation: The Myth of the Frontier in Twentieth Century America*. New York: Atheneum, 1992.

Spackman, Barbara. *Fascist Virilities: Rhetoric, Ideology, and Social Fantasy in Italy*. Minneapolis: University of Minnesota Press, 1996.

Steedly, Mary. *Hanging without a Rope: Narrative Experience in Colonial and Post-colonial Karoland*. Princeton: Princeton University Press, 1993.

Steedman, Carolyn. *Landscape for a Good Woman: A Story of Two Lives*. London: Virago Press, 1986.

Steiger, Brad, and Hayden Hewes. *Inside Heaven's Gate*. New York: Signet, 1997.

Sterne, Laurence. *The Life and Opinions of Tristram Shandy*. New York: Norton, 1980.

Stewart, Kathleen. "Bitter Faiths." In *Technoscientific Imaginaries: Conversations, Profiles and Memoir*, ed. George Marcus. Chicago: University of Chicago Press, 1994.

———. "Nostalgia—a Polemic." *Cultural Anthropology* 3 (1988): 227–41.

———. *A Space on the Side of the Road: Cultural Poetics in an "Other" America*. Princeton: Princeton University Press, 1996.

Stewart, Kathleen, and Susan Harding. "Bad Endings: American Apocalypsis." *Annual Review of Anthropology* 28 (1999): 285–310.

Stewart, Susan. *On Longing: Narratives of the Miniature, the Gigantic, the Souvenir, the Collection*. Durham, N.C.: Duke University Press, 1993.

Strange, Susan. *Casino Capitalism*. Oxford: Basil Blackwell, 1986.

Strozier, Charles B., and Michael Flynn. *The Year 2000: Essays on the End*. New York: New York University Press, 1997.

Sturken, Marita. *Tangled Memories: The Vietnam War, the AIDS Epidemic, and the Politics of Remembering*. Berkeley: University of California Press, 1997.

Tabbi, Joseph. *Postmodern Sublime: Technology and American Writing from Mailer to Cyberpunk*. Ithaca: Cornell University Press, 1995.

Tadiar, Neferti X. "Manila's New Metropolitan Forms." In *Discrepant Histories: Translocal Essays on Filipino Cultures*, ed. Vicente L. Rafael. Philadelphia: Temple University Press, 1995.

Takamura Kōtarō. "Midori-iro no taiyō" (Green Sun). *Subaru Journal*, April 1910, 35–36.

Taussig, Michael. *Defacement: Public Secrecy and the Labor of the Negative*. Stanford: Stanford University Press, 1999.

———. *The Magic of the State*. New York: Routledge, 1996.

Taylor, Joshua C. *Futurism*. New York: Museum of Modern Art catalog, n.d.

Thomas, Bob. *Liberace: The True Story*. New York: St. Martin's Press, 1987.

Thompson, E. P. "Time, Work-Discipline, and Industrial Capitalism." In *Customs in Common: Studies in Traditional Popular Culture*. New York: New Press, 1993.

Tiptree, James [Alice Sheldon]. "The Girl Who Was Plugged In." In *Warm Worlds and Otherwise*. New York: Ballantine, 1975.

Titus, A. Constandina. *Bombs in the Backyard: Atomic Testing and American Politics*. Reno and Las Vegas: University of Nevada Press, 1986.

Toffler, Alvin. *Future Shock*. New York: Random House, 1970.

Tolentino, Roland, ed. *Geopolitics of the Visible: Essays on Philippine Film Culture*. Quezon City: Ateneo de Manila University Press, 2000.

Tomas, David. "Feedback and Cybernetics: Reimaging the Body in the Age of Cybernetics." In *Cyberspace/Cyberbodies/Cyberpunk: Cultures of Technological Embodiment*, ed. Mike Featherstone and Roger Burrows. London: Sage, 1995.

Trow, George. *Within the Context of No Context*. New York: Atlantic Monthly Press, 1997.

Tsing, Anna. "Inside the Economy of Appearances." *Public Culture* 12, no. 1 (2000): 115–44.

——. *In the Realm of the Diamond Queen*. Princeton: Princeton University Press, 1993.

Tufte, Edward. *The Visual Display of Quantitative Information*. Cheshire, Conn.: Graphics Press, 2001.

Turner, Frederick Jackson. "The Significance of the Frontier in American History." In *Rereading Frederick Jackson Turner*, ed. John Mack Faragher. New York: Henry Holt, 1994.

Tuveson, Ernest Lee. *Redeemer Nation: The Idea of America's Millennial Role*. Chicago: University of Chicago Press, 1968.

Ullman, Ellen. "Out of Time: Reflections on the Programming Life." In *Resisting the Virtual Life: The Culture and Politics of Information*, ed. James Brook and Iain A. Boal. San Francisco: City Lights, 1995.

Urban, Greg. *Metaculture: How Culture Moves through the World*. Minneapolis: University of Minnesota Press, 2001.

U.S. General Accounting Office. *Security Clearances: Consideration of Sexual Orientation in the Clearance Process*. Washington, 1994.

Wallace, Anthony F. C. "Revitalization Movements." *American Anthropologist* 58 (1956): 264–81.

Weart, Spencer R. *Nuclear Fear: A History of Images*. Cambridge: Harvard University Press, 1988.

Weber, Max. *The Protestant Ethic and the Spirit of Capitalism*. New York: Scribners, 1958.

Weber, Samuel. "Upsetting the Setup: Remarks on Heidegger's 'Questing after Technics.' " In *Mass Mediauras: Form, Technics, Media*, ed. Alan Cholodenko. Stanford: Stanford University Press, 1996.

Welsome, Eileen. *The Plutonium Files: America's Secret Medical Experiments in the Cold War*. New York: Dial Press, 1999.

Williams, Raymond. *Marxism and Literature*. New York: Oxford University Press, 1977.

Worster, Donald. *Rivers of Empire: Water, Aridity, and the Growth of the American West*. New York: Oxford University Press, 1992.

——. *Under Western Skies: Nature and History in the American West*. New York: Oxford University Press, 1992.

Wright, Erik Olin. *Class Counts: Comparative Studies in Class Analysis*. Cambridge, U.K.: Cambridge University Press, 1996.

Yeo, Richard. *Encyclopaedic Visions: Scientific Dictionaries and Enlightenment Culture*. Cambridge, U.K.: Cambridge University Press, 2001.

NOTES ON CONTRIBUTORS

SASHA ARCHIBALD is an associate editor of *Cabinet* magazine.

SUSAN HARDING is a professor of anthropology at the University of California, Santa Cruz.

JAMER HUNT is an associate professor of design at the University of the Arts, Philadelphia.

PAMELA JACKSON received her Ph.D. from the Department of Rhetoric at the University of California, Berkeley.

SUSAN LEPSELTER received her Ph.D. from the Department of Anthropology at the University of Texas, Austin.

JONATHAN LETHEM won the National Book Critics Circle Award in 1999 for *Motherless Brooklyn*. His most recent novel is *Fortress of Solitude*.

JOSEPH MASCO is an assistant professor of anthropology at the University of Chicago.

CHRISTOPHER NEWFIELD is a professor of English at the University of California, Santa Barbara.

ELIZABETH POLLMAN currently studies law at Stanford University, where she completed her undergraduate degree in anthropology and art.

VICENTE RAFAEL is a professor of history at the University of Washington.

DANIEL ROSENBERG is an assistant professor of history in the Robert D. Clark Honors College at the University of Oregon.

MIRYAM SAS is an associate professor of Japanese and comparative literature at the University of California, Berkeley.

KATHLEEN STEWART is an associate professor of anthropology at the University of Texas, Austin.

ANNA TSING is a professor of anthropology at the University of California, Santa Cruz.

INDEX

Science fiction, 135, 147, 182, 300, 309; as *anime*, 211; as community, 176–77; language and, 183, 207

Security: national security state, 42, 260; risk and, 246–47; technoscience and, 23. *See also* Risk

Silicon Valley, 245–50

Speculation: as erratic temporality, 69, 74. *See also* Chance; Contingency; Gambling; Investment

Speed, 6, 15, 157, 203, 207–8, 211–13, 216, 228, 324, 329; as "single second bursts," 215–17; technology and, 88; temporal acceleration, 64–65. *See also* Waiting

Still-life, 328–31; defined, 328; graphomania and, 333–34. *See also* Narrative

Structure of feeling, 265, 278 n. 21

Sublime: in Futurist aesthetics, 161–62, 206–8; technology and, 206. *See also* Uncanny

Suburbia: aesthetics of, 336; built to be destroyed, 28; as ironic site of mass suicide, 300, 305; shopping malls in, 94

Suicide: as escape to future, 312, 315; mass, 146, 300–302, 307, 312; as misogynist technology, 209, 220. *See also* Escape

Surrealism, 155–56, 164–68

Taruho, Inagaki, 204, 213–19

Technology, physical: beauty and, 205; as gifts from aliens, 259; for nuclear containment, 32–37; as prostheses, 82, 144. *See also* Cell Phones; Testing

Technology, social: crowd as, 91–93; Martha Stewart as, 329–30; restoring something lost and, 137–40

Testing, 273–74; Nevada Test Site, 25–32

Texting, 80–88; "Generation Txt" in Philippines, 84, 86–88

Timelines, 5, 283–95; of aliens, 256. *See also* Linearity

Time travel, 137, 146–47

Tokyo, 203–5, 208, 210, 219

Traffic jam, as metaphor, 90, 187–99

Trauma time, 323, 328, 331–38; defined, 325; modernity and, 328; as specter of future, 338

UFOS, 37–42, 257–62, 266–68, 273–76

Uncanny, 258–62, 265, 273–75, 278 n. 16; real and, 273; as "secret meaning," 265. *See also* Sublime

Utopia, 23, 97, 133; as abolition of social hierarchy, 91; cleanliness and, 326; as cultural imaginary, 207; dystopia and, 23–24, 183; literary, 148, 179; paranoid, 39; technological, 77, 206

Velocity. *See* Speed

Waiting: in crowd, 95–96, 99; in traffic, 187–99; on transforming resource frontier, 61–62

Waste: food matter as, 155; as future aesthetic, 175, 181; nuclear, 23, 27; urban garbage, 90; at Yucca Mountain, 33–37. *See also* Decay

West, 13, 23, 28; as figure for past, 269; as salvation, 275; "Wild," 69, 72

Y2K, 6–7. *See also* Millennium

Acknowledgment of other photographs and artwork:

Daniel Rosenberg, pages 52, 76, 172, 186, 202, 232, 298, 322.

Japanese Futurist Manifesto. Courtesy of the Museum of Modern Japanese Literature, page 226.

Alien Time Line, © Joe Nickel, *Skeptical Inquirer* (1997), page 256.

Library of Congress Cataloging-in-Publication Data
Histories of the future / edited by Daniel Rosenberg and Susan Harding.
Includes bibliographical references and index.
ISBN 0-8223-3485-2 (cloth: alk. paper)
ISBN 0-8223-3473-9 (pbk.: alk. paper)
1. Forecasting. I. Rosenberg, Daniel, 1966– II. Harding, Susan Friend.
CB158.H57 2005   303.49—dc22   2005000324